THE STUDIA PHILONICA ANNUAL
Studies in Hellenistic Judaism

Program in Judaic Studies
Brown University
BROWN JUDAIC STUDIES
Edited by

Shaye J. D. Cohen, Ernest S. Frerichs, Calvin Goldscheider

Editor for Studia Philonica: Shaye J. D. Cohen

Number 287
THE STUDIA PHILONICA ANNUAL
Studies in Hellenistic Judaism

edited by
David T. Runia

THE STUDIA PHILONICA ANNUAL
Studies in Hellenistic Judaism

Volume V

1993

Editor:
David T. Runia

Associate Editors:
Alan Mendelson
David Winston

Book Review Editor:
Gregory E. Sterling

Scholars Press
Atlanta, Georgia

THE STUDIA PHILONICA ANNUAL
Studies in Hellenistic Judaism

The financial support of
C. J. de Vogel Foundation, Amsterdam
Coe College, Cedar Rapids, Iowa
University of Notre Dame
is gratefully acknowledged

Copyright © 1993 by Brown University
Copyright © 2007 by the Society of Biblical Literature

All rights reserved. No part of this work may be reproduced or transmitted in any form or by any means, electronic or mechanical, including photocopying and recording, or by means of any information storage or retrieval system, except as may be expressly permitted by the 1976 Copyright Act or in writing from the publisher. Requests for permission should be addressed in writing to the Rights and Permissions Office, Society of Biblical Literature, 825 Houston Mill Road, Atlanta, GA 30329, USA.

ISBN: 1-55540-917-2 (cloth binding : alk. paper)
ISBN: 978-1-58983-469-9 (paper binding : alk. paper)

Printed in the United States of America
on acid-free paper

THE STUDIA PHILONICA ANNUAL
STUDIES IN HELLENISTIC JUDAISM

EDITORIAL BOARD

EDITOR: David T. Runia, *Universities of Leiden and Utrecht*

ASSOCIATE EDITORS:
Alan Mendelson, *McMaster University*
David Winston, *Graduate Theological Union, Berkeley*

BOOK REVIEW EDITOR: Greg Sterling, *University of Notre Dame*

ADVISORY BOARD

David Hay, *Coe College, Cedar Rapids* (chair)
Hans Dieter Betz, *University of Chicago*
Peder Borgen, *University of Trondheim*
Jacques Cazeaux, *CNRS, University of Lyon*
Lester Grabbe, *University of Hull*
Robert G. Hamerton-Kelly, *Stanford University*
Richard D. Hecht, *University of California at Santa Barbara*
Pieter W. van der Horst, *Utrecht University*
Jean Laporte, *Paris*
Burton L. Mack, *Claremont Graduate School, Claremont*
Birger A. Pearson, *University of California at Santa Barbara*
Robert Radice, *Sacred Heart University, Milan*
Jean Riaud, *Catholic University, Angers*
James R. Royse, *San Francisco*
Abraham Terian, *Andrews University*
Thomas H. Tobin S.J., *Loyola University, Chicago*
Herold D. Weiss, *St. Mary's College, Notre Dame*

The Studia Philonica Annual accepts articles for publication in the area of Hellenistic Judaism, with special emphasis on Philo and his *Umwelt*.

Contributions should be sent to the Editor, Prof. D. T. Runia, Rijnsburgerweg 116, 2333 AE Leiden, The Netherlands. Please send books for review to the Book Review Editor, Prof. G. Sterling, Dept. of Theology, University of Notre Dame, Notre Dame, IN 46556, U.S.A.

Contributors are requested to observe the 'Instructions to Contributors' located at the end of the volume. Articles which do not conform to these instructions cannot be accepted for inclusion.

CONTENTS

ARTICLES

P. W. VAN DER HORST, 'Thou shalt not Revile the Gods': the LXX Translation of Ex. 22:28 (27), its Background and Influence 1

N. G. COHEN, The Greek Virtues and the Mosaic Laws in Philo: an Elucidation of *De Specialibus Legibus* IV 133–135 9

G. P. CARRAS, Dependence or Common Tradition in Philo *Hypothetica* viii 6.10 – 7.20 and Josephus *Contra Apionem* 2.190–219 24

L. H. FELDMAN, Josephus' Portrait of Balaam 48

R. McL. WILSON, Philo and Gnosticism 84

D. ZELLER, Notiz zu den "immerfließenden Quellen der göttlichen Wohltaten" 93

SPECIAL SECTION: PHILO AND MIDDLE PLATONISM

INTRODUCTORY NOTICE 95

G. E. STERLING, Platonizing Moses: Philo and Middle Platonism 96

D. T. RUNIA, Was Philo a Middle Platonist? a Difficult Question Revisited 112

D. WINSTON, Response to Runia and Sterling 141

T. H. TOBIN, S.J., Was Philo a Middle Platonist? Some suggestions 147

J. DILLON, A Response to Runia and Sterling 151

INSTRUMENTA

J. R. ROYSE, Reverse Indexes to Philonic texts in the Printed Florilegia and Collections of Fragments 156

BIBLIOGRAPHY SECTION

D. T. RUNIA and R. RADICE, Philo of Alexandria: an Annotated Bibliography 1990 180

SUPPLEMENT: Provisional Bibliography 1991-93 197

BOOK REVIEW SECTION

F. SIEGERT, *Philon von Alexandrien. Über die Gottesbezeichnung 'wohltätig verzehrendes Feuer' ('De Deo'): Rückübersetzung des Fragments aus dem Armenischen, deutsche Übersetzung und Kommentar.* Reviewed by James ROYSE 208

F. SIEGERT, *Drei hellenistisch-jüdische Predigten. Ps.-Philon, "Über Jona", "Über Jona" (Fragment) und "Über Simson", II: Kommentar nebst Beobachtungen zur hellenistischen Vorgeschichte der Bibelhermeneutik.* Reviewed by Pieter W. VAN DER HORST 219

D. M. HAY (ed.), *Both Literal and Allegorical: Studies in Philo of Alexandria's Questions and Answers on Genesis and Exodus.* Reviewed by Sze-kar WAN 222

G. VERMES and M. D. GOODMAN, *The Essenes According to the Classical Sources.* Reviewed by Gregory E. STERLING 227

F. PETIT, *La Chaîne sur la Genèse: Édition intégrale chapitres 1 à 3.* Reviewed by David T. RUNIA 229

G. BOCCACCINI, *Middle Judaism: Jewish Thought, 300 B.C.E. to 200 C.E.* Reviewed by David WINSTON 233

H. CONZELMANN, *Gentiles-Jews-Christians: Polemics and Apologetics in the Greco-Roman Era.* Reviewed by Gregory E. STERLING 238

H.-J. KLAUCK, (ed.), *Monotheismus und Christologie. Zur Gottesfrage im hellenistischen Judentum und im Urchristentum.* Reviewed by Dieter ZELLER 242

NEWS AND NOTES 246

NOTES ON CONTRIBUTORS 248

INSTRUCTIONS TO CONTRIBUTORS 250

'THOU SHALT NOT REVILE THE GODS'
The LXX translation of Ex. 22:28 (27), its background and influence

PIETER W. VAN DER HORST

One of the many riddles that the LXX sets before us is its rendering of Ex. 22:27a (in the LXX 28a). The Hebrew text (MT) runs as follows: *'elohim lo' t^eqallel*, that is, 'you shall not revile God', whereas the Old Greek has: 'you shall not revile (the) gods' (θεοὺς οὐ κακολογήσεις). Verse 28b follows with: 'nor shall you curse a ruler [LXX: rulers] of your own people'.

The King James Version, like the Vulgate, follows the LXX and has: 'Thou shalt not revile the gods'; but the Jerusalem Bible, the New English Bible, the Revised English Bible, the Moffatt translation, the Revised Standard Version and the New Revised Standard Version all have: 'You shall not revile God' (but curiously enough, the Berkeley Version follows the ancient Targumim in translating: 'Heap no abuse upon judges').[1] Most other modern translations render *'elohim* with a singular. Also in modern commentaries one mostly finds the opinion that a singular (i.e. God) is meant here. It is of course a fact that the Hebrew word *'elohim* is formally (and originally) a plural, but nonetheless the LXX translators almost never hesitate in rendering this apparent plural with the singular θεός. Only when the context makes it unequivocally clear that by *'elohim* pagan gods are meant, as for instance in Exodus 20:2,23; 23:32-3, is the rendering θεοί chosen. Why do the translators of the book of Exodus here prefer the rendering with the plural θεοί? One can only guess at the reason(s). The context does not give any support for this translation, so we cannot but assume that the translator willfully made the text say what it now says, namely that one should not revile the gods, that is, the pagan gods with which he and his readers were confronted in their daily life in Alexandria. If one wants to make a guess as to the background of this translation, one could think of a sincere tolerance towards believers of other religions,[2] or even a tendency

---

[1] Both Onkelos and Pseudo-Jonathan render *'elohim* with 'judges' in conformity with Rabbinic exegesis of our text; see the note by B. Grossfeld, *The Targum Onkelos to Exodus* (Edinburgh 1988) 63 n. 5.
[2] For instance R. Le Déaut speaks of 'l'espèce de tolérance d'Ex 22,27' in his article 'La Septante: un Targum?', in R. Kuntzmann & J. Schlosser (edd.), *Études sur le judaïsme hellénistique* (Paris 1984) 181; see also A. le Boulluec & P. Sandevoir, *La Bible d'Alexan-*

towards compromising with paganism, as that can be observed for instance in the *Letter of Aristeas* when its author says that the God of Israel and Zeus do bear different names but are in fact identical (*Ep. Arist.* 16).[3] It is possible, however, also to look in a different direction, namely by taking this translation as a piece of Jewish apologetics.

From the third cent. BCE onwards, that is to say, beginning in the time that the LXX version of the Pentateuch came into existence, up till the first cent. CE, several pagan Alexandrian authors depicted Moses in their works as an apostate Egyptian priest who for many years exercised a reign of terror over his people (the Egyptians), in which he desecrated their temples, destroyed the images of their gods, forbade the worship of these gods, and took other measures directed against Egyptian religion.[4] We know from Jewish sources other than the LXX that, in reaction to these and similar manifestations of anti-Judaism in Alexandria, there developed a Jewish apologetic literature in which Moses is depicted as a benefactor of humanity as a whole (not only of the Jewish people); one author, Artapanus, even goes so far as to make Moses the founder of Egyptian religion![5] This strong emphasis on Moses as a benefactor can be found in many Alexandrian Jewish authors, both historians and poets.[6] Characteristic of this apologetics is a picture of Moses as someone who does no harm to other religions, or, to put it another way: *as someone who does not revile gods*. So it is well conceivable that the LXX translators of Exodus came to render our verse in the way they did because they were inspired by such apologetic motives as sketched here. If Moses himself could be shown to have forbidden in the Law any evil-speaking

---

drie, 2: *L'Exode* (Paris 1989) 230: 'Elle fait preuve ainsi d'une sorte de tolérance'. In his article 'Use, Authority, and Exegesis of Mikra in the Writings of Josephus', in M. J. Mulder (ed.), *Mikra*, CRINT II 1 (Assen-Philadelphia 1988), L. H. Feldman says that Josephus takes over this LXX-rendering of Ex. 22:27 'in the spirit of tolerance' (496). On Josephus see further below in our text.
[3] V. Tcherikover, *Hellenistic Civilization and the Jews* (New York 1959) 352, interprets the verse in this sense.
[4] These texts, mostly preserved in Josephus' *Contra Apionem*, are now easily accessible in M. Stern, *Greek and Latin Authors on Jews and Judaism* I-II (Jerusalem 1974–80). For a good discussion see J. Gager, *Moses in Greco-Roman Paganism* (Nashville–New York) 1972, 113–133.
[5] See my article 'The Interpretation of the Bible by the Minor Hellenistic Jewish Authors', in my volume *Essays on the Jewish World of Early Christianity* (Fribourg-Göttingen) 1990, 187–219; also my 'Schriftgebruik bij drie vroege joods-hellenistische historici: Demetrius, Artapanus, Eupolemus', in my volume *De onbekende god: Essays over de joodse en hellenistische achtergrond van het vroege christendom* (Utrecht 1988) 158–174.
[6] The relevant material can be found in Gager's *Moses* (n. 4) and in my 'The Interpretation of the Bible by the Minor Hellenistic Jewish Authors' (n. 5).

of other gods, how could he have committed the sacrilegious crimes that he was accused of?[7]

It is possible that we should also judge in light of this apologetic motive the striking fact that in the Jewish-Alexandrinian writing *Joseph and Aseneth*, which deals with the conversion of the daughter of an Egyptian priest to Judaism, we find no negative statements about the deities she had renounced.[8] We can establish that the Greek speaking Jewish writers who quote or allude to Ex. 20:28 took this text seriously. Unfortunately there are only a few of them,[9] but the relevant passages in their work are very illuminating.

The first author in whose writing we can see our biblical passage at work is the Jewish philosopher Philo of Alexandria. In his *De specialibus legibus* 1.53 he says that Moses commanded the Israelites not to 'revile with an unbridled tongue the gods whom others acknowledge, lest they on their part be moved to utter profane words against Him who truly is'. Philo sees as motive behind the interdiction the lawgiver's care to prevent that God will be reviled among the heathen as a possible consequence of the people of Israel's reviling their gods. In the *De Vita Mosis* 2.203–205 Philo explains not Exodus 22:28 itself but Leviticus 24:15–16 in light of the text from Exodus.[10] Philo seems to read the Leviticus passage in such a way that v. 15 ('anyone who curses God shall bear the sin') refers to something different than the immediately following verse 16 ('one who blasphemes the name of the Lord shall be put to death'): he praises Moses because he punishes the mentioning of the name of the Lord more heavily than cursing God/god, for by the word 'god' Moses means not the Most High but in general the gods of the different cities who are falsely so called. 'We must refrain from speaking insultingly of these, lest any of Moses' disciples get into the habit of treating lightly the name 'god' in general, for it is a title worthy of the highest respect and love' (§205). We see here that Philo interprets the passage in Lev. 24 in light of Exodus 22:28. In his *Quaestiones in Exodum* 2.5 (preserved only in

---

[7] That the Jews hold the gods in contempt (or are ἄθεοι) is a frequently recurring motif in pagan literature of the Hellenistic and Roman periods; see for instance Tacitus, who says that the first thing Jews teach a proselyte is *contemnere deos* (to disdain the gods), *Hist.* V 5.2, with many parallels in W. Fauth *ad locum* in H. Heubner & W. Fauth, *P. Cornelius Tacitus: Die Historien* V (Heidelberg 1982) 73. For a suggestion that is somewhat similar to ours see J. W. Wevers, *Notes on the Greek Text of Exodus* (Atlanta 1990) 355.
[8] See D. Sänger, 'Bekehrung und Exodus: Zum jüdischen Traditionshintergrund von 'Joseph und Aseneth'', *JSJ* 10 (1979) 19–20.
[9] A.-M. Denis' *Concordance grecque des pseudépigraphes d'Ancien Testament* (Louvain 1987) makes clear that our text is not quoted in any of the Jewish-Greek pseudepigrapha.
[10] E. P. Sanders, *Jewish Law from Jesus to the Mishnah* (London–Philadelphia 1990, 59, thinks that Philo here contrasts Lev. 24:11 and 16, which I doubt.

Armenian translation)[11] Philo deals with the question: Why does Scripture say that we should not revile the gods? His answer is threefold: (1) it is not in the lawgiver's nature to deal scathingly with the beliefs of those of different opinion, for praise is always better than revilement; (2) criticism of each other's gods always leads to war, whereas the Law wants to be a source of peace; (3) to refrain from negative language about other gods may have as a positive consequence that others (pagans) may speak well of and even praise the only true God. Here Philo sees the prohibition in Ex. 22:28 even in terms of attracting others to belief in the God of Israel.

In *Contra Apionem* 2.237 Josephus says that he would prefer to refrain from investigating the laws and institutions of other nations, 'for it is our traditional custom to observe our own laws and to refrain from criticism of those of aliens. Our legislator has expressly forbidden us to deride or blaspheme the gods recognized by others, out of respect for the very word 'God'. But since our accusers expect to confute us by a comparison of the rival religions, it is impossible to remain silent'. Josephus here follows Philo in seeing respect for the word 'God' as the motive behind the injunction in Ex. 22:28. In *Antiquitates* 4.207, in a paraphrase of the laws of the book of Deuteronomy, Josephus combines our verse in Ex. 22 with Deut. 7:5, 25 as follows: 'Let none blaspheme the gods which other cities revere, nor rob foreign temples, nor take treasure that has been dedicated in the name of any god'. To be sure, Deut. 7 actually stipulates that one *should* destroy the altars of pagan gods, smash their pillars, burn their images, etc., but Josephus is so much concerned to present the Jewish people as the opposite of desecrators of what is holy to others that he does not hesitate to enlist Ex. 22:28 for the purpose of turning Deut. 7 into its contrary.[12] Louis Feldman presumes that it is for exactly this same reason that in *Antiquitates* 9.118, in his rendering of the story of Jehu's eradicating of the Baal service, Josephus omits the element that this god's temple was turned into a latrine (2 Kings 10:27).[13]

Let us now turn to the *Wirkungsgeschichte* of Ex. 22:28 in early Christian literature. Neither in the New Testament nor in the literature of the second century is our text used.[14] The first author to make explicit use of

---

[11] I summarize here the translation by Ralph Marcus in the Philo LCL edition.
[12] On this passage see also G. Delling, Josephus und die heidnische Religionen, in his *Studien zum Neuen Testament und zum hellenistischen Judentum* (Göttingen 1970) 46f.
[13] Feldman in Mulder, *Mikra* (n. 2) 496; cf. *ibid.* 517.
[14] In the NT one might suspect a vague reminiscence of our text at John 10:34-36. For the second century see the *Biblia patristica: Index des citations et allusions bibliques dans la littérature patristique*, vol. 1 (Paris 1975).

the text is Origen in his *Contra Celsum* 8.38. In this passage Origen reacts to what Celsus in his *True Doctrine* had asserted about the Christians' attitude towards images of gods in the following terms: 'Christians say, Look, I stand by the image of Zeus or Apollo or any god indeed, and I blaspheme it and strike it, but it takes no vengeance on me'.[15] Origen's response is as follows:

> He does not notice that in the divine legislation there is the command, 'Thou shalt not speak evil of gods', that our mouth may not get accustomed to speaking evil of any being. For we have heard the command, 'Bless and curse not' [Rom. 12:14], and we are taught that 'Revilers shall not inherit the kingdom of God' [1 Cor. 6:10]. Who among us is so foolish as to say this and not to see that this sort of thing can do nothing to destroy the notion held about the supposed gods?

Origen brings our biblical text to bear on the supposed godlessnes of the Christians, supports this interpretation with two quotations from Paul (that in fact deal with a different matter), and states that no one who believes such things will be so foolish as to make derogatory remarks about another persons' beliefs. Elsewhere, however, Origen probably makes the gods of Ex. 22:28 refer to judges (see *Contra Celsum* 4.31, *in fine*: the judges 'were called 'gods' by a traditional Jewish usage'),[16] a tradition also reflected in the Targumim (see n. 1 above). Moreover, in a fragment from Origen in the *Catenae* on the Psalms it seems that he sometimes took 'gods' to refer to Christian priests.[17]

It is interesting to see how this same tradition was used and reinterpreted by Origen's contemporary, the anonymous author of the Syriac *Didascalia apostolorum*. In Chapter 9 the author says that one may never revile a bishop or a deacon, for it is written in the Law, 'Thou shalt not revile gods': 'Let no one think that the Lord speaks (here) about idols of stone, but he calls 'gods' those who preside over you!'.[18] Cyprian, who also wants our verse to refer to leaders or princes of the people, facilitates such a move by quoting it as follows: *non maledices neque principi populi tui detraxeris*, omitting the word *deos*, which is not the reading of the Vetus Latina (*Testimonia ad Quirinum* III 13).

The idea that 'gods' refers to earthly rulers will gain a wide following. One sees the motif, for instance, in Eusebius of Caesarea, who in his exposition of Psalm 49:1 (MT 50:1), θεὸς θεῶν κύριος ἐλάλησεν, remarks

---

[15] Translation by H. Chadwick, *Origen, Contra Celsum* (Cambridge 1953) 479; Greek text in S. Rizzo, *Celso: Contro i Cristiani* (Milan 1989) 268.
[16] See Chadwick *ad locum*, 208 n. 1.
[17] See the Greek text in J. B. Pitra, *Analecta Sacra* III (Venice 1883) 340.
[18] See R. H. Connolly, *Didascalia Apostolorum*, Oxford 1929, 92–93. A. Vööbus, *The Didascalia Apostolorum in Syriac, I: Chapters I-X*, CSCO 402 (Louvain 1979) 103, translates the final words as 'those who stand as representing you'.

that one sees more often that the Bible uses the term 'gods' in the meaning of 'rulers' (*Commentaria in Ps.* 49:1, PG 23.433), and illustrates this by quoting Ps. 81(82):1 ('God has taken his place in the divine council, in the midst of the gods he holds judgment') and Ex. 22:28. John Chrysostom too appeals to the same biblical verses in his exposition of Psalm 49 in order to prove that 'gods' refers to worldly rulers, here with an explicit reference to the *archontes* in the second half of Ex. 22:28 (*Expos. in Ps.* 49:1, PG 55.241). Elsewhere this Church father has the 'gods' of our text refer to priests in the church, whom he apparently regards as rulers (*Expos. in Ps.* 137:1, PG 55:407).[19] As late as the middle of the sixth century we find John Philoponus making the 'gods' in our text refer to ecclesiastical and worldly rulers and kings (*De opificio mundi* 261).

In the Pseudo-Clementine *Homiliae* 16.5–9 we encounter a disputation between Peter and Simon Magus, in which the latter asserts that the Jewish Scriptures say there are more gods than one and that God cherishes no wrath against them, because he had himself spoken of many gods in his Scriptures. Then he quotes a long series of proof-texts, among others Gen. 3:22, 'See, man has become like one of us', followed by Ex. 22:28, 'Thou shalt not revile the gods' (16.6). Peter then tries to refute his opponent by quoting texts to prove Scripture's monotheism, but Simon ripostes with the remark that, when the Scriptures contain so much material that supports both contradictory positions, they apparently mislead us (16.9). In the parallel passage in the Pseudo-Clementine *Recognitiones* (2.39–42) Simon again cites Gen. 3:22 (alongside Gen. 1:26 and 11:7) and Ex. 22:28 to the effect that the Old Testament recognizes polytheism. Now Peter answers that the second half of Ex. 22:28 ('you shall not curse the leaders of your people') makes clear that also in the first half of the verse the 'gods' are nothing but the rulers of the nations (*principes gentium*) and not real gods. Again we see here how the text functions in a framework of polemics, albeit in a very different way than in Origen's work. It was of course in the nature of this text to function in polemical settings. It is therefore not at all surprising that this continues to take place.

A pagan philosopher, whose identity unfortunately cannot be established with certainty—was he Porphyry, Julian, Hierocles, or still another?[20]—is combatted by Macarius Magnes (c. 400) in his *Apocriticus* 4.23.[21] Again we see Ex. 22:28 functioning in the context of a debate on

---

[19] Ps.John Chrysostom, *Synopsis Scripturae Sacrae: Exodus*, PG 56.327, also emphasizes that one should read Ex. 22:28a in light of 28b: the text does not speak about gods but about rulers.
[20] For discussion and references see G. Rinaldi, *Biblia gentium* (Rome 1989) 88–89, 153–54.
[21] Edition by A. von Harnack, *Kritik des Neuen Testaments von einem griechischen*

'gods' in Scripture. The pagan philosopher turns out to know the Bible very well:

> I could also give proof to you of that insidious name of 'gods' from the Law, when it cries out and admonishes the hearer with much reverence, 'Thou shalt not revile gods, and thou shalt not speak evil of the ruler of thy people'. For it does not speak to us of gods other than those already recognized by us, from what we know in the words, 'Thou shalt not go after gods' (Jer. 7:6 LXX),[22] and again, 'If you go and worship other gods' (Deut. 13:3 LXX). It is not men, but the gods who are held in honour by us that are meant, not only by Moses, but also by his successor Joshua. For he says to the people, 'And now fear him and serve him alone, and put away the gods whom your father served' (Jos. 24:14 LXX). And it is not concerning men, but incorporeal beings that Paul says, 'For though there be so-called gods, whether on earth or in heaven, yet to us there is but one God and Father, of whom are all things' (1 Cor. 8:5-6). Therefore you make a great mistake in thinking that God is angry if any other is called a god and obtains the same title as Himself. For even rulers do not object to the title from their subjects nor masters from slaves. And it is not right to think that God is more petty-minded than men. Enough then about the fact that gods exist and ought to receive honour.

We see here that a non-Christian brings not only Ex. 22:28 but also other biblical, even New Testament, texts into position in order to attack monotheism. It is the Bible itself, says the anonymous author, that indicates not only that other gods exist but also that they should be worshipped. For the commandment not to revile the gods implies that they should also be honoured.

Julian the Apostate makes a similar use of our text in his great work *Contra Galilaeos*.[23] In one of the preserved fragments we read the following:[24]

> For the Hebrews have precise laws concerning religious worship, and countless sacred things and observances which demand the priestly life and profession. But though the lawgiver forbade them to serve any gods save only that one whose 'portion is

---

Philosophen des 3. Jahrhunderts, TU 37.4 (Leipzig 1911) 90. Harnack defends the thesis that the philosopher was Porphyry; he prints the text as fr. 78 in his edition of the fragments of Porphyry's *Adversus Christianos*. Text and translation in Rinaldi, *Biblia gentium* 278-9, no. 135 (I have made some minor modifications to the translation).
[22] All biblical quotations by this author are rather free and apparently done from memory.
[23] For a brief but good discussion of Julian's *Contra Galilaeos* see Rinaldi, *Biblia gentium* 146-151; further A. Meredith, 'Porphyry and Julian Against the Christians', in *ANRW* II 23.2 (Berlin –New York 1980) 1119-1149.
[24] I use the text and translation in Rinaldi, *Biblia gentium* 297, no. 167. The fragment concerned is in Cyril of Alexandria's *Pro christiana religione* 238C and may be found at pp. 207-208 in the edition by C. J. Neumann, *Iuliani imperatoris librorum contra Christianos quae supersunt* (Leipzig 1880) and at pp. 388-390 in vol. 3 of the LCL edition of Julian by W. C. Wright (London 1923) (Rinaldi prints Wright's translation).

Jacob, and Israel an allotment of his inheritance' (Deut. 32:9 LXX), he did not say this only, but methinks he added also, 'Thou shalt not revile the gods'. Yet the shamelessness and audacity of later generations, desiring to root out all reverence from the mass of the people, has thought that blasphemy accompanies the neglect of worship.

Here we observe an opinion that is also found in other pagan authors of late antiquity, namely that Moses was wise enough to recognize the existence of other gods even though he prohibited their worship—hence praise for Moses—but that later generations had corrupted the original Mosaic religion, in which there still was a place for other gods, so as to make it into a rigid exclusivism.[25] As Julian states here and elsewhere in his work against the Christians,[26] for Moses the God of Israel was one of the many gods of the many nations. Hence Julian had nothing against incorporating Moses' God into his own pantheon. But the later Jewish exclusivism, that had been taken over by the Christians, was rejected by him categorically, a view which he felt was given support by Ex. 22:28 LXX.[27]

By way of summary we can say that relatively little use of our text was made in early patristic literature, and that when it did occur, it was often forced upon the Patres by the fact that their pagan opponents attacked them with exactly this verse as prooftext on behalf of polytheism. Outside this polemical context the text is mainly quoted to convince the Christian readers that they should honour (and obey) their worldly and ecclesiastical rulers, an interpretation that was sometimes supported with a reference to the fact that in the second half of the verse earthly rulers are indeed mentioned. It is only in the Jewish apologists Philo and Josephus that one finds the positive interpretation to the effect, namely that God gave this commandment to humanity in order to teach them to always be respectful in dealing with the word 'god', even in the plural form 'gods', and to prohibit his own people from reviling other gods lest He himself be reviled by adherents of other gods. It might even be, Philo says, that by such an attitude of God's people others will come to take a positive stance towards Israel's God. As Philo remarks in this connection: reviling each other's gods always causes war, and the Torah is meant to be a source of peace.[28]

University of Utrecht

---

[25] See e.g. Gager, *Moses* (n. 4) 106.
[26] See the references in D. Rokeah, *Jews, Pagans and Christians in Conflict* (Jerusalem-Leiden 1982) 164–165.
[27] It is interesting to see that the thesis of an original Israelite polytheism has been revived in modern research on ancient Israel, but on completely different grounds.
[28] *QE* 2.5.

THE GREEK VIRTUES AND THE MOSAIC LAWS IN PHILO
An Elucidation of *De Specialibus Legibus* IV 133–135

NAOMI G. COHEN

The present article is focused on the Philonic text *De Specialibus Legibus* 4.133–135.[1] It falls rather naturally into two distinct, albeit connected, parts. The first deals with Philo's equation of the Greek 'virtues' and the Mosaic 'laws', while the second focuses on his association of the Greek philosophic *topos* which demands that 'words, thoughts and actions' be in mutual harmony with the Septuagint version of Deut. 30:14 which contains the combination 'mouth, heart and hands'.

Before us are two more examples of the thesis propounded in a previous article,[2] namely that in any specific instance the first, and often the most relevant question to be posed, is not whether the frame of reference is 'philosophic' or 'Jewish', but rather *how* the two have been indissolubly intertwined.

Of course one must be able to identify Jewish and Hellenistic parallels in order to do this, but it is not the separate 'building blocks', but their combination, which is the literary artifact under consideration and it is this rather than the discrete elements which contains Philo's message.

I

Section 133 serves as a bridge between the principle of organization of the commandments under the discrete rubrics of the Decalogue which has been followed in *Spec*. I–IV until now, and the ensuing material which Philo describes as 'belonging to the Decalogue as a whole'. The text reads:[3]

τούτων μὲν δὴ ἅλις. οὐ δεῖ δ' ἀγνοεῖν, ὅτι ὥσπερ ἰδίᾳ ἑκάστῳ τῶν δέκα συγγενῆ τινα τῶν ἐπὶ μέρους ἐστίν, ἃ πρὸς ἕτερον γένος οὐδεμίαν ἔχει κοινωνίαν, οὕτως ἔνια κοινὰ πάντων συμβέβηκεν, οὐχ ἑνὶ ἢ δυσίν, ὡς ἔπος εἰπεῖν, τοῖς ⟨δὲ⟩ δέκα λογίοις ἐφαρμόττοντα.

---

[1] It is a chapter in my forthcoming book which is provisionally entitled: *Philo as His Contemporaries Read Him*.
[2] This thesis is presented in some detail in my article 'The Jewish Dimension of Philo's Judaism—An Elucidation of *de Spec. Leg.* IV 132–150,' *JJS* 38 (1987) 169–172. We have done our best not to repeat what we have written there.
[3] Though we have used Colson's English translation in the Loeb edition as the base, it has been freely modified, either to achieve greater accuracy, or for stylistic reasons.

(133) Enough then of this. But we must not fail to recognize that just as each of the ten separately has some particular laws akin to it having nothing in common with any other, so there are some common to all which fit in not with a particular number such as one or two, but in a manner of speaking, with the Decalogue as a whole.

Sections 134–135 harness Greek philosophical truisms in the service of praising a commitment to traditional Judaism, for the text continues immediately:

ταῦτα δ' εἰσὶν αἱ κοινωφελεῖς ἀρεταί· καὶ γὰρ ἕκαστος ἰδίᾳ τῶν δέκα χρησμῶν καὶ κοινῇ πάντες ἐπὶ φρόνησιν καὶ δικαιοσύνην καὶ θεοσέβειαν καὶ τὸν ἄλλον χορὸν τῶν ἀρετῶν ἀλείφουσι καὶ προτρέπουσι, βουλαῖς μὲν ἀγαθαῖς ὑγιαίνοντας λόγους, λόγοις δὲ σπουδαίας πράξεις συνείροντες, ἵνα τὸ ψυχῆς ὄργανον εὐαρμόστως ὅλον δι' ὅλων συνηχῇ πρὸς ἐμμέλειαν βίου καὶ συμφωνίαν ἀνεπίληπτον. περὶ μὲν οὖν τῆς ἡγεμονίδος τῶν ἀρετῶν, εὐσεβείας καὶ ὁσιότητος, ἔτι δὲ καὶ φρονήσεως καὶ σωφροσύνης εἴρηται πρότερον, νυνὶ δὲ περὶ τῆς ἐπιτηδευούσης ἀδελφὰ καὶ συγγενῆ ταύταις

(§134) These are the virtues of universal value; for each of the Ten Commandments separately and all in common drill and inculcate[4] *phronesis* (wisdom) and *dikaiosyne* (justice) and *theosebeia* (worship of G-d) and the rest of the company of virtues—combining[5] good thoughts and intentions with health-giving words, and words with actions of true worth—so that the soul, being well attuned in all its parts may sound the melody of a life of impeccable harmony and accord. (§135) Of the queen of the virtues, *eusebia* and *hosiotes* (piety and holiness),[6] we have spoken earlier and also of *phronesis* and *sophrosyne* (wisdom and temperance). Our theme must now be that whose ways are close akin to them, that is *dikaiosyne* (justice).

Colson, in his note to §133[7] has expressed the view that what is being referred to here are the 'virtues' introduced in the opening words of §134: '*These* are the virtues of universal value' thereby disagreeing with Heinemann who understood them to be 'the Mosaic Laws'. As we have already argued elsewhere[8] it is our conviction that very often Philo did not mean *either/or*. Here too, he is not referring *either* to 'the Greek virtues' *or* to 'the Mosaic Laws', but wished at one and the same time to allude *both* to the 'virtues of universal value' (αἱ κοινωφελεῖς ἀρεταί) mentioned at the beginning of §134, which is a clearly Hellenistic idiom,[9] *and* the Mosaic Laws, artfully equating the two.

---

[4] See LSJ *s.v.* ἀλείφω, 'youths undergoing gymnastic training'. Hence we have rendered Philo's ἀλείφουσι καὶ προτρέπουσι by 'drill and inculcate'.
[5] Note that the subject here is the Ten Commandments.
[6] A *hendiadys*—i.e. the expression of a concept by two words connected by *and*. Cf. inter alia Philo *Dec*. 119, as well as Plato *Euthyphro* 12e.
[7] See PLCL 8.90 note *b*, who in this disagrees with Heinemann at GT 2.258.
[8] 'Jewish Dimension', *loc. cit.* (n. 2).
[9] And indeed it is even very difficult to find a Hebrew equivalent for it. The terms usually used in common parlance— מדות טובות and מעלות טובות are similarly untranslatable idioms. Literally: טובות = 'good', מדה = 'measure', and מעלה = 'degree'.

As a literary device this facilitated the transition between the classification of the 'particular laws' under the rubrics of each of the Ten Commandments and what follows, i.e. the discussion of commandments, '(133) common to all which fit in not with some particular number ... but in a manner of speaking with the Decalogue as a whole.' At the same time it also served as the vehicle for Philo's didactic/homiletic message that since the commandments 'drill and inculcate ... the whole company of (Greek) virtues', the 'virtuous life' in terms of the Greek frame of reference is to be achieved by ordering one's life in accord with the precepts of the Mosaic revelation.[10]

One misses much of what Philo has to say if when reading his writings one does not take this stylistic idiosyncracy constantly into account, while its recognition makes it possible for us to fathom the multi-levelled dimension—the sophisticated nuances—which Philo's contemporary readers must have enjoyed.[11]

At the same time, before proceeding it will be well to bear in mind that the presentation of Judaism as a philosophy is not really specifically Philonic, for the conceptualization of Judaism in philosophic terms was almost certainly taken for granted at least on the part of Greek speaking Jewry in the first century CE and an integral part of its accepted 'truths'. In any event Josephus has spoken of it in these terms in the *Wars*, in the *Antiquities*, and in *Contra Apion*—even though they stem from different periods of his life.

Thus, Josephus *BJ* 2.119 reads:[12]

(119) Jewish *philosophy*, in fact takes three forms. The followers of the first school are called Pharisees, of the second Sadducees, of the third Essenes.

The Greek of the passage commences: τρία γὰρ παρὰ 'Ιουδαίοις εἴδη φιλοσοφεῖται κτλ which thus takes for granted that the appropriate frame of reference for discussing these 'schools' is philosophical. Josephus is here talking about 'three schools of philosophy'. We today would probably term them either 'trends' or 'parties'—but however termed, it is to 'Judaism' to which they belong, both in Josephus' and in our own eyes.

---

[10] See also 'Jewish Dimensions', loc. cit. (n. 2).
[11] This is why we find ourselves at loggerheads with some of the categorical conclusions of I. Heinemann in his classic study, *Philons griechische und jüdische Bildung: kulturvergleichende Untersuchungen zu Philons Darstellung der jüdischen Gesetze* (Breslau 1932, Hildesheim 1962²). Though we agree that the term discussed was understood by Philo in a 'Hellenistic philosophic' sense, this rarely exhausts the subject as far as understanding what Philo wished thereby to say; cf. also V. Nikiprowetzky, *Le commentaire de l'Écriture chez Philon d'Alexandrie* (Leiden 1977) 241, *et passim*.
[12] Translation quoted according to H. St. John Thackeray, in the Loeb edition.

Although this returns us to the insoluble conundrum 'What is a Jew', and its corollary, 'What is Judaism', in any event, an integral part of the differences between the Pharisees, Sadducees, and Essenes, both in the traditional Jewish literature as well as in other sources, always include differences respecting the religious beliefs and practices of Judaism. And the same is true respecting what we may for convenience call Philo's Mosaic philosophy. If pressed Philo too would hardly have called it anything but 'Judaism'.

Similarly, we read in *Ant.* 13.171:[13]

> Now at the time there were three schools (τρεῖς αἱρέσεις) of thought among the Jews ... the first being that of the Pharisees, the second that of the Sadducees, and the third that of the Essenes.

One of the meanings of the term αἵρεσις is of course 'system of philosophic principles', and a form of the word (αἱρετισταὶ) was also used in *BJ* 2.119—the pericope whose beginning has just been quoted—as well as in 162; and just because the word *hairesis* does not mean 'philosophic sect' exclusively, it is all the more fitting in this context. And note further that the direct continuation in *Ant.* 13.172 discusses the differences concerning *heimarmene* (Fate, or perhaps as it has been suggested,[14] Providence), an eminently philosophic dimension.

Most striking however is what Josephus has written in *Contra Apion* II, for like here in the Philonic pericope under present consideration—as we have understood it—so too in *Contra Ap.* 2.170 Josephus has also explicitly stated that Judaism encompasses within it all the virtues.[15] We read there:

> οὐ γὰρ μέρος ἀρετῆς ἐποίησεν τὴν εὐσέβειαν, ἀλλὰ ταύτης μέρη τἆλλα, λέγω δὲ τὴν δικαιοσύνην, τὴν σωφροσύνην, τὴν καρτερίαν, τὴν τῶν πολιτῶν πρὸς ἀλλήλους ἐν ἅπασι συμφωνίαν.

> (170) For he (Moses) did not make religion a department of virtue, but the entire complement of the virtues—I mean justice, temperance, fortitude and mutual harmony ... departments of religion.

This text clearly describes Judaism in an identical manner to Philo in our section; not only as the best of all philosophies, but as *subsuming within it the entire complement of the virtues as well.*[16]

---

[13] Translation quoted according to Ralph Marcus in the Loeb edition.
[14] See note in Loeb ed. *ad loc.*
[15] Translation quoted according to H. St. John Thackeray, in the Loeb edition, except that we have rendered τἆλλα as 'the entire complement of'.
[16] And even should one argue some sort of direct dependence of Josephus upon Philo (hardly likely here in our view), this would at the very least corroborate our under-

Clearly then, when in *Spec. Leg.* 4.133–135 Philo refers to 'the whole family of virtues' *et sim.*, he is talking of the practice of Judaism, and his contemporary readers took this for granted without requiring it to be explicitly stated; and indeed, the understanding of Judaism as a philosophy is quite natural to the frame of reference of ancient 'philosophic' thought, for the definition of philosophy in the ancient world was not that to which we have become accustomed since the Middle Ages and which we accept today without giving it a second thought.

As we all know but often fail to bear in mind, in the ancient world, at least from the time of Plato and those who followed in his wake, 'philosophy' was looked upon as *'the acquisition of that knowledge which leads to the good life'*, though of course the different philosophical schools espoused different views respecting the nature of the discrete components of this equation. Further, with the advent of the Stoa and other Hellenistic philosophic schools which originated outside of Greece proper, the major stress turned from 'the theory of knowldege' to *the knowledge of the right road to be followed*; and in the Hellenistic Roman period to which Philo and Josephus belonged, the different philosophic traditions had become virtual recipes for 'right living'.

Hence since the Greco-Roman world had no word for *religion* in the modern sense of the term[17] it was natural for Judaism, a religion for whom the ethical imperative was axiomatic, and which believed that it had been vouchsafed divinely inspired laws and commandments for every facet of life whose observance would enable the devotee to live 'the good life', to be defined as a 'philosophy', with the 'virtues' being departments of this religion; and it could only have been in this sense that Josephus wrote that the Pharisees 'bear a resemblance to what among the Greeks are called the Stoics (Josephus, Vita 12).' Though pagan writers might conceivably have erred in this respect,[18] Josephus

---

standing of the Philonic passage.

[17] M. Smith, 'Palestinian Judaism in the First Century', in M. Davis, *Israel: Its Role in Civilization* (New York 1956) 79, mentioned by J. G. Gager, *The Origins of Antisemitism–Attitudes Towards Judaism in Pagan and Christian Antiquity* (New York–Oxford 1983) 85, has even suggested that the modern equivalent for the term *philosophia* in the Greco-Roman world ought to be 'the cult of wisdom' rather than 'philosophy'. Already in Eduard Zeller's classic *Outlines of the History of Greek Philosophy*, which was written over a century ago, in the introduction to ch. 57, Hellenistic Philosophy (13th ed., revised by Wilhelm Nestle, ET L. R. Palmer, Trinity College, Cambridge, 1931, repr. New York 1955) 226, we find the statement that Hellenistic philosophy took on many aspects of what we consider to be religion, and we even find the categorical statement that 'religion and philosophy now tended to become united.'

[18] Greek authors–particularly from the very inception of the Hellenistic period on–are quoted (for the most part in sources which clearly stem from Greco-Roman times) as portraying the Jews as a people of 'philosophers' replete with 'philosophic' views on a

could hardly have been referring to any similarities in cosmogonic speculations.

Be that as it may, clearly, in *Spec. Leg.* 4.134–5 the 'philosophic virtues' and the 'Jewish' parameters of the subject not only cannot but also should not be separated out, for what Philo is telling us is that '(134) each of the Ten Commandments separately and all in common drill and inculcate ... (the entire) company of virtues,' thus making the Decalogue the 'realization' of both Platonic and Aristotelian pronouncements on the subject of the ideal relationship between the 'classic virtues' and the ideal, or at least the good laws.[19]

For example, Plato writes in *Laws* I 631a:

> *Ath.*: ... you were quite right in beginning with virtue, and saying that this was the aim of the giver of the law ...

So too we find in Aristotle, *Nic. Eth.* II 1, 1103b1-7, and V 2, 1130b23-25:[20]

> (1103b) Similarly we become just by doing just acts, temperate by doing temperate acts, brave by doing brave acts. This truth is attested by the experience of states: lawgivers make the citizens good by training them in habits of right action—this is the aim of all legislation ... this is what distinguishes a good form of constitution from a bad one.

> (1130b) For the actions that spring from virtue in general are in the main identical with the actions that are according to law, since the law enjoins conduct displaying the various particular virtues and forbids conduct displaying the various particular vices.

However, Philo's argument is far more sophisticated than this. In order to fathom its multi-dimensional levels we must take a closer look at the choice of the specific virtues here listed and the order in which they are presented. While in *Spec. Leg.* IV 134-5 Philo *does* allude to what eventually became known as the 'cardinal virtues', this is hardly an adequate description of the section's contents, for his overall design goes far beyond a simple enumeration of the virtues. His contemporary readers must have readily and almost intuitively grasped the multi-faceted associations inherent in his presentation, but for us this is hardly the case. If we wish to be able to discern even its major outlines we are

---

variety of subjects For a list and description of these ancient authors see M. Hengel, *Judaism and Hellenism* (ET, London 1974) 255ff., Gager, *op. cit.*, 39, and of course the separate entries in M. Stern, *Greek and Latin Authors on Jews and Judaism* (Jerusalem 1974–84).

[19] Cf. also Wolfson, *Philo* (Cambridge Mass. 1947, 1968[4]) 2.200–225.

[20] I cite the translation of Rackham in the LCL; cf. also *Nic. Eth.* X 9, 1179b32: 'And it is difficult to obtain a right education in virtue from youth up without being brought up under right laws.'

forced to laboriously dissect the section and to separate out each discrete component. This is most unfortunate since the original zest and flavour of the section is thereby destroyed and the net result is similar to what happens when one has to explain a *bon mot* to one's listeners. It loses its charm. The reader should bear in mind, however, that it is we and not Philo who has laboured the point—for it took him only about thirty words. In any event, since I see no other way to make the 20th century reader aware of Philo's elegant and polished literary exercise, this is the manner by which we shall perforce proceed; and once these associations are perceived, they do, I think, become obvious not only to Philo's erudite contemporary audience, but to us as well.

First: Philo takes for granted that the existence of the classic virtues as well as their specific identity as *wisdom (phronesis), justice (dikaiosyne), temperance (sophrosyne)* and *courage (andreia)* is an integral part of his reader's stock of associations, for without further ado he refers at the beginning of §134 to two of these 'virtues', *wisdom (phronesis)*, and *justice (dikaiosyne)*. But instead of completing the list with *temperance (sophrosyne)* and *courage (andreia)* as we would *prima facie* have expected were the frame of reference exclusively 'the four cardinal virtues', he has completed it with: '*theosebeia* (worship of G-d) and the rest of the company of virtues'. To this we shall return shortly.

Second: when, immediately following in§135, Philo states that *wisdom (phronesis)* and *temperance (sophrosyne)* (sic!) were spoken of earlier, this obviously cannot be taken to be a reference to the virtues mentioned at the beginning of §134, for there it is *wisdom (phronesis)* and *justice (dikaiosyne)*, and not *wisdom (phronesis)* and *temperance (sophrosyne)* which have been listed.

We therefore conclude that what Philo meant in §135 was that *wisdom (phronesis)* and *temperance (sophrosyne)* were the virtues discussed in *Spec. Leg.* I-IV as a whole,[21] for this naturally introduces the statement which immediately follows, that the next virtue to be discussed will be *justice (dikaiosyne)*, while the list of the four virtues is eventually completed by *courage (andreia)* introduced at the beginning of the ensuing treatise *De Virtutibus* which opens with the words:

(§1) The subject of *justice (dikaiosyne)*, and all the relevant points which the occasion requires having already been discussed, I will take the next in sequence—*courage (andreia)*.

---

[21] This has already been remarked in notes to both the German and the French translations—viz. that of I. Heinemann in PCH, vol. 2 ((Breslau 1910) 285 n.1 and of A. Mosès in PAPM vol. 25 (Paris 1970) *ad loc.*

Our second point thus explains the mention of the 'virtues' *phronesis, sophrosyne* and *dikaiosyne* in §135 and brings the four traditional virtues into focus as the framework for *Spec. Leg.* through *Virt.* (which completes the list with *andreia*)—and it also fits our suggested understanding of what *'these'* were at the beginning of §134.

But what then is the significance of the beginning of §134 where *'wisdom' (phronesis), 'justice' (dikaiosyne)*, and *'worship of G-d' (theosebeia)* have been listed together? And to what is Philo referring by the opening words of §135, 'Of the queen of virtues, *piety and holiness (eusebia and hosiotes)* we have spoken earlier'? The key which unlocks the meaning here is the realization that although the concept 'four virtues' was a commonplace in pagan Greek philosophic thought, nevertheless in ancient philosophical sources what is today referred to as 'the four cardinal virtues' were not the *sole* referrent.

True, as one can see from Cicero *de Officiis* I v 15–17[22] it was clearly standard in Philo's day.[23] But at the same time one must not lose sight of the fact that although in Plato's *Rep.* IV 427ff. 433b, *Prot.* 361b and elsewhere the four virtues *wisdom (phronesis), justice (dikaiosyne), temperance (sophrosyne)* and *courage (andreia)* were considered *'the virtues' par excellence*, Plato also sometimes included *holiness (hosiotes)* in the list of virtues (which then number five)—e. g. *Prot.* 330b and 349b, and Aristotle also enlarges the list of the 'principal virtues' without further ado.

Plato and Aristotle have also time and again equated one 'virtue' with another, and each of them has in fact assigned to a single specific virtue a position of primacy encompassing all the rest. Further, I think that one can hardly doubt that whether or not Philo's contemporary readership could quote a specific source such as:

(a) *Laws* I 631, 'virtue' ... was the aim of the giver of the law, ... *wisdom (phronesis)* is chief and leader ...

or (b) *Protagoras* 361b: all things are *knowledge (episteme)*, including *justice (dikaiosyne)* and *temperance (sophrosyne)* and *courage (andreia)*,

they were certainly cognizant of the fact that at the base of Plato's philosophy was the assumption that *knowledge* or *wisdom* (the first 'virtue' in Philo's list at the beginning of §134) was the epitome of all the virtues.[24]

And indeed, although Philo has listed the four virtues in differing

---

[22] And *ibid.* in greater detail till the summary in *id.* xliii 152.
[23] Later, Ambrose and Augustine (4th cent. CE) added three 'theological virtues' and called the lot the 'seven cardinal Christian virtues'. (See J. Hastings (ed.), *Encl. of Religion & Ethics* (New York 1955) 11.430–1, s.v. *Seven virtues.*)
[24] In this frame of reference *episteme, phronesis* and *sophia* are of course synonymous, and sometimes one and sometimes another is used by Plato; cf. *sophia: Prot.* 329e; *episteme: id.* 330b; *sophia: id.* 333a–b; *phronesis: Laws* I 631c, III 688b; *sophia: Rep.* IV 428b; etc.

orders in different contexts, in view of the incontrovertibly strong Platonic component in his philosophic *Weltanschauung*, it is hardly entirely fortuitous that the Platonic 'super-virtue', *wisdom*, is the virtue mentioned first in all them—including *Spec. Leg.* IV 134.[25]

At the same time Philo and his readers must also have been very much aware that *justice* was considered to be the epitome of 'virtue itself' by Aristotle; see e.g. *Nic. Eth.* V 1, 1129b26 –1130a10 where *inter alia* we read:[26]

> (1129b31) Justice then in this sense is perfect virtue, ... This is why *justice (dikaiosyne)* is often thought to be *the chief of virtues* ... and we have the proverb—'In *justice* is all virtue found in sum' (*Theognis* 147) ... (1130a7) Justice *(dikaiosyne)* in this sense then is not a part of virtue, but *the whole of virtue.*

Thus it is now clear why Philo has begun the list in *Spec.* 4.134 with *wisdom (phronesis)*, which was a sort of 'super-virtue' in the Platonic tradition including within it all the other 'virtues', and continued it with the Aristotelian 'pre-eminent virtue' *justice (dikaiosyne)*. By adding *the worship of G-d (theosebeia)* to the list as a third 'pre-eminent' or 'super' virtue (with all the rest of the virtues lumped together under the general category of 'the rest of the company of virtues') Philo has gracefully reiterated the point which he makes time and again—that *the worship of G-d*, like *wisdom* and *justice*, encompasses within it all the other virtues.

But we must still take one step further with him, for at the beginning of §135 Philo has elegantly added *'piety and holiness'*—which is of course synonymous with *'the worship of G-d' (theosebeia)*—to the four cardinal virtues, at the same time crowning it as 'the queen of virtues'[27] thereby vouchsafing us a repetition *cum* explication of the point just made that it too must be considered a 'super-virtue' subsuming within it all excellence.

So too, in *Vita Mosis* 2.216 we also find *'piety and holiness'* appended to the list of the cardinal virtues which all together are conceived as being the summation of Judaism. We read in this passage:

> (§216) Even now ... the Jews every seventh day occupy themselves with the philosophy of their fathers, dedicating that time to the acquiring of *knowledge (episteme)* and the *study* of the truths of nature (θεωρίᾳ τῶν περὶ φύσιν). For what are our places of prayer throughout the cities but schools of *wisdom (phronesis)* and *courage (andreia)*

---

[25] For example, *Leg.* 2.18 alludes to *wisdom, temperance, justice* and *bravery*, while *Spec.* 2.62 to *wisdom, temperance, courage* and *justice*, and *Mos.* 2.216 which will be quoted shortly, lists *wisdom, courage, temperance* and *justice*.
[26] And cf. similarly, *id. id.* V 2, 1130b 6–7.
[27] And cf. similarly *Spec.* 4.147 and *Praem.* 53 where *piety*—probably short for *piety and holiness*—is labelled 'the queen of virtues'.

and *temperance* (*sophrosyne*) and *justice* (*dikaiosyne*) and *piety and holiness* (*eusebeia kai osiotes*) and every virtue by which duties to G-d and men are discerned and rightly performed.

The context in *Vita Mosis* II 216 differs from *Spec.* 4.134-5, and therefore the order of the mention of the different virtues differs accordingly, but the message is very similar: that *Torah* and 'truths of nature',[28] the traditional 'cardinal virtues' and '*piety and holiness*' (=*worship of G-d*) all fit together as parts of a unified whole.

While I do not wish to suggest that Philo had this frame of reference in mind every single time he mentions the virtues, I *do* think that it helps us understand the specific choice of virtues enumerated in several other passages in *Spec. Leg.* I-IV as well. For example, *Spec.*1.277 contains a description — or perhaps one should rather say, almost a definition of — G-d were that thought to be possible. We read there:

> (§277) ... being as He is, the primal good, the consummation of perfection, the perennial fountain of wisdom (*phronesis*) and justice (*dikaiosyne*) and every virtue ...

Clearly, the choice of these two virtues specifically as the consummation of perfection is not arbitrary, but a function of their being the Platonic and the Aristotelian conceptions respecting virtue *par excellence* and hence the epitome of 'good', of which G-d is 'the perennial fountain'. So too it is very likely that implicit in *Spec.* 2.12, 2.259, and 4.170 is the threefold pattern just described—where 'the worship of Gd' (*theosebeia*) or its synonym 'piety and holiness' (*eusebeia* and *hosiotes*) is identified or put on a par with what for lack of a better term we have called the Platonic and Aristotelian 'super-virtues'.

One final point: the locution '*piety and holiness*' (*eusebeia and osiotes*) which Philo has used as a synonym for the term '*worship of G-d*' (*theosebeia*), and which he time and again describes as being '*the queen of virtues*' clearly meant for him 'the observance of the traditional commandments' in contexts such as these. We will not try to prove this, but merely to illustrate it by a single quotation which I am sure will convince the reader that this is indeed so. *Spec.* 1.186 reads:

> When the third special season has come in the seventh month at the autumnal equinox there is held at its outset the sacred-month-day also called 'trumpet day'[29] ... On the tenth day is the fast,[30] which is carefully observed not only by the zealous for *piety and holiness* (εὐσεβείας καὶ ὁσιότητος) but also by those who never act religiously (εὐαγὲς οὐδὲν δρᾶται) in the rest of their life.

---

[28] Cf. also *Mos.* 2.211: θεσμοῖς φύσεως.
[29] I.e. *Rosh Hashanah, Yom Teruah*.
[30] I.e. The Day of Atonement (*Yom Kippur*).

Apparently then as now the Day of Atonement had special significance for the non-observant, assimilated Jew, who has on that day, as Philo put it, also acted like those 'zealous for piety and holiness'.

In sum: once we take due cognizance of the fact that many of the associations common to Philo and his readers are not automatically called into our own consciousness, we see that there is often rhyme and reason for what to us at first appeared to be merely a verbose and unsystematic recapitulation of philosophic jargon. While such nuances cannot be identified in the usual translations alone,[31] careful attention to the fine points of the Greek text often unveils heretofore unsuspected literary, intellectual and aesthetic facets of Philo's writings.

II

We now turn to the second part of the discussion of *Spec.* 4.133–135: the consideration of the clause in §134 which in our translation given above we placed between the dashes as follows:

—combining[32] good *thoughts* and intentions with health-giving *words*, and words with *actions* of true worth–

Here too a Greek quasi-philosophic 'truth' has been drafted into the service of enhancing Jewish religious commitment.[33] This maxim,—that thoughts, words and actions should be in harmony with each other—which is found *inter alia* in Plato as well as in later Stoic sources,[34] is time and again reiterated by Philo. A particularly felicitous example is *Mos.*

---

[31] For example: in *Spec.* 2.12 in the Loeb edition Colson has translated ὁσιότης as 'righteousness' rather than as 'holiness', which confuses the picture, and in *id. id.* 259, though Colson does give the alternative 'holiness' in the footnote, the running text reads 'religion'; and though this is of course correct, and even relays the meaning in the context better than 'holiness', nevertheless it does not preserve the nuance. It should also be noted that here, as in *id.* 4.170, requires taking into account the underlying Biblical allusion.

[32] As pointed out above, the subject here is the Decalogue.

[33] See *e.g.* the remarks of D. Winston, at the beginning of his article, 'The Philonic Sage' (Hebrew), *Da'at* 11 (Summer 1983) 9–10, where it is pointed out that this is a philosophic commonplace. The English Summary at the end of the Journal begins with the statement that 'Philo's portrait of the wise man is essentially identical with that of the Stoics, faithfully echoing the well-known paradoxes which they had applied to him.'

[34] See *op. cit.*, 9–10, and particularly n. 4 end and n. 5 where parallels of varying degrees of affinity are mentioned by Winston; so Democritus, *Tritogeneia* (the name of the goddess is allegorically taken to suggest right mind, speech and activity), Plato, *Statesman* 498e, Seneca, *Letters* 75.4; 20.2, 24.19, 52.8, 108.36, 114, Marcus Aurelius 10.16, and Iamblichus, *Life of Pythagoras* 176.

1.29,[35] for it is there explicitly stated that this was a philosophical commonplace. Speaking of Moses, Philo writes:

> (§29) He (Moses) exemplified his *philosophical creed* by his daily actions. His *words* expressed his *feelings*, and his *actions* accorded with his words, so that speech and life were in harmony, and thus through their mutual agreement were found to make melody together as on a musical instrument.

But while one can hardly doubt that its philosophic pedigree weighed heavily in its favour, this hardly exhausts the gamut of associations which Philo presumably expected his readers to have in connection with this 'truth'. Thus in *Post.* 85[36] Philo has explicitly identified Deut. 30:14[37] to be an expression of this philosophical construct and he there does not even bother to explain why this is so, but takes it for granted that his readers will recognize it for he writes:

> (§85) And *in a thoroughly philosophic way* he (Moses) makes a threefold division of it: saying 'It (viz. 'the good') is in thy *mouth* and in thy *heart* and in thy *hand*' (Deut. 30:14).

Elsewhere too, Philo explicitly associates Deut. 30:14 with the idiomatic philosophic commonplace respecting *'words ... thoughts ... and actions'*. While I do not wish to claim that in all the instances without exception in which it appears in his writings, Philo has drafted it to serve in the cause of one of his major theses, namely that the actual practice of the Torah commandments was indeed 'philosophically' de *rigueur*, I do think that this was very often the case.

Our final example is found in the closing book of the *magnum opus* which having begun with *De opificio mundi* proceeded from a primarily philosophical/allegorical stance to an ever more literal/halakhic approach finally ending with the *Rewards and Punishments* (*Praem.*). In this final treatise Philo does not merely implicitly associate this philosophical commonplace with a paraphrase of the *Septuagint* version of Deut. 30:11-14. He has spelled this out. We read at *Praem.* 79-81:

---

[35] Brought by Winston, *op. cit.* In the running text Winston brings the parallel in *Post Caini* 88. The other parallels listed by him in note 4: *Spec.* 1.138 (corrected); Spec. 2.52; *Mos.* 1.29; *Mos.* 2.48, 130, 140, 150; *Virt.* 184; *Praem.* 81-83 (discussed by us *infra*); *Prob.* 96, 155; *Jos.* 230; *Fug.* 150; *Mut.* 237; *Somn.* 1.182; *Decal.* 102; *QG* 4.7, 84, 110; *QE* 1.5. He further refers the reader to W. Völker, *Fortschritt und Vollendung bei Philo von Alexandrien* (Leipzig 1938) 276 who he notes has minimized the Greek influence.

[36] Winston *op. cit.* has quoted from §88 of this same pericope, which section we will discuss in greater detail elsewhere.

[37] The biblical verse is embedded in the text quoted immediately from *Post.* 85.

(§79) A clear testimony is recorded in the Holy Scriptures. ... If, he says, you keep the Divine commandments in obedience to his ordinances and accept his precepts, not merely to hear them *but to carry them out by your life and conduct* ...(§80) For the commandments are not too huge and heavy for the strength of those to whom they will apply, nor is the good far away either beyond the sea or at the end of the earth, ... nor has it suddenly left the earth to settle in Heaven, ...

Note the allusion here to Deut. 30:11-13:

(v.11) Now what I am commanding you today is not too difficult for you or beyond your reach. (v.12) It is not up in heaven, so that you have to ask, 'Who will ascend into heaven to get it and proclaim it to us so we may obey it?' (v.13) Nor is it beyond the sea, so that you have to ask, 'Who will cross the sea to get it and proclaim it to us so we may obey it?'

At this point we reach Philo's paraphrase of the (*Septuagint*) version of Deut. 30:14. The Sept. text reads:[38]

(v.14) ἔστιν σου ἐγγὺς τὸ ῥῆμα σφόδρα ἐν τῷ στόματί σου καὶ ἐν τῇ καρδίᾳ σου καὶ ἐν ταῖς χερσίν σου αὐτὸ ποιεῖν. (= For the word is very near you; it is in your mouth and in your heart, *and in your hands* to do it.)

Philo then continues:

(§80 cont'd) No, it is close by, very near, firmly set in three of the parts of which each of us is constituted, mouth and heart and hand, representing in a figure respectively speech and thought and action.

And then Philo proceeds with his homiletic explanation:

(§81) For if our *words* correspond with our *thoughts* and intentions and our *actions* with our words and the three mutually follow each other, bound together with indissoluble bonds of harmony, 'happiness' prevails and this is the most authentic *knowledge and wisdom* (σοφία καὶ φρόνησις) *knowledge for the worship of G-d, wisdom for the regulation of human life*.[39] (82) Now while the commandments of the laws are only on our lips our acceptance of them is little or none, but when we add thereto deeds ... deeds shown in the whole conduct of our lives ... (83) For who ... would not admit that surely that nation alone is *wise and full of knowledge* (σοφὸν ... καὶ ἐπιστημονικώτατον)[40] whose history has been such that it has not left the divine exhortations (θείας παραινέσεις) voided and forsaken by the *actions* which are akin to them, but has fulfilled the words (τοὺς λόγους) with laudable *deeds*?

---

[38] A comparison of the MT and the Septuagint to this verse is presented below.
[39] My rendering here differs from that of Colson's: The Greek text reads: τουτέστιν ἡ ἀψευδεστάτη σοφία καὶ φρόνησις, σοφία μὲν [γὰρ] πρὸς θεραπείαν θεοῦ, φρόνησις δὲ πρὸς ἀνθρωπίνου βίου διοίκησιν.
[40] Cf. this to Septuagint Deut. 4:6 λαὸς σοφὸς καὶ ἐπιστήμων. The paraphrase at this point could hardly be closer. The similarity and difference between *Praem.* 81 and 83, and the Septuagint parallel will I hope be further discussed in my forthcoming book.

As Colson has recognized,[41] Philo is here urging the necessity of not merely hearing, but also carrying out the 'law'[42]—for in certain contexts the Greek word *logos* indeed means '(*Torah*) commandments'; cf. e.g. the term *Decalogue* (δέκα λόγοι) for the Ten Commandments. A single but clear example will suffice here for our present purposes.[43] In *Decal*. 32 we read:

> The Ten Words or oracles, *in reality laws or statutes* (= τοὺς δέκα λόγους ἢ χρησμούς, νόμους ἢ θεσμοὺς πρὸς ἀλήθειαν ὄντας)

Before closing let us consider the pre-history of this midrashic/ homiletic association between the philosophic *topos* and the Biblical verse. That this indeed had a clearly identifiable pre-Philonic history is attested by the fact that either the translators of the *Septuagint*, or its redactors, or at the very least a copyist/glossar of the text *before* Philo, must have been influenced by this association, for the phrase '*and in your hands*' (καὶ ἐν ταῖς χερσίν σου) *has been added* in the Sept. version to MT Deut. 30:14—something which clearly reflects the influence, *conscious or otherwise*, of this Hellenistic *topos*.[44]

A juxtaposition of the MT and the Septuagint texts will make this point clear. In contrast to the Sept. (brought above) which has the words '*and in your hands*' (καὶ ἐν ταῖς χερσίν σου) MT Deut. 30:10-14 reads:

MT: ‏(14)כי קרוב אליך הדבר מאד בפיך ובלבבך לעשותו‏
(= For the word is very near you; it is in your mouth and in your heart to do it.)[45]

The Sept.'s words: καὶ ἐν ταῖς χερσίν σου (= '*and in your hands*') are not a rendering of MT ‏לעשותו‏ (= 'to do it'), for the Septuagint has translated this latter by: αὐτὸ ποιεῖν (= 'to do it'). Do the indelible fingerprints of this midrashic association need any further brushing to become clearly visible?

So much for the *pre-history*; the general outlines of this midrashic *topos* can also still be discerned—albeit in a somewhat different form,

---

[41] PLCL 8.310.
[42] And cf. similarly *Virt*. 183–184–which work immediately follows *Spec*. IV and immediately precedes *Praem*.–where Deut. 30:11-14 is also paraphrased and explained in a similar vein.
[43] We shall discuss this point at greater length in its proper place in my forthcoming book.
[44] In view of the existence of this Hellenistic *topos* it is hardly likely to have dropped out of the MT in the Hellenistic period, not to mention the proverbially great care taken to preserve the exact text of the Hebrew Pentateuch.
[45] I have brought the NIV translation into a more literal relation with the MT, by rendering MT ‏לעשותו‏ as: 'to do it', rather than NIV 'so you may obey it.'

and of course accomodated to the MT–in Rabbinic midrash which surfaces centuries *later*. In BT *Eruvin* 54a we read:

> R. Isaac said, This may be derived from the following: *But the word is very nigh unto thee, in thy mouth, and in thy heart, that thou mayest do it.* (MT לעשותו ובלבבך בפיך). When is it very near you? When it is in your mouth and in your heart so you may do it (לעשותו).

Since the addition found in the Septuagint: 'in your hands' is not part of the MT, the final word of the sentence in the MT, לעשותו (= 'so that you may do it'), had to be drafted in its stead. Nevertheless the same verse is here brought and homiletically expounded in the same manner in order to form the same triad and to project the same message.

Here this 'Hellenistic-philosophic' *topos* is relayed in the name of R. Yitshak, whose particular expertise was the transmission of *haggadic* lore. At the same time it should also not be overlooked that as is often the case in examples of Rabbinic midrash, what R. Yitshak has relayed is not the ancient tradition in its entirety but merely a precipitate thereof, divested of all of its meta-associations, and more likely than not neither R. Yitshak nor his listeners were anything but entirely oblivious to its original 'philosophic' infrastructure.[46]

I conceive this as being, *mutatis mutandis,* somewhat similar to the manner in which the contemporary spiritual descendents of R. Yitschak approach the writings of medieval Jewish philosophy. In the vast majority of instances they too are entirely innocent of even the slightest inkling of the Aristotelian and Neoplatonic infrastructure of medieval Jewish philosophic thought.

Thus we see that this homiletic association of the Hellenistic philosophic *topos* with Deut. 30:14, 'mouth, heart, and hands' and with the obligation to keep the commandments, was already a part of the common stock which informed the Septuagint version used by Philo, while vestiges of it are discernible in Rabbinic midrash centuries later, albeit as a precipitate of the original Hellenistic thought pattern, with the 'philosophic' associations filtered out and no longer a part of the frame of reference of either the midrashist or his readers.

Haifa University
Haifa, Israel

---

[46] Suggested paths of contact are discussed in my book.

DEPENDENCE OR COMMON TRADITION IN PHILO *HYPOTHETICA* VIII 6.10 – 7.20 AND JOSEPHUS *CONTRA APIONEM* 2.190–219

GEORGE P. CARRAS

The present study will consider two questions.[1] First, what traditions and sources did Philo use in the *Hypothetica*? Second, how may the traditions and sources used by Philo in this treatise help inform us about the traditions and sources used by Josephus in his *Contra Apionem*? Specifically, our concern will be to determine whether *Contra Apionem* used the *Hypothetica* as a source for his summary of the Law. An affirmative answer to this question has been adopted for nearly the past 100 years.[2]

Basic to both of these concerns is the assumption that it is possible to uncover traditions and sources used by Philo in the *Hypothetica* and by Josephus in *Contra Apionem*. The general question of determining traditions and sources forms a central methodological issue of the scholarly debate both within Josephus and Philonic studies. In addition to those Josephus scholars already named, E. Kamlah and L. Troiani should be added as important contributors to the debate.[3] Two significant studies

---

[1] The present contribution is a revised version of a paper read at the 1990 Philo Seminar at the Society of Biblical Literature Annual Meeting. The paper 'Philo's *Hypothetica*, Josephus' *Contra Apionem* and the Question of Sources' was published in the *SBL Seminar Papers* 29 (1990) 431–450.
[2] P. Wendland, 'Die Therapeuten und die philonische schrift vom beschaulichen Leben', *Jahrbuchücher für classische Philologie*, Supplementband 22 (1896) 715; B. Motzo, 'Le 'Υποθετικά di Filone', *Atti della R. Accademia delle Scienze di Torino* 47 (1911–12) 571; A. Momigliano, 'Intorno al Contro Apione', *Quinto contributo alla storia degli studi classici e del mondo antico* (Rome 1975) 2.768; S. Belkin, *Philo and the Oral Law* (Cambridge Mass. 1940) 25; cf. also 'The Alexandrian Source for Contra Apionem II', *JQR* 27 (1936–7) 1–32; N. Bentwich, *Philo Judaeus of Alexandria* (Philadelphia 1940) 222; G. Vermes, 'A Summary of the Law by Flavius Josephus', *NovT* 23 (1982) 301–2 n. 50. G. Sterling, 'Philo and the Logic of Apologetics' in D. J. Lull (ed.), *1990 SBL Seminar Papers* (Atlanta 1990) 415 suggests Josephus was 'in some sense dependent' on Philo. Sterling, however, clarifies his view: 'rather than direct dependence, we should think of shared traditions'. See also the unpublished paper of E. Hilgert, 'A Survey of Previous Studies on Philo's *Hypothetica*', delivered at the Philo Seminar, 1990 SBL Annual Meeting, New Orleans, 5–6.
[3] E. Kamlah, 'Frömmigkeit und Tugend: Die Gesetzapologie des Josephus in C. Ap. 2.145 - 295', in O. Betz, K. Haacker, M. Hengel (edd.) *Josephus-Studien*, Festschrift für O. Michel (Göttingen 1974) 220–32; L.Troiani, *Commento storico al Contro Apione' di Giuseppe* (Pisa 1975) passim. For other scholars see n. 50 below.

on Philo that have helped to shape the discussion are by R. G. Hamerton-Kelly[4] and B. L. Mack.[5] These scholars maintain that in order to assess Philo's contribution to Alexandrian Jewry the traditions used by him must be considered.[6] In the light of this it is striking that no systematic evaluation of Jewish traditions or sources has yet been attempted in the case of the *Hypothetica*.[7] This is what the first part of this study will investigate, before we proceed to the relationship between traditions in the *Hypothetica* and those of *Contra Apionem*.[8] The thesis I will argue in this study is that there is inadequate evidence to support the view that Josephus in his *Contra Apionem* used Philo's *Hypothetica* as a source for his summary of the Law.

1. Setting the Context

Before we address ourselves to the issues sketched above, several remarks on the character, title, and structure of the *Hypothetica* are required. Sandmel classified the works of Philo under four categories. The first of these is called the 'historical'. This means 'non-biblical' treatises—those that do not reflect an interpretation of scripture.[9] It is to this category that the *Hypothetica* is allocated.

---

[4] R. G. Hamerton-Kelly, 'Sources and Traditions in Philo Judaeus', *SPh* 1 (1973) 3–26.
[5] B. L. Mack, 'Exegetical Traditions in Alexandrian Judaism: A Program for the Analysis of the Philonic Corpus', *SPh* 3 (1974–5) 71–112; 'Philo and Exegetical Traditions in Alexandria', *ANRW* 21.1 (1984) 228–71.
[6] Other contributors to the discussion on Philo are: V. Nikiprowetzky, *Le Commentaire de l'Écriture chez Philon d'Alexandrie* (Leiden 1977); I. Heinemann, *Philons griechische und jüdische Bildung* (Breslau 1932, repr. 1962) 137–54; H. Wolfson, *Philo* (Cambridge Mass. 1947) 1.57–73; H. Hegermann, *Die Vorstellung vom Schöpfungsmittler im hellenistischen Judentum und Urchristentum*, TU 82 (Berlin 1961) 27–87; W. Bousset, *Jüdisch-christlicher Schulbetrieb in Alexandrien und Rom* (Göttingen 1915); E. R. Goodenough, 'A Neo-Pythagorean Source in Philo Judaeus' *Yale Classical Studies* 3 (1932) 115–64.
[7] Several scholars have discussed the issue: e.g. Heinemann, *Philons Bildung* 352–58; M. Petit, 'A propos d'une traversé exemplaire du désert du Sinaï selon Philon (Hypothetica vi 2–3.8: texte biblique et apologétique concernant Moïse chez quelques écrivains juifs', *Semitica* 26 (1976) 137–42; F.H. Colson, *Philo* LCL vol. 9 (Cambridge Mass. 1943) 407–443; J. Bernays, 'Philon's Hypothetica und die Verwunschungen des Buzyges in Athen', *Gesammelte Abhandlungen* (Berlin 1885) 1.262–82; Motzo, 'Filone' 560. It is noteworthy, however, that G. Boccaccini, *Middle Judaism: Jewish Thought 300 B.C.E. to 200 C.E.* (Minneapolis 1991) makes no mention of the *Hypothetica* and only a few passing citations of *Contra Apionem* in his description of 'Middle Judaism'.
[8] For an evaluation of traditional ideas in *C. Ap.* 2.190–219 see my 'Paul, Josephus and Judaism: The Shared Judaism of Paul and Josephus' (Oxford D. Phil. 1989) where this is investigated.
[9] S. Sandmel, 'Philo Judaeus: An Introduction to the Man, his Writings, and his Significance', *ANRW* II 21.1 (1984) 6. Sandmel's classification in general follows L. Massebieau, 'Le classement des œuvres de Philon', *Bibliothèque de l'École des Hautes Études: Sciences Religieuses* Paris 1889 (1) 1–91.

In treating the *Hypothetica* several difficulties emerge: first, the work has survived in the form of two extracts preserved by Eusebius in his *Praeparatio Evangelica* viii 6.1–7.20 and viii 11.1–8). Consequently, some guesswork is required concerning the precise context of several passages (e.g. 6.2, 7.1, 7.10, 11.1). In addition, it is unclear what the overall intention of the work is. The problem is enhanced by the difficulty of the work's title. An understanding of the name *Hypothetica* could help us to gain a better idea of the aims of the work, but the precise meaning is disputed. The title occurs before the first extract of the treatise, where Eusebius describes Philo as 'speaking in defense of the Jews against their accusers' (viii 5.11). Several different suggestions have been made concerning the meaning of the title: (1) suppositions about the Jews;[10] (2) exhortations, moral advice;[11] (3) imputations.[12] Ὑποθετικά understood as 'suppositions' about the Jews seems unlikely, since it would only fit the initial portion of the work. The second option, moral advice, has the following points in its favour. First, ὑποθετικοὶ λόγοι elsewhere refers to treatises which contain moral advice in distinction from theoretical speculation on ethics. Second, Philo uses the word ὑποθῆκαι not infrequently in the sense of 'counsels', 'admonitions', 'teaching' (*Spec.* 1.299, 3.29; *Virt.* 70). However, this view of the title is difficult to reconcile with 5. 11 cited above, where the *Hypothetica* is defined as an apologetic work. This latter interpretation is reinforced if the *Hypothetica*, the work referred to as 'the Apology to the Jews' (Ὑπὲρ Ἰουδαίων ἀπολογία), and the work called περὶ Ἰουδαίων are all the same work. Consequently, it has been suggested that the title *Hypothetica* is best understood as 'imputations', i.e. false opinions about the Jews which are being refuted. This understanding is supported by the statement at 6.6: ἢ τοὺς μὲν ἀπολέμους καὶ ἀνάνδρους εἶναι καὶ παντελῶς ὀλίγους ὑποθώμεθα. This would also cohere with the character of the *Hypothetica* given at 5.11 as an ἀπολογία.[13]

Assuming that an apologetic emphasis is appropriate in characterizing the *Hypothetica* we can make several observations on the literary structure of our treatise. Since our interest is in Philo's summary of the Law we shall restrict ourselves to 6.10 – 7.20. There are a number of

---

[10] This meaning is noted by Colson, *Philo*, 410. However, cf. E. Schürer, *The History of the Jewish People in the Age of Jesus Christ*, rev. ed. G. Vermes, F. Millar and M. Goodman (Edinburgh 1987) 3.866–7 (by J. Morris).
[11] Bernays, 'Philons Hypothetica' 262–82.
[12] Massebieau, *Classement* 55–9.
[13] I owe the above points to Schürer, *Jewish People*, 886–87. The apologetic nature of the *Hypothetica* supported here is also maintained by L. Troiani, 'Osservazioni sopra l'apologia di Filone: gli *Hypothetica*', *Athenaeum* 56 (1978) 312. For the view that ὑποθετικά should be understood as a 'hypothetical syllogism' as used in Stoic logic, see Sterling 'Apologetics', 419–22.

structural indicators that are found within the treatise. It begins with the statement that the Jewish laws are clear and simple. This is followed by a number of offenses which carry the death penalty (7.1). This 'if-then' structure continues in the next paragraph, where on three different occasions the words 'so too' occur. The implication is that what was stated already regarding the cause-effect relationship between offence and punishment continues.

7.3–5 begins with the statement that there are 'other rules of various kinds'. What follows is a list of rules directed to wives, parents, sons, rulers, etc. At 7.6 the author summarizes what has already been given as well as what follows: 'besides these there is a host of other things which belong to unwritten laws, customs, and institutions or are contained in the laws themselves'. This is the clearest statement of the content of the summary.

Philo then gives a further list of injunctions of various sorts that extend to 7.8. These include treatment of the poor, animals, dead people, abortion against a foetus, etc. The list concludes with the comment that the injunctions just given are more important and serious than those that will follow (7.9). Then a further list occurs. After these less serious matters the comment is made that violation of the rules entails the vengeance of God. The treatise concludes with a longer section on the sabbath and the sabbatical year, which is more rhetorical and explanatory in nature (7.10–20).

It is notable from the structure of Philo's summary of the Law that he consistently presents the admonitions, prohibitions, and injunctions in list-form. Apart from the final section on the sabbath and the sabbatical year, the summary consists of lists classified under the heading 'unwritten law, customs, institutions, and laws', i.e. those found in the Torah. This list-like form suggests that the content may reflect 'traditional' material: whatever may be the objective value of the summary, the structure and form of the material suggest that Philo considered the summary to be one of 'basic principles.'[14] He takes it as obvious that common ideals of Jews are being given. This interpretation can only be tested by considering each injunction in turn in order to determine if and to what extent the formulation of the Law in the *Hypothetica* is traditional and what may be possible sources for his ideas.

We now turn to an investigation of traditions in *Hypothetica* viii 6.10–7.20. The approach we shall adopt is to survey the laws, customs, and

---

[14] This point is made by E. P. Sanders, 'Judaism and the Grand 'Christian' Abstractions: Love, Mercy and Grace,' *Int* 39 (1985) 357–372, who focusses on *C. Ap.* 2.190ff. (but this summary is similar in context, aims and structure to the *Hypothetica*).

institutions of Philo's summary of the Law in order to determine whether the material reflects traditional ideas. In this vein, we shall consider the *Hypothetica* in relation to several different categories of Jewish evidence. These consist of: (1) biblical law; (2) OT non-legal material; (3) Jewish material from the close of the OT prior to the time of Philo; (4) material shared by Philo with his contemporaries; (5) ideas shared by the *Hypothetica* and *Contra Apionem*; (6) material unique to the *Hypothetica*; (7) ideas in the *Hypothetica* that were common in antiquity, among Jews as well as non-Jews. By considering the *Hypothetica* in the light of these analytical categories it may be possible to reach a verdict on its use of and appeal to Jewish traditions. Our approach will be to consider first each injunction separately. We shall conclude by bringing together evidence under each of these categories.

2. *Laws: 'Clear and Simple'*

Our extract commences with the statement that the laws of the Mosaic constitution are clear and simple (7.1 ἁπλᾶ καὶ δῆλα, cf. *C. Ap.* 2. 190). The context for this statement is the question whether there are among the Jews evaders of the Law of Moses.[15] Philo replies in the negative: no such people are found among Jews. In addition, this opening section forms a defence against Gentile charges that the Jews were adulterers, and of a violent nature, that they ill-treated the free man and servants alike, stole from the Temple, and were impious in their acts. To counter these charges Philo affirms that the Jews are not fickle in character when it comes to the Law; first, they know their Law, second, they are acquainted with its implicit cause-and-effect dimension—disobedience results in punishment.

Now Philo produces his list of laws, beginning with those on sex. For violating laws against pederasty, adultery, rape and prostitution Philo states that the penalty is death. Prohibitions against pederasty, adultery, and rape (in general circumstances)[16] are in accord with biblical law (Lev 18:22, 20:10, 22:23–7; Deut 21:10ff). These offenses are equally found among later Jewish witnesses.[17]

---

[15] As noted by Troiani, 'Filone' 309.
[16] See also in this connection the injunction against committing 'outrage' on the person of a slave or free man (7.2).
[17] Pederasty: *Sib. Or.* 2.13; 3. 185; *Arist.* 152; Ps.-Phoc. 3a, 190, 170–83, also Philo *Spec.* 3.37–42; adultery: Wisdom 14. 26; Ps.Phoc. 3a, 170–83; Jos. *Ap.* 2.199; *Arist.* 152; rape: *Ap.* 2.215 (cf. Ps.Phoc. 198, where rape is denounced but it is not said to be a capital offence). See Heinemann, *Philons Bildung,* 286ff.; for other texts; L. M. Epstein, *Sex Laws and Customs in Judaism* (New York 1948) 179ff.

The matter is different regarding prostitution. Philo's example may appear to be in conflict with the Bible (Judg 11:1; Josh 2) and Rabbinic Judaism (e.g. R. Judah-ha-Nasi: t.Tem. 4.8) where prostitution is known and practiced. Josephus in his summary of Judaism at *Ant*. 4.206 notes the practice, though he states that payment received by a prostitute for her hire may not be used to purchase a sacrifice. Philo, on the other hand, states at *Spec*. 3.51 that a harlot (πόρνη) is to be stoned. In addition to *Hypoth*. 7.1 this view also occurs at *Ios*. 43, where a harlot from among the commonwealth of Israel is not permitted to live. This is given in a context where visiting prostitutes is attributed to nations other than Jews. If it is correct that Philo's view is based on the LXX Deut 23:18, where a daughter of Israel is prohibited from being a prostitute, we may detect a different emphasis in the diaspora. This may have been in part because 'some Jews attempted to forbid prostitution entirely within their communities (a step which was not required in Palestine, where the problem of Gentile ethics did not press so heavily) and make Jews take the step to be distinctive'.[18] (Compare here Ps.Phoc. 177–8, where the wife is not to be induced to prostitution whereas Lev 19:29 forbids the daughter). However, neither Pseudo Phocylides nor Lev 19:29 adds the death penalty.

The death penalty is also extended to other forms of misconduct. First is the confining, kidnapping, or selling of a person, whether slave or free man. This is similar to the injunction at Exod 21:16, where, as in the *Hypothetica*, the penalty is death. Second, impiety towards God and parents, either verbally or by action, is considered to be a violation of the Law. This can clearly be documented from the Torah at Lev 24:13ff., where the person who curses God is to be stoned. The death penalty incurred for parental disobedience also occurs in the Torah at Exod 21:17 and Deut 21:18–21. The former passage states that anyone who curses his mother and father will be put to death; the latter prescribes (as in the *Hypothetica*) that death will be by stoning.

The view that Philo gives is also present in *C. Ap.* 2. 206: 'If a son does not respond to the benefits provided him by his parents he will be stoned'. It is evident from this that the tradition which Josephus and Philo follow derives from the OT Law. Pseudo-Phocylides makes the same general point regarding discipline of children[19] but does not

---

[18] E. P. Sanders, 'Paul and Sex', paper delivered in the NT Seminar, Oxford, 19 June 1986, p. 11. See also more recently *Paul* (Oxford 1991) 110.
[19] J. Bernays, 'Über das Phokylideische Gedicht', *Gesammelte Abhandlungen* (Berlin 1885) 1.244. Several studies that demonstrates the common material in the *Hypothetica*, *Contra Apionem* and the Pseudo-Phocylidean *Sentences* are: M. Küchler, *Frühjüdische Weisheitstraditionen* (Göttingen 1979) 221ff., K.W. Niebuhr. *Gesetz ind Paränese:*

include the penalty of death for disobedience:[20] 'And if a child sins against you, let the mother cut her son down to size, or else the elders of the family or the chiefs of the people'. The Mishnaic tradition, however, greatly restricted the circumstances under which the rebellious son was to be condemned to death. For example, *m. San.* 8.1-6 indicated several criteria: the parents must both wish for the execution to take place; the child may not have any physical defects; the child must have been previously chastised by his parents and the elders of the community; the youth must not be under 13 years and one day old and must have stolen from his parents; finally, he must be guilty of having consumed large quantities of food and drink. With these sort of criteria to convict a rebellious son, the success of any actual case became a virtual impossibility.[21] Philo did not have such a restrictive outlook: violation of the parents' wishes resulted in stoning.

The precept to honour and obey parents assumed here is deeply rooted in the Jewish tradition.[22] In the *Hypothetica* we find impiety to God placed alongside that against parents; this point also occurs in *C. Ap.* 2. 217. In a different context in Josephus a person's attitude to God is related to behaviour towards parents: 'Honour to parents the Law ranks second only to honour to God' (*C. Ap.* 2. 206). One example that echoes Josephus occurs at Ps.Phoc. 8: 'Honour God first and foremost and thereafter your parents'. Similar is the *Sib. Or.* 3. 593f.; 'they honour Him alone who reigns for ever, the Eternal, and after him their parents'. But it should be borne in mind that honour to parents was also a recurring theme in Greek and Roman literature.[23]

We can see from this that Philo is clearly following a traditional line

---

Katechismusartige Weisungsreihen in der Früjüdischen Literatur, (Tübingen 1987) 5–72.

[20] P.W. Van der Horst, *The Sentences of Pseudo-Phocylides* (Leiden 1978) 248. For the date and destination of these texts I follow Van der Horst, who argues that the content of the document 'seems to favor a date between 50 B.C.–100 A.D.' This is based on the fact that the *Pseudo-Phocylides* were probably written in Alexandria at a time when relations between Jews and Greeks had not yet become too tense. Van der Horst narrows this down to some time during the reign of Augustus (30 B.C.–A.D. 14) or Tiberius (A.D. 14–37). See more recently his 'Pseudo-Phocylides' in J.H. Charlesworth (ed.), *Old Testament Pseudepigrapha* (London 1985) 2.567–8 and 'Pseudo-Phocylides Revisited', *JSP* 3 (1988) 3–30. For another proponent of Alexandrian provenance for this document see P. M. Fraser, *Ptolemaic Alexandria* (Oxford 1972) 2.539.

[21] S. Riskin, 'The Halakah in Josephus as Reflected in *Against Apion* and the *Life*' (Yeshiva University M.A. thesis 1970) 16.

[22] Decalogue (Exod 20:12; Deut 5, 16), biblical law (Lev 19:3), the wisdom tradition (Prov 1:8, 19:26, 23:22–5, 28:24; Sir. 3:1–6), the apocalyptic tradition (*Jub.* 7.20), and the rabbinic tradition (*Meklita* on Exod 20...12) (cf. Philo *Spec.* 2. 235; *Decal.* 51).

[23] J. W. Hewitt, 'Gratitude to Parents in Greek and Roman Literature', *AJPh* 52 (1931) 30–48; Van der Horst, *Sentences* 116.

in his outlook towards God and parents. However, he reflects a distinct view when he adds that impiety towards one's benefactor will also result in stoning. This punishment for reviling a benefactor is absent from the Torah and from Philo's treatise *On the Special Laws*, as well as other known sources.[24]

There is a third form of misconduct which according to the *Hypothetica* incurs the death penalty; it is the stealing of sacred things. Troiani maintains that the context of this statement is the charge of Philo's accusers that Jews as a group steal from the Temple.[25] Philo's rebuttal is that Jews who behave in such a way will be punished by death. Therefore, there is strong incentive to avoid Temple theft. There are several examples from Jewish material where Jews are known to have stolen from the Temple: *Ps. Sol.* 8.12; *T. Levi.* 14.15. CD 6.15 indicates that anyone who has stolen from the Temple is not suitable as a candidate for admission into the community. There is also an example given by Josephus in *Ant.* 18.81–4 of a Jew who 'played the part of an interpreter of the Mosaic law and its wisdom'. With three confederates he enlisted a female proselyte to give money to the Temple in Jerusalem. However, they took the money and used it for their own gain (cf. Acts 19:31; *Ant.* 4. 18).[26]

These examples are presented to illustrate that Jews stole from the Temple; they do not show that Jews incurred punishment for plundering the Temple of its goods. It is this that is noteworthy in the present context. Inspite of the fact that stealing is a violation of the Decalogue (Exod 20:15; Deut 5:19), the verdict of death for Temple stealing does not seem to occur except in the *Hypothetica*. This also applies to stealing in general, the other feature which Philo includes: the penalty is death for the stealing of things *profane* as well as sacred.

This first section of the *Hypothetica* has shown that Philo was dependent on ideas from the Bible as well as other Jewish literature for many of his ideas; pederasty, adultery, rape, impiety towards parents, and the binding, kidnapping or stealing of a person. However, we found scant precedent for Philo's verdict against prostitution. Regarding the indictment that Jews who stole from the Temple should be put to death, it appears that Philo is giving his own distinct view. This applies also to the statement that a person should receive the death penalty if he acts in an impious manner toward his benefactor.

---

[24] Colson, *Philo* 423d.
[25] Troiani, 'Filone' 309.
[26] Cf. F. B. Watson, *Paul, Judaism and the Gentiles* (Cambridge 1986) 111.

3. 'Other Rules of Various Kinds'

We shall now proceed to the second section of the *Hypothetica* (7.3–5) in order to test our initial judgment on Philo's appeal to traditional ideas. This section begins with the statement that what follows is 'other rules of various kinds'. The impression given by this is that the subject matter is loosely bound together under the guise of a single theme. The topics included broadly confirm this, since the passage deals with the role of women in relation to their husbands, parental guidance, and situations in which vows are to be kept.

First, Philo defines role differences between husband and wives: 'wives must be in servitude to their husbands, a servitude not imposed by violent ill-treatment but by promoting obedience in all things' (7.3). Similarly, at 7.4 it is the husband who is to transmit knowledge of the Law to his wife.[27] There is an injunction at 7.8 which reflects the man's role as protector to his wife: the husband is not to be separated from his wife even if taken captive. Josephus shares this general outlook in *C. Ap.* 2. 201: 'The woman, says the Law, is in all things inferior to the man. Let her accordingly be submissive, not for her humiliation, but that she may be directed; for the authority has been given by God to the man'. This view of Philo and Josephus may have had its origin in Gen 3:16 (LXX). Furthermore, according to Josephus, it was a view held by the Essenes (*War* 2. 121; *Ant.* 18.21).

Philo next considers parental guidance. We have already seen in a different context (7.2) how children are to behave towards their parents. Here Philo presents another aspect of the parent-child relationship, this time from the perspective of the parent: they are to have rule/power (ἀρχεῖν) over their children. This is for the preservation and care of the offspring. There is a similar statement at 7.8, where children are not to be parted from their parents even if they are held captive. The purpose of the formulation at 7.2 may be polemical, since the idea of gratitude to one's parents was a recognized topos among both Greeks and Romans.[28] In this way Jewish children would not appear to have less regard for their parents than non-Jews. It may also be possible to see in Philo the influence of the Roman *patria potestas*.[29]

---

[27] See A.-M. Durbarle, 'Paul et l'antiféminisme', *RSPT* 60 (1976) 263–8, for a survey of attitudes towards women in antiquity and the suggestion that the view of Philo is typical. In this regard, one may consult J. E. Crouch, *The Origin and Intention of the Colossian Haustafel* (Göttingen 1972) 107–9. Also R.A. Baer, *Philo's Use of the Categories Male and Female* (Leiden 1970), esp. 41–3, 94–5; D. Sly, *Philo's Perception of Women* (Atlanta 1990).
[28] Hewitt, 'Gratitude' 30ff.
[29] This has been suggested by Heinemann, *Philons Bildung*, 251, with reference to *Spec.*

It may equally be that this dictum is to be understood in relation to Deut 21:18–21: that is, parents in the interest of the preservation and well-being of the child exercise rule or power over the child so that what is prescribed in Deut 21:18–21 will not come to fruition. This would make the view of the *Hypothetica* similar to *C. Ap.* 2.206 and Ps.Phoc. 208–9 (cf. *Spec.* 2.232).

Whichever of these suggestions is the more cogent, the following points are clear from Philo's statement: (1) parents have rule over their children; (2) the intention of this is to ensure the child's safety and preservation; the parents are to be guardians of the children; (3) there is no explicit suggestion that parental honour is a concern; (4) there is no penalty prescribed for disobedience to parental rule.

The third topic considered in this section may be classified under the heading of the keeping of vows (7.3b–5). The basic premise regarding a person's possessions is first stated: a person's belongings are his own unless they have been given over to God. The following paragraphs give conditions which apply to this basic premise. (1) If a person makes a vow to God, even by means of a casual verbal promise, his belongings are not his to handle or touch. (2) If a man has promised to God what was intended for his wife to keep herself, he must refrain from giving it to her. (3) If a father has promised to God a gift destined for his son, he must consider it the property of God. (4) The ruler cannot give to his servants what he has previously apportioned to God. There are two further prohibitions given: you must not commit sacrilege in the temple of gods by robbing what belongs to the gods; you must not steal what others have committed to God.

The idea of keeping vows occurs in the Pentateuch (Num 30:2–16; Deut 22:21–3). We also find in the OT the strong injunction to keep a vow once it has been made: 'If you have made a vow you shall be careful to perform what has passed through your lips' (Deut 21:23). There are also explicit conditions given that are to be observed. Num 30:2–16 is a good example. Conditions are first directed to the man (30:2), followed by those to the woman (30:3).

We also know that vow-keeping was practiced in the first century. Luke in the Acts records that Paul made a vow to shave his head (18:18; 21:23–4).[30] We do not find, however, in the Pentateuch or elsewhere the conditions given by Philo in the *Hypothetica*. Nor do we find a penalty given for failing to keep a vow. Nor do we know of (except from later rabbinic texts) any means of absolution from a vow made such as occur

---

3.232, where a similar sentiment to that in *Hypothetica* is expressed.
[30] Other passages which record the keeping of vows are: *Ant.* 19.294; *War* 2.313; Philo, *Ebr.* 2; *m. Ned.* 6. 1ff.

in the *Hypothetica*: 'the chief and most perfect way of releasing dedicated property is by the priest refusing it, for he is empowered by God to accept it or not'.[31]

Our survey of the three topics thus suggests that Philo's view of the place of women in relationship to men was a commonly held one which had its roots in the OT but developed among Philo's general contemporaries. On the other hand, we found the statement regarding the authority or power which parents are to have over their children less clear: here the background could have been either Jewish or Graeco-Roman. Finally, we saw that vow-keeping as a practice could be documented from the OT and from first-century witnesses. What we did not find except in the *Hypothetica* were (1) the particular conditions set by Philo; (2) the statement that a person might incur punishment for failure to keep a vow. In the case of absolution from vows, a parallel can only be found in the later rabbinic literature.

4. 'A Host of Other Things'

The third section of our extract occurs at 7.6–9. It is introduced by the comment: 'Besides these there is a host of other things which belong to unwritten customs and institutions or are contained in the laws themselves.' The method Philo uses to present these 'other things' is simply to state them in the form of a list with little or no explanation. Our aim will be to observe each injunction and determine whether it reflects Jewish tradition.

The first injunction concerns how to treat other people: 'what a person would not want to suffer he should not do to others' (7.6). The closest OT text which reflects this view stated in the positive form is Lev 19:18 'thou shall love your neighbour as yourself'.[32] The formulation of Philo, however, was familiar in Judaism. *Tob* 4.15 states 'what you hate do not do to anyone'. Similarly, from a later time Hillel summarized and explained Lev 19:18 by quoting the negative form of the golden rule to a proselyte: 'What is hateful to you, do not do to your neighbour, that is the whole law, everything else is commentary, go and learn' (*b. Shabb.* 31a). The injunction also occurs in the NT at Matt 7:12 'whatever you wish that men would do to you, do so to them'. If it is accurate to think of Matthew as a convert from Judaism,[33] then what we have within his Christian ethics is something that is fundamentally Jewish.

---

[31] There is an elaborate system among the rabbis for absolution of vows, e.g. *m. Ned., passim; b. San.* 68a. See L. I. Rabinowitz, Art. 'Vows', *EncJud* 16 (1974) 227.
[32] Colson, *Philo* 426 note c.
[33] R. T. France, *Matthew: Evangelist and Teacher* (Exeter 1988) 70–3.

It is also the case that the general sentiment of concern for others, which the more specific formulation of Philo assumes, was widely current within Judaism.³⁴ However, the injunction to treat others as you want to be treated is not only found among Jews; it was also affirmed by non-Jews. 'Do not do to others that which angers you when they do it to you' (Isocrates, *Nicocl.* 39c; also Herodotus 3. 142; Menander, *Mem.* 40; Diog. Laert. 5. 21; cf. Confucius, *Analects* 15. 23). We can see that the injunction on how to treat others reflects traditional ideas both among Jews and Greeks.³⁵

The prohibition against stealing is given next; a person is not to take up what he had not laid down; he must not filch anything, however small. While the precise formulation is not found in the OT, the general condemnation of stealing is deeply rooted in the Decalogue (Exod 20. 15; Deut 5. 19) and is consonant with the Law, (Deut 22:1–3; Lev 6:2–3; Lev 6:2–3). It is also reflected in Josephus' summary of the Law, where the prohibition against stealing is similar in form to that of *Hypoth.* 2. 208: 'none may appropriate goods which he did not place on deposit, or lay hands on any of his neighbour's property'. Bernays notes that the present injunction occurs as a piece of moralizing ascribed to Solon (Diog. Laert. 1. 57) and described by Plato at *Leg.* 913c.³⁶ Regardless of this similarity to Greek moralizing, Philo reflects a sentiment which is shared by Josephus and is generally rooted in the Pentateuch.

A third prohibition is now given which is shared only by Philo and Josephus. The injunction is to share the basic necessities of life with all people. These include fire and water (*C. Ap.* 2. 211; *Hypoth.* 7.6). Josephus also adds the necessity of food.³⁷ These three elements: fire, water and food accurately summarize 'basic necessities'. This injunction is absent from the Law and from Palestinian literature generally. Prov 25:21, comes closest to the injunction of Philo and Josephus: 'If your enemy is hungry, give him bread to eat; and if he is thirsty, give him water to drink'. This doctrine concerning basic necessities is strong evidence for the view that Philo and Josephus shared a common source.³⁸

---

³⁴ Eg. *Arist.* 207; Sir. 10. 6; *C. Ap.* 2. 211ff.; *t. Naph.* 1. 6; 2 *En.* 61. 1–2; *Tg. Yer.* 1 to Lev 19:18; *ARN* 15).
³⁵ See A. Dihle, *Die goldene Regel* (Göttingen 1962); W. D. Davies and D. C. Allison, *The Gospel According to Saint Matthew* (Edinburgh 1988) 1.686–7; Bernays, 'Hypothetica' 274 n. 1.
³⁶ Bernays, *ibid.* 273.
³⁷ There is another difference, namely that Philo states his concern in the negatives 'do not grudge to one' while Josephus gives the positive statement 'furnish...to all'.
³⁸ There are stories of Greek gods disguising themselves as destitute travelers to test people's hospitality and punishing them if they failed to give a meal and shelter (cf. Ovid, *Met.* 8.626ff). Individuals punished with exile were to be refused fire and water by

The summary proceeds to a theme similar to that which we have just considered, the admonition to offer help to the less fortunate (the poor and the crippled). At 7.6 there is an injunction not to worsen the plight of a person in dire straits. Both of these admonitions are different sides of the same injunction: show help to the needy. This concern can be well documented from a variety of Jewish sources. From the OT we have: 'If there is among you a poor man... you shall open your hand to him and lend him sufficient for his need whatever it may be' (Deut 15:7f.). Wisdom literature: 'She opens her hand to the poor, and reaches out her hands to the needy' (Prov 31:20, cf. 19:17, 22:12, 31:9; *Sir.* 4:4–5); Pseudo-Phocylides: 'Of that which God has given you, give of it to the needy' (29; also 10, 19b, 23b, 28); Josephus, *Contra Apionem*: 'He who refuses a suppliant the aid which he has power to give is accountable to justice' (2.207).[39]

This brings us to the injunction concerning burial of the dead. This admonition, like the previous one, was traditional among Jews. But the witnesses differ on whom the Jews were to bury. In the OT (e.g. Deut 21:22–3), where we are given guidelines for the burial of a criminal, the context implies that the criminal referred to was one who had been stoned on the orders of the 'elders of the city'. The prescription would thus apply to the covenant people of God, not to Gentiles. Similarly, in three separate places Tobit mentions the responsibility of burying the dead. At 1:17 and 2:7 the reference is to the Jewish people, while 4:3 mentions his own father. Sirach, on the other hand, keeps the recipient of the rite of burial more general (38:16). This is also the case in Philo: 'He must not debar dead bodies from burial but throw upon them as much earth as piety demands' (*Hypoth.* 7.7). A further Jewish expression of abhorrence from leaving the dead unburied is Ps.Phoc. 99, which, like Philo, speaks of burial very literally in terms of the corpse being covered with earth as well as keeping the recipients quite general. There is, however, one contemporary Jewish voice who considers it the duty of Jews 'not to leave the corpse of others unburied'. The context here suggests that the 'others' are Gentiles. The sole Jewish witness for this idea from a contemporary of Philo is Josephus in *C. Ap.* 2. 211: see on this point *b. Gitt.* 61a. There is thus good reason to suppose Philo

---

all members of the community—the underlying assumption being that normally these basic essentials would be shared.

[39] See K. Berger, *Gesetzesauslegung Jesu* (Neukirchen-Vluyn 1972) 369–81, for a commentary on several of these texts. Also A. Nissen, *Gott und der Nächste im antiken Judentum* (Tübingen 1974) 166 n. 299; Van der Horst, *Sentences*, 134. In this vein, Küchler, *Weisheitstraditionen* 222ff, considers the *Hypothetica* 7.1–9 as an example of 'hellenistiche Weisheitslehre'.

includes burial of the dead as a recognized principle among Jews.[40]

It must be emphasized, however, that burial of the dead was not just a distinctive concern of Jews in the ancient world; it was a concern shared by non-Jews as well. Apollonius of Tyana, who was reputed to condemn possessions and outward honours, 'hurried, when he heard of his father's death, to Tyana, and interred him with his own hands beside his mother's grave' (Philostratus, *Vita Apoll.* 1. 13). Here, therefore, we find Philo sharing ideas with non-Jews. Hengel has summarized the matter thus: 'Refusal of burial had always been considered among Greeks and Jews as an unheard of act of impiety and as the severest of punishments for criminals. Basically there was on this point no difference between Jews and Gentiles. Burial of the dead was for ancients always both a human and a religious duty'.[41]

Abortion, a concern of Jews in antiquity, is the next prohibition. Philo states that men and women are to take no part in anything that interferes with normal human reproductive processes (7.7). While there is no law in the Pentateuch that forbids abortion, the LXX translation of Exod 21:22-3 seems to have been the starting-point for these reflections.[42] This can be seen by comparing the MT and LXX texts. The first has: 'When men strive together, and hurt a woman with child, so that there is a miscarriage, and yet no harm follows, the one who hurt her shall be fined, according as the woman's husband shall lay upon him; and he shall pay as the judge determines. If any harm follows, then you shall give life for life.' The Septuagint version 'If two men wrestle with one another and hit a pregnant woman, and the child comes forth and is not formed yet, then the penalty shall be money. But if it was formed then thou shalt give life for life.' It is clear from Exod 21 (LXX) that a formed foetus was a human being. Therefore, whoever kills such a one has committed murder and will be punished by death. Although Philo makes no distinction between a formed and unformed foetus, his view seems to presuppose that of Exod 21 (LXX) by the fact that he includes the prohibition against abortion in a group of injunctions which he classifies as greater in importance and more serious in nature than the minor offenses listed in 7.9; but he still maintains that these minor

---

[40] The central importance of burying the dead in the rabbis is clearly reflected in the following: 'He who is confronted by a dead relative is freed from reciting the Shema, from the Eighteen Benedictions, and from all commandments stated in the Torah' (*m. Ber.* 31a). It is also assumed as a central feature of Jewish life in the NT (Mt. 8:21-22 and Lk. 9:59-60).
[41] M. Hengel, *The Charismatic Leader and His Followers* (Edinburgh 1981) 10.
[42] Van der Horst, *Sentences*, 234; D. M. Feldman, *Birth Control in Jewish Law* (New York 1973) 257-8.

deeds are punishable by destruction from God. If these minor misdemeanours are punishable in this way, can abortion be treated with any less severity?

Furthermore, Philo's lack of distinction between a formed and unformed foetus may be in part explained by the fact that Philo was writing as a Jew in the diaspora to an audience that included at least some pagans. In such a context Philo wished to portray the view of Jews on aborting a foetus in distinct contrast to those of surrounding pagans who considered such measures as well as the exposure of a foetus to various prey as a form of birth control.[43]

This view of abortion in Philo is also shared by Josephus: 'a woman who deliberately causes a miscarriage or the destruction of a foetus is regarded as one who commits infanticide.' (C. Ap. 2.202).[44] There is a further text on the theme of abortion that runs parallel to Philo and Josephus, Ps. Phoc. 184–5: 'A woman should not destroy the unborn babe in her belly'. The view that we observe in Josephus, Philo, and Pseudo-Phocylides is echoed in the rabbinic writings as well. For example, the *Mekilta* Exod 21. 13 clearly states that 'the killing of a viable foetus is forbidden'. There is thus multiple testimony to support the view that Philo's attitude to abortion reflects a common Jewish sentiment.

The proper treatment of animals is the next item Philo includes in his description of the Mosaic constitution.[45] The topic is discussed here and in the following section (7.9ff.), where Philo states that he takes up 'little things of casual occurrence'. The main injunction against the maltreatment of animals is found at 7.7; its motive is that it is contrary to the wishes of God and Moses, the giver of the Law.

The general humane treatment that animals are to receive indicates Philo's acquaintance with the Pentateuch (Deut 14:3, 22:1–4, 25:4; Lev 11:2–23). It also indicates that Philo and Josephus share a similar sentiment towards animals (C. Ap. 2.213–14).[46] More specific injunctions against improper use of animals shared by the OT, Philo, Josephus, and Pseudo-Phocylides are the prohibition against separating parent birds from their young. This originates at Deut 22:6 and is echoed in C. Ap. 2.

---

[43] See on the theme of exposure A Cameron, 'The Exposure of Children and Greek Ethics' CR 46 (1932) 105–114.

[44] L. Troiani, *Commento*, 189; Belkin, 'Alexandria' 9. For a survey of several relevant texts from Philo on abortion see Belkin, *Philo and Oral Law* 129–33, 136 n. 135.

[45] See A. Terian, 'Some Stock Arguments for the Magnanimity of the Law in Hellenistic Jewish Apologetics,' *Jewish Law Association Studies 1: The Touro Conference Volume* (ed. B.S. Jackson) (Chico 1985) 141–9 for a treatment on how the laws on the treatment of animals illustrate the magnanimity of the law.

[46] See Terian, 'Magnanimity', 142–144 on the similarities and differences between the *Hypothetica* and *Contra Apionem*.

214 and Ps.Phoc. 84–85. It would appear this may be what is intended by Philo's statement 'do not render desolate the nesting home of birds' (*Hypoth.* 7.9).⁴⁷

Philo and Josephus include an injunction, not found in the OT or the Ps. Phoc., that animals which take refuge in a person's home should be treated as suppliants (*C. Ap.* 2.213; *Hypoth.* 7.7).⁴⁸ A creature that has taken refuge in someone's home may not be killed by the occupants. Since this injunction is restricted to Philo and Josephus, this is a further example which would suggest that both authors shared a common source.

Finally, we find in the *Hypothetica* a prohibition that is confined to the Philonic account. The seed of animals is not to be destroyed; animal defrauding is also not allowed. The vagueness of both of these injunctions may contribute to the view that these injunctions are unique to Philo. Nevertheless, the teaching of Philo that one should show kindness toward animals is in accord with ancient Judaism generally.

The summary next moves to a prohibition against fraudulent crimes (7.8). Philo mentions three in particular: no unjust scales, no false measurement, no use of fraudulent coins. These crimes may be classified under the heading of unfair play concerning weights and measures. Comparative evidence to show Philo's appeal to tradition is extensive.⁴⁹

The section concludes with a piece of common-sense advice on friendship. 'The secrets of a friend must not be divulged in enmity.' This precise injunction is found neither in the Pentateuch (cf. Lev 19:16ff.; also Prov 11:13) nor in the rabbinic literature (cf. *m. San.* 3.7; *b. San.* 4b). Yet it occurs in *C. Ap.* 2.207 in a clearer form than in Philo: 'We must conceal nothing from our friends, nor divulge secrets.' It is generally considered⁵⁰ that the statement of *Contra Apionem* is similar to that of Josephus at *War* 2.141, when, referring to Essenes, he says that they 'neither hide anything from those of their sect nor reveal to others any of their sect though urged by death.' These secrets referred to in the *War* are concerned with a prohibition directed at new initiates, so that they

---

⁴⁷ Colson, *Philo* 430 note a.
⁴⁸ Van der Horst, *Sentences*, 172f. The fact that Philo and Josephus reflect the same attitude is assumed by Colson, *Philo* 430 note b.
⁴⁹ The evidence for unfair play is as follows: Lev 19:35–6; Deut 25:13–16; Prov 11:1, 16. 11, 20. 10, 23; Sir. 42. 4; Amos 8:4ff.; Hos 12:7–8; Mic 6:11; Ezek 45:10–12; *Ap.* 2. 216; Ps.-Phoc. 14–15; (cf. *b. Baba Bathra* 88b–89a).
⁵⁰ Troiani , *Commento*, 191; Kamlah, 'Gesetzesapologie' 229 n. 32; H. St. J. Thackeray, *Josephus: Against Apion*, LCL (Cambridge Mass. 1926) 1.376; J. G. Müller, *Des Flavius Josephus Schrift gegen den Apion* (Basel 1877) 325; Th. Reinach, *Flavius Josèphe: Contre Apion* (Paris 1930) 95.

will not disclose the secrets of the community to others (cf. IQS 8.11ff., 5.15–16). But the statement of *Contra Apionem* has nothing at all to do with prohibitions to be observed by an initiate. Rather, what is being referred to is an 'ideal of Jewish friendship'.[51] It is here that Philo and Josephus agree. The only parallel to the prohibition relating to friendship thus comes from a diaspora source.

At this stage without attempting to summarize our results from this third section of the *Hypothetica* (7.6–7, 8), we can already see that Philo has predominantly used traditional Jewish ideas. However, in several instances (e.g. burying the dead) we noted that he uses ideas also common among non-Jews. And finally, in the case of the statement on ideal friendship we saw that the only source sharing the same view is *Contra Apionem*.

5. Final Topics

There are two further topics with which the treatise is concerned. These occur in the final section (7.10–20). First the sabbath is considered, and then the sabbatical year. In contrast to the previous sections, where injunctions presented in the form of lists predominated, the present section is more varied. It includes rhetorical questions, an exposition of Jewish practices on the sabbath day and during the sabbatical year, as well as an explanation or rationale for the ideas expounded. However, this change in form is not a hindrance to our overall objective of determining whether Philo's views are 'traditional'.

The section begins with a question: 'Is it not a marvel that for a whole day they should have kept from transgressing on any occasion any of the ordinances?' (7.10). The apologetic aspect of the treatise seems evident from the way in which the section opens. It is evident also at 7.14 in the statement 'but any one of them whom you attack with enquiries about their ancestral institutions can answer you readily and easily'. Philo is answering the view of the accusers that the Jews as a group are known for their vices, such as stealing, immorality, ill-treatment of persons, etc. It is from this point of reference that the question at 7.10 is best considered. Philo's rebuttal is to show that it was not an accident that the Jews kept the laws and ordinances. It was consistent with the plan of Moses. The section then proceeds to sketch the process which helps the Jews to keep the laws. First, they become experts in the ancestral laws and customs. The actual method is then sketched. (1) Jews assemble together on the Sabbath. (2) They are instructed by the priests and elders

---

[51] Belkin, 'Alexandrian Source' 22.

by means of an exposition from the 'holy laws'. (3) The result is that the Jewish people will become experts in the law and 'advance in piety'. (4) One effect is that when Jews are questioned about their laws they will not be proved to be ignorant. (5) The Torah is to be passed on by a man to his wife and children; the same responsibility applies to a master toward his slave.

This scenario from the *Hypothetica* is not unique to Philo. It is consonant with the Jewish vision of education and transformation within the community (see also Philo, *Mos.* 2.216; Jos. *C. Ap.* 2.175). Josephus at *C. Ap.* 2.204, in quite a different context from that of Philo's *Hypothetica* presents a similar view. Josephus affirms that festivals are not the only occasion on which sobriety is to be observed: the rule also applies in the bringing up of children (cf. *C. Ap.* 1.60; *Ant.* 4.211). They are to be taught the Torah and the deeds of their forefathers so that Jewish children may not be ignorant of the Torah or transgress its laws. This injunction to teach one's children is firmly rooted in Jewish tradition. The link between the education of children and Jews in general and Torah observance demonstrates the central place which study of the Torah held as a religious ideal for Jews. The *locus classicus* in the OT for teaching children the Torah is Deut 6:4–9. Following the giving of the appeal of the Shema 'Hear, O Israel: The Lord our God is one Lord', the Israelites were exhorted diligently to teach the commandments of Moses at all times to their children (cf. Deut 11:19, 32:6).

Not only are parents to teach their children, but children are to learn from or obey the instruction of their forefathers. It is here that the *Hypothetica* supports the view of the OT and Josephus. In *Hypoth.* 7.13 we are told that it is the priests and elders who read and expound the Torah so that those who listen to their teaching will 'advance in piety'.[52] One result in Torah instruction is to ensure that Israel's children will have a confident knowledge of their laws. Philo elaborates this point at 7.14. He maintains that when a Jew is attacked with enquiries about his ancestral institutions he will be able to answer these objections and not need to resort to the assistance of a learned person (i.e. a professional in moral and legal matters), because Jews know their Law. We can see, then, that while Philo and Josephus are addressing different issues their views on Jewish education in the Law are consistent with each other as well as with the general view of the OT.[53]

---

[52] This function of priests occurs also in the Law: Deut 21:5ff.
[53] On Jewish education see G.F. Moore, *Judaism* (Cambridge Mass. 1927) 1.316ff., B. I. Viviano, *Study as Worship: Aboth and the New Testament* (Leiden 1976), esp. 155; M. Greenberg, Art. 'Sabbath' *EncJud* 14 (1972) 564–5; A. Demsky, Art. 'Education (Jewish)' *EncJud* 6 (1972) 583.

This brings us to the last topic of the treatise, which considers the sabbatical year. The theme of sabbath continues to the matter of allowing the land to rest. Just as the sabbath day is a time for the Jew to take respite from the affairs of the world by Torah study, so the sabbatical year is a time for the land to rest so that it can have a fresh start. Philo states that this was proof that Jews cared for things important to human society.

This idea of a sabbath year is clearly documented from the OT: 'Six years you shall sow your field, and six years you shall prune, but in the seventh year there shall be a sabbath of solemn rest for the land' (Lev 25:3–4; also 25:18–22; Exod 23:10–11). Furthermore, we know that the sabbatical year was observed during the Second Temple Period.[54] One example is from Josephus, who informs us that during the dictatorship of Julius Caesar Jews were exempt from paying tribute to the High Priest since 'they neither take fruit from trees nor do they sow' (*Ant.* 14.202; cf. *Ant.* 11.338).

6. *Conclusions*

Let us now draw together some conclusions from our analysis of the *Hypothetica*. The aim of our investigation was (1) to assess the traditions within Philo's *Hypothetica* 6.10 – 7.20, and by so doing contribute to the continuing search for 'traditions', 'traditional influences' and 'sources' within the Philonic corpus; (2) to consider the possibility that a source for Josephus' *Contra Apionem* 2.190ff. was the *Hypothetica*. We have now completed the first task. The conclusions to be drawn from the first part of our study will be set out by placing the central ideas of the *Hypothetica* in relation to the various different categories of material listed at the beginning of our study—Bible, intertestamental material prior to Philo, contemporaries of Philo, etc. Since we will find several of the same ideas in different categories of material this enforces the point that Philo is using traditional ideas. Our conclusions regarding the second task will emerge. We will formulate these more explicitly at the end of the investigation. In our consideration of *Hypoth.* 6.10 – 7.20 we suggested that there were a number of traditional Jewish ideas reflected in this material. A list of ideas which the *Hypothetica* shares with the Bible would include the following points. (1) There is a prescribed sexual ethic. Failure to observe these laws will result in the death penalty: pederasty, adultery, and rape are prohibited and punishable by death. (2) Impiety towards God will result in the penalty of death. (3) Children are to obey

---

[54] A. Rothkoff, 'Sabbatical Year,' Art. *EncJud* 14 (1972) 583.

their parents; the consequence of failing to do so is death. (4) Kidnapping or stealing a person is punishable by death. (5) Keeping vows one has made is prescribed in the Law. (6) Treating others as you want to be treated is a fundamental aspect of the biblical view. (7) Jews are to behave toward others in a prescribed manner. They must not steal or refuse help to a person in need but give a hand to the needy and the poor. (8) Burying the dead is a necessary duty. (9) Education in the Torah is a fundamental aspect of the Jewish religion. (10) Animals are to be treated in a humane way. (11) The practice of fraud concerning weights and measures is prohibited. (12) The observance of the sabbath day and the sabbatical year is an integral part of the Law of God.

A second category of material relevant to assessing traditions in the *Hypothetica* consists of Jewish ideas that may, broadly speaking, be contemporary with Philo (apart from Josephus' *C. Ap.* 2.190ff). The evidence in this category indicates that the *Hypothetica* shared a number of ideas with contemporary Judaism. (1) Honour to God and parents is a religious ideal to be emulated. (2) Women are to be subservient to their husbands. (3) Care for the poor and needy is a prescribed duty. (4) Abortive measures against the generative process are prohibited. (5) Burying the dead is universally obligatory. (6) Humane treatment of animals is expected. (7) Unfair play regarding weights and measures is prohibited.

A third category of material is that which the *Hypothetica* shares with ancient writers regardless of whether they are Jews or Gentiles. These ideas are: (1) respect for parents; (2) the necessity of burying the dead; (3) the injunction to treat others as you want to be treated; (4) the prohibition against 'taking up' what does not belong to you.

The fourth category of material by which to evaluate the *Hypothetica* are ideas contained in *Contra Apionem*. Observation of the ideas shared between these two documents will enable us, in due course, to speculate on the question of source relationships between the texts. A list of common agreements between the summary of the Law in these two documents would include the following. (1) Animals are to be treated humanely, and are even to be granted refuge in one's own home. (2) Women are to have a subservient role to their husbands. (3) Instruction in the Torah serves the religious and social function of learning the Jewish tradition, advancing in piety, and the avoidance of ignorance. (4) Helping the needy is a religious duty. (5) People are to be given help with basic necessities such as water, fire (and also food in *Contra Apionem*). (6) Abortive measures against the generative process are prohibited. (7) Impiety towards God and parents is punishable by death. (8) Burying the dead is a duty. (9) The authority of parents is acknowledged. (10) Confidentiality should be observed in friendship; misuse of information that has been divulged in trust is not permissible, even if a time of estrangement should arise.

This brings us to a fifth type of data, ideas found in *Contra Apionem* but absent from the *Hypothetica*. Several that are noteworthy are: (1) a belief in a future salvation; (2) accessibility of the Jewish religion to non-Jews; (3) the observance of purity laws in relation to the marriage union and following a funeral ceremony; (4) the practice and existence of the Temple, cultus, and prayer; (5) the central importance of one God and the prohibition against the making of false images; (6) the need for youths to respect their elders; (7) the prohibition against charging interest to fellow Jews; (8) the stipulation that sacrifices are an occasion for sobriety; (9) the prohibition against taking a wife by violence and against committing an outrage against a woman prisoner; (10) the prohibition against the destruction of an orchard where warfare has taken place.

A sixth category of material relevant to our discussion consists of ideas in *Hypothetica* which are absent from *Contra Apionem*: (1) the stipulation of a sabbatical year for the land to rest; (2) the conditions regarding the making of vows; (3) prohibition against stealing sacred things; (4) appeal to the negative form of the love commandment; (5) the requirement that children should remain with their parents if they are taken captive (the same applies to wives remaining with captive husbands); (6) duty of a master to instruct his slaves in the Torah.

There are two further types of material which may be included in our survey. These are ideas and formulations that are peculiar to the *Hypothetica* and *Contra Apionem*. Those in the *Hypothetica* include the following. (1) Impiety against a benefactor may carry with it the death penalty. (2) Failure to observe the strict obligation of a vow results in death, but one could be absolved from a vow if the priest refused to accept it. (3) Children are not to be held as captives without their parents; this injunction also applies to the wife and husband. (4) The punishment for theft (in general) is death. (5) Jews who stole from the Temple will receive the death penalty.

The ideas peculiar to the *Contra Apionem* are as follows. (1) At sacrifices precedence is given to prayers for the community. (2) The consequence of accepting bribes is death. (3) The burning of the country of an enemy is not allowed. (4) The despoiling of a fallen combatant is prohibited. (5) An animal used in labour is not to be killed.

From the above summary we can see that the *Hypothetica* uses a varied and complex collection of traditions and sources to create a multifaceted, idealized portrayal of Judaism. We can now ask how probable it is that *Contra Apionem* used the *Hypothetica* as a, or even as *the* main, source for his summary of the Law. There are three possibilities.

(1) The *Hypothetica* and *Contra Apionem* shared a common source. (2) *Contra Apionem* did use the *Hypothetica*. (3) *Contra Apionem* used the *Hypothetica* but in the form of a loose paraphrase.

Let us consider first of all the view that there is a common source. This position is supported by G. Klein (1909), I. Heinemann (1932), I. Lévy (1965), J. Crouch (1972) and E. Kamlah (1974).[55] We suggested above that there were ten points in which the *Hypothetica* and *Contra Apionem* shared material. However, of these cases eight were drawn explicitly from the OT, whereas no more than two can be documented from the *Hypothetica* and *Contra Apionem* only. The former category includes burying the dead, the authority of parents, humane treatment of animals, the centrality of Torah study, helping the needy, impiety to God and parents. Those shared exclusively by *Contra Apionem* and the *Hypothetica* are: the theme of secrecy in friendship and the injunction to provide basic necessities for others. In addition, we found that there were two items that had their origin in the OT yet came to fuller expression in later literature, the *Hypothetica* and *Contra Apionem* being two examples. These were the prohibition against aborting the generative process and the stipulations concerning the role of woman.

We also observed several ideas whose general sentiment was found in the OT but which appear in the *Hypothetica* and *Contra Apionem* in a form peculiar to these works. These include the statements that one purpose of Torah study is to avoid ignorance and that animals in need of help are to be granted refuge. It must be added that in the case of Torah study the emphasis on the avoidance of ignorance seems to be assumed in the OT (e.g. Josh 4.21–2). Regarding help offered to animals, there is a difference in a detail: whereas the *Hypothetica* says that if animals make appeals for help they should not be refused, *Contra Apionem* states that if you take an animal into your home you are not permitted to kill it. There was also one case (burying the dead) where common tradition is reflected. The distinct formulation in the *Hypothetica*, however, is documented only in one other source—not, in fact, *Contra Apionem*, but Pseudo-Phocylides.

From these observation we can affirm that the *Hypothetica* and *Contra Apionem* shared common sources and traditions for some of their ideas. We also maintain that other ideas came directly or originated from the OT; still others are best explained as coming from post-biblical traditions.

---

[55] G. Klein, *Der älteste christliche Katechismus und die jüdische Propaganda Literatur* (Berlin 1909); Heinemann, *Philons Bildung* 354–6; I. Lévy, *Recherches esséniennes et pythagoriciennes* (Geneva–Paris 1965) 51–66; Crouch, *Haustafel* 84–111; Kamlah, 'Gesetzapologie' 220 n. 3.

The common source theory thus can only be supported in a qualified sense. It may rather be better to explain the shared ideas in the *Hypothetica* and *Contra Apionem* by suggesting a multiplicity of sources.

Within this context we shall now consider the view that Josephus in *Contra Apionem* used the *Hypothetica* as his source. There are several factors that seem to argue against this conclusion. First, both witnesses show reliance on the OT and especially on biblical law. Often they share the same ideas. (We have indicated this where relevant in our analysis of the *Hypothetica*.) The implication of this is that *Contra Apionem* could have used the OT as a primary source rather than obtaining the themes second hand from the *Hypothetica*. Second, both share some ideas with contemporary Judaism, a fact which may suggest that their ideas form part of a common Judaism. (I have listed above the points regarding the *Hypothetica*; those for *Contra Apionem* are found in my study already referred earlier.[56]) Third, there are ideas in the *Hypothetica* and *Contra Apionem* that are distinct from each: some occur in the *Hypothetica* and are absent from *Contra Apionem*, and vice versa. If *Contra Apionem* used the *Hypothetica*, what is Josephus' source for his distinctive ideas? One might also ask why he chose to omit Jewish ideas from his summary that are known from other sources to have been central to Judaism. For example, the *Hypothetica* omits all references to monotheism, purity laws, prohibition against idolatry, and the hope for a future salvation. Josephus equally has his omissions: the sabbath (though it is mentioned in *War* 2.289, and could be assumed to form the occasion of instructing children at *C. Ap.* 2.204), the keeping of vows, the sabbatical year, the love commandment (yet he does say that Jews were to emulate the 'practice of virtue', *C. Ap.* 2.192, in ways that amount to the love commandment). In conclusion, it seems that the view which maintains that Josephus in writing *Contra Apionem* used the *Hypothetica* as his source is inadequate to explain the relationships between the two texts.

There is a third hypothesis which has been suggested to explain the relationship between the texts, namely that *Contra Apionem* is a loose paraphrase of the *Hypothetica*. In our view it is difficult to maintain this position with any degree of certainty. In order to sustain this thesis we would need clear and certain criteria to decide the matter; we would need to devise a way to determine the original idea and the paraphrase when the ideas expressed are fairly similar. Since of the ten items which the *Hypothetica* and *Contra Apionem* share there are only two that must have come from a common source, there are too few instances to permit any real test. Clearly here the paraphrastic option breaks down.

---

[56] See my *Paul, Josephus and Judaism*, pp. 23–86.

It therefore seems plausible to accept that the common-source theory is the most suitable, with the qualification that other sources also played a central role.[57] Josephus and Philo then shared a common source and body of traditions in their respective summaries of the Law. However, many of the traditions used were part of a common Judaism that consisted of a wide variety of Jewish witnesses and influences, which are attributed to different locations within the diaspora; Alexandria and Rome, as well as Palestine. The fact that Josephus writing in Rome and Philo in Alexandria appeal to similar ideas suggests the presence of a common Judaism that was not tied to a single location or to a single synagogue. A recognition of this dimension in understanding Philo may enable us better to appreciate his relationship within the hellenistic synagogue and to understand that he and Josephus form part of a rich tradition within diaspora Jewry.

Department of Near Eastern Studies
University of California at Berkeley

---

[57] *Pace* Motzo, 'Filone' 561-2 it seems inadequate to maintain that in the *Hypothetica* and *Contra Apionem* Mosaic ideas are simply dressed up in a Greek way, since a number of the ideas in both documents can be found in biblical law or the OT or reflect common Jewish tradition. It is also incorrect to suggest that Josephus' motive for including an idea was that Philo had done so before him. We have shown in our analysis that each author has distinct ideas not shared by the other.

JOSEPHUS' PORTRAIT OF BALAAM

LOUIS H. FELDMAN

1. *Introduction*

That Josephus' paraphrase (*Ant.* 4.102–158) of the story of Balaam[1] was of great interest to him may be deduced from the extraordinary amount of space that he gives to the narrative. Thus, whereas the Hebrew (Num 22:2–25:9) has 164 lines and the Septuagint 261 lines, Josephus has 363 lines.[2] This gives a ratio of 2.21 for Josephus as compared with the

[1] Of the studies that have thus far been attempted of Josephus' version of the Balaam pericope, J. R. Baskin, *Pharaoh's Counsellors: Job, Jethro, and Balaam in Rabbinic and Patristic Tradition* (Chico, California 1983) 96–99, very briefly summarizes Josephus' account and is particularly interested in comparing it with the rabbinic tradition. She concludes that the portrait of Balaam in Josephus is relatively mild in comparison with the rabbinic depiction but gives few details. Even the otherwise exhaustive (526 pages) treatment by H. Rouillard, *La Péricope de Balaam (Nombres 22–24): La Prose et les 'Oracles'* (Paris 1985), of the three chapters in Numbers containing the Balaam episode has only a few scattered and extremely brief references to Josephus' account. P. Villalba i Varneda, *The Historical Method of Flavius Josephus* (Leiden 1986) 227–229, contains little more than a brief paraphrase of Josephus' narrative. J. T. Greene, 'Balaam: Prophet, Diviner, and Priest in Selected Ancient Israelite and Hellenistic Jewish Sources,' *SBLSP* (Atlanta 1989) 57–106, is concerned primarily with an analysis of the biblical text about Balaam and attempts to show that Balaam was a figure utilized by various warring groups of priests and prophets against each other's ideal self-concept and type-concept; he has very little to say specifically about Josephus' version. The only full-scale treatment of Josephus' interpretation of the Balaam episode is by L. Moscovitz, 'Josephus' Treatment of the Biblical Balaam Episode' (M.A. thesis, Yeshiva University, New York 1979), done under my direction. This excellent study, however, hardly exhausts the topic, and, in particular, takes into account only intermittently the relationship of Josephus' treatment of Balaam to his treatment of other biblical episodes.

[2] As evidence that Josephus used a Hebrew text (probably in addition to a Greek text) for his account of Balaam we may note that whereas the Hebrew text (Num 23:2) indicates that one of the animals sacrificed by Balak and Balaam was a bullock, the Septuagint speaks of it as a calf, and Josephus (*Ant.* 4.113) identifies the animals as bullocks. Again, we read there (as well as in the Aramaic Targumim) that Balak and Balaam offered a bullock and a ram on every altar, whereas according to the Septuagint (and Philo, *Mos.* 1.277), Balak alone sacrificed the bullock; and according to Josephus (*Ant.* 4.113) it is Balaam alone who offered the sacrifice. (On this latter point we may perhaps suggest that Josephus may have considered it logical for Balaam to do the sacrificing inasmuch as it was he who would be uttering the curse and who required divine approval.) Likewise, we may see from Josephus' paraphrase (*Ant.* 4.125) of Numbers 24:4 and 16 that he used a Hebrew text, inasmuch as he speaks of Balaam 'falling upon his face,' rendering *nofel*, 'falling down,' whereas the Septuagint reads 'he

Hebrew and 1.39 for Josephus as compared with the Septuagint. This contrasts with a ratio of 2.70 as compared with the Hebrew for the account of Saul, 2.16 for Jeroboam, 2.01 for Jehu, 2.00 for Joseph (5.45 for the episode of Joseph and Potiphar's wife and 3.28 for the narrative dealing with Joseph's dreams and subsequent enslavement), 1.98 for Ahab, 1.95 for David, 1.93 for Jehoram of Israel, 1.87 for Samuel, 1.83 for Absalom, 1.54 for Samson, 1.52 for Elijah, 1.32 for Daniel, 1.15 for Jonah, 1.11 for Elisha, .97 for Hezekiah, .91 for Manasseh, 1.20 for Ezra (.72 compared with the Septuagint), and .24 for Nehemiah (.18 compared with the Septuagint). For the episode of the Israelite men and the Midianite women (Num 25:1-9) the ratio of Josephus' 176 lines (*Ant.* 4.131-158) to the Hebrew text of 15 lines is no less than 11.73 (9.26 as compared with the Septuagint).[3] The fact that Josephus mentions Balaam again after the conclusion of the episode with the Midianite women (*Ant.* 4.158) and says that 'on this narrative readers are free to think what they please' shows that he regarded the whole account as a single narrative.

There are several reasons for Josephus' interest in this pericope. In the first place, Josephus is very much concerned with the phenomenon of prophecy, since he regarded himself as having a special gift for prediction, like his biblical namesake Joseph, as he shows in foretelling (*War* 3.400-402) that Vespasian will become emperor. Indeed, Josephus apparently looked upon himself as a latter-day Jeremiah,[4] as we can see from the explicit reference to Jeremiah in his speech to the Jews (*War* 5.391-392). Moreover, Josephus in his youth (*Life* 10) spent considerable time with the Essenes, who from their early years were particularly well versed in the prophetic books (*War* 2.159) and who, indeed, had a special gift for prediction themselves. Similarly, the Pharisees, with whom Josephus eventually allied himself (*Life* 12) after experimenting with the three sects of Jews, were said to have a special gift of foreknowledge (πρόγνωσιν, *Ant.* 17.43), as we can see from the predictions of Pollio the Pharisee (*Ant.* 15.3-4) and his disciple Samaias (*Ant.* 14.172-175).

---

saw in his sleep' (εἶδεν ἐν ὕπνῳ). For the Hebrew I have used the standard edition of the biblical text with the commentary of M. L. Malbim (New York, no date); for the Septuagint I have used the text of A. Rahlfs, vol. 1 (Stuttgart 1935). For Josephus I have used the LCL text, vol. 4, translated by H. St. J. Thackeray (London 1930).
[3] The ratio of Josephus' 187 lines (*Ant.* 4.102-130) to the Balaam story (Num 22:2-24:25) proper of 149 lines (that is, without including the narrative of the Midianite women) is 1.26; the ratio to the Septuagint's 242 lines is .77.
[4] On Josephus' identification with Jeremiah see C. Wolff, *Jeremia im Frühjudentum und Urchristentum* (Berlin 1976) 10-15; D. Daube, 'Typology in Josephus,' *JJS* 31 (1980) 18-36 and S. J. D. Cohen, 'Josephus, Jeremiah, and Polybius,' *History and Theory* 21 (1982) 366-381.

Furthermore, Josephus the historian saw an integral relationship between history and prophecy,[5] inasmuch as, in defending the accuracy of the biblical narrative (*Ag. Ap.* 1.37), he declares that only the prophets had the privilege of recording the history of the Jewish people, and that the accuracy and consistency of their records are guaranteed by the fact that they were divinely inspired. Finally, the prophets had standing even among pagans, if we may judge from their popularity in the second century among philosophers, such as Numenius of Apamea, the Pythagorean, who, according to Origen (*Against Celsus* 4.51), quoted not only Moses but also the prophets in many passages in his writings.

In general, in his portraits of biblical figures Josephus focuses upon their personalities and aggrandizes their qualities of character.[6] Balaam, however, is different in that he is a non-Jew and, at least according to the simple reading of the biblical text, a wicked figure at that. Josephus was here clearly confronted with a dilemma: if he showed too much regard for Balaam, he would be giving credence to a pagan prophet who had sought to curse Israel; on the other hand, if he downgraded Balaam, he would betray his prejudice against non-Jewish men of wisdom. For Balaam, nevertheless, as we shall see, Josephus gives a relatively

---

[5] See my 'Prophets and Prophecy in Josephus,' *JThS* 41 (1990) 397–400.
[6] See my 'Hellenizations in Josephus' Account of Man's Decline,' in J. Neusner (ed.), *Religions in Antiquity: Essays in Memory of Erwin Ramsdell Goodenough*, Studies in the History of Religions 14 (Leiden 1968) 336–353; 'Josephus' Portrait of Noah and Its Parallels in Philo, Pseudo-Philo's *Biblical Antiquities*, and Rabbbinic Midrashim,' *PAAJR* 55 (1988) 31–57; 'Abraham the Greek Philosopher in Josephus,' *TAPA* 99 (1968) 143–156; 'Abraham the General in Josephus,' in F. E. Greenspahn, E. Hilgert, B. L. Mack (edd.), *Nourished with Peace: Studies in Hellenistic Judaism in Memory of Samuel Sandmel*, Scholars Press Homage Series 9 (Chico, California 1984) 43–49; 'Josephus as a Biblical Interpreter: the '*Aqedah*,' *JQR* 75 (1984–85) 212–252; 'Josephus' Portrait of Jacob,' *JQR* 79 (1988–89) 101–151; 'Josephus' Portrait of Joseph,' *RB* 99 (1992) 379–417, 504–528; 'Josephus' Portrait of Moses,' *JQR* 82 (1991–92) 285–328; 83 (1992–93) 7–50; 'Josephus' Portrait of Joshua,' *HThR* 82 (1989) 351–376; 'Josephus' Portrait of Deborah,' in A. Caquot et al. (edd.), *Hellenica et Judaica: Hommage à Valentin Nikiprowetzky* (Leuven-Paris 1986) 115–128; 'Josephus' Version of Samson,' *JSJ* 19 (1988) 171–214; 'Josephus' Portrait of Samuel,' *AbrN* 30 (1992) 103–145; 'Josephus' Portrait of Saul,' *HUCA* 53 (1982) 45–99; 'Josephus' Portrait of David,' *HUCA* 60 (1989) 129–174; 'Josephus as an Apologist to the Greco-Roman World: His Portrait of Solomon,' in E. S. Fiorenza (ed.), *Aspects of Religious Propaganda in Judaism and Early Christianity* (Notre Dame 1976) 69–98; 'Josephus' Portrait of Hezekiah,' *JBL* 111 (1992) 597–610; 'Josephus' Interpretation of Jonah,' *Association for Jewish Studies Review* 17 (1992) 1–29; 'Josephus' Portrait of Daniel,' *Henoch* 14 (1992) 37–96; Josephus' Portrait of Nehemiah,' *JJS* 43 (1992) 187–202; 'Hellenizations in Josephus' Version of Esther,' *TAPA* 101 (1970) 143–170; and, for an overall survey, 'Use, Authority, and Exegesis of Mikra in the Writings of Josephus,' in M. J. Mulder and H. Sysling (eds.), *Mikra: Text, Translation, Reading and Interpretation of the Hebrew Bible in Ancient Judaism and Early Christianity*, CRINT II 1 (Assen 1988) 455–518.

unbiased portrayal,[7] especially when it is compared with Philo,[8] with the rabbinic tradition,[9] with the New Testament,[10] or with the Bible itself;[11]

---

[7] G. Vermes, *Scripture and Tradition in Judaism*, 2nd ed. (Leiden 1973) 174, remarks that Josephus minimizes Balaam's wickedness slightly by imputing all of Balaam's wrongs to a desire to please Balak, but that apart from these specific slants, he shows the same general bias that is exhibited in the rest of the Palestinian tradition and in the New Testament. It is our argument that the changes are much more substantial. Interestingly, the portrayal by Pseudo-Philo, *Biblical Antiquities* 18.3, is even more favorable to Balaam than is Josephus, as Baskin (*op. cit.* (n. 1)) 99, has noted. Origen (*PG* 12.683d) is surprisingly even-handed, blaming him for inspiring idolatry and immorality but praising him when the word of G-d is placed in his mouth. See J. Braverman, 'Balaam in Rabbinic and Early Christian Traditions,' in S. B. Hoenig and L. D. Stitskin (edd.), *Joshua Finkel Festschrift* (New York 1974) 41–50. The chief reason, however, why Balaam is viewed more positively in patristic literature is that he was regarded as prophesying the coming of Jesus.

[8] Philo, *Cher.* 32, *Conf.* 159, and *Migr.* 113, portrays Balaam as foolish and vain. *Det.* 71 delineates him as an empty sophist, a conglomerate of incompatible and discordant notions. *Deus* 181, *Conf.* 159, and *Mut.* 202 portray him as a dealer in the vanity of unfounded conjecture and as the very antithesis of true prophecy. *Mos.* 1. 263–300, presents an extremely unfavorable picture of Balaam, charging him, in particular, with avarice.

[9] To be sure, the rabbis (*Sipre Deut.* 357.2, ed. Finkelstein, 430), commenting on the verse (Deut 34:10) that there has not arisen a prophet in Israel equal to Moses, assert that among the nations such a prophet did arise, namely Balaam. In fact, the rabbis were ready to grant (*ibid.*) that in some respects Balaam was actually superior to Moses; thus Moses did not know who spoke with him, whereas Balaam did know; moreover, Moses did not know when G-d would speak with him until he was actually addressed by G-d, whereas Balaam knew in advance. The reason, say the rabbis (*Seder Eliyahu Rabbah* 26 (ed. Freedman, p. 142)) why G-d raised Balaam to such heights was so that the Gentiles would not be able to say that if they had had a prophet of the stature of Moses they would have accepted the Torah. Indeed, an anonymous rabbinic tradition (*b. B. Bat.* 14b) regarded the Balaam episode as so important that it singles it out as a separate book distinct from the rest of the Torah, this being the understanding of the statement that Moses wrote his own book and the portion of Balaam. But even those rabbinic passages which acknowledge his greatness as a prophet denigrate him for his greed, envy, immorality, and bestiality (cf. b. Sanh. 105a, where he is said to have committed bestiality with his ass) and depict him (*b. Sanh.* 105a–106b) as subjected to all four of the modes of capital punishment. He is known as Balaam the Wicked (*b. Sanh.* 105b) and, indeed, is looked upon (*b. Sanh.* 106b) as the very epitome of wickedness because of his skill in being able to gauge the exact moment when G-d is angry. He is, thus, worse than any of the others who are denied a portion in the world to come (m. Sanh. 10.2). His greatest wickedness (*b. Sanh.* 105b) consisted of his seeking to strike at the very heart of the Israelites through cursing them that they should possess no synagogues or schools. Indeed (*b. Sanh.* 106a), he is identified as one of Pharaoh's counsellors who advised him to cast into the Nile River the new-born male children of the Israelites. The Mishnah (*ʾAbot* 5:19) berates him for his evil eye, his haughty spirit, and his proud soul. Though he was at first an interpreter of dreams and then a prophet, he sank to the level of sorcerer (*Tanḥuma B* 4.134). There are even those who find a veiled reference to Jesus in the passage (*b. Sanh.* 106b) which states that a *min* (heretic) asked Rabbi Ḥanina how old Balaam was, whereupon he replied that since, according to the Psalm (55:24),

but, most significantly, he shifts the focus from his personality to the historical, political, and military confrontation between the Israelites and their enemies. Indeed, to a considerable degree, the episode, as described by Josephus, is a prologue to the war against the Midianites. Furthermore, Josephus employs the prophecies of Balaam to present, to be sure in a veiled form, his vision of the future of the Jewish people.

2. *Balaam the Soothsayer*

Clearly, Josephus was confronted with a dilemma when he came to classify Balaam. On the one hand, if he knew the rabbinic tradition, as there is good reason to think that he did,[12] he realized the high regard in

---

'Bloody and deceitful men shall not live out half their days,' it follows that Balaam was 33 or 34 years (since a normal lifetime is seventy years), whereupon the *min* stated that he had seen Balaam's Chronicle in which he read that Balaam the lame was 33 years old when Phinehas the Robber put him to death. The theory, however, that Balaam is Jesus, that the Chronicle is the Gospel, and that Phinehas is Pilate has been generally disputed. See, for example, L. Ginzberg, *The Legends of the Jews*, vol. 6 (Philadelphia 1928) 123–124, n. 722; and J. Klausner, *Jesus of Nazareth* (New York 1925) 32–35.

[10] Cf., e.g. 2 Pet 2:15: 'Forsaking the right way, they (the heretics) have gone astray; they have followed the way of Balaam, the son of Beor, who loved gain from wrongdoing, but was rebuked for his own transgression; a dumb ass spoke with human voice and restrained the prophet's madness.' The same theme of Balaam's unholy search for gain is to be found in Jude 1:11: 'Woe to them (i.e. false teachers), for they walk in the way of Cain and abandon themselves for the sake of gain to Balaam's error.' Finally, In the vision of Jesus in Rev 2:14 there is a bitter reference to Balaam as the one who inspired the Israelites to perform the cardinal sins of idolatry and immorality.

[11] When Balaam is mentioned after the scene from Numbers in which he is central he is depicted in negative tones. Thus in Deut 23:5 we read that G-d would not listen to Balaam but that, instead, he turned his curse into a blessing. Almost exactly the same motif is found in Jos 24:10 and in Neh 13:2.

[12] That Josephus was acquainted with traditions which are found recorded in later rabbinic tradition is evident from Josephus' remarks (*Life* 8–9) on his excellent education, presumably in the legal and aggadic traditions of Judaism, which he received in his native city of Jerusalem, which was then the center of Jewish learning. Josephus says that he received a reputation for his excellent memory and understanding (μνήμη τε καὶ σύνεσις) and that while he was only fourteen years of age he already had won universal applause for his love of learning (φιλογράμματον). While it is probably true that Josephus is not averse to boasting, he had so many enemies that it seems unlikely that he would have made such broad claims unless there were some basis to them. See B. J. Bamberger, 'The Dating of Aggadic Materials,' *JBL* 68 (1949) 115–123, who has argued convincingly that the Talmud and Midrashim are compilations of traditional material which had existed orally for a considerable time before they were written down. He notes that extra-rabbinic sources, notably the Septuagint, the Apocrypha, the Pseudepigrapha, Hellenistic Jewish writings, and the New Testament—all apparently older than rabbinic writings in their present form—contain innumerable parallels to the rabbinic aggadah. L. Prijs, *Jüdische Tradition in der Septuaginta* (Leiden 1948) cites numerous

which that tradition held Balaam as a prophet. Moreover, inasmuch as Balaam is included, with virtually no introduction, in a text discovered in 1967 indicates that the name of Balaam was well known to the pagan people to whom the inscription (apparently dating from the eighth century BCE) was addressed, so that we may infer that his was a tradition of long standing.[13]

On the other hand, Josephus was surely aware of the portrayal of

---

instances where the Septuagint parallels rabbinic tradition. For example, inasmuch as the second-century Rabbi Meir (b. Meg. 13a) states, as does the Septuagint (Esth 2:7), that Mordecai had married Esther, it is more likely that the translators of the Septuagint were acquainted with this ancient tradition than that Rabbi Meir consulted the Septuagint. Similarly, the plague of ʿarob is understood by the second-century Rabbi Nehemiah to consist of stinging insects (Exod. Rab. 11.3), whereas the Hebrew is generally understood to refer to varied wild beasts; again, this is the explanation of the Septuagint (Exod 8:17). Moreover, one of the paintings of the third-century CE Dura Europos synagogue depicts Hiel (1 Kgs 16:34), a confederate of the priests of Baal, crouching beneath the altar while a snake approaches to bite him; but such a story is not mentioned in a Hebrew source until much later midrashim (Exod. Rab. 15.15, Pesiq. R. 4.13a) and not fully until the thirteenth-century Yalquṭ (on 1 Kgs 18:26). Hence that tradition must have been more ancient. S. Rappaport, Agada und Exegese bei Flavius Josephus (Wien 1930) cites 299 instances where Josephus parallels rabbinic traditions that are not recorded until a later, often a much later, period. To these may be added numerous other instances cited in my various articles dealing with Josephus. For example, as I have noted ('Josephus' Portrait of Jacob,' art. cit. (n. 6) 130–133), Josephus was apparently aware of the equation of Esau and Rome, which is later found in rabbinic tradition. We may also add that the fact that many midrashic traditions, now extant only in later medieval collections, are found in such Church Fathers as Origen and especially Jerome confirms their antiquity. That the rabbis carefully preserved the statements of their predecessors and did not ascribe to them remarks that they had not made would seem to be borne out by the strong statement in b. Megillah 15a, in which the third-century Rabbi Eleazar ben Pedath is reported to have said in the name of Rabbi Ḥanina that whoever reports a saying in the name of its originator brings deliverance to the world. Most recently R. Kalmin, 'Talmudic Portrayals of Relationships between Rabbis: Amoraic or Pseudepigraphic?' Association for Jewish Studies Review 17 (1992) 165–197, has concluded, in opposition to the view frequently expressed by J. Neusner (e.g., Making the Classics in Judaism: The Three Stages of Literary Formation (Atlanta 1989) 19–44), that aspects of Amoraic attitudes, at least so far as expressions of praise and special respect, most likely originate close to the time of the rabbis involved, and are not later editorial fabrications. Further evidence against Neusner's skepticism may be seen in Kalmin's recent study, 'Collegial Interaction in the Babylonian Talmud,' JQR 82 (1991–92) 383–415, in which he convincingly demonstrates that the interactions among contemporary amoraim in the Talmud are not the product of the fancy of the redactor but are historically grounded. Again, in a forthcoming essay, 'Dreams and Dream Interpreters in Ancient Rabbinic Literature,' Kalmin shows, through an analysis of rabbinic statements and stories about dreams, that several differences between early (prior to the third century CE) and later (from the early third to the early sixth century) rabbis are most likely accurate historically, reflecting real changes in rabbinic attitudes, and are not the product of the redactor.

[13] See J. A. Hackett, The Balaam Text from Deir ʿAllâ (Chico, California 1980).

Balaam as the epitome of wickedness. One is not disappointed in one's expectation that Josephus will distinguish carefully, in his terminology, between pagan and Jewish prophets and even between the classical prophets and those latter-day prognosticators such as himself. The Septuagint, we may note, reserves the term προφήτης[14] for the one who reveals the Divine will, but uses the word μάντις and its cognates when referring to heathen soothsayers.[15] The prophet declares nothing which is his own. Josephus, in general, seems to maintain the classical difference between μάντις and προφήτης,[16] namely that the former has foresight and knowledge of future events, as Cicero (*Div.* 1.1) puts it (hence this can continue after the cessation of prophecy, which occurred during the reign of Artaxerxes, according to *Ag. Ap.* 1.41), whereas the task of the προφήτης is to be the voice of G-d and to declare the knowledge of G-d to those who come for advice. The role of the prophet is that of a mediator, serving both as G-d's spokesman to man and vice versa. As Krämer[17] remarks, it is not until the second century CE, under Christian influence, that the term προφήτης refers to one who foretells the future. The μάντις, as Rose[18] remarks, is not an inspired prophet but a craftsman (δημιουργός), associated with leeches and carpenters in Homer (*Od.* 17.384).

To be sure, Josephus never applies the word προφήτης to Balaam or, for that matter, to himself. Instead, he uses the terms μάντις, μαντεία, μαντεῖον, and μαντεύομαι with reference to pagan prophecies (particularly those derived from dreams), for example, of the Egyptian seers (*Ant.* 2.241; *Ag. Ap.* 1.236, 256, 257, 258 (2), 267, 306) or Balaam (*Ant.* 4.104 (2), 112, 157) or the Witch of Endor (*Ant.* 6.330, 331, 338) or Babylonian soothsayers (*Ant.* 10.195) or a seer in Alexander the Great's army (*Ag. Ap.* 1.203, 204) or the Emperor Tiberius (*Ant.* 18.217, 223) or the Delphic Oracle (*Ag. Ap.* 2.162) or soothsayers in general (*Ant.* 6.327, 331, 17.345, *War* 2.112).[19]

---

[14] R. Rendtorff, 'Προφήτης: Navi in the Old Testament,' in *TDNT*, vol. 6 (Grand Rapids 1968) 812, remarks that in the Septuagint *navi* is always translated by προφήτης. Προφήτης is also the translation in a few instances for *ro'eh* (1 Chr 26:28, 2 Chr 16:7, 10) and *ḥozeh* (2 Chr 19:2, 29:30, 35:15).
[15] One reason perhaps why Josephus avoids using the term μάντις for biblical prophets is that the word is associated with the words μαίνομαι, 'to be mad,' and μανία, 'madness.'
[16] H. J. Krämer, 'Προφήτης,' in *TDNT*, vol. 6 (Grand Rapids 1968) 790.
[17] Krämer, art. cit. (n. 16) 795.
[18] H. J. Rose, 'Divination (Greek),' in J. Hastings (ed.), *Encyclopaedia of Religion and Ethics*, vol. 4 (New York 1914) 796.
[19] In this respect Josephus parallels the pagans, who restrict the use of the term προφήτης to a religious sphere, where it indicates 'one who speaks in the name of a god (as in the etymology from πρό + φημί) declaring the divine will and counsel in the oracle.' Historical seers and prophets not connected with the oracle—the biblical parallel would be those not connected with G-d—are called not προφῆται but χρησμολόγοι or the

Indeed, in this respect Josephus diminishes the stature of Balaam not merely by declining to call him a προφήτης but also by stating that he was the best μάντις of his day (τῶν τότε), the implication being that he was not the best diviner of all time (the Bible does not refer to him as either a prophet or a seer of any kind).[20]

And yet, Josephus (*Ant.* 4.113), like Pseudo-Philo (*Bib. Ant.* 18.10), succeeds in giving added importance to Balaam by having Balaam offer the sacrifice before he prophesies; in contrast, in the Hebrew text (Num 23:2) Balaam and Balak offer the sacrifice together,[21] and in the Septuagint and in Philo (*Mos.* 1.277) it is Balak who does so. Nevertheless, Josephus (*Ant.* 4.113) avoids blaming Balaam by declaring, in an addition to the biblical text (Num 23:4), that Balaam realized that his prophecy was governed by inflexible Fate.

Again, the fact that Josephus usually abbreviates biblical poetry and presents it in indirect discourse, whereas in the case of Balaam he actually gives it added emphasis by combining his three discourses into a single long, powerful prophecy, and by keeping it in direct discourse serves to highlight the tribute to Balaam as one who is a gentile prophet.

---

like. But since Josephus wishes, on the whole, to restrict the use of the word προφήτης to those who qualify as prophets according to the Bible, he also applies these terms (μάντις, etc.) to Jews, notably Judas the Essene (*War* 1.79, *Ant.* 13.312, 313) and even himself (*War* 4.625). As we can see from the fact that he uses the term μαντεῖον with reference to the Delphic Oracle, Josephus here departs from classical usage (see J. E. Fontenrose, 'Prophetes,' *OCD*, rev. ed. (Oxford 1970) 887), which reserved the term προφήτης for one attached to an established oracular shrine and which employed the term μάντις for an unattached seer; perhaps his purpose is to stress that the μάντις merely predicts the future and is not a spokesman for the divine.

[20] Philo (*Mos.* 1.264) likewise avoids calling him a prophet and instead refers to his widespread fame for soothsaying (μαντείᾳ). Pseudo-Philo, in his *Biblical Antiquities* (18.2), likewise avoids calling him a prophet and instead refers to him as an interpreter of dreams (*interpretem somniorum*). For Origen (*Commentary on John* 28.12 (*PG* 14.707)) there is a question whether Balaam was or was not a prophet. Finally, he concludes that Balaam was not a prophet, inasmuch as his prophecies were involuntary and shortlived and inasmuch as he is referred to not as a prophet but as a soothsayer (μάντις). Yet, just as Josephus is not consistent and precise in his terminology of slavery (see J. G. Gibbs and L. H. Feldman, 'Josephus' Vocabulary for Slavery,' *JQR* 76 (1985–86) 281–310) or in his use of the terms for 'city' or 'village,' so here, though he avoids the term for Balaam, he does use the word 'prophet' for an Egyptian prophet (*Ag. Ap.* 1.312), for Cleodemus-Malchus the historian (*Ant.* 1.240), and the prophets of Baal opposed by Elijah (*Ant.* 8.339). Josephus also uses the word μαντεία in referring to predictions by Jews who were not prophets, such as Jotham (*Ant.* 5.253), the diviners banished by King Saul (*Ant.* 6.327), Judas the Essene (*War* 1.80, *Ant.* 13.312), the anonymous critics of Herod (*Ant.* 17.121), the diviners skilled in interpreting dreams who were sent for by the ethnarch Archelaus (*Ant.* 17.345), and Josephus himself (*War* 4.625).

[21] So also Targum Onkelos and Targum Pseudo-Jonathan on Num 23:2.

3. Other Positive Qualities of Balaam

There is almost no quality more deeply appreciated in antiquity than hospitality, as we can see most notably in Homer, both positively, in the case of the Phaeacians (*Od.* books 6-8), and negatively, in terms of condemnation when it is violated, as in the case of Polyphemus the Cyclops (*Od.* book 9). Indeed, a standard epiphet of Zeus, the king of the gods, is Ξένιος, the god of hospitality. Hence, Josephus' amplification (*Ant.* 6.326) of the repayment made by David for the hospitality shown to him by Achish, king of the Philistines, would lead to greater admiration for David.[22]

Similarly, the reader will form a distinctly positive picture of Balaam by virtue of Josephus' additions to the Biblical statement. Thus, whereas the latter (Num 22:8) asserts simply that Balaam told the envoys from Balak to remain overnight, Josephus (*Ant.* 4.105) elaborates that Balaam received them in friendly fashion (φιλοφρόνως, 'lovingly,' 'cordially,' 'affectionately,' 'benevolently,' 'kindly,' 'politely,' 'joyfully,' 'gladly' —the same word which is used with regard to the hospitality shown by David (*Ant.* 7.30)) and with hospitality (ξενίᾳ). Josephus then adds that Balaam, the gracious host, gave them supper.

The portrait of Balaam is likewise improved by Josephus' addition to Balak's rebuke of Balaam after the latter had praised the Israelites. Whereas the Bible (Num 23:25) says, very simply, that Balak told Balaam neither to denounce them nor to bless them, Josephus (*Ant.* 4.118) expands considerably and dramatically by describing Balak's fuming (δυσχεραίνοντος, 'feeling displeasure,' 'being indignant,' 'being annoyed,' 'being angry,' ' being dismayed,' 'being vexed,' 'being distressed,' 'being troubled') at Balaam and his accusing him of transgressing the covenant according to which he had obtained his services.

4. Apologetics

a. Refutation of the Charge that Jews Hate Non-Jews

To a high degree, as I have tried to indicate elsewhere,[23] Josephus in

---

[22] We likewise see a picture of David the gracious host in Josephus' addition (*Ant.* 7.30) to the statement (2 Sam 3:20) that David made Abner and his men a feast. Josephus adds to the portrait by stating that David received him in friendly (φιλοφρόνως) fashion and entertained him with splendid and lavish feasts that lasted many days. The same quality of hospitality is to be found in Josephus' extra-biblical comment (*Ant.* 7.54), to which nothing in the Bible (2 Sam 5:3) corresponds, that when the tribal leaders came to pay homage to David at Hebron, he entertained and treated them hospitably (φιλοφρονησάμενος) and then sent them to bring all the people to him.

[23] See my essays cited in note 6 above.

the *Antiquities* is endeavoring to do what he does systematically in his essay *Against Apion*, namely, defend the Jews against the charges of their enemies.

One of the recurrent charges against the Jews is hatred of mankind. Even Hecataeus (*ap.* Diod. Sic. 40.3.4), who is otherwise well disposed toward the Jews, describes the Jewish way of life as 'somewhat unsocial' (ἀπάνθρωπόν τινα) and hostile to foreigners (μισόξενον). Throughout his *Antiquities* Josephus is concerned with refuting these charges.[24] Indeed, Josephus (*Ant.* 1.241) is proud of the fact that two of Abraham's sons fought along with Heracles and that the daughter of one of them married Heracles himself. Moreover, he notes that Abraham is moved with compassion for his friends and neighbors the Sodomites (*Ant.* 1.176), that Joseph sells grain to all people and not merely to native Egyptians (*Ant.* 2.94 and 2.101), that David, far from being a misanthrope, is described as φιλάνθρωπος, and that Solomon asks that G-d grant the prayers not only of Jews but also of foreigners (*Ant.* 8.116–117). Furthermore, presumably in the interests of tolerance, he omits (*Ant.* 9.138) the conversion of the Temple of Baal into an outhouse. Again, significantly, though he generally follows the Apocryphal Addition C, containing Esther's prayer to G-d, rather closely, Josephus omits the abhorrence of foreigners expressed by Esther (C 26–27): 'I detest the bed of the uncircumcised and of any alien.' Jews, says Josephus (*Ant.* 4.207 and *Ag. Ap.* 2.237), following the Septuagint (Exod 22:28), are forbidden by the Torah to blaspheme the gods of others out of respect for the very word 'god.'[25]

Undoubtedly, one of the contributing factors to the view that Jews hate non-Jews is the fact that Jews sundered themselves off from others. It is this that leads a Tacitus (*Hist.* 5.5.1–2) to remark that Jews sit apart at meals and sleep apart and feel only hate and enmity toward every other people.

The presentation of the Balaam narrative was a real challenge for

---

[24] See my 'Use, Authority and Exegesis of Mikra in the Writings of Josephus' (*art. cit.*, n. 6) 494–496; and my *Jew and Gentile in the Ancient World: Attitudes and Interactions from Alexander to Justinian* (Princeton 1993) 133–142.

[25] Inasmuch as Josephus is writing for a primarily non-Jewish audience, he could hardly afford to offend these pagan readers. Hence, it is not surprising that he totally omits (*Ant.* 12.290) the reference in I Maccabees (3:49) to the incident in which the 'nations' (ἔθνη) drew the likenesses of their idols upon a scroll of the Law. Again, whereas we read in I Maccabees (3:25) that after Judah crushed Seron the fear and dread of Judah and his brothers began to fall upon the nations (ἔθνη) around them, Josephus (*Ant.* 12.293) omits mention of the effect upon the nations. Indeed, in the one place (*Ant.* 12.327) where Josephus does refer to the 'nations,' he is speaking not of the heathens generally but rather of the nations geographically surrounding Judaea. See my 'Use, Authority, and Exegesis of Mikra in the Writings of Josephus' (*art. cit.*, n. 6) 470–471.

Josephus, inasmuch as Balaam was a non-Jew, and Josephus is constantly aware of the charge that Jews are guilty of hating non-Jews. Indeed, we find in Balaam's words in the Bible (Num 23:9) the statement that the Israelites are a people that shall dwell alone and shall not be reckoned among the nations. Significantly, in his version of this passage, Josephus (*Ant.* 4.114), clearly aware of this charge, avoids presenting the Israelites as sundered off from all other peoples and instead presents the statement in terms of the *excellence* of the Israelites as compared with other peoples, and states that G-d has lavished upon the Israelites the means whereby they may become the *happiest* of all peoples. No one could object to such prophecy of the Israelites' happiness; the objection, which Josephus carefully avoids mentioning, is to having them cut themselves off from other peoples.

Indeed, in the course of Josephus' version of the Balaam narrative he has the Midianite women (*Ant.* 4.137), when they successfully persuade the Israelite youths to give up their way of life, remark that the Israelites have customs and a way of life wholly alien ἀλλοτριώτατα, 'belonging to another,' 'different,' 'not comparable,' 'hostile') to all mankind, 'inasmuch as your food is of a peculiar sort (ἰδιοτρόπους) and your drink is distinct from that of other men'—remarks frequently found in Graeco-Roman pagan writers.[26]

Another indication of Josephus' desire to avoid attacking the religious institutions of non-Jews may be seen in his complete omission (*Ant.* 4.112) of the fact that it was to the high places of the pagan god Baal that Balak took Balaam in order to inspect the Israelites.

It is particularly effective, in terms of Josephus' overall goals of apologetic for the Jews, to have a non-Jew praise them. Whereas Balaam in the Bible (Num 23:21) declares that G-d has not beheld any wrong or perverseness in the Israelites, Josephus (*Ant.* 4.118) has Balaam go one step further in positively pronouncing them, on his own authority, the most blessed of men.

It is likewise extremely effective to have Balaam, in an extra-biblical remark, state (*Ant.* 4.127–128) that the Israelites will never be overwhelmed by utter destruction since Divine providence is watching over them. It surely would have been a source of great consolation to Josephus' Jewish readers to read that a non-Jewish seer had predicted (*Ant.* 4.128) that the misfortunes that the Israelites will encounter will be slight and momentary, and that thereafter they will flourish once more.

---

[26] See my 'Anti-Semitism in the Ancient World,' in D. Berger (ed.), *History and Hate: The Dimensions of Anti-Semitism* (Philadelphia 1986) 30–32.

b. Jews Do Not Hate the Romans

Again, Josephus (*Ant.* 4.115) does not hesitate to have Balaam present a prophecy that the Israelites will occupy the land to which G-d has sent them and that the whole earth will be filled with their fame. If Josephus (*Ant.* 4.125) foretells the calamities that will befall kings and cities of the highest celebrity (some of which, he says, have not yet been established), he is careful to keep this prophecy cryptic enough so that Gentile readers will not necessarily identify this as referring to Rome, just as he has a similarly cryptic prophecy in his pericope of Daniel (*Ant.* 10.210).

The most striking indication of Josephus' ambiguity with regard to the Romans may be seen in his evasiveness (*Ant.* 10.210) with regard to the meaning of the stone which, in Nebuchadnezzar's dream, destroyed the kingdom of iron (Dan 2:44-45).[27] His excuse is that, as an historian, he is expected to discuss the past and not to predict the future, although Josephus certainly saw a kinship between the prophet and the historian,[28] particularly since he must have been aware of the dictum of Thucydides (1.22.4), one of his favorites, that 'whoever wishes to have a clear view of the events which have happened and of those which will some day, in all human probability, happen again in the same or a similar way' will find his history useful.[29] Indeed, this is the only place where Josephus makes such a statement; and, in fact, no other ancient historian makes any such remark.[30]

There is a similar cryptic passage in Josephus' pericope of Balaam (*Ant.* 4.125), in which he declares, in an extra-biblical remark, that Balaam foretold what calamities were to come for kings and cities of the

---

[27] The perceptive reader might well have connected this with the passage (*Ant.* 10.276) in which Josephus states explicitly that Daniel wrote about the empire of the Romans, though admittedly there is no necessary connection between the two passages. G. Stemberger, *Die Römische Herrschaft im Urteil der Juden* (Darmstadt 1983) 33-37, concludes that Josephus is more critical toward Rome in the *Antiquities* than in the *War* and stands in the apocalyptic tradition. Perhaps we should say not that he is more critical but that he is more ambiguous.
[28] See my 'Prophets and Prophecy in Josephus,' (*art. cit.*, n. 5) 397-400.
[29] Conversely, a prophet is concerned with recording the past, as may be seen from the fact that Moses (*Ant.* 4.320), at the close of his life, 'prophesies' to each of the tribes the things that are past.
[30] The very fact that Josephus (*Ant.* 1.240) refers to the historian Cleodemus-Malchus as 'the prophet' is a further indication of the kinship between historian and prophet. We may add that one basic reason for Josephus' great interest in the prophets—and he regarded Daniel as a prophet (*Ant.* 10.246, 249, 268)—was that he viewed them as his predecessors as historians of the past. Moreover, Josephus (*Ag. Ap.* 1.41) remarks that the reason why the historical works from the time of Artaxerxes in the mid-fifth century BCE to his own time are less reliable is that they did not have the prophets to attend to them.

highest celebrity (some of which had not yet been founded), 'along with other events which have already befallen men in bygone ages, by land or sea, down to times within my memory. And from all these prophecies one may infer what the future also has in store.'

Of course, inasmuch as Josephus, especially in his paraphrases of the prophets, is highly selective, he might have simply omitted this passage, as he did a paraphrase of the passage (Dan 2:44) predicting a Messianic kingdom which would destroy all previous kingdoms and which itself would last forever, as well as the passage in Daniel (7:18), in which it is made clear that the fifth, world-wide, and everlasting empire would be ruled by a people of 'saints of the Most High,' that is the Jews—a passage which would, to the obvious embarrassment of Josephus as spokesman for the Romans, imply the overthrow of Rome.[31] The fact that he does not omit the interpretation of Nebuchadnezzar's dream or this statement of Balaam's prophecies is an indication of deliberate ambiguity in his attempt to reach both of his audiences, the non-Jews and the Jews, for the latter of whom the references were apparently to a Messianic kingdom which would make an end of the Roman Empire. Perhaps he felt that to omit them altogether would have been regarded by the latter as a clear indication that he had sold out to the Romans. In fact, Klausner[32] goes so far as to argue that Josephus' trip to Rome in 64, despite his statements in the *War* that Rome's ascendancy was part of a Divine plan, may have actually increased his enthusiasm for the cause of the revolutionaries, inasmuch as he must have been impressed with Rome's decadence and hence saw that it was only a matter of time before Rome would fall; and the passages in *Antiquities* 4.125 and 10.210 may be a clue to his real feelings.[33]

In the passage (Num 24:17–18) corresponding to *Antiquities* 4.125, however, Balaam predicts that a star out of Jacob and a scepter out of

---

[31] D. Flusser, 'The Four Empires in the Fourth Sybil and in the Book of Daniel,' *IOS* 2 (1972) 148–175, concludes that Josephus (*Ant.* 10.276–277) could not speak of the common interpretation of the four empires in Daniel because of its anti-Roman character; but that in *Antiquities* 15.385-387, where no danger could arise, he has given the common Jewish sequence of the four empires—Babylonia, Persia, Macedonia, and Rome. We may remark, however, that there is no indication in the latter passage that the Roman Empire is destined to be overthrown.

[32] J. Klausner, *History of the Second Temple* (Hebrew), vol. 5 (Jerusalem 1949) 167–168.

[33] Moscovitz (*op. cit.*, n. 1) 27, suggests that it is very likely that Balaam's prophecy here is the famous 'ambiguous oracle' mentioned by Josephus (*War* 6.314), which Josephus thus left in all its obscurity. We may counter, however, that this seems unlikely, inasmuch as Josephus (*Ant.* 4.125) says that some of the prophesied events had already befallen men in bygone ages, whereas the ambiguous prophecy was one that was yet to come to pass.

Israel will conquer Edom and Seir. That this was an eschatological prophecy is clear from Balaam's statement (Num 24:14) that he will advise Balak what the Israelites will do to the Moabites at the end of days. That this was a Messianic prophecy seems to be hinted at in the Septuagint's version of Numbers 24:7: 'There shall come a man out of his (i.e. Israel's) seed, and he shall rule over many nations; and the kingdom of Gog shall be exalted, and his kingdom shall be increased.' In any case, this was interpreted messianically shortly after the time of Josephus in the case of Bar Kochba (y. Ta'an. 69d) by Rabbi Akiva. Of course, such a Messianic explanation was avoided by Josephus because of his subservience to the Romans.[34]

And yet, Josephus (Ant. 4.125) is eager to avoid giving the impression that the Israelites are out to destroy their enemies mercilessly, as would seem to be evident from the biblical passage (Num 24:8) in which Balaam predicts that the G-d of Israel will 'eat up the nations that are His adversaries and break their bones in pieces.' In Josephus' much milder version we are informed merely that Balaam foretold what calamities were in store for the opponents of the Israelites without spelling out precisely what those calamities were.[35]

c. Jews Do Not Rebel

As one who had participated in the war against the Romans and who had come to the conclusion that resistance to Rome was futile and that Rome was divinely destined to rule the world, Josephus constantly seeks to prevail upon his compatriots to give up the dream of national independence. Whereas in the Bible the promise of Canaan's land to Abraham is constantly renewed,[36] Josephus shifts the stress from the

---

[34] Josephus likewise omits all reference to the Kittim (Num 24:24), who are identified with the Romans, at least in later rabbinic literature (b. ʿAbod. Zar. 2b, b. Šebu. 6b, etc.), as well as perhaps at Qumran. See E. Schürer, *The History of the Jewish People in the Age of Jesus Christ (175 B.C.–A.D. 135)*, vol. 1 (edited by G. Vermes and F. Millar) (Edinburgh 1973) 241–242, n. 30.
[35] Cf. Josephus, *War* 5.367: 'G-d, who went the round of the nations, bringing to each in turn the rod of empire, now rested over Italy.' M. de Jonge, 'Josephus und die Zukunftserwartungen seines Volkes,' in O. Betz, K. Haacker, M. Hengel (edd.), *Josephus-Studien: Untersuchungen zu Josephus, dem antiken Judentum und dem Neuen Testament Otto Michel zum 70. Geburtstag gewidmet* (Göttingen 1974) 211, deduces from the use of the word 'now' in the above quotation that Josephus regarded the Romans as being powerful at the time that he was writing but not forever. We may reply, however, that the use of the word 'now' is perfectly natural in the context, namely the speech delivered by Josephus to his fellow-countrymen. He is making an appeal to realism: right now (but without reference to the future, which really is irrelevant) the Romans are in firm control of the world; hence revolution makes no sense.
[36] See B. H. Amaru, 'Land Theology in Josephus' *Jewish Antiquities*,' *JQR* 71 (1980–81)

covenanted Land of Israel, so dear to the revolutionaries, to the biblical personalities themselves and to the role of the Diaspora. In fact, Josephus never uses the word 'covenant' (διαθήκη), which is the Septuagint's equivalent for the Hebrew *berith*.[37] Instead of promises that the Jews will have the land of Canaan we have, in general, predictions.[38] Thus, in the incident of Jacob's wrestling with the angel, in the biblical version there is a simple statement (Gen 32:29) that the angel blessed Jacob, with no indication of the contents of the blessing, let alone of a blessing for his posterity; in Josephus' account (*Ant.* 1.332) the angel assures him that his race will never be extinguished.[39] Again, in Jacob's dream (Gen 46:3-4) in the biblical version there is no mention either of the land of Israel or of dominion and glory for Jacob's posterity, whereas in Josephus' paraphrase (*Ant.* 2.175) G-d predicts that there will be a long era of dominion and glory for his posterity and that He will establish them in the land.

We may see another instance where Josephus avoids terminology pertaining to an independent state in his remark (*Ant.* 4.114) that G-d has granted untold blessings to the Israelites and has vouchsafed to them His own providence as their perpetual ally (σύμμαχον) and guide (ἡγεμόνα). This is clearly, as Attridge[40] has pointed out, not merely a device for translating the biblical concept of covenant but is actually a replacement for it. The key is that the Israelites will thus be happy (εὐδαίμων, *Ant.* 4.114) rather than that they will dominate the world. It is with their fame (*Ant.* 4.115)—rather than, it would seem, with their

---

201-229.
[37] A. Paul, 'Flavius Josephus' 'Antiquities of the Jews': An Anti-Christian Manifesto,' *NTS* 31 (1985) 473-480, suggests that Josephus' substitution of the word παῦλαν ('truce') for the word *berith* (Gen 9:9, Septuagint διαθήκη) arises from his desire to dissociate himself from the New Testament's emphasis on the doctrine of the 'new covenant.' But see my reply in 'The Portrait of Noah in Josephus, Philo, Pseudo-Philo's *Biblical Antiquities*, and Rabbinic Midrashim' (*art. cit.*, n. 6) 26-27.
[38] Thus Josephus omits the passage (Gen 36:3-5) which relates G-d's blessing to Isaac promising the land to Abraham's descendants. It is significant that while in the Bible (Gen 27:27-29) Isaac's blessing of Jacob (whom he thinks to be Esau) asks G-d for agricultural abundance and power to demand respect from other nations, in Josephus (*Ant.* 1.272) the national aspect is totally omitted, and instead we have a prayer for personal happiness and satisfaction. Happiness, we may note, is likewise the state which G-d, according to Balaam's prophecy (*Ant.* 4.114), will lavish upon the Israelites.
[39] Hence, Josephus has given us a 'gereinigten' text, wherein the name 'Israel' assumes an eschatological rather than a political significance. So A. Butterweck, *Jakobs Ringkampf am Jabbok: Gen. 32,4 ff. in der jüdischen Tradition bis zum Frühmittelalter* (Frankfurt am Main 1981) 51-56. For other examples where Josephus omits phrases which have political significance and which may be offensive to the Romans, see my 'Josephus' Portrait of Jacob' (*art. cit.*, n. 6) 137.
[40] H. W. Attridge, *The Interpretation of Biblical History in the Antiquitates Judaicae of Flavius Josephus* (Missoula 1976) 79-80.

sheer force—that the whole earth will be filled, as we see in another of Josephus' extra-biblical additions. In particular, we may note that in place of the Bible's picture (Num 23:24) comparing the Israelites to lions that do not lie down until they have eaten their prey and drunk their blood, Josephus (*Ant.* 4.115-116) avoids the bloodthirsty elements and speaks only of the land that the Israelites will occupy. Indeed, Josephus (*Ant.* 4.116) clearly shifts the focus from the land of Israel to the Diaspora when he has Balaam declare that whereas now the Israelites are contained by the land of Canaan, the habitable world (τὴν οἰκουμένην), that is the Diaspora, lies before them as an everlasting habitation.[41]

Josephus was similarly aware that the Romans were sensitive to the great expansion of the Jewish population, especially through proselytism. Hence, whereas when Isaac blesses Jacob before sending him off to find a wife, the Bible (Gen 28:3) invokes G-d's blessing to 'make thee fruitful and multiply thee, that thou mayest become a multitude of people,' and (Gen 28:4) to let Jacob inherit the land which G-d gave to Abraham, Josephus (*Ant.* 1.278) omits this.[42]

Hence, we can understand Josephus' sensitivity when he came to the passage in Balaam's prophecy (Num 23:10) with regard to the population explosion of the Israelites: 'Who hath counted the dust of Jacob or numbered the fourth part of Israel?' Josephus diplomatically omitted this altogether.

d. Jews Are Not Busybodies

We can see another of the charges against the Jews, for example, in the order (*Ant.* 19.340-342) given by Marsus, the governor of Syria, to Agrippa I, to break up the conference of various kings which the latter had convened at Tiberias because of the suspicion that Agrippa was trying to organize a conspiracy against the Romans. Hence, in an extra-biblical detail, Josephus (*Ant.* 4.102), in introducing the narrative of Balaam, remarks that Balak, the king of the Moabites, had formed an alliance with the Midianites when he saw the Israelites growing so great and became concerned that they would seek to expand at his expense. He

---

[41] This is clearly a plea for the viability of Jewish life in the Diaspora, as noted by A. Schalit, trans., Josephus, *Antiquitates Judaicae* (in Hebrew), vol. 1 (Jerusalem 1944), Introduction, lxxxi. We may see a parallel in Josephus' version of G-d's blessings to Jacob (Gen 28:13-15; *Ant.* 1.280-283): Jacob, he says, will have good children who will rule over both the land of Israel and who will fill all other lands (*Ant.* 1.282).

[42] Furthermore, while the Bible (Gen 28:14) declares, in G-d's promise in Jacob's dream, that his seed will be 'as the dust of the earth' and that 'thou shalt spread abroad to the west and to the east and to the north and to the south,' Josephus (*Ant.* 1.282) predicts that the number of Jacob's direct descendants will be vast, but he is careful to avoid any indication that they will seek to convert others to Judaism.

had not learned, says Josephus, that the Hebrews were not for interfering with other countries, G-d having forbidden them to do so. The verb which is here used for 'interfering,' πολυπραγμονεῖν, implies being meddlesome, being an inquisitive busybody, and is almost always employed in a pejorative sense.[43]

Moreover, it is significant that whereas in the biblical statement (Deut 2:9) G-d forbids the Israelites to attack the Moabites, inasmuch as He had not given the Moabites' land to the Israelites but had given it to the Moabites as the descendants of Lot, Josephus (Ant. 4.102) here broadens this to a sweeping general principle, namely that the Israelites do not interfere in the affairs of all other countries. Moreover, whereas G-d in the Bible prohibits the Israelites from engaging in battle with the Moabites for the sake of acquiring their land, Josephus has broadened this into a prohibition against any kind of interference with their affairs.

e. Reduction in Gentile Anti-Judaism

Josephus is also concerned to attribute hatred of the Jewish people not to whole nations but rather to individuals. Thus, whereas in the Bible (Exod 17:8–16) it is the Amalekites as a nation who beset the Israelites in the desert, in Josephus (Ant. 3.40) it is the kings of the Amalekites who are to blame for sending messages to the kings of neighboring tribes exhorting them to make war against the Israelites.

Hence, whereas in the rabbinic tradition (Tanḥuma (ed. Buber) 4.134, Num. Rab. 20.4, Sipre Num. 157 (ed. Horowitz, p. 209), Sanh. 105a), the Moabites and Midianites join forces, despite the fact that they are bitter enemies of one another, because their hatred of the Jews is even greater, Josephus (Ant. 4.102) assiduously avoids giving the impression that Gentiles by nature hate Jews and instead depicts the two nations as being long-time friends and allies. The motive of these nations in going to war with the Israelites, according to Josephus (Ant. 4.103), is thus not hatred; in fact, in an extra-biblical addition, Josephus specifically says that it was not Balak's intention to fight with men fresh with success and who were found to be only the more emboldened by reverse; rather his aim was to check their aggrandizement. This, consequently, casts the Moabites and the Midianites in a much better light.

Moreover, far from imputing anti-Jewish hate to Balaam, Josephus (Ant. 4.106) presents Balaam as counselling the envoys who had been sent by Balak to renounce the hatred which they bore to the Israelites, whereas the rabbinic view (Tanḥuma Balak 6, Tanḥuma (ed. Buber, 4.136–137), Midr. Aggadah on Num 22:13 (ed. Buber, 2.134)) and that of Philo

---

[43] Cf., e.g., Hdt. 3.15; Xen., Anab. 5.1.15; Aristoph., Pl. 913; Pl., Rep. 433a.

(*Mos.* 1.266) is that Balaam was not at all sincere in refusing to accompany the envoys. In contrast, in the Bible (Num 22:13) Balaam does not give advice on his own but merely reports that it is G-d who has refused to allow him to accompany them.

Moreover, this favorable picture of Balaam is sustained by the fact that, unlike the rabbinic tradition,[44] which seeks to connect Balaam's desire to gratify the ambassadors with his hatred of the Israelites, Josephus has Balaam explicitly inquire of G-d what His intention was with regard to the invitation of the envoys. When G-d informs him (Num 22:12) that he is not to curse the Israelites, in the biblical version (Num 22:13) Balaam tells the envoys that they must return, inasmuch as G-d refuses to allow him to accompany them. To be sure, in Josephus' version (*Ant.* 4.105) Balaam does seem to be more anti-Israelite, inasmuch as he makes plain to the envoys his readiness (προθυμίαν) and zeal (σπουδήν) to comply with their request to curse the Israelites but says that G-d has refused to allow him to do so. From this we see, however, that Balaam's motive is not hatred for the Israelites but rather loyalty to his sovereign. Moreover, in stating that G-d has vetoed his request he piously adds to the biblical narrative a statement of his recognition that the G-d who refused him is the G-d who had brought him to his high renown for truth's sake and for the prediction (πρόρρησιν)[45] thereof.

The favorable portrayal of Balaam may also be seen in the scene (*Ant.* 4.112) in which he is said, in an extra-biblical addition, to have received a magnificent reception from Balak. According to the Bible (Num 22:37), Balak berates Balaam, asking why he had not hitherto come to him and whether it was because Balak was not able to honor him sufficiently. Josephus, on the other hand, is here clearly stressing that the relationship between Balak and Balaam is, in the first instance, motivated by friendship rather than by hatred of the Israelites. In contrast, we find that the rabbis[46] describe the reception which Balak gave to Balaam as very cheap and poor; and Philo (*Mos.* 1.275), who, to be sure, remarks that the interview began with friendly greetings, proceeds immediately to note that these were followed by Balak's words of censure for Balaam for his slowness and failure to arrive more readily.

---

[44] *Tanḥuma Balak* 5, 8, 12; *Tanḥuma* (ed. Buber) 4.136, 137, 142; *Num. Rab.* 20.12, 20.19; *Eliyahu Rabbah* 29 (ed. Friedmann, p. 142), *Aggadath Bereshith* 65 (ed. Buber, p. 131).

[45] The fact that Josephus here uses the word πρόρρησις does not indicate that he regards Balaam as a prophet comparable to the Hebrew prophets, inasmuch as πρόρρησις is used of predictions in a dream (e.g., Joseph's dream, *Ant.* 2.15; the butler's dream, *Ant.* 2.65; the baker's dream, *Ant.* 2.72; Amram's dream, *Ant.* 2.217) or a prediction in general (e.g., of Pharaoh's seer, *Ag. Ap.* 1.258).

[46] 2 *'Abot R. Nat.* 23 (ed. Schechter, p. 48); *Tanḥuma Balak* 11; *Tanḥuma* (ed. Buber) 4.140.

Again, the meeting is presented by Josephus not as an occasion to exhibit hatred for the Israelites but rather to plan militarily to defeat them. Thus, it is the Israelites' camp (στρατόπεδον, *Ant.* 4.112, clearly a military term) that Balak and Balaam go to inspect, rather than, as the Bible would have it (Num 22:41) 'a portion of the people.' And the mountain to which they, in an extra-biblical addition, go in order to inspect the Israelites' camp is located (*Ant.* 4.112) with respect to its distance from the camp. Moreover, it is implied in the biblical text (Num 22:41) that it was Balak who took the initiative to escort Balaam, whereas in Josephus it is Balaam who apparently asked to be conducted to one of the mountains in order to inspect the disposition—which would certainly include the readiness to fight—of the Israelites' camp.

Indeed, Balaam is depicted in Josephus (*Ant.* 4.107) as succumbing only to persistent pressure by Balak. Thus the Bible (Num 22:15) states very simply that Balak sent yet again princes, more in number and more honorable than those whom he had sent previously. In Josephus (*Ant.* 4.107) his entreaties δέησιν, 'supplication,' 'plea') are urgent and persistent, and he agrees to consult G-d anew not out of audacity or greed, but only in order to give these new envoys some gratification. Indeed, it is this desire to gratify Balak and his representatives that Josephus notes as Balaam's motive in several other additions (*Ant.* 4.121, 123, 127) to the biblical text. Even when, instructed by G-d to accompany them, he agrees to do so, Josephus (*Ant.* 4.107), in an extra-biblical addition, not only does not blame Balaam but even seems to castigate G-d, since we are told that Balaam did not realize that G-d had deluded him in giving him this order.[47] To be sure, Josephus defends G-d's action by remarking that He was angry that Balaam should have tempted Him thus a second time; it is Balaam, however, that Philo (*Mos.* 1.268) puts in a more unfavorable light by stating that Balaam's second consultation of G-d was once again pure pretense. Even Balak emerges in a more favorable light, inasmuch as Josephus (*Ant.* 4.107) totally omits the attempt (Num 22:17-18) made by Balak, according to the Bible, to influence Balaam with the promise of power and money in order to get him to curse the Israelites.

Josephus makes every attempt to depict Balaam's purpose in cursing the Israelites as due to his friendship with Balak rather than to hatred of the Israelites or greed, as we find in Philo (*Mos.* 1.267-268), the New Testament (2 Pet 2:15, Jude 11), and rabbinic literature (*m.* ʾ*Abot* 5.19, 1

---

[47] As Baskin (*op. cit.*, n. 1) 97, has noted, Josephus here appears to be in accord with the rabbinic tradition (*Num. Rab.* 20.9, 20.11) in indicating that it was G-d who had led Balaam astray in acceding to the request of the envoys.

'Abot R. Nat. 29 (ed. Schechter, p. 88), and 2 'Abot R. Nat. 49 (ed. Schechter, p. 125). Thus, in an extra-biblical addition, Balaam (Ant. 4.120-121) declares that it was his earnest prayer to do no despite to Balak's desire to have him curse the Israelites but that G-d is mightier than that determination of his 'to do this favor.' Again, he reiterates (Ant. 4.123) that it was his earnest desire to gratify Balak and the Midianites and that, indeed, it was unseemly to reject their request. Hence, when, against the biblical version (Num 23:27), in which it is Balak who proposes to Balaam a second attempt to curse the Israelites, it is Balaam who proposes that new altars be erected and additional sacrifices be offered, the change is intended to depict that Balaam's motive was his close friendship with Balak.

Indeed, whereas in the Bible (Num 22:34), when the angel rebukes him, Balaam responds penitently, declaring that he had sinned unknowingly and offering to return home, Philo (Mos. 1.274) remarks that Balaam was dissimulating, 'for why should he ask about a matter so evident?' and that his real intention remained to harm the Israelites.[48] In Josephus' version, however, there is no indication of any lack of sincerity on the part of Balaam; in fact, in an extra-biblical remark (Ant. 4.111), the blame is actually put upon G-d, who has to exhort him to pursue his intended way.

Commentators have long asked why the Midianites are introduced into the account, when actually the story concerns only Balak the king and Balaam the prophet of Moab. In reply, we may suggest that Josephus (Ant. 5.336) was well aware that Ruth, a Moabite, was the ancestress of King David; and hence he was careful not to impute such groundless hatred to the people as a whole. Indeed, whereas in the biblical text the Moabites are mentioned thirteen times and the Midianites only twice, in Josephus' version the ratio is almost exactly reversed, with the Moabites mentioned only twice and the Midianites nine times. In particular, whereas in the Bible (Num 25:1) the harlotry is with the daughters of Moab, with the Midianites merely participating in it (Num 25: 6-18), in Josephus, although in his parting advice (Ant. 4.126-130), Balaam tells the Midianite princes to instruct their women to seduce the Israelite youths and to get them thus to worship the gods of the Midianites and the Moabites, the actual seduction is by the Midianite women and the war that follows is against the Midianites (Ant. 4.131-164), with no mention of the role of the Moabites in the entire narrative. Again, it is not the Midianites as a nation, as in the Bible, but rather

---

[48] So also Philo (Mos. 1.274) and the rabbinic tradition (Num. Rab. 20.14-15, Tanḥuma (ed. Buber, 4.139).

their leaders (*Ant.* 4.126) who are responsible for the device whereby the Midianite women seduced the Israelite men.

As to the Israelites, in contrast to the Bible (Num 22:13), which states that Balaam told the envoys sent by Balak that they should return because G-d had refused to allow him to accompany them to curse the Israelites without giving the reason for G-d's veto, Josephus (*Ant.* 4.106) uses the opportunity to speak apologetically for the Israelites by declaring that the reason why G-d had refused his request was that the Israelites were in favor with Him.

If we wonder why Josephus omitted mention of the death of Balaam, this may be due to the fact that he was killed in battle, together with the Midianite kings (Num 31:8). To be sure, Josephus (*Ant.* 4.161) does mention this battle; but if he had included Balaam in it it is quite conceivable that this would have underscored the impression that Balaam was anti-Jewish. Hence, as Moscovitz[49] remarks, by omitting such a detail Josephus is consistent in stressing the view that Balaam was not a conspirator against Israel but rather simply a professional soothsayer.

f. Appeal to Stoicism

The very fact that Josephus compares the religious groupings of the Jews to the Greek philosophical schools, asserting (*Life* 12) that the Pharisees, the leading sect, are very similar to the Stoic school,[50] is an indication of the philosophical interests that he expected his audience to have, especially since such comparisons would hardly appear to be central to one who viewed the religious dimensions of these groups. Inasmuch as Stoicism was the favorite philosophy of Hellenistic intellectuals,[51] it is not surprising that he should attempt to appeal particularly to them in his recasting of biblical material.[52] If Josephus

---

[49] Moscovitz (*op. cit.*, n. 1) 30.
[50] See now S. Mason, *Flavius Josephus on the Pharisees: A Composition-Critical Study* (Leiden 1991), especially 138–140, 154–156.
[51] See W. W. Tarn and G. T. Griffith, *Hellenistic Civilisation* (London 1952³) 325; L. H. Martin, 'Josephus' Use of *Heimarmene* in the *Jewish Antiquities* XIII, 171–3,' *Numen* 28 (1981) 127–137.
[52] Indeed, at the very beginning of his account, Josephus employs Stoic terminology in his extra-biblical statement (*Ant.* 1.46) that G-d had decreed for Adam and Eve a life of happiness unmolested (ἀπαθῆ) by all ill. We should note that the term ἀπαθής, as well as the corresponding noun ἀπάθεια (freedom from emotional disturbance), is a common Stoic term with reference to freedom from emotion. For Josephus' use of Stoic terminology in his versions of Abraham and Isaac see my 'Abraham the Greek Philosopher in Josephus' (*art. cit.*, n. 6) 146–149; and 'Josephus as a Biblical Interpreter: the ʿAqedah' (*art. cit.*, n. 6) 222–224.

does speak of G-d it is in terms of the Stoic conception of Providence (πρόνοια) and in order to attack the Epicureans.⁵³ Indeed, this term, πρόνοια, appears no fewer than seventy-four times in the first half of the *Antiquities*.⁵⁴ The fact that Josephus chose to conclude his account of Daniel and, indeed, of this whole book—as well as the first half of the entire work—with no fewer than five paragraphs (*Ant*. 10.277–281) to demonstrate how mistaken the Epicureans are in asserting (*Ant*. 10.278) that the world runs by its own movement (αὐτομάτως)⁵⁵ without knowing a guide (ἡνιόχου, 'charioteer') or another's care (ἀφρόντιστον) is an indication of how much importance he attached to this lesson of the power of Providence in human affairs.⁵⁶ We may suggest that the vehemence with which he attacks the Epicureans reflects his consonance with the rabbinic view that one must know what to answer to an *Apiqoros* (ʾ*Abot* 2.14).⁵⁷

---

⁵³ See Attridge (*art. cit.*, n. 40) 103–104 and literature cited on page 103, n. 1. W. C. van Unnik, 'An Attack on the Epicureans by Flavius Josephus,' in W. den Boer *et al.* (eds.), *Romanitas et Christianitas, Studia Iano Henrico Waszink ... Oblata* (Amsterdam 1973) 341–355, notes original elements in Josephus' views here of providence and concludes that this originality refutes those who assert that Josephus was merely copying handbooks. We may, however, reply that in this case, at least, the argument is inconclusive, since almost all of the primary sources for Epicureanism are lost.
⁵⁴ See my 'Use, Authority and Exegesis of Mikra in the Writings of Josephus' (*art. cit.*, n. 6) 499–500.
⁵⁵ S. Lieberman, 'How Much Greek in Jewish Palestine?' in A. Altmann (ed.), *Philip W. Lown Institute of Advanced Judaic Studies, Brandeis University: Studies and Texts*, vol. 1: *Biblical and Other Studies* (Cambridge, Mass. 1963) 123–141, notes that the word *automaton* occurs in only one passage in rabbinic literature, namely *Midrash Psalms* (ed. Buber, 1.22), where the reference is to the heretics—probably the Epicureans—who say that the universe is an *automaton*. Lieberman remarks that Epicurus was chosen by the rabbis as the archsymbol of heresy not only because of his immense popularity but also because of the particular danger inherent in his philosophy.
⁵⁶ The attack on the Epicureans in *Against Apion* 2.180 is similarly centered on their denial of G-d's providential care (πρόνοια) for mankind. So also in Philo, *Conf*. 114.
⁵⁷ The rabbis (m. *Sanh*. 10.1) go so far as to mention specifically *Apikorsim* among those who forfeit their share in the world to come. We may understand the appropriateness and the vehemence of Josephus' attack if we bear in mind the rabbinic view, as later codified by Maimonides (*Mishneh Torah, Teshuvah*, 3.8), defining the *apiqoros* as one who either denies prophecy, and therefore the possibility of communion between G-d and man, or divine revelation, or divine knowledge of the deeds of man. The story of Daniel is, we may say, centered on these very doctrines. Specifically, in the case of the miracle of the Red Sea, Josephus (*Ant*. 2.347) is ready to consider the possibility that it occurred through accident (κατὰ ταὐτόματον), whereas in the Daniel pericope, using the same expression (*Ant*. 10.280), he vehemently denies the possibility of *automatism* (αὐτοματισμῷ). G. Delling, 'Die biblische Prophetie bei Josephus,' in O. Betz, K. Haacker, M. Hengel (edd.), *Josephus-Studien: Untersuchungen zu Josephus, dem antiken Judentum und dem Neuen Testament Otto Michel zum 70. Geburtstag gewidmet* (Göttingen 1974) 118, suggests that it is perhaps not accidental that the first half of the

In the case of Balaam, the statement (*Ant.* 4.113), which is an addition to the biblical text (Num 23:4), that when Balaam carried out his sacrifice before prophesying he saw the indications of inflexible Fate (ἄτροπον, Thackeray's brilliant emendation) is a sign that he looked upon such interpretations as did the Stoics.

The concept of Providence, so central in Stoic thought, is introduced several times by Josephus in the Balaam pericope. Thus, Balaam proclaims (*Ant.* 4.114) that G-d has vouchsafed His own providence to the Israelites as their personal ally and guide. Further he declares (*Ant.* 4.117) that the Israelites have been invested by the providence of G-d with superabundant valor. Again, in his parting advice, he tells Balak that G-d's providence is watching over the Israelites to preserve them from all ill (*Ant.* 4.128). Finally, we are told (*Ant.* 4.157) that it was by divine providence (θείᾳ προνοίᾳ) that Balaam was prevented from cursing the Israelites.

Likewise, in the biblical text, after Balak and Balaam offer their sacrifices, G-d (Num 23:16) plays an active role in putting words into Balaam's mouth, whereas Josephus (*Ant.* 4.114), with his stress on the concept of Providence, is clearly appealing to a Stoic audience in remarking that Balaam realized that G-d had bestowed untold blessings upon the Israelites and had granted His own providence (πρόνοιαν) as their perpetual ally and guide.

5. *Emphasis on Military Details*

A major change in nuance in Josephus' version of the Bible is to be seen in the fact that Josephus portrays the Israelites as an army and Moses as their general. Indeed, this emphasis on military details is precisely what one would expect from one who had served as a general, as Josephus did in Galilee during the early stages of the war against Rome. Undoubtedly, moreover, Josephus saw a need to stress the military capacity of the Israelites because the Jews had been reproached with cowardice by such detractors as Apollonius Molon (*Ag. Ap.* 2.148).

It is significant that when Josephus (*Ant.* 1.13) enumerates the main topics of the Bible he lists 'all sorts of surprising reverses, many fortunes of war, heroic exploits of generals, and political revolutions.' One is thus struck by the emphasis on military matters. Indeed, in his final

---

Antiquities ends with the prophet who speaks of the rescue of the Jewish people from their seemingly hopeless situation at the time when Josephus completed his work. If so, this would reinforce the view that Josephus, despite his obvious feeling of indebtedness to his imperial hosts, adopts a tone of ambiguity here in deference to the Jewish readers whom he is also attempting to reach.

encomium of Moses (*Ant.* 4.329), he remarks that as a general he had few to equal him and that as a prophet he had no rivals.[58]

Not only are we given in Josephus an extended portrait of Moses as a general, but his people are presented as soldiers. Thus Balaam (*Ant.* 4.106) tells the envoys who have come to him that the army whom he has been requested to curse is in favor with G-d; thus the confrontation between the Moabites-Midianites and the Israelites is put on a military basis, and not on the basis of anti-Jewish hatred. Indeed, the Israelites are referred to several times (*Ant.* 4.106, 116, 122, 140) as an army where this military aspect is missing in the biblical original. Moreover, whereas the Bible (Num 22:41) states that Balak took Balaam and brought him into the high places of Baal, whence he saw a portion of the people, in Josephus (*Ant.* 4.112) Balaam is presented as a kind of general who desires to be conducted to inspect the disposition of the Israelites' camp (στρατόπεδον). Likewise, Josephus (*Ant.* 4.116) has Balaam refer to the Israelites as a blessed army (στρατός). The military phraseology continues with Josephus' statement (*Ant.* 4.117) that not even one of the enemies of the Israelites will return victorious so as to gladden the hearts of child and wife. That the latter phrase has military associations is clear from the fact that it is so similar to the language used by Homer (*Il.* 5.688) with regard to the warrior Sarpedon and, negatively, by Tyrtaeus (frag. 6–7, line 6) with regard to the opposite of the warrior, namely the beggar who wanders with his little children and his wedded wife.

This emphasis (*Ant.* 4.112) on the military aspects of the confrontation between the Moabites–Midianites and the Israelites serves to underscore

---

[58] Josephus' listing of Moses' achievement as a general before he mentions his role as a prophet would seem to indicate an order of importance; and, in any case, Josephus' attitude is clearly to be contrasted with that of the Bible, which speaks (Deut 34:7–12) only of Moses' supremacy as a prophet. Furthermore, in his apologetic treatise *Against Apion* (2.157–63), in summaring Moses' achievements, the first point that he makes is that it was he who took command of the multitudes who left Egypt and guided them safely through a huge desert and defeated their enemies. Throughout this, says Josephus, he proved the best of generals. Similarly, the offices in which Joshua succeeds Moses (*Ant.* 4.165) are those of prophet and general, whereas, in the corresponding biblical passage (Num 27:18), Joshua is described as a man in whom there is spirit, but there is no mention of his military abilities. Finally, after Moses announces to the Israelites that he is to die and proceeds to exhort them to obey the laws which he has given them, it is his role as general which they indicate they will miss most (*Ant.* 4.194). At such an emotional point in the history of the nation, Josephus (*Ant.* 4.194–95) tells us that what they remember is his bravery, namely the risks which he had run in their behalf and his ardent zeal for their salvation. This depiction of the Israelites in military terms is especially clear in the exhortation which Moses gives to the Israelites before his death (*Ant.* 4.177), where he addresses them as 'comrades in arms' (συστρατιῶται) and partners in long tribulation. On Moses' role as general see further my 'Josephus' Portrait of Moses' (*art. cit.*, n. 6) 13–28.

the military prowess of the Israelites, just as the emphasis on Moses as a general[59] does likewise.

Josephus frequently, in extra-biblical additions,[60] stresses the courage and skill in battle of the biblical heroes. He is especially motivated to do so because, as we have noted, the Jews had been reproached with cowardice by such Jew-baiters as Apollonius Molon (*ap. Ag. Ap.* 2.148). Moreover, Josephus himself had been subjected to such a charge (*War* 3.358). Hence, it is particularly effective that Balaam (*Ant.* 4.117) remarks that the Israelites have been invested by the providence of G-d with superabundant valor (ἀνδρείας). Moreover, there is greater effect in Balaam's blessing of the Israelites because he originally intended, as Josephus (*Ant.* 4.120–122) indicates, to curse them.

6. *Miracles*

If, indeed, as we have indicated, Josephus was addressing a predominantly non-Jewish literate audience,[61] perhaps the most difficult task confronting him was what to do with the various miracles in the Bible. On the whole, Josephus tends to downgrade miracles,[62] as we see especially when we compare, for example, his view of Abraham and Moses as talented generals with the rabbinic portraits of these leaders as prevailing because of G-d's miraculous assistance.[63] Josephus frequently

---

[59] It is significant that whereas in the Septuagint Moses is never called στρατηγός (general) or even ἡγεμών (leader), in Josephus he is referred to fifteen times in the *Antiquities* (2.241, 268; 3.2, 11, 12, 28, 47, 65, 67, 78, 102, 105; 4.82, 194, 329) and once in the *Against Apion* (2.158) as a στρατηγός; in addition, the verb στρατηγέω, 'to be a field-commander,' 'to lead an army,' is used of him once (2.243); and the noun στρατηγία, 'army command,' 'office of supreme commander,' is used with reference to him twice (2.255, 282). Furthermore, the noun ἡγεμών is used of him six times (2.268, 4.11; *Ag. Ap.* 1.238, 261; 2.156, 159).
[60] See my 'Use, Authority and Exegesis of Mikra in the Writings of Josephus' (*art. cit.*, n. 6) 490–491, and my *Jew and Gentile in the Ancient World* (*op. cit.*, n. 24) 222–223.
[61] See my 'Use, Authority and Exegesis of Mikra in the Writings of Josephus' (*art. cit.*, n. 6) 470–471.
[62] Thus, the prediction (Gen 18:10) that the angel will return and that Sarah will bear a son 'according to this season of life,' that is a year from then, is toned down in Josephus, so that we have merely the statement (*Ant.* 1.197) that one of the angels will return some day in the future. Then, when the birth does occur, Josephus (*Ant.* 1.214) says simply that it occurred during the following year. Again, the scene of the ram being caught in a thicket by its horns (Gen 22:13) may have seemed grotesque and too much of a miracle for a rationalizing Greek intellectual. Hence, Josephus omits it and says merely that G-d brought the ram from obscurity into view, implying that it had always been there. See my critical bibliography on the subject of Josephus' treatment of miracles in *Josephus and Modern Scholarship* (Berlin 1984) 477–480. See also my 'Use, Authority and Exegesis of Mikra in the Writings of Josephus' (*art. cit.*, n. 6) 506–507.
[63] See my 'Abraham the General in Josephus' (*art. cit.*, n. 6) 43–49.

(*Ant.* 1.108, 3.81, 3.268, 3.322, 4.158, 8.262, 10.281, 17.354, 19.108; *War* 5.257) employs the time-honored formula, found not merely in Dionysius of Halicarnassus (1.48.1, 1.48.4, 2.40.3, 2.74.5, 3.36.5), Lucian (*Hist. Conscr.* 10), and Pliny (*Hist. Nat.* 9.18), but also earlier in Herodotus (2.123, 5.45) and Thucydides (6.2.1), allowing the reader to make up his mind, which, as Delling and MacRae[64] have remarked, is an expression of courtesy to his pagan readers more than a confession of his own doubt about the veracity of these accounts. Thus, when referring to the miracle of the splitting of the Red Sea, realizing that such a miracle would seem incredible to most of his readers, Josephus cites the parallel (*Ant.* 2.348) of the Pamphylian Sea, which retired before the advance of the army of Alexander the Great, though, even so, he adds, 'However, on these matters everyone is welcome to his own opinion.'[65]

[64] G. Delling, 'Josephus und das Wunderbare,' *NovT* 2 (1957–58) 291–309; G. W. MacRae, 'Miracle in *The Antiquities* of Josephus,' in C. F. D. Moule (ed.), *Miracles: Cambridge Studies in Their Philosophy and History* (London 1965) 136–142.
[65] Of course, the story of Jonah presented Josephus with a number of miracles—the swallowing of Jonah by the big fish, Jonah's prayer from within the big fish, the episode of Jonah emerging from the big fish, the conversion of the whole city of Nineveh, the plant that grew within one night, the destruction of the plant on the next day by a single worm, and the huge dimensions of Nineveh. In the case of the miracle of Jonah remaining alive for three days in the belly of the big fish and then emerging from it, this was apparently regarded as a major miracle, so that Celsus, in the second century (*ap.* Origen, *Against Celsus* 7.53), sarcastically declares that Christians should worship not Jesus but Jonah or Daniel, whose miracles outdo the resurrection. Even three centuries later, to judge from Augustine (*Epistulae* 102.30), who quotes Porphyry's lost work *Adversus Christianos*, this incident was a source of ridicule among the pagans in general. Josephus might have omitted the story as being incredible (as he did the other miraculous events enumerated above), or he might have left it to the reader to decide, or he might have modified it to conform with the somewhat similar stories told about Heracles and Hermione and Perseus and Andromache, where the fish is maimed by the hero; but Josephus chose not to depart from the biblical version, perhaps because it was so well known, while dissociating himself from necessarily believing it. He does so by the device of stating that the story (λόγος) has it that Jonah was swallowed by a huge fish, just as in a somewhat similar account, that of Arion who was rescued by a dolphin, Herodotus (1.24) declares, without taking responsibility for the tale, that 'they say' (λέγουσι) that the dolphin took him on his back. Moreover, whereas the biblical narrative (Jonah 2:1–9) has Jonah miraculously address G-d while he is still in the big fish, Josephus has eliminated the miraculous element by having him do so after he has emerged from the fish. Furthermore, in the Bible (Jonah 2:1–2) Jonah, praying from the belly of the fish, declares that G-d has answered him (Jonah 2:7), whereas it is clear that the deliverance has not yet taken place. The Septuagint version corrects this by having the optative, 'May my prayer come to Thee.' The Targum resolves the problem by referring the rescue to the future: 'And it is revealed before you to raise my life from destruction.' Josephus neatly resolves the matter by having Jonah pray (*Ant.* 9.214) after emerging from the belly of the fish. Furthermore, in the Hebrew version (Jonah 2:10) we read that the L-rd spoke to the fish that had swallowed Jonah and that it vomited Jonah upon the dry land. Josephus (*Ant.* 9.213), obviously sensitive to the charge of

Undoubtedly, one of the greatest challenges that Josephus faced with regard to credulity was what to do with the story of Balaam's ass that spoke. Josephus might have omitted the incident,[66] as he did several other episodes in the Bible—the cunning of Jacob in connection with Laban's flock (Gen 30:37-38), the Judah-Tamar episode (Gen 38), Moses' slaying of the Egyptian (Exod 2:12), the building of the golden calf (Exod 32), Miriam's leprosy (Num 12), the story of Moses' striking the rock to bring forth water which speaks of Moses' disgrace (Num 20:10-12), and the story of the brazen serpent (Num 21:4-9) whereby Moses cured those who had been bitten by the fiery serpents. Instead, only at the very end of the whole episode of Balaam do we have the familiar words of Josephus (*Ant.* 4.158): 'On this narrative readers are free to think what they please.'[67]

We may guess that Josephus was not afraid to include the narrative of the speaking ass because his audience was probably familiar with the account of Achilles' horse (Homer, *Il.* 19.408-417), Xanthos, which likewise speaks after being unfairly accused by his master. And just as Balaam's ass speaks because G-d willed it, so Xanthus is said to have spoken because the goddess Hera gave him speech. Thus both narratives clearly acknowledge that human speech is not natural for animals.

Even so, Josephus has taken several steps to make the narrative of the miracle more credible. In the first place, whereas the story of the speaking ass is the subject of fifteen verses in the Bible (Num 22:21-35), in Josephus this is reduced to four short paragraphs (*Ant.* 4.108-111). In the second place, in the Bible Balaam smites his ass three times, whereas Josephus mentions this only once (*Ant.* 4.108-109). Thirdly, the Bible has

---

credulity, says nothing about G-d's action in speaking to the fish and instead resorts to the passive voice with the statement that after three days and as many nights Jonah was cast up on the shore of the Black Sea. So also Pseudo-Philo, *Homily on Jonah* 19-25, replaces the prayer with a more appropriate supplication. It is interesting that the great twelfth-century scholar Ibn Ezra, in his commentary on Jonah 2:2, notes that there were commentators who stressed the fact that Jonah prayed not in the fish but from the fish and hence deduced that he prayed after he had emerged from the fish.

[66] Pseudo-Philo, *Bib. Ant.* 18.9, though mentioning the ass, says nothing about the ass speaking.

[67] Moscovitz (*op. cit.*, n. 1) 18 suggests that it is possible that Josephus postponed his customary declaration that the reader may believe as he pleases to the end of the Balaam narrative, where it is added as an afterthought, because the whole incident of the ass was so trivial and insignificant in Josephus' eyes. The incident, however, hardly seems trivial in view of the fact that Josephus does devote four paragraphs to it. More likely, the reason for the postponement was that it is not only the incident of the ass that might strike readers as incredible, since the very idea that someone had the power to curse a whole nation and that he could be prevented by divine intervention might likewise stretch credibility.

the ass speaking twice, whereas Josephus has her speak only once (*Ant.* 4.109). Fourthly, whereas the Bible (Num 22:28) states that the L-rd actually opened the mouth of the ass, Josephus (*Ant.* 4.108) is less direct in asserting that the ass became conscious of the divine spirit approaching her. Fifthly, instead of saying that G-d actually opened the mouth of the ass, Josephus (*Ant.* 4.109) says that the ass broke out in human speech because G-d so willed it. Sixthly, readers might well have wondered why an ass that has the supernatural power to speak should be sensitive to pain, as is clear from the Bible (Num 22:28); and so Josephus (*Ant.* 4.108) seems to be more consistent in asserting that the ass was insensible to the blows with which Balaam smote her. Seventhly, whereas in the Bible (Num 22:29) when the ass speaks, Balaam gives no indication of his amazement that his animal should be speaking, Josephus, aware that his readers would obviously wonder that a man hearing an animal speak should not be astonished, specifically declares (*Ant.* 4.110) that Balaam was aghast (ταραττομένου, 'confounded,' 'put into confusion,' 'embarrassed,' 'frightened,' dismayed,' 'bewildered') at hearing his ass speak thus with a human voice. Similarly, when the angel (Num 22:32) rebukes Balaam for striking the ass, the Bible (Num 22:34) gives no indication that Balaam was at all surprised, whereas Josephus (*Ant.* 4.111), clearly aware that his readers would wonder that Balaam was not amazed, states that Balaam was terrified (καταδείσας).

In any case, the picture painted of Balaam in this incident is much harsher in the Bible than in Josephus; in the former, Balaam is spoken of as angry (Num 22:27), and he even threatens (Num 22:29) to kill the animal, whereas in Josephus neither of these remarks is made, and, indeed, Balaam is, in effect, excused (*Ant.* 4.109) on the ground that he had failed to understand that it was G-d's purpose that debarred the ass from serving him on his mission.[68] Moreover, whereas in the Bible (Num 22:30) the ass speaks in direct discourse reproaching Balaam, the strength of the ass' rebuke is considerably diminished by having it merely reported in Josephus (*Ant.* 4.109).

7. *Preaching against Assimilation*

Just as Livy, in the preface to his history, laments the decline of morals in the Roman Empire, so Josephus, as a responsible historian, cites lessons to be learned from his history. One major lesson, perhaps with a

---

[68] In the Targumim it is the ass herself which reproaches Balaam for failing to understand the ways of G-d, whereas in Josephus it is the historian's comment that Balaam failed to understand G-d's purpose.

view toward what was happening to some of Josephus' contemporaries, is that Jews must avoid assimilation with Gentiles.⁶⁹

The theme of moralizing about the effects of assimilation may be seen particularly in Josephus' portrayal of Joseph as resisting temptation and lecturing Potiphar's wife on the folly of passion (*Ant.* 2.51-52). It may also be perceived in Josephus' assertion in his version of the Samson story that one must not debase (παρεχάρασσεν—used of coins) one's rule of life (δίαιταν) by imitating foreign ways (*Ant.* 5.306). It is likewise present in Josephus' discussion of Anilaeus and Asinaeus, the two Jewish brothers who established an independent state in Mesopotamia in the first century only to lose it when, at the very peak of their success, Anilaeus (*Ant.* 18.340) had an affair with a Parthian general's wife. The closely connected theme, that one must not submit to one's passionate instincts is frequent in Josephus⁷⁰ and may be seen particularly in his portrayal of Antony (*War* 1.243) as a slave to his passion for Cleopatra.

A dilemma confronted Josephus in his interpretation of the episode of the Midianite women: if he gave a favorable view, he would be condoning the assimilation and intermarrige forbidden by the Torah (Deut 7:3); and yet, he was aware that too strenuous an objection against intermarriage would play into the hands of those opponents of the Jews who charged them with misanthropy and illiberalism.

On the one hand, as we have noted, Josephus is careful to avoid offending non-Jews and their religion; on the other hand, assimilation and even, to some degree, intermarriage were problems in his own day. That this was, indeed, a serious issue is intimated by Josephus' remark (*Ant.* 4.140) that as a result of the seduction a sedition (στάσις) far worse even than that of Korah descended upon the Israelites. Of course,

---

⁶⁹ It would seem that Josephus had two audiences in mind for his *Antiquities*. On the one hand, the very fact that in his prooemium he cites (*Ant.* 1.10) as a precedent for his work the translation of the Torah into Greek for King Ptolemy Philadelphus is clearly designed as a justification for his directing his work to Gentiles with apologetic intent, inasmuch as he apparently realized that normally it is prohibited to teach the Torah to Gentiles (*b. Ḥag.* 13a, *b. Sanh.* 59a). The fact that he asks (*Ant.* 1.9) whether any of the Greeks have been curious to learn 'our' history and that he specifically declares (*Ant.* 1.5) that his work was undertaken in the belief that the whole Greek world would find it worthy of attention indicates that he was directing the *Antiquities* to pagans. Again, the fact that at the end of the work (*Ant.* 20.262) he boasts that no one else would have been equal to the task of issuing so accurate a treatise for the Greeks indicates that he directed the work to the non-Jewish world, since the term 'Greeks' for Josephus is used in contrast to Jews. And yet, that Josephus is also directing his work to Jews seems clear from his apologetic statement (*Ant.* 4.197), defending his reorganization of the details of the Jewish code of law,' lest perchance any of my countrymen who read this work should reproach me at all for having gone astray.'

⁷⁰ See my 'Josephus' Version of Samson' (*art. cit.*, n. 6) 211-212, n. 94.

Josephus might have omitted the incident as he does a number of others. But apparently Josephus felt the need to lecture to his contemporary Jews;[71] and so, he not only includes it but, as Van Unnik[72] has stressed, Josephus' account (*Ant.* 4.131-155) of the Israelites' sin with the Midianite women (Num 25:1-9) has been expanded from nine verses to twenty-five paragraphs.

That Josephus has the danger of intermarriage in mind would seem to be indicated by the fact that in his version of the incident he adds (*Ant.* 4.132) that the men implored the women to be their brides and that the women, in turn (*Ant.* 4.135), declared that they were content (ἀγαπήσομεν) to end their lives with them as wedded wives. That Josephus has the contemporary situation of the Jews in mind would seem to be indicated by the fact that he omits the particular names, such as Shittim and Baʿal Peʿor, thus making the story a generic tale that presumably has direct application to the situation in which he is writing, when Jews were likewise being seduced by the temptations of Hellenism.[73]

In particular, the speech of Zambrias (*Ant.* 4.145-149) sounds very much like the summary of arguments that assimilated Jews would have used,[74] namely attacking the tyranny (*Ant.* 4.146, 149, a word twice repeated) of the commandments and advocating liberty (ἐλευθέρων, *Ant.* 4.146, a key word throughout the *Antiquities*)[75] of action. Apparently, the danger which Josephus is highlighting is intermarriage: significantly, it is intermarriage between Jewish men and Moabite-Midianite women that he mentions (*Ant.* 4.135, 148), whereas Philo (*Mos.* 1.295-304), Pseudo-Philo (*Bib. Ant.* 18.13-14), and the rabbis (*b. Sanh.* 106a) present

---

[71] See L. Troiani, 'I lettore delle 'Antiquitates Judaicae' di Giuseppe,' *Athenaeum* 64 (1986) 343-353.
[72] W. C. van Unnik, 'Josephus' Account of the Story of Israel's Sin with Alien Women in the Country of Midian (Num. 25.1 ff.),' in M. S. H. G. Heerma van Voss (ed.), *Travels in the World of the Old Testament: Studies Presented to Professor M. A. Beek* (Assen 1974) 241-261.
[73] See my 'Josephus' *Jewish Antiquities* and Pseudo-Philo's *Biblical Antiquities*,' in L. H. Feldman and G. Hata (edd.), *Josephus, the Bible, and History* (Detroit 1989) 66.
[74] So Van Unnik (*art. cit.*, n. 72) 258-259 and S. Schwartz, *Josephus and Judaean Politics* (Leiden 1990) 177.
[75] That liberty was a key concept for the Romans may be seen in the fact that when the conspirators to assassinate the Emperor Gaius Caligula choose a password (*Ant.* 19.54), the word they select is 'liberty' (ἐλευθερίας). Josephus goes out of his way to stress the Jews' devotion to the ideal of liberty, as we see, for example, in the great effort (*Ant.* 2.290) which Moses devotes to procuring his people's liberty from the oppressive Egyptians. Indeed, when the Israelites angrily complain against him because of their lack of food and water in the desert Moses (*Ant.* 3.19) answers them by declaring that it was not from negligence that G-d had thus tarried in helping them but rather to test their manhood and their delight in liberty (ἐλευθερίαν).

the view that the great sin committed by the Israelites was surrender to illicit passion. Similarly, we may remark, Josephus has elaborated his account of Samson's relations with alien women (Judg 14:1–16:3, *Ant.* 5.286–317)[76] as a lesson to the Hellenized Jews of his own day who sought assimilation with the Gentiles through intermarriage.

8. *'Improvements' in the Story: Clarifications, Increased Drama*

One basic reason for Josephus' writing of a paraphrase of the Scripture was that he sought to avoid apparent contradictions in the biblical text.[77] One major difficulty in the pericope is that in Numbers 22:20 G-d instructs Balaam to accompany the envoys that have been sent to him, whereas a mere two verses later (Num 22:22) G-d expresses his anger that Balaam accompanies the envoys. The rabbis (*Tanḥuma Balak* 8; *Tanḥuma* (ed. Buber) 4.137; *Num. Rab.* 20.12) resolve this contradiction by insisting that since Balaam wanted to act wickedly he was permitted to do so, inasmuch as 'A man is divinely assisted in treading the path he desires.' Josephus (*Ant.* 4.107) resolves the problem by having G-d express indignation that Balaam should have tempted Him and by having Balaam misunderstand G-d's sarcasm in permitting him to go with the envoys.

Josephus also tries to increase the dramatic interest of the biblical narrative. If we ask why Josephus chose to paraphrase the Bible when it had already been translated into Greek more than three centuries earlier in the form of the Septuagint, the answer would seem to be that he sought to make the stories in the Bible more attractive to his readers, particularly to non-Jews.[78] We may see an example of this in Josephus' version (*Ant.* 4.113) of the incident where, having seen the Israelites, Balaam began to prophesy. According to the Bible (Num 23:5) G-d first puts a word into Balaam's mouth and tells him to return to Balak, and only later does Balaam take up his parable. On the other hand, in Josephus' version (*Ant.* 4.113) G-d plays no direct role, and instead Balaam proceeds directly and more dramatically to prophesy immediately after his sacrifice. Moreover, in the biblical version Balaam presents

---

[76] See my 'Josephus' Version of Samson' (*art. cit.*, n. 6) 194–204, 210–214.
[77] Thus, for example, the Bible (Gen 2:17) declares that G-d told Adam that he would die on the day that he would eat from the tree of knowledge. The fact, of course, is that not only did Adam not die but he lived until the age of 930. Josephus (*Ant.* 1.40) resolves the problem by simply omitting the phrase 'on the day' and by generalizing that if they touched the tree it would prove the destruction of Adam and of Eve.
[78] See my 'Use, Authority and Exegesis of Mikra in the Writings of Josephus' (*art. cit.*, n. 6) 500–501.

three brief prophetic discourses; Josephus' Balaam (*Ant.* 4.114–117) is dramatically much more effective by combining these prophecies into a single discourse. The fact, noted by Moscovitz,[79] that Josephus presents this prophecy in direct discourse, whereas Josephus generally either omits biblical poetry or refers to it in brief summary (e.g., Jacob's benediction (*Ant.* 2.194–195), the Song at the Red Sea (*Ant.* 2.346), Moses' farewell songs (*Ant.* 4.303, 4.320), the song of Deborah (*Ant.* 5.205–209), David's mourning for the deaths of Saul and Jonathan (*Ant.* 7.6), David's lament for Abner (*Ant.* 7.42), David's songs (*Ant.* 7.305), and Jeremiah's lamentations (*Ant.* 10.78)), serves to highlight the importance of this prophecy.

Furthermore, the description of Balaam (*Ant.* 4.118) as one who is no longer his own master (οὐκ ὢν ἐν ἑαυτῷ) is definitely reminiscent of the Platonic (*Phdr.* 245A) concept of ecstatic possession, whereby the god enters, for example, into the Pythian priestess at Delphi and uses her vocal organs as if they were his own (Plato, *Leg.* 672b).[80] That Josephus is using the concept of ecstasy in a sense different from the Septuagint, where it means a deep sleep, is especially clear in the Balaam pericope. In the Bible, we recall (Num 23:26), Balaam says, 'All that the L-rd will speak, that must I do.' Josephus (*Ant.* 4.119) has not only expanded this but has used Hellenistic terminology in explaining that it does not rest with a person to be silent or to speak when he is possessed by the spirit of G-d, 'for that spirit gives utterance to such language and words as it will, whereof we are all unconscious.' To be sure, there is a difference between this view of ecstasy and the view that the Pythian priestess at Delphi was actually possessed by the god Apollo, who used her vocal chords as if they were his own and hence presented Apollo's utterance in the first person, whereas Balaam presents G-d's view in the third

---

[79] Moscovitz (*op. cit.*, n. 1) 20.

[80] See E. R. Dodds, *The Greeks and the Irrational* (Berkeley 1951) 77 and 94–95, note 84. The god who is within the diviner speaks from the person in a strange voice or in an unintelligible way (cf. Eur., *Bacc.* 300, 1124). Indeed, Euripides (*Bacc.* 298 ff., has Teiresias claim that Dionysus is the god of ecstatic prophecy. Understanding is no longer in the individual (cf. Pl., *Ion* 534B). Cf. Philo (*QG* 3.9), who similarly defines the ecstasy of prophets as a state when the mind is divinely possessed and becomes filled with G-d, so that it is no longer within itself, inasmuch as it receives the divine spirit to dwell within it. Moscovitz (*op. cit.*, n. 1) 56, n. 9, states that Josephus' references to himself as being 'inspired' (ἔνθους, *War* 3.353, 4.33) make it extremely unlikely that he is referring to ecstatic possession in the Hellenistic sense; but the important question is how his non-Jewish readers would interpret that word. It seems likely that they would understand it as Plato, notably, uses it in his dialogues. In that case, it seems reasonable to assume that Josephus, who knew Plato's works (see my 'Josephus as a Biblical Interpreter: the ʿAqedah' (*art. cit.*, n. 6) 225, n. 39), would have been aware of the connotations of the word.

person. Again, Josephus (*Ant.* 4.121) presents the prevalent theory of ecstasy in stating that one is wholly impotent who pretends to such foreknowledge of human affairs drawn from his own breast as to refrain from speaking what G-d suggests and to violate His will. In particular, his use of the phrase that 'once G-d has gained prior entry, nothing within us is any more our own,' is typical of Platonic and Hellenistic descriptions of ecstasy.

There is further increased drama in Josephus' version of the event surrounding Balaam's parting advice. In the Bible (Num 24:25) after Balaam blesses the Israelites he and Balak go their respective ways. In Josephus' version (*Ant.* 4.126), Balak expresses his fury by summarily dismissing Balaam, dignifying him with no reward. And then, just as he is on the point of crossing the Euphrates, Balaam, in Josephus' version, sends for Balak and the Midianite princes and presents them with a scheme for overcoming the Israelites.

Inasmuch as Josephus is addressing a primarily non-Jewish audience, as we have noted, and inasmuch as he realized that the reader's interest could hardly be maintained through twenty books of political and military history without digressions of purple passages and especially romantic narratives, Josephus frequently inserts such passages, thus following in the path particularly of Herodotus (one thinks, in particular, of the episode of the Scythian youths and the Amazon women, Hdt. 4.111–116). We may cite, above all, the development of erotic episodes in his version of the stories of Abraham, Jacob, Joseph, Moses, Samson, and Esther.[81]

Whereas the Bible itself does not actually immediately connect the apparent end of the Balaam episode (Num 24:25) with the incident involving the Israelite youths with the Moabite women (Num 25:1-5) and does not until a later point (Num 31:16) indicate a connection of Balaam with the incident, Josephus, like the rabbis,[82] develops the theme that it was Balaam who gave the advice to use this method to overcome the Israelites. Van Unnik[83] notes the significant fact that Josephus expands at great length (*Ant.* 4.126-151) the story of the seduction of the Israelite youths by the women, whereas he deals only briefly with the Phinehas episode (*Ant.* 4.152-155), even though they are of approximately equal length in the Bible (Num 25:1-5 and 6-13). In

---

[81] See my 'Use, Authority and Exegesis of Mikra in the Writings of Josephus' (*art. cit.*, n. 6) 501-503.
[82] See *b. Sanh.* 106a and parallels cited by Rappaport (*op. cit.*, n. 12) 126, n. 180. In Philo (*Virt.* 34-35) the advice is that of the Midianites rather than of Balaam.
[83] Van Unnik (*art. cit.*, n. 72) 243.

particular, as Braun[84] has remarked, Josephus, like Philo (*Mos.* 1.294–304 and *Virt.* 34–42), shows a strong interest in the erotic psychology upon which Balaam's advice is based, whereas this is not touched upon at all in the Talmudic parallels. Josephus' version is considerably more romantic than that of Philo in that the women (Josephus has changed them from Moabites to Midianites, as does the Bible itself (Num 25:6)) at first surrender to the youths without any conditions; but once they perceive that the Israelite youths have been ensnared by passion, they, following Balaam's advice (*Ant.* 4.130), leave them. The men, now, in a most romantic touch, in the depths of despondency, offering the women all that they possess, implore the women, in the manner typical of the later Hellenistic novels, with tears, which they affirm with oaths, ironically, despite their immorality, invoking their G-d as arbiter of their promises, so as to render themselves an object of the women's compassion (*Ant.* 4.133), and they entreat them to stay. The women, in turn, demand (*Ant.* 4.134–138) that they give up their laws and customs.

9. Summary

The importance of the Balaam pericope for Josephus may be seen from the extraordinary amount of space that he gives to the narrative, especially to the incident of the Israelite youths and the Midianite women. Josephus was clearly in a dilemma in his portrait of Balaam in that if he gave too positive a portrayal he would not only be going against the simple meaning of the biblical text but he would also be praising one who sought to curse the Jews. On the other hand, Josephus wished to avoid the charge that Jews look down upon non-Jewish men of wisdom. The result is a relatively unbiased portrait in sharp contrast with the negative picture painted by Philo, the New Testament, and the rabbis. He does this by shifting the focus from Balaam's personality to the historical, military, and political confrontation between Israel and her enemies.

To be sure, Josephus never applies the term προφήτης to Balaam but rather refers to him as a μάντις. But Josephus adds stature to Balaam by elaborating on the hospitality that he shows to Balak's envoys.

To a high degree, Josephus seeks in his paraphrase of the Bible to answer the charges of those who are hostile to the Jews. One of these

---

[84] M. Braun, *History and Romance in Graeco-Oriental Literature* (Oxford 1938) 104. Braun notes a parallel in Aristophanes' *Lysistrata*, where similarly the women break off relations with their husbands and threaten to leave them unless they fulfill certain political conditions, whereupon the men submit.

charges is that Jews hate non-Jews, as shown by their sundering themselves off from them. In the Balaam pericope Josephus, by skilful changes from the biblical narrative, shifts the emphasis from the Jews' separatism for its own sake to their excellence and their goal of happiness. It is particularly effective to have a non-Jew, Balaam, praise the Israelites, even beyond the biblical text.

Josephus was confronted with a dilemma in what to do with Balaam's prophecy which was understood by near-contemporary rabbinic tradition to refer to the coming of a messiah and the overthrow of the Roman Empire. His solution, as with a similar prophecy in the Book of Daniel, is to be ambiguous, so that Jews would not accuse him of omitting it and non-Jews would not accuse him of disloyalty to the Roman Empire. Again, in place of covenant theology which would be regarded by the Romans as a challenge to their rule of Judaea, Josephus has predictions of future fame and happiness of the Jews, rather than of political domination by them. Moreover, he shifts from the centrality of Canaan to the dispersion of the Jews in the Diaspora. Furthermore, he omits Balaam's reference in the Bible to the population explosion of the Jews, since the Romans were so sensitive about the tremendous increase in the number of the Jews, particularly through proselytism. In addition, Josephus is careful to stress, as an important principle of their policy, that the Israelites do not interfere in the affairs of other countries.

Inasmuch as an important goal of Josephus' revision of the Bible is to counter hatred of the Jews, it is particularly significant that Balaam urges Balak's envoys to give up this hatred. As for Balaam himself, in Josephus' view his motive in seeking to curse the Israelites is not Jew-hatred but rather loyalty to his sovereign. As for the meeting of Balak and Balaam, it is presented not as an exercise in Jew-hatred but as a planning session to find a way to defeat the Israelites militarily. In any case, Balaam is depicted as succumbing only to persistent pressure by Balak. Balaam's initial decision to desist from cursing the Israelites is presented as sincere; indeed, the blame for the reversal is actually put on G-d Himself.

Josephus makes a particular appeal to his non-Jewish readers by his constant reference to Providence (πρόνοια), a central concept in Stoic thought. Though he realizes that miracles, particularly that of the speaking by Balaam's ass, might make his narrative less credible, he nonetheless does mention it, perhaps because readers would think of the parallel of Achilles' speaking horse; however, he takes a number of steps to make it more plausible.

The fact that Josephus not only includes but very considerably expands the narrative of the Midianite women is apparently due to his desire to preach to his Jewish readers about the dangers of intermarriage. This expansion, replete with erotic motifs and with the description of the ecstatic state of Balaam in prophesying, clearly increases the drama of the entire episode.

Yeshiva University
New York

PHILO AND GNOSTICISM*

R. McL. WILSON

'That some relationship exists between Gnosticism and the religious philosophy of Philo can hardly be doubted.'[1] The debated question is however just what that relation is. Birger Pearson, from whom these words are quoted, begins his *ANRW* survey with two alternative opinions: 'Philo has been understood by some scholars as a Gnostic, indeed as the first Gnostic, or at least heavily influenced by Gnosticism. Alternatively, he has been taken as representing a stage in the development of Gnosticism, or even as a formative factor in certain mythico-philosophical systems of second-century Gnosticism. In general, more recent scholarship has tended toward the latter alternative, preferring to view Philo as representing a kind of 'pre-Gnostic' pattern of religious thought rather than a full-blown Gnosticism.'[2]

---

* A paper presented to the Philo seminar at the annual meeting of SNTS in Madrid, July 1992. This paper was intended to serve as a basis for discussion, not to provide a comprehensive and definitive treatment of the subject; it was hoped that other members of the group would bring their own contributions to the discussion. Accordingly, the emphasis is mainly on the raising of the relevant questions and the indication of some of the problems, with a fairly extensive bibliography for those who may wish to pursue the matter further. [In responding to my request whether he would offer his paper for publication Prof. Wilson remarked in a *postscriptum* that it was fifty years since he commenced his doctorate on this subject (under the supervision of W. L. Knox). We welcome the opportunity to benefit from such lengthy reflection on a fascinating theme that even now is far from settled. EDITOR]

[1] B. A. Pearson, 'Philo and Gnosticism', ANRW II.21.1 (Berlin–New York 1984) 295–342 (quotation from p. 296). See also his 'Philo, Gnosis and the New Testament', in *Gnosticism, Judaism and Egyptian Christianity* (Minneapolis 1990) 165–182 (originally published in A. H. B. Logan and A. J. M. Wedderburn (edd.), *The New Testament and Gnosis* (Edinburgh 1983) 73–89; updated for 1990 volume). Reference may also be made to R. McL. Wilson, *The Gnostic Problem* (London 1958); idem, 'Philo of Alexandria and Gnosticism', *Kairos* 14 (1972) 213–219; H. Hegermann: *Die Vorstellung vom Schöpfungsmittler im hellenistischen Judentum und Urchristentum*, TU 82 (Berlin 1961) (see index s.v. Gnosis).

[2] *Ibid.* 295. In a footnote he refers for the first alternative to H. Graetz, *Gnosticismus und Judenthum* (Krotoschin 1846) 5, but his comment that in Graetz' view Philo's speculative system 'was the chief representative of that 'Alexandrinismus' out of which Gnosticism developed' might seem to link it more appropriately with the second. Cf. the opinions of Harvey and Bréhier mentioned below. The reference to a 'pre-Gnostic' pattern of thought seems to reflect the definitions proposed at the Messina colloquium in 1966, for which see U. Bianchi (ed.), *Le Origini dello Gnosticismo* (Leiden 1967) xxviff.

Close on twenty years earlier, Marcel Simon[3] also listed a number of divergent views: for Emile Bréhier, 'Philon n'a pas pris comme point de départ la philosophie grecque, mais cette théologie alexandrine qui devait produire les systèmes gnostiques.' E. R. Goodenough however, while admitting 'many similarities to Gnostic and Neo-Platonic formulations', declares that Philo 'could yet have had no sympathy with that travesty of philosophy, the type of mythological presentation to which we give the collective name of Gnosticism'. H. A. Wolfson wrote two large volumes on Philo's thought, but 'on cherche en vain dans l'index les mots de gnose et de gnosticisme'. For Hans Jonas, finally, 'la pensée philonienne représente la première forme de la gnose'. More than a century ago, in his edition of Irenaeus, W. W. Harvey wrote: 'Philo Judaeus was mainly instrumental in causing the rise of Gnosticism, by bringing about that union of Jewish interpretations of Biblical Truth with Platonism, that more than anything else directed the attention of the schools to the Theosophy of the East.'[4]

It will be evident that the title of this paper itself requires some measure of exegesis: what have we in mind when we speak of 'Philo and Gnosticism'? This is not so simplistic a question as it may appear to be. On the one hand we have a specific author, whose works have been preserved in considerable quantity, so that we can form a fair assessment of his views and opinions, although we must always beware of the danger of undue systematization, of making Philo a much more coherent and consistent thinker than he actually was; one thinks here of Wolfson's claim that Philo was 'no mere dabbler in philosophy, but a philosopher in the grand manner', indeed 'the most dominant influence in European philosophy for wellnigh seventeen centuries'. One wonders what significance should be attached to the fact that Wolfson had earlier written about Spinoza; and some might wish to mention

---

[3] 'Eléments gnostiques chez Philon', *Le Origini* (n. 2), 359–374 referring to E. Bréhier, *Les idées philosophiques et religieuses de Philon d'Alexandrie* (Paris 1925) 317; E. R. Goodenough, *An Introduction to Philo Judaeus* (Oxford 1962) 17 and *By Light, Light* (New Haven 1935) 119; H. A. Wolfson, *Philo* (Cambridge Mass. 1948); H. Jonas, *Gnosis und spätantiker Geist*, II.1 (Göttingen 1954) 70–121. Jonas, it may be added, speaks of 'Philos geistergeschichtliche Zwischenstellung zwischen Judentum, Griechentum und Gnostizismus (p. 74). A heading on p. 77 reads 'Die Wurzeln des Philonischen Agnostizismus'! Simon's article is reprinted in *Le christianisme antique...*, WUNT 23 (Tübingen 1981) 1, 336ff. See also his 'Situation du Judaisme alexandrin dans la Diaspora', *ibid.* 356ff.
[4] *Sancti Irenaei Adversus Haereses* (Cambridge 1857) 288 n.2. J. Helderman (in M. Krause (ed.) *Essays on the Nag Hammadi Texts*, NHS 6 (Leiden 1975) 40) claims that 'der Einfluss Philos auf spätere Kreise Ägyptens, wie die der Valentinianer, stärker ist als oft angenommen wird'; but later (42f.) he suggests that this influence was not direct but indirect.

Plotinus. Then there is the other danger, of making Philo 'too much the mirror of his times': the sheer bulk of his extant writings is such, and the quantity of other material so meagre, that one is tempted to quote Philo over and over again as representative of 'Diaspora Judaism'—as if every diaspora Jew was another Philo. It is not even certain that he should be regarded as representative of Alexandria, or Alexandria as representative of the Diaspora,[5] although he probably was representative of a fairly considerable number of Alexandrian Jews. It is a question of getting things into proper focus, of striking the right balance, and in the absence of other material that can be difficult.

The other side of the equation is rather more problematic, since there can be differences of opinion as to what we are talking about when we speak of Gnosticism or, as our German colleagues prefer, of Gnosis. How far are they one and the same thing, how is it to be defined, where does it begin—the problems are endless. There are even problems with the little word 'and' which in our title connects the two poles. Recently I saw a cross-word puzzle clue: 'The forty-first thief'—and the required answer was 'Ali Baba'. Now anyone who recalls the story will remember that Ali Baba was not one of the thieves, but their opponent who eventually overcame them. The 'and' in 'Ali Baba and the Forty Thieves' does not associate them as it does in 'Robin Hood and his Merry Men'; it brings them together, indeed, but it also sets them in opposition. So in our title Philo and Gnosticism are brought together—but it is for purposes of comparison, and possibly of contrast.

But what of Gnosticism? According to Bultmann,[6] 'It first appeared and attracted the attention of scholars as a movement within the Christian religion, and for a long time it was regarded as a purely Christian movement, a perversion of the Christian faith into a speculative theology, the 'acute Hellenization of Christianity'. Further research has, however, made it abundantly clear that it was really a religious movement of pre-Christian origin, invading the West from the Orient as a competitor of Christianity.' I should add at once that in the original German the term used is not *der Gnostizismus* but *die Gnosis*—which does make a difference. To put the matter briefly, British scholars have generally tended to think in terms of Gnosticism, with reference particularly to the 'classic' Gnostic systems of the second century; German scholars on the other hand prefer (as they have every right to do) to speak of *die Gnosis*, with reference to the whole Gnostic movement—and therefore often in a somewhat wider sense. When translators render *die*

---

[5] Cf. Simon, *Le christianisme antique* 1.356ff.
[6] *Primitive Christianity in its Contemporary Setting* (ET London–New York 1956) 162.

Gnosis by 'Gnosticism', British readers inevitably think in terms of the second century—which may be quite misleading. Attempts have been made to clarify the situation by making distinctions, but without much success; indeed they may only have made confusion worse confounded. There is much to be said for Pearson's view[7] that we should abandon both these 'slippery words'[8] and speak rather of the Gnostic religion or the Gnostic movement. That would at least provide us with a single term for the whole Gnostic phenomenon, from its earliest (and still obscure) beginnings to its most developed forms; but the problem of Gnostic origins would still remain—when and where does it begin? Are we to await the full development before we can speak of the Gnostic religion, or is it already present from the first tentative movement in a 'Gnostic' direction?

In his *Interpretation of the Fourth Gospel*, C. H. Dodd writes 'there is a sense in which orthodox Christian theologians like Clement of Alexandria and Origen, on the one hand, and Hellenistic Jews like Philo, and pagan writers like the Hermetists, on the other, should be called Gnostics; and in this wide sense the terms ['Gnostic' and 'Gnosticism'] are used by many recent writers, especially in Germany'.[9] He himself however uses the term Gnostic 'in the way in which it has been generally used for many years by theologians in this country, as a label for a large and somewhat amorphous group of religious systems described by Irenaeus and Hippolytus ..., and similar systems known from other sources'. He frankly admits that this use has no warrant in any ancient authorities, 'but it is convenient, and need not be misleading'. Convenient it may have been; whether it 'need not be misleading' is, in the light of subsequent discussion, rather a different matter. What is important about his observation is however the recognition that there can be an orthodox Gnosis—it is what they considered a Gnosis falsely so called that Irenaeus and others opposed. This merely adds a further complication to the problem: for Gnosis in the widest sense could then be conceived as a kind of atmosphere, an attitude, an outlook, a way of thinking, prevalent in the later stages of the Hellenistic age and in the early Roman Empire, a matter of trends and tendencies which had an influence in all kinds of areas. Initially it could be described as 'neutral', but with the passing of time there came a parting of the ways: one

---

[7] E.g. in C. W. Hedrick and R. Hodgson (edd.), *Nag Hammadi, Gnosticism and Early Christianity* (Peabody Mass. 1986) 17; cf. also his *Gnosticism, Judaism and Egyptian Christianity* (Minneapolis 1990) *passim*.
[8] See *Expository Times* 89 (1978) 296–301.
[9] Cambridge 1953, 97.

branch, certainly dependent on Philo,[10] developed into the Christian Gnosis of a Clement of Alexandria; another grew into the classic second-century systems of heretical Christian Gnosticism; and there may well have been others. One of our problems is to identify the branches, to trace their development, to determine precisely where the parting of the ways took place, and why.

In the light of all this we may refine our topic into a number of questions: what is the relation between Philo and Gnosticism? Is he himself a Gnostic, and if so, in what sense? Is he influenced by a Gnosticism already in existence before his time, and thus evidence for a pre-Christian Gnosticism? Or is he, as Harvey and others thought, himself instrumental in the development of Gnosticism? Or are the parallels which can be detected to be explained in some other way? Against any thought of influence from an already existing Gnosticism there is the fact that we have no documentary evidence for anything of the sort, unless we are to accept the view of Friedländer,[11] that the allegorists whom Philo criticises for rejecting observance of the Law in its literal sense because of their allegorical interpretation (*Migr.* 86–93) were actually Gnostics. This is a clear example of the dangers of holding up a mirror to a text in the effort to identify the opposition confronted. Antinomian they may have been, but that does not make them Gnostic. Again, against Harvey's view that Philo was instrumental in the development of Gnosticism we must bear in mind Pearson's warning against the suggestion 'that Philo's religious philosophy lies in a trajectory that logically and chronologically issues in Gnosticism'.[12] Hans Jonas long ago warned against thinking in terms of a conveyor-belt in a modern factory,[13] and in fact there are Jewish elements in Gnosticism which are not to be found in Philo's extensive writings.[14]

The best way to approach the question is probably first to outline the

---

[10] 'The fact is beyond any doubt that Clement knew Philo virtually by heart and did not refrain from including many excerpts of his writings in his *Stromateis* (especially in the first and second books)' (S. R. C. Lilla, *Clement of Alexandria: A study in Christian Platonism and Gnosticism* (Oxford 1971) 5 n. 1). The dependence can be clearly seen in the numerous parallels cited by Lilla. See now also the study by A. van den Hoek, *Clement of Alexandria and his Use of Philo in the Stromateis: an Early Christian Reshaping of a Jewish Model*, VChr.S 3 (Leiden 1988) *passim*.
[11] *Der vorchristliche jüdische Gnostizismus* (Göttingen 1898, repr. Farnborough 1972). Cf. Simon art. cit. (n. 3) 360–362; also Pearson, 'Friedländer Revisited', *Gnosticism, Judaism and Egyptian Christianity* (Minneapolis 1990) 10–28 (originally in *SPh* 2 (1973) 23–39; edited and updated); *idem, ANRW* II 21.1 296–303, 321.
[12] Pearson, *ibid.* 340.
[13] In one of the discussions at the Messina colloquium.
[14] Cf. Wilson, *The Gnostic Problem* (London 1958) 262.

main features of the classical Gnosticism, and then consider possible affinities in the writings of Philo. It is however important to pay due attention not only to the similarities but also to the differences. Even the use of the same or similar terminology may not be indicative of some relationship: we have to examine the use of such terms and concepts, and whether Philo and the Gnostics employ them in the same way and with the same significance.

In brief, Gnosticism attempts to set out a solution to the human predicament; in the words of Charles Bigg more than a century ago, 'It was an attempt, a serious attempt, to fathom the dread mystery of sorrow and pain, to answer that spectral doubt, which is mostly crushed down by force—Can the world as we know it have been made by God?'[15] The Gnostic answer is emphatically in the negative: this world is not the creation of the true and supreme God, but the work—variously explained—of an inferior being, often described as the Demiurge. Now this term goes back at least to the *Timaeus* of Plato, but as Dodd long ago observed it is there 'applied to God Himself, as it also is by Philo and by most of the Hermetic writers'.[16] 'The restriction of the term δημιουργός to a single secondary god, on the ground that the supreme God does not create, appears first in these second-century writers (i.e. 'Valentinus and other Christian or semi-Christian Gnostics'). But the application of the term δημιουργός to a secondary creator is earlier'[17]—Philo in *Fug.* 68-70 uses it in his interpretation of the plural ποιήσωμεν in Gen 1:26: ἀναγκαῖον οὖν ἡγήσατο τὴν κακῶν γένεσιν ἑτέροις ἀπονεῖμαι δημιουργοῖς, τὴν δὲ τῶν ἀγαθῶν ἑαυτῷ μόνῳ. This is a neat example of the need for discrimination between the various uses of the same terms in our sources: for Philo, these lesser δημιουργοί are agents of the supreme God, and serve as a buffer between him and the human race, so that he has nothing whatever to do with evil; the Gnostic Demiurge on the other hand stands over against the supreme God, as a usurper who (wrongly) thinks himself supreme, and is frequently hostile to the human race.

Philo does speak of the impious falsehood of admiring the cosmos rather than the Creator (*Opif.* 7; cf. *Abr.* 69), but his own view of the

---

[15] *The Christian Platonists of Alexandria* (Oxford 1886) 28. G. A. G. Stroumsa, *Another Seed: Studies in Gnostic Mythology* (Leiden 1984) 17 writes: 'At the root of the Gnostic rejection of the material world and its creator lies an obsessive preoccupation with the problem of evil'. This in his view reflects a Platonic heritage. 'Yet, as important as this heritage may be, it apparently did not give rise to Gnostic mythology, but rather influenced its literary expression or provided philosophical and conceptual background.' One question to be borne in mind is that of the extent to which similarities between Philo and Gnosticism may be due to this Platonic heritage.
[16] *The Bible and the Greeks* (London 1935) 136.
[17] *Ibid.* 137 notes 2-3; cf. also 155.

cosmos is positive rather than negative: Simon[18] notes that the limits of the Philonic 'Gnosticism' are set by the recurring refrain in the biblical Creation story 'and God saw that it was good', citing *Opif.* 21: εἰ γάρ τις ἐθελήσειε τήν αἰτίαν ἧς ἕνεκα τόδε τὸ πᾶν ἐδημιουργεῖτο διερευνᾶσθαι, δοκεῖ μοι μὴ διαμαρτεῖν σκοποῦ φάμενος, ὅπερ καὶ τῶν ἀρχαίων εἰπέ τις, ἀγαθὸν εἶναι τὸν πατέρα καὶ ποιητήν· οὗ χάριν τῆς ἀρίστης αὐτοῦ φύσεως οὐκ ἐφθόνησεν οὐσίᾳ μηδὲν ἐξ αὐτῆς ἐχούσῃ καλόν, δυναμένῃ δὲ πάντα γίνεσθαι, and *Leg.* 3.78: τοῖς γοῦν ζητοῦσι, τίς ἀρχὴ γενέσεως, ὀρθότατα ἄν τις ἀποκρίνοιτο, ὅτι ἀγαθότης καὶ χάρις τοῦ θεοῦ, ἣν ἐχαρίσατο τῷ μετ' αὐτὸν γένει. Philo can refer to the cosmos as son of God (*Spec.* 1.96; cf. *Ebr.* 30 τὸν μόνον καὶ αἰσθητὸν υἱὸν, τόνδε τὸν κόσμον), or as τὸν μέγιστον καὶ τελεώτατον ἄνθρωπον, τόνδε τὸν κόσμον (*Migr.* 220). The distinction he would make is between this universe as the younger son of God and the intelligible universe as the elder (*Deus* 31f.)—it is those who are bound to the world of sense, and do not seek after the intelligible, whom he would condemn. This may at times seem akin to the Gnostic repudiation of this world and all that belongs to it, yet are there are differences on closer examination. As Simon pertinently notes,[19] the origin of evil is for the Gnostics built into the very creation of the cosmos; for Philo, the creation and the 'incarnation' of man are both ultimately the work of God, and therefore good.

Simon sees the 'Gnostic affinities' of Philo as lying in anthropology rather than in cosmology,[20] and this is undoubtedly correct: man is mortal in respect of his body, immortal in respect of his mind (*Opif.* 135); every man is allied to divine reason in respect of his mind, but in the structure of his body is allied to the world (*Decal.* 134; *Det.* 83f.). This is not so far from the Gnostic idea that man in his essential nature belongs not to this world but to a higher realm, to which he seeks to return. Yet even here there are differences to be observed: Philo is concerned to give a 'philosophical' interpretation of the Old Testament, particularly in terms of Platonism, but does not appear to speak of the soul as a spark of the divine fire imprisoned in matter as the Gnostics did. His allegorical interpretation of the Fall in Genesis has been neatly summed up as converting it into a story 'of how mind was misled by pleasure into an unhallowed union with sense'.[21] The fall is not the primordial fall of an

---

[18] *Art. cit.* (n. 3) 363.
[19] *Ibid.* 365.
[20] *Ibid.* 366.
[21] C. H. Dodd, *The Bible and the Greeks*, London 1935, 148, who notes a parallel in the Hermetic *Poimandres*. See *Opif.* 151–156 and cf. J. Drummond, *Philo Judaeus* (London 1888) 2.279; S. Sandmel, *Philo's Place in Judaism* (New York 1971) 161. W. L. Knox, *St. Paul and the Church of the Gentiles* (Cambridge 1939) 83, 98f., treats the fall of Adam as a fall into

aeon, a Sophia, which sets the whole cosmic process in motion. The shortcomings which Philo censures are those of people who surrender themselves to pleasure, to the natural instincts of the body, instead of devoting themselves to 'philosophy'. At times he does come very close to the Gnostic view, but we must constantly seek to discriminate.

The affinities are even closer when we turn to what he says about the body: the natural gravitation of the body pulls down with it those of little mind, strangling and overwhelming them with the multitude of the fleshly elements (*Spec.* 4.114). The body is wicked and a plotter against the soul (*Leg.* 3.69), of itself a corpse and a dead thing (cf. *Gig.* 15), a composition of clay, a moulded statue, carried as a corpse from birth to death (*Agr.* 25, cf. *Leg.* 3.69, *Migr.* 21), a dwelling place of endless calamities (*Conf.* 177), a foul prison-house (*Migr.* 9). Mind is in the body as a prison (*Ebr.* 101). The business of wisdom is to become estranged from the body and its cravings (*Leg.* 1.103f.). Philo can speak of genuine philosophers who study to die to the life of the body (*Gig.* 14), or of the 'killing' of the body for the release of the soul (*Ebr.* 69ff.). All this is reminiscent of the Gnostic disparagement of the body, but once again we must look more closely. For Philo is using the Platonic σῶμα-σῆμα concept (cf. *Spec.* 4.188; *Leg.* 1.108; *Somn.* 1.139). The Gnostics also used it, but in their own way and for their own purposes. We may note also Philo's use of the Platonic trichotomy (e.g. *Spec.* 4.92ff.), and his disparagement of the lower desires; but that trichotomy is not employed as by the Valentinians, to classify mankind as spiritual or psychic or hylic. Philo's concern rather is with those who are prepared to devote themselves to the search for God, to the study of 'philosophy', over against those who are content to carry on their lives on the lower level of sense. He can allegorize the patriarchs as representative of different classes of men, but this does not appear to be determinative for their future salvation. Indeed, Hegermann writes: 'Philos Interesse an dem Schicksal der Seele nach dem Tode ist auffallend gering.'[22]

More might be said—on Philo's doctrine of God, on the nature of the soul, and so on—but this may suffice to provide a basis for further discussion. To sum up, we need to observe not only the similarities but also the differences. It is all too easy to draw unwarranted conclusions from a superficial similarity, when in fact there are distinctions which also require to be made. If by 'Gnosticism' we mean the classic systems of the second century Christian Gnostics, then Philo is definitely not a Gnostic. If however we widen the definition, and speak of Gnosis, then

---

matter, which would bring Philo close to Gnostic ideas.
[22] *Op. cit.* (n. 1) 41.

there is a sense in which he could be called Gnostic. Here however it is well to ponder Hans Jonas' words, in the peroration to a paper read in 1964: 'A Gnosticism without a fallen God, without benighted creator and sinister creation, without alien soul, cosmic captivity and acosmic salvation, without the self-redeeming of the Deity—in short: a Gnosis without divine tragedy will not meet specifications.'[23] This was directed in particular against Gershom Scholem's use of the terms Gnosis and Gnosticism in relation to Merkabah mysticism, but is more widely applicable: we need to be clear as to what we see as the essential elements of the Gnostic religion before we can determine whether any ancient author should be considered to belong to it, or to have contributed to its development. In my view Philo is sometimes very close, but not so close that he should be regarded as belonging; and it is by no means certain that he should be considered to have contributed. Rather he provides us with evidence for the climate of the times, the kind of ideas which were current, and which eventually, in a particular kind of combination, were to develop into the classic Gnosticism.[24]

St. Andrews

---

[23] In J. P. Hyatt (ed.) *The Bible in Modern Scholarship* (Nashville 1965) 293.
[24] According to H. Chadwick (in A. H. Armstrong (ed.) *Cambridge History of Later Greek and Early Mediaeval Philosophy* (Cambridge 1970²) 146), some of the raw material of Gnosticism can be found in Philo, but he is not, except in the vaguest sense, himself a Gnostic. Elsewhere, in his article 'St. Paul and Philo of Alexandria', *BJRL* 48 (1965-66) 305, Chadwick writes that similarities between Philonic, gnostic and apocalyptic teaching 'are probably best explained as arising from a common use of the same OT texts (although it is also possible that gnostic parallels at this point arise from a deviant use of Christian or Philonic teaching).' Much the same position is taken by Pearson in his *ANRW* article (cited in n. 1), 340: '1. Philo cannot be described as a 'Gnostic' in the technical sense of the word. If, however, we use the designation 'philosophical gnosis' for that development in the history of Graeco-Roman philosophy wherein philosophy becomes oriented to religion and metaphysics, we may include Philo's thought in that category. ... 2. Philo is not dependent upon, or influenced by, Gnosticism ... 3. Philo can therefore be placed in the category of 'pre-Gnosticism', as defined by the Messina Colloquium.' On this last point, as already indicated, Pearson warns against the suggestion 'that Philo's religious philosophy lies in a trajectory that logically and chronologically issues in Gnosticism.' The problems are rather more complex than that!

Notiz zu den "immerfließenden Quellen der göttlichen Wohltaten"

DIETER ZELLER

Philon gebraucht im Zusammenhang mit den göttlichen χάριτες öfter das Bild von den ἀέναοι πηγαί. In einer Studie *Charis bei Philon und Paulus* habe ich Vermutungen über die Herkunft dieses poetisch anmutenden Ausdrucks in metaphorischem Gebrauch angestellt.[1] Eine eindeutige klassische Quelle war nicht auszumachen.

Inzwischen habe ich mit Hilfe eines Computerausdrucks, den mir freundlicherweise D. T. Runia erstellte, den *Thesaurus Linguae Graecae* ausgewertet und bin bei meiner Untersuchung griechischer Gnomologien auf einige weitere Stellen gestoßen. Hier ist das Ergebnis.

1. Im wörtlichen Sinn kommen "immerfließende Quellen"—im Unterschied zu im Sommer versiegenden—erwartungsgemäß oft vor, vor allem in naturwissenschaftlichen Werken. Sie bilden aber auch—meist neben "Flüssen"—einen Teiltopos im stoisch-jüdisch-christlichen Aufweis der Schöpfungsordnung: Cic., ND II 98 *fontium gelidas perennitates*; Orac. Sib. bei Theoph. Ant., Autol. II 36,45 ἀέναα χεύματα πηγῶν; Orac. Sib. IV 15 ἀενάων στόμα πηγῶν; 1 Clem. XX 10,3 ἀεναοί τε πηγαί, hier mit dem Bild von den Brüsten der Mutter Erde, das auch Philon, opif. 133 in Auslegung der "Quelle" von Gen 2,6 verwendet (vgl. 38), allerdings ohne das Attribut ἀέναος. Vgl. ferner Hom. Clem. III 35,3,2; Theoph. Ant., Autol. I 6,11; Athan, virg. I 15; Eus., laus Const. I 4,5.

2. Im übertragenen Sinn wird πηγή schon früh verwendet.[2] So auch in der Bedeutung von "Prinzip" im pythagoreischen *Carmen Aureum*.[3] Es nennt Z. 48 die Tetraktys παγὰν ἀενάου φύσεως (Quelle der immerwährenden Natur). Hier ist freilich das Adjektiv nicht auf "Quelle" bezogen, wohl aber in der Anwendung auf die vier Elemente bei Eus., laus Const. VI 5,7. Philon, opif. 47.52 kennt die Bezeichnung der Vierheit als πηγή, zitiert aber das Gedicht nicht ausdrücklich.

3. Metaphorisch kann leicht von dem "immerfließenden Quell der Schlechtigkeit"—so ein unbekannter Autor in Comicorum Atticorum

---

[1] Stuttgarter Bibelstudien 142 (Stuttgart 1990) 40f mit Anm. 37.
[2] Vgl. W. Michaelis, Art. πηγή in: *TWNT* VI 112–117, 113.3ff (zu Philon 114,20–37).
[3] Vgl. D. Young (ed.), *Theognis*, Bibliotheca Scriptorum Graecorum et Romanorum Teubneriana, Leipzig 1971, 91. Die Stelle wird oft zitiert, etwa bei Sext. Emp. und Neuplatonikern.

Fragmenta 353,2—wie von dem der Güte gesprochen werden. Letzteres bezeugt mit etwas anderem Vokabular das Fragment eines Gedichts, das bei Hephaistion aus Alexandrien erhalten ist:[4]

βλύζει τὸ ῥεῖθρον εὐμενὲς τὸ τῶν χαρίτων
(Es sprudelt der gütige Fluß der Wohltaten)

Die χάρις wird dadurch nicht zu einem Fluidum, sondern bleibt konkrete Tat, wie das auch bei Philon festzustellen ist.[5]

4. Das aus Stobaeus zusammengestellte *Gnomologium Epicteteum*[6] vergleicht die mit der Tugend verkehrende Seele einer "immerfließenden Quelle" (ἀένναος πηγή). "Denn sie ist etwas Reines, Ungetrübtes, Trinkbares, Ergiebiges, Sich-Mitteilendes, Reiches, Unschädliches und Nicht-Verderbliches".

5. Ein später Epigrammatiker, Macedonius (6. Jh. n. Chr., AP XI 374) beschreibt, wie eine alternde Hetäre ihren Liebreiz (χάρις) verströmt hat, da sie ja nicht aus einer "immerfließenden Quelle" schöpft.

6. Philons Anwendung des Bildes auf Gott als die Quelle alles Guten findet sich in christlichen Texten. So sagt Gott in der Einleitung zum 4. Esra, der auf ein griechisches Original zurückgeht, in einem Trostwort:[7]

exuberant fontes mei et gratia mea non deficiet (2.32).

Von Philon beeinflußt sein könnten Eus., or. ad coet. sanct. V 1,4, wo von der "immerfließenden Quelle der ἀρεταί Gottes" (parallel zu εὐεργεσίαι) die Rede ist; ders., laus Const. XII 2,6 (Der Logos läßt vom guten Vater wie aus einer immerfließenden und unerschöpflichen Quelle Gutes heraufsprudeln); Gr. Nyss., bapt. Chr. IX (S. 241,3), wo Gott als καθαρὰ καὶ ἀέννaος τῆς ἀγαθωσύνης πηγή bezeichnet wird. Vgl. auch Oecumenius, Apoc. 22,1 (S. 248): χαρίσματα ἅτινα ἀεννάως εἰς τοὺς ἁγίους κέχυται.

Fazit: Die Metapher ist griechischen Schriftstellern schnell zur Hand, zumal in poetischen Texten. Mit theologischem Bezug begegnet sie zuerst bei Philon; ein konkreter Anknüpfungspunkt für ihn ist kaum noch zu ermitteln.

Mainz

---

[4] Vgl. H. Lloyd-Jones, P. Parsons (edd.), *Supplementum Hellenisticum*, Texte und Kommentare 11 (Berlin–New York 1983) Nr. 1054. Allerdings in einer Epitome, so daß Wilamowitz unseren Vers sogar als byzantinisch verdächtigen kann.

[5] Vgl. *op. cit.* (n. 1) 125 Anm. 358.

[6] Ed. H. Schenkl, *Epicteti dissertationes*, Bibliotheca Scriptorum Graecorum et Romanorum Teubneriana, Nachdruck Stuttgart 1965, 476. Ein ähnlicher Vergleich bei Marc. Ant. VIII 51,1.

[7] Text als 5 Esra bei W. Lechner-Schmidt, *Wortindex der lateinisch erhaltenen Pseudepigraphen zum Alten Testament*, Text und Arbeiten zum Neutestamentlichen Zeitalter 3 (Tübingen 1990).

SPECIAL SECTION
Philo and Middle Platonism

On November 22 1992 in San Francisco a special session of the Philo Seminar, which is held every year during the Annual Conference of the Society of Biblical Literature (for further information see the News & Notes section in this Annual), was devoted to the subject of Philo and his relation to Middle Platonism.

Thirty years ago, before the seminal contributions of Pierre Boyancé and Willy Theiler, and some time before the publication of John Dillon's well-known survey of the field, it would have seemed odd to call Philo a Middle Platonist or ask what his relation to Middle Platonism was. This becomes clear if one consults the standard comprehensive studies on Philo by Bréhier and Wolfson, where the description is nowhere to be found. Cornelia De Vogel, who published her third volume of *Greek Philosophy* in 1959, still speaks of 'Prae-neoplatonism'. Now both the term Middle Platonism and the tendency to relate Philo to this philosophical school have become a commonplace. It seemed to the organizers of the seminar a good idea to take stock and ask how the relation between the two should be seen and whether it is in fact legitimate to call Philo a Middle Platonist at all. Since this is a question of vital importance for Philonic studies and is also of wider interest for historians of philosophy and others, it also seemed a good idea to publish the resultant papers and responses in the Annual.

The papers were pre-circulated to the members of the seminar before the meeting and subsequently lightly revised in the light of the ensuing discussion. The first two responses were presented at the session and subsequently reworked in written form. John Dillon, the author of the third response, was most unfortunately unable to attend the session. In spite of a very busy schedule, he was able to find time to read the two papers and present a short written response. We thank him most cordially, and also wish to extend our thanks to Thomas Tobin S.J. for his willingness to contribute as respondent to the session. All who attended were in agreement that it was an instructive and memorable occasion.

THE EDITORS

PLATONIZING MOSES
Philo And Middle Platonism

GREGORY E. STERLING

In the course of his etymological interpretation of Jubal (Gen 4:21), Philo introduces the King's Road which the Hebrews traveled on their way to the promised land. The Alexandrian explains that since God is the king, the road is the way leading to the Deity. The road itself is ἀληθὴς καὶ γνήσιος φιλοσοφία which the law calls θεοῦ ῥῆμα καὶ λόγος.[1] On another occasion Philo sets out the standard Stoic definition of philosophy: ἔστι γὰρ φιλοσοφία ἐπιτήδευσις σοφίας, σοφία δὲ ἐπιστήμη θείων καὶ ἀνθρωπίνων καὶ τῶν τούτων αἰτίων.[2] These two texts represent the occasions in which Philo offers a definition of philosophy. They also illustrate the fundamental difficulty of formulating an assessment of his relationship to philosophy: on the one hand, he knows technical philosophical concepts; on the other, he identifies these with his ancestral scriptures. The result of this symbiosis is an intriguing, but complex corpus. Ancient attempts to describe Philo's relationship to philosophy are varied. The earliest *testimonium*, that of Josephus, offers the simple statement: Φίλων ... φιλοσοφίας οὐκ ἄπειρος.[3] Others were much more specific. For example, Clement of Alexandria and Sozomen dubbed him ὁ Πυθαγόρειος.[4] A more famous judgment is preserved in the *bon mot*: ἢ Πλάτων

---

[1] *Post.* 100–102. Biblical references to the 'King's Road' include Num 20:17; 21:22.
[2] *Congr.* 79. Sextus, *M.* 9.13 (*SVF* 2.36), provides the Stoic definition: τὴν φιλοσοφίαν φασὶν ἐπιτήδευσιν εἶναι σοφίας, τὴν δὲ σοφίαν ἐπιστήμην θείων τε καὶ ἀνθρωπίνων πραγμάτων. Cf. also Cicero, *Off.* 2.5: ... nec quicquam aliud est philosophia ... praeter studium sapientiae. sapientia autem est, ut a veteribus philosophis definitum est, rerum divinarum et humanarum causarumque, quibus eae res continentur, scientia; and Seneca, *Ep.* 89.5. On the scope of philosophy in Philo see also *Congr.* 144; *Somn.* 1.55–58, 205; 2.165; 3.1, 191; *QG* 2.41. Philo also knows the threefold division of philosophy common in Stoic circles and follows the standard Stoic arrangments: logic-ethics-physics, *Leg.* 1.57; *Ebr.* 202; *Spec.* 1.336; physics-ethics-logic, *Agr.* 14–16; *Mut.* 74–76. Cf. also *Prob.* 80, where he mentions all three but does not list them in order. For Stoic statements see Aëtius, *Placita* I *Proem.* 2 (*SVF* 2.35); Plutarch, *Moralia* 1035a (*SVF* 2.42); Sex. Emp., *Adv. Math.* 7.16 (*SVF* 2.38); 7.22 (*SVF* 2.44); Diogenes Laertius 7.39 (*SVF* 2.37); 7.40 (*SVF* 2.38, 43). Antiochus of Ascalon (*apud* Cic., *Acad.* 1.19) and Eudorus (*apud* Sen., *Ep.* 89.9–17) appear to have preferred the order ethics-physics-logic.
[3] *Ant.* 18.259 (PCW 1.lxxxxv). Cf. also the Armenian preface to *De Providentia* (PCW 1.lcvi). Anastasius Sinaita, *Viae dux* 14 (PCW 1.cviii–ix) and *In Hexaemeron* 7 (PCW 1.cix), calls him φιλόσοφος.
[4] Clement, *Strom.* 1.360 (PCW 1.lxxxxv); 2.482P (PCW 1.lxxxxvi); Sozomen, *Hist. eccl.*

φιλωνίζει ἢ Φίλων πλατωνίζει.[5] Eusebius knew both connections and claimed that Philo surpassed all of his contemporaries in his zeal for the systems of Plato and Pythagoras.[6] These statements make it clear that while the ancients recognized the basic components of Philo's philosophical views—although no one called him a Stoic—they did not unanimously situate him within a particular tradition.

The complexity of the Philonic corpus coupled with the fragmentary nature of our knowledge of philosophy in the first century BCE and first century CE have placed us in a position similar to that of the ancients: we have not reached unanimity. Within the twentieth century attempts to situate Philo in ancient philosophy have labelled him as eclectic,[7] a philosopher 'in the grand manner' (i.e., the creator of the synthesis that dominated Medieval philosophy),[8] a Middle Platonist,[9] and some have

---

1.12.9 (PCW 1.cvi).
[5] First attested in Jerome, *De vir. ill.* 11 (PCW 1.ciii), who explained it in these words: id est aut Plato Philonem sequitur aut Platonem Philo; tanta est similitudo sensuum et eloquii. For other examples see Isidore of Pelusium, *Ep.* 3.81 (PCW 1.cviii), whose explanation is similar to Jerome's: καὶ Φίλων δέ, ἄνθρωπος Πλάτωνος ἢ ὁμιλητὴς ἢ ὑφηγητής τις εἶναι δόξας; Photius, *Biblioth. Cod.* 105 (PCW 1.cx), who thinks it expresses the Greeks estimation of Philo's eloquence; Suidas, s.v. Φίλων (PCW 1.cx), offers the same judgment as Jerome; Theodorus Metochita, *Miscell.* 16 (PCW 1.cxi–cxiii), thought this praise of Philo's wisdom inappropriate if understood literally, but acceptable if understood as a statement of Philo's philosophical allegiance: τῷ ὄντι γὰρ καὶ τῆς τοῦ Πλάτωνος φιλοσοφίας αἱρεσιώτης ἐστὶν ὁ Φίλων. Augustine, *c. Faust.* 12.39 (PCW 1.cv), does not cite the proverb, but says that the Greeks consider Philo's eloquence equal to Plato's.
[6] *HE* 2.4.2 (PCW 1.lxxxxviii).
[7] This was very common at the end of the nineteenth and beginning of the twentieth century. There is a famous quotation from E. R. Dodds which captures the general sentiment. In 'The *Parmenides* of Plato and the Origin of the Neoplatonic "One"', *CQ* 22 (1928) 132 he wrote: 'any attempt to extract a coherent system from Philo seems to me foredoomed to failure; his eclecticism is that of a jackdaw rather than the philosopher'. Among the recent advocates of such a position see H. Chadwick, 'Philo and the Beginnings of Christian Thought', in A. H. Armstrong (ed.), *The Cambridge History of Later Greek and Early Medieval Philosophy* (Cambridge 1970) 141, 155 (Chadwick argues religion rather than philosophy determines Philo's thought (138, 155–56)) and J. Morris, 'The Jewish Philosopher Philo', in E.Schürer, *The History of the Jewish People in the Age of Jesus Christ (175 B.C.–A.D. 135)*, 3 vols. rev. G. Vermes, F. Millar, and M. Goodman (Edinburgh 1973–87) 3.872.
[8] H. A. Wolfson, *Philo: Foundations of Religious Philosophy in Judaism, Christianity, and Islam*, 2 vols. (Cambridge 1947) 1.93–115, 2.439–60.
[9] The most important representatives of this view are W. Theiler, 'Philo von Alexandria und der Beginn des kaiserzeitlichen Platonismus', in K. Flasch (ed.), *Parusia: Studien zur Philosophie Platons und zur Problemgeschichte des Platonismus (Festgabe für Johannes Hirschberger)* (Frankfurt/Main 1965) 199–219; U. Früchtel, *Die kosmologischen Vorstellungen bei Philo von Alexandrien: Ein Beitrag zur Geschichte der Genesisexegese*, ALGHJ 2 (Leiden 1968) esp. 1–4; J. Dillon, *The Middle Platonists (80 B.C. to A. D. 220)* (Ithaca, New York 1977) 139–83, esp. 182–83, where he argues that Eudorus and Philo

denied him the sobriquet 'philosopher'.[10] The importance of the issue is difficult to overstate: it compels Philonists to state the interpretative framework in which we read Philo; it requires students of ancient philosophy to determine whether Philo can be used as evidence for a particular philosophical tradition.

In this article I will attempt to clarify an aspect of the debate by arguing that Philo's marriage of Jewish scripture and Greek philosophy through allegorical exegesis was one example of the effort to bridge the East and the West within the philosophical tradition. Previous studies have correctly pointed out the connections between Philo's allegorical exegesis and that of his Jewish predecessors and contemporaries,[11] his indebtedness to the Stoics' allegorical readings of Homer,[12] his parallels

provide evidence for Platonism in Alexandria; idem, 'Preface', in D. Winston, Philo of Alexandria: The Contemplative Life, the Giants, and Selections, Classics of Western Spirituality (New York 1981) xiii; idem and A. A. Long (edd.), The Question of 'Eclecticism': Studies in Later Greek Philosophy, Hellenistic Culture and Society 3 (Berkeley 1988) 8; idem, Review of Clara Kraus Reggiani and Robert Radice, Filone de Alessandria: La Filosofia Mosaica (La Creazione del Mondo secondo Mosè); (Le Allegorie delle Leggi) SPhA 2 (1990) 178–80, where he appears to nuance his earlier position by 'denying that Philo is a faithful adherent of any particular Greek philosophical sect' and affirming that he is 'an exponent of the philosophy of Moses', a philosophy Dillon understands to be coherent; D. Winston, Philo of Alexandria 2–3; idem, Logos and Mystical Theology in Philo of Alexandria (Cincinnati 1985) 11–12; T. H. Tobin, The Creation of Man: Philo and the History of Interpretation, CBQMS 14 (Washington, D.C. 1983) 9–19; R. M. Berchman, From Philo to Origen: Middle Platonism in Transition, BJS 69 (Chico 1984) 23–53, who argues Philo developed Jewish Platonism in the Middle Platonic tradition; and H. Tarrant, 'The Date of Anon. In Theaetetum', CQ 33 (1983) 173–78, who argued that Philo represents a mildly skeptic form of Middle Platonism.
[10] The most important recent representatives include V. Nikiprowetzky, Le Commentaire de l'Ecriture chez Philon d'Alexandrie, ALGHJ 11 (Leiden 1977) esp. 180–81, 192, 238–39, 242, where he argues that Philo is an exegete who wrote 'un commentaire de l'Ecriture au sens technique du terme'; D. T. Runia, Philo of Alexandria and the Timaeus of Plato, PhilAnt 44 (Leiden 1986) 485–519, esp. 504–19; and idem, 'Redrawing the Map of Early Middle Platonism: Some Comments on the Philonic Evidence', in A. Caquot, M. Hadas-Lebel, J. Riaud (edd.), Hellenica et Judaica: Hommage à Valentin Nikiprowetzky (Leuven 1986) 104; reprinted in D. T. Runia, Exegesis and Philosophy: Studies on Philo of Alexandria, CSS 332 (Hampshire 1990), who compares him to the Middle Platonists and finds the divergencies too great to place Philo among them. Runia prefers to consider Philo a Platonizing expositor. For a carefully nuanced analysis of the positions see Runia's paper 'Was Philo a Middle Platonist? a Difficult Question Revisited' below pp. 112–140.
[11] Wolfson, Philo 1.115–38; D. M. Hay, 'Philo's References to Other Allegorists', SPh 6 (1979–80) 41–75, who provides a detailed treatment of Philo's explicit references to Jewish allegorists; and D. Dawson, Allegorical Readers and Cultural Revision in Ancient Alexandria (Berkeley 1992) 74–82, who treats Aristobulus and Pseudo-Aristeas.
[12] E.g., Ed. Zeller, Die Philosophie der Griechen in ihrer geschichtlichen Entwicklung, 3 vols. (Leipzig 1923^5) 3.2:397–98; J. Pépin, Mythe et Allégorie: Les origines grecques et les contestations Judéo-Chrétiennes, Philosophie de l'Esprit (Aubier 1958) 231–42; and J. Dillon, 'Ganymede as the Logos: Traces of a Forgotten Allegorization in Philo', SPh 6

to Middle Platonic techniques,[13] as well as his similarities to the later Neoplatonic commentaries on Plato and Homer.[14] The lacuna in these studies which I propose to address is the presence of first and second century CE philosophers who read sacred oriental traditions through the lenses of occidental philosophies by means of allegorical exegesis. I believe that an examination of Chaeremon, Plutarch, and Numenius will demonstrate the philosophical nature of Philo's enterprise.[15]

Philo of Alexandria

Before turning to the other examples, it will be helpful if I clarify my own understanding of Philo's presentation of philosophy. For the Alexandrian Torah exegete Moses was at once the philosopher *par excellence* and *the* recipient of divine revelation. At the outset of *De opificio mundi* he claimed that Moses 'had both reached the apex of philosophy and had been taught by oracles the most significant and essential aspects of nature'.[16] The two are in perfect harmony since 'the cosmos is in harmony with the law and the law with the cosmos'.[17]

This unity of law and nature appears in Philo's statements about Jewish and Greek philosophy. According to Philo, Moses, the πάνσοφος,[18] is the greatest of philosophers since he lived his own philosophy.[19] We may therefore speak of the philosophy of Moses,[20] of the πάτριος φιλοσο-

---

(1979–80) 37–40; Winston, *Philo of Alexandria* 4–6. Our best access to the Stoic material is Heraclitus' *Homeric Allegories*. The standard text is F. Buffière (ed.), *Héraclite, Allégories d'Homère*, Budé (Paris 1989²).

[13] I. Christiansen, *Die Technik der allegorischen Auslegungswissenschaft bei Philon von Alexandrien*, BGBH 7 (Tübingen 1969).

[14] The most important treatments are J. Dillon, 'The Formal Structure of Philo's Allegorical Exegesis', in David Winston and John Dillon (edd.), *Two Treatises of Philo of Alexandria: A Commentary on De Gigantibus and Quod Deus Sit Immutabilis*, BJS 25 (Chico, CA 1983) 77–87, who finds similarities in the division of the text into *lemmata*, the progression of exegetical levels in each κεφάλαιον, and the doxographic nature of the commentaries; and R. Lamberton, *Homer the Theologian: Neoplatonist Allegorical Reading and the Growth of the Epic Tradition*, The Transformation of the Classical Heritage 9 (Berkeley 1989) 44–54, who treats Philo as a representative of Middle Platonic exegesis.

[15] In this article I will deal with Philo's attitude towards philosophy generally. I, however, share the common perception that his fundamental affinity is with the Middle Platonic tradition.

[16] *Opif.* 8. Cf. also *Her.* 301, where Philo calls Moses φιλόσοφος καὶ θεοφράδμων ἀνήρ.

[17] *Opif.* 3. Cf. also *Opif.* 143; *Mos.* 2.48–49; *Praem.* 23; *Contempl.* 2. For Philo the law is ὁ ὀρθὸς λόγος: *Ebr.* 141–42; *Ios.* 29–31 (cf. Cicero, *Rep.* 3.33); *Prob.* 46, 62; *Aet.* 59.

[18] *Abr.* 13.

[19] *Mos.* 1.18–29, esp. 29, 48, 66; *QE* 2.20.

[20] *Prob.* 43, refers to him as γυμνῆς ... ἀσκητὴς φιλοσοφίας which is probably a play off of the gymnosophists. *Contra* F. H. Colson, PLCL 9.35 n. c.

φία of the Jewish people,[21] or of specific groups whose practices embody the highest principles of Jewish philosophy.[22] The philosophy which they practice is embedded within the Torah. As Philo interpreted Gen 4:2 he promised: 'we will attempt—as much as it is possible—to accurately specify the implied philosphical thought'.[23] The key to unlocking the philosophical secrets of the Torah is allegorical exegesis. In a statement which ostensibly reports the practices of the Therapeutae, but which appears to reflect Philo's own convictions he wrote: 'For they read the sacred writings and practise their ancestral philosophy through allegorical interpretation,[24] since they regard the words of the literal meaning as symbols of a hidden nature which is revealed through the underlying meanings'. Similarly, when Philo explained the high priest's robe in QE 2.117, he said: 'But I wonder at and am struck with admiration by the theologian's allegorizing of his philosophical beliefs'.[25]

On the other hand, there are a number of texts where Philo explained the origin of philosophy within the context of encomia on sight. Drawing his inspiration from Plato's *Timaeus* (47a–c) and its subsequent interpretation, Philo suggested that philosophy arose as a result of human observation of the celestial bodies. To cite but one example, in *De opificio mundi* 77, he spoke of the creation of the ἄνθρωπος in these terms: '(God) willed that when he came into existence he should lack none of the things that contribute to living and to living well'. He expanded: 'The supplies and bounties of the things contributing to enjoyment furnish the former; the contemplation of the (bodies) in the heavens the latter', explaining, 'since the mind is amazed through contemplation (of these) and acquires a love and longing for knowledge of them'. He then added: 'From this process philosophy sprang up by which a human although mortal becomes immortal'.[26] These texts are Philo's bow to the Greek philosophical tradition.[27]

---

[21] *Somn.* 2.127; *Mos.* 2.216; *Contempl.* 28; *Legat.* 156. Cf. also *Legat.* 245, where it is called ἡ 'Ιουδαϊκὴ φιλοσοφία.
[22] The Therapeutae in *Contempl.* 26, 28, 67, 69, 89; and the Essenes in *Prob.* 88.
[23] *Sacr.* 1. Cf. also *Migr.* 34–35, which I think refers to Philo's writing of the *Allegorical Commentary*; *Spec.* 3.1–6, where he looks back on the writing of the *Allegorical Commentary*.
[24] Or 'practise philosophy by allegorically deriving their ancestral philosophy', if τὴν πάτριον φιλοσοφίαν is the object of ἀλληγοροῦντες rather than the cognate accusative of φιλοσοφοῦσι.
[25] Cf. also *QG* 4.89, 241.
[26] For other encomia see *Opif.* 53–54; *Abr.* 164; *Spec.* 1.322; 3.185–91; *QG* 2.34. Cf. also *QG* 2.41; 4.1. In *Spec.* 1.336, Philo affirms that it was νοῦς that καὶ τὸ μέγιστον ἀγαθόν, φιλοσοφίαν, ἐγέννησε ...
[27] So also Nikiprowetzky, *Le Commentaire de l'Écriture chez Philon d'Alexandrie* 98–99 and Runia, *Philo of Alexandria and the Timaeus of Plato* 270–76.

How does he relate these two explanations? For Philo Moses is the *fons* of philosophical thought.[28] He develops this in several ways. In some instances he argued for direct dependence. So, for example, Philo claimed that Heraclitus derived from Moses the principle that opposites are from the same whole[29] and that life in the body is death.[30] The Torah served as Zeno's source for his stance on the paradoxical value of slavery.[31] More recent philosophers learned the value of the good directly from Moses.[32] In other cases Philo claimed temporal priority for Moses and implied dependence without directly affirming it. He claimed that both Pythagoras and Aristotle expressed their views on felicity after Moses[33] and that Zeno's ethical norm of living according to nature was first expressed by a much higher authority.[34] In yet other instances, Philo compared Hellenes to Jews and found that they came up short: the Therapeutae were superior to Anaxagoras and Democritus;[35] Terah was better than Socrates.[36] Nor was his argument restricted to philosophy: Moses preceded Hesiod;[37] the Greeks derived their laws from Jews.[38]

This evidence appears to suggest that Philo can cite Greek philosophy since it is derived from Moses.[39] The matter is not, however, so simple. There are at least two factors which complicate the situation. First, there are places where Philo gives some priority to the Greeks. In his panegyric celebrating the *Wunderkind* Moses, Philo found it necessary to have Moses educated by Greeks.[40] In another text, he recognized the universal

---

[28] There are several significant recent treatments of this topos: A. J. Droge, *Homer or Moses? Early Christian Interpretations of the History of Culture*, HUT 26 (Tübingen 1989) 47–48 and P. Pilhofer, *Presbyteron Kreitton: der Altersbeweis der jüdischen und christlichen Apologeten und seine Vorgeschichte*, WUNT 2.39 (Tübingen 1990) 173–92.
[29] *Her.* 214; *QG* 3.5. For Heraclitus' views see G. S. Kirk, J. E. Raven, and M. Schofield, *The Presocratic Philosophers* (Cambridge 1983²) 188–93 (nn. 199–209).
[30] *Leg.* 1.108; *QG* 4.152. Philo interprets this saying in light of the σῶμα–σῆμα play. Cf. Plato, *Gorg.* 493a; *Crat.* 400b–c. For the views of Heraclitus see Kirk–Raven–Schofield, *The Presocratic Philosophers* 205–06 (nn. 233–34).
[31] *Prob.* 53–57, esp. 57.
[32] *QG* 4.167.
[33] *QG* 3.16.
[34] *Prob.* 160. For Zeno's position see Diogenes Laertius 7.87.
[35] *Contempl.* 13–16.
[36] *Somn.* 1.58. Cf. also *QG* 2.6.
[37] *Aet.* 17–19.
[38] *Spec.* 4.61.
[39] So J. Mansfeld, 'Philosophy in the Service of Scripture', in *The Question of "Eclecticism"* 71–72, 85.
[40] *Mos.* 1.18–24, esp. 21 and 23. He also mentions Egyptians. Philo is careful not to reverse the possible flow of influence by explaining that Moses advanced so rapidly ὡς ἀνάμνησιν εἶναι δοκεῖν, οὐ μάθησιν (21).

validity of Pythagoras' dictum, 'do not walk on the highways'.[41] He even called the Stoics Boethus of Sidon and Panaetius θεόληπτοι.[42] Second, the acceptance of Greek philosophy is a *fait accompli* for Philo. We can grasp this by comparing Philo to one of his predecessors. Aristobulus attempted to forge a rapprochement between Hellenic philosophy and Jewish faith in the second century BCE by arguing that the former was directly derived from the latter.[43] Since the earliest philosophers antedated the LXX, Aristobulus argued that there were partial translations of the Torah into Greek prior to the LXX.[44] Greek philosophy was acceptable because it was in reality Mosaic. Although Philo knew the 'theft of philosophy' argument, he did not exploit it to the same degree. The examples of Greek dependence on Moses cited above are virtually all those within the Philonic corpus. What was a central thesis for Aristobulus—if our fragments convey an accurate picture of his thought—is a subpoint for Philo.[45]

How do we explain this shift in emphasis? For Philo there is only one correct understanding of reality. So he can claim that what the law does for Jews, philosophy does for its adherents: it is the road to virtue or to wisdom.[46] It is, however, much more than this: it gives them the knowledge of the one true God. In a statement which anticipates the more famous formulation of another Alexandrian, Philo wrote: 'For what comes to the adherents of the most esteemed philosophy, comes to the Jews through their laws and customs, namely the knowledge of the highest and most ancient Cause of all and the rejection of the deception of created gods'.[47] Philosophy provides humans with the power to see

---

[41] *Prob.* 2–3.
[42] *Aet.* 76.
[43] The fragments are in A.-M. Denis (ed.), *Fragmenta pseudepigraphorum quae supersunt Graeca una cum historicorum et auctorum Judaeorum hellenistarum fragmentis*, PVTG 3 (Leiden 1970) 217–28. There are convenient German and English editions: N. Walter, 'Fragmente jüdisch-hellenistischer Exegeten: Aristobulos, Demetrios, Aristeas', in W. G. Kümmel (ed.), *Unterweisung in lehrhafter Form*, JSHRZ 3.2 (Gütersloh 1975) 261–79 and A. Yarbro Collins, 'Aristobulus', in J. H. Charlesworth (ed.), *The Old Testament Pseudepigrapha*, 2 vols. (Garden City 1983–85) 2.831–42. For the fragments which accentuate Greek dependence see F2 (*PE* 8.10.4); F3 (*PE* 13.12.1–2); F4 (*PE* 13.12.4–8); F5 (*PE* 13.12.10–11, 13–16).
[44] F3 (*PE* 13.12.1–2).
[45] On Philo's position see Runia, *Philo of Alexandria and the* Timaeus *of Plato* 528–35 and Pilhofer, *Presbyteron Kreitton* 187–90.
[46] To virtue: *Leg.* 1.57; *Congr.* 142; *Somn.* 2.170. Cf. also *Ios.* 86–87; *QG* 3.43. It is contrasted with pleasure in *Cher.* 93; *QG* 4.191. Cf. also *Dec.* 15. Philo claims philosophy leads to wisdom in *Congr.* 79; *Somn.* 2.170–71; *Abr.* 164; *Contempl.* 28; *QG* 1.57; 3.43.
[47] *Virt.* 65. Cf. also *Spec.* 2.164–67. Clement of Alexandria's formulation is in *Strom.* 1.5.28. Cf. also Augustine, *Civ. Dei* 8.12, who argues that Platonism is the most appropriate form of philosophy, but warns that even Plato succumbed to polytheistic worship.

beyond the limits of corporeal existence, to try—although the apophatic nature of Philo's thought considers this ultimately impossible—to perceive God.[48] It therefore leads to service to God and even immortality.[49] For Philo Judaism and Platonism intersected at the most pivotal of all points, the understanding of God.[50] It was on the basis of this *similarity* rather than *dependence* that Philo argued Middle Platonism and the Jewish Torah were but two expressions of the same reality.[51]

But—to borrow the words of another first century Jew—'what is the advantage of the Jew'? Like his contemporary Christian counterpart, Philo understood the advantage to lay in the possession of the sacred oracles. Moses offered a *definitive* statement, but it was not *exclusive*. Are there other examples of philosophical figures who worked with similar understandings? I think there are.

Chaeremon of Alexandria

One of Philo's contemporaries and political opponents in Alexandria was the Stoic philosopher Chaeremon.[52] He is particularly intriguing because he was both a ἱερογραμματεύς (T6 and F4, 12, 13)[53] and a φιλόσοφος (T3, 4), more particularly a Στωϊκός (T9, 10 and F3, 10, 11, 14). We know only a few things about his life: he was the head of the Alexandrian school of grammarians (T4), a member of the anti-Jewish delegation from Alexandria in 40 CE (T5),[54] and a tutor to Nero (T4).

What makes Chaeremon important for our purposes is that he applied Stoic allegorical exegesis to Egyptian mythology. Porphyry claimed that Origen 'made use of the works of Chaeremon the Stoic and Cornutus from which he learned the allegorical method of the mysteries

---

[48] *Spec.* 1.37–40. It is the road to God in *Post.* 101–02; *QE* 2.13. Philo also claims that philosophy enables humans to perceive the aetiological ideas in *QG* 4.21, 22.
[49] *Congr.* 114 and *Opif.* 77 respectively.
[50] For an attempt to set up some of the specifics of this identification cf. H. Conzelmann, *Gentiles–Jews–Christians: Polemics and Apologetics in the Greco-Roman Era* (Minneapolis 1992) 135–39.
[51] I am thus in agreement with the basic assessments of Dillon, *The Middle Platonists* 143 and Winston, *Philo of Alexandria* 1.
[52] Recent treatments at P. W. van der Horst, *Chaeremon: Egyptian Priest and Stoic Philosopher*, EPRO 101 (Leiden 1984); and M. Frede, 'Chaeremon der Stoiker', ANRW II.36.3 (Berlin 1989) 2067–2103. All references to *testimonia* and fragments are from van der Horst's edition.
[53] F10 and 11 describe the Egyptian priests. He is credited with a work entitled *Hieroglyphica* (T1, 2, 6 and F12, 13), a work only possible for a priest.
[54] For his anti-Jewish sentiment see T8 and F1. For an analysis of the relationship between Philo and Chaeremon in the political situation see my 'Philo and the Logic of Apologetics: An Analysis of the *Hypothetica*', SBLSP 29 (Atlanta 1990) 412–30.

among the Greeks and applied it to the Jewish scriptures' (T9).[55] Although we only have a few fragments, several of them substantiate Porphyry's statement about Chaeremon's methodology. In keeping with his Stoicism, Chaeremon allegorically interpreted the Egyptian myths to refer to material realities. Porphyry wrote:[56]

> For he saw that those who say that the sun is the Demiurge interpret the stories about Osiris and Isis and all the priestly myths as referring to either the stars and their appearances and seclusions and their rising in their revolutions or to the waxings and wanings of the moon or to the course of the sun or to the nocturnal hemisphere or the diurnal hemisphere or the river, in short, everything to the physical (εἰς τὸ φυσικά) and nothing to the incorporeal and living beings (εἰς ἀσωμάτους καὶ ζώσας οὐσίας).

The result of this process is a mixture of Egyptian religious ideas and Stoic philosophy.[57]

On what basis did Chaeremon combine the two? We have a good indication in a fragment preserved by Michael Psellus who mentioned Chaeremon in connection with the centuries long debate over whether the Egyptians or Babylonians discovered astronomy. Psellus wrote: 'When I read the wise Chaeremon ... I found that the wisdom of the Chaldeans is older than that practiced among the Egyptians, although neither taught the other but both have their champions' (F2). I find this concession nothing short of astounding. Chaeremon's most famous literary predecessor, the third century BCE Egyptian priest Manetho, would never have concurred. Manetho's *Aigyptiaka* accentuated the antiquity of Egypt in an effort to claim cultural superiority over all other civilizations—oriental and occidental.[58] Even the rather thick-headed scribe who composed the *Excerpta Latina Barbari* understood the force of Manetho's presentation when he wrote: 'We learn that the kingdom of the Egyptians is the oldest of all kingdoms'.[59] In stark contrast, Chaeremon granted the Mesopotamians their chronological due—although he did

---

[55] Cf. also T12.
[56] F5. The same type of interpretation appears in F6, 7, 9, 12. Among the *Fragmenta dubia* see F17d and 19d.
[57] Cf. Van der Horst, *Chaeremon* xi: 'Chaeremon's ideas are an interesting syncretistic mixture of Egyptian religious ideas, Stoic philosophic concepts, magical and astrological interests, and anti-Semitic sentiments. He is important to the students of the environment and background of the early Church as one of those who strove after an amalgamation of Egyptian and Greek concepts, and as such he gives valuable insight into the world of a syncretistic, intellectual élite in the time of the first generations of Christianity'. H. Strathmann, 'Chairemon', *RAC* 2 (1954) 990–93 (esp. 991), following H. R. Schwyzer, *Chairemon*, Klass.-phil. Studien 4 (Leipzig 1932), is of a similar opinion.
[58] For details see my *Historiography and Self-Definition: Josephos, Luke-Acts and Apologetic Historiography*, NovTSup 64 (Leiden 1992) 117–35.
[59] *FGrH* 609 F4.

not concede dependence. The reason he could make this concession is that his frame of thought was different. It was no longer a question of dependence but of independent recognition of the same reality. So he said: 'neither taught the other'. I suggest that it was on this same basis that he argued for the presence of Stoic philosophy in Egyptian mythology.[60]

The general similarities between Chaeremon and Philo are patent. The ties may, however, go further. There are at least two pieces of more specific evidence to indicate that Chaeremon and Philo had similar objectives. First, Chaeremon presented the Egyptian priests as philosophers, even bestowing the term upon them (F10, 11). The literary form he used to describe the priests is the same as that used by Philo to present the Therapeutae; in fact, it is so similar that a number of scholars have concluded that Philo was dependent on Chaeremon's description of the priests.[61] I would prefer to argue that both were dependent on a common literary form in which authors presented select groups as embodiments of the ideals of the larger groups to which they belonged.[62] These ideals are, however, those of Greek philosophy. In either case, it is clear that Chaeremon and Philo shared a common agenda. Second, Philo appears to know that hieroglyphs were interpreted allegorically. While Chaeremon is not the only possible source for this information, he is at least a leading candidate.[63]

I do not think that this evidence substantiates Philo's dependence on Chaeremon. What I do think that it points to is the presence in first century CE Alexandria of Egyptian priests and Jewish exegetes using Stoic and Platonic philosophy to forge a rapprochement between their ancestral traditions and Hellenic thought.[64]

Plutarch of Chaeronea

There is an example of a Middle Platonist who found the Isis and Osiris

---

[60] Frede, 'Chaeremon der Stoiker' 2085–92, has a very helpful discussion of this point.
[61] For bibliography see van der Horst, *Chaeremon* 56. Add to this: J. Leipoldt, *Griechische Philosophie und frühchristliche Askese*, Berichte über die Verhandlungen der sächlichen Akademie der Wissenschaften zu Leipzig, philologische-historische Klasse 106.4 (Berlin 1961) 25–27, who argues for Philo's dependence on Chaeremon.
[62] On the form see A. J. Festugière, 'Sur une nouvelle Édition du "De Vita Pythagorica" de Iamblique', *REG* 50 (1937) 476–78 and Strathmann, 'Chairemon' 991.
[63] *Mos.* 1.23. Mansfeld, 'Philosophy in the Service of Scripture' 77, argues that this indicated Philo's knowledge of Chaeremon's work on hieroglyphs.
[64] Runia, 'Was Philo a Middle Platonist?' likewise recognizes the similarity between Philo and Chaeremon, although he denies that Philo is a Platonist in the sense that Chaeremon is a Stoic; see below p. 132–133.

myth engaging.⁶⁵ Plutarch's *De Iside et Osiride* is aware of Stoic interpretations, but operates with a Platonic perspective.⁶⁶ The Chaeronean wrote it toward the end of his life (c. 120 CE) while serving as a priest at Delphi.⁶⁷ He addressed it to Clea, a priestess of both Dionysus and Osiris, who served with him at Delphi.⁶⁸ The work probably reflects their common interest in and discussions on Egyptian myths and religion.⁶⁹

Like Chaeremon, Plutarch used allegory to interpret the sacred Egyptian myths. His method is standard and includes etymologies⁷⁰ as well as moral and physical allegory.⁷¹ This is somewhat surprising given his reticence in *De audiendis poetis* where his attitude is much closer to Plato's. He stated the rationale for his use clearly: 'one must not use the myths as if they were entirely factual, but take what is fitting (πρόσφορον) from each as it accords with truth (κατὰ τὴν ὁμοιότητα)'.⁷² His tool for uncovering what is fitting is philosophy: 'For this reason it is necessary that especially with regard to these matters we should take the reason that comes from philosophy as our guide and piously reflect on each of the things that are said or done'.⁷³

---

⁶⁵ There are two full commentaries on the text: T. Hopfner, *Plutarch über Isis und Osiris*, 2 vols., Monographien des Archiv Orientální. Untersuchungen, Texte und Übersetzungen 9 (Prague 1940–41; reprint, Darmstadt 1967) and J. G. Griffiths, *Plutarch's De Iside et Osiride* (Cambridge 1970). C. Froidefond (ed.), *Plutarque: Oeuvres Morales* 5.2, Budé (Paris 1988), has an extensive introduction. I have used Griffiths edition. For a bibliography see Luc Deitz, 'Bibliographie du platonisme impérial antérieur à Plotin: 1926–1986', *ANRW* II.36.1 (Berlin 1987) 158–60.

⁶⁶ The Stoics are mentioned by name in 367c, 367e, and 369a. For a summary of research see Griffiths, *Plutarch's De Iside et Osiride* 85–88. Whether Plutarch knew Chaeremon's work is open to question. The fragmentary nature of the latter and the attestation of a good deal of the material in other sources, ensures the speculative nature of an answer.

⁶⁷ That he wrote it—or at least parts of it—at Delphi, is suggested by 378c–d. On the date see Griffiths, *Plutarch's De Iside et Osiride* 16–18 and Froidefond, *Plutarque* 14–23.

⁶⁸ *Mor.* 351c, 352c, 364d–e, where he asks: 'That he (Osiris) is the same as Dionysus, who should know better than you, O Clea, you who are a priestess of the Thyiades at Delphi and were dedicated to the Osirian rites by your father and mother'? Griffiths, *Plutarch's De Iside et Osiride* 431, suggests that her parents were devotees of Serapis and dedicated their daughter to the cult.

⁶⁹ For the theological and philosophical reasons why Plutarch chose Egyptian mythology see Froidefond, *Plutarque* 67–80.

⁷⁰ E.g., 354c–d, 355a, 356d–e, 359b, 359c, 362b–d, 365e, 371c, 374b, 375c–76a.

⁷¹ For details see Griffiths, *Plutarch's De Iside et Osiride* 100–01; Froidefond, *Plutarque* 80–92; and Dawson, *Allegorical Readers and Cultural Revision in Ancient Alexandria* 58–66.

⁷² 374e. Cf. also 355b, 358e–59a.

⁷³ 378a. Cf. also 352c, where he states that a true devotee of Isis examines everything rationally (λόγῳ ζητῶν καὶ φιλοσοφῶν περὶ τῆς ἐν αὐτοῖς ἀληθείας); and 353e, where he insists that nothing should be irrational (οὐδὲν γὰρ ἄλογον οὐδὲ μυθῶδες οὐδ' ὑπὸ δεισιδαιμονίας).

Like the Alexandrian Jew, he knew the traditions about Greeks who visited Egypt. He wrote that Greeks confirmed the devotion of the Egyptians to sacred wisdom: 'The wisest of the Greeks attest (to this): Solon, Thales, Plato, Eudoxus, and Pythagoras, and as some say, Lycurgus, who all came to Egypt and associated with the priests'. He cautioned, however, that the lines of communication did not flow one way. In the same context he stated that Pythagoras 'was admired and admired these men'.[74] Later he noted that Greeks who emigrated taught the countries they visited Greek names for their deities. So he argued that Osiris was a Greek compound of ὅσιος and ἱερός.[75] Lines of dependence were not, however, his prinicpal concern. He wrote: 'Therefore we should engage in as little rivalry as possible about names; although I would be more willing to concede Sarapis to the Egyptians than Osiris since the former is a foreign name but the latter Greek, yet I consider both to belong to one god and one power'.[76] While Plutarch does not manage to extricate himself completely from the rival claims of cultural superiority, he makes it clear that he can see past parochial claims to a broader unity.

The basis of this unity is that the myths contain truths about the Deity. In a famous passage Plutarch wrote:

> There is nothing to be alarmed about if, in the first place, they preserve the gods in common with us and neither make them the gods of the Egyptians alone nor understand by these names the Nile and only the land the Nile waters nor claim that the marshes and lotus-flowers are the only work of the gods. Since this would deprive other people who do not have a Nile or Buto or Memphis of great gods. But all have and know Isis and the gods with her: even though some only recently learned to address them by Egyptian names; they have known and honored the power of each from the beginning.[77]

He is thus similar to Philo in recognizing that statements about the Deity were the common ground between the Platonism of the West and the religions of the East.[78]

Plutarch's treatise represents a different perspective than the works of Chaeremon or Philo. The perspective in Plutarch's work moves from the Occident to the Orient rather than the reverse. It is not surprising to find the Hellenic element emphasized in Plutarch just as the Jewish is in Philo.

---

[74] 354d–e. Cf. also 364d.
[75] 375d–e.
[76] 376a.
[77] 377c–d. Cf. also 351c–e, 354b–c, 355b–c, 369b–d, 376a.
[78] For a more nuanced summary of his relationship to Egyptian religion see Griffiths, *Plutarch's* De Iside et Osiride 18–33 and Froidefond, *Plutarque* 93–177, esp. 126–77.

Numenius of Apamea

One of the most interesting figures in second century CE Platonism is Numenius of Apamea.[79] All that we know of his life is that he was from Apamea. Johannes Lydus refers to him as ὁ ‛Ρωμαῖος (F57) which may either be a nod or reflect a period of time when Numenius was active in Rome.[80] His *floruit* was the middle of the second century. Even though we only have fragments, we do know of several works he composed including the following: Περὶ τἀγαθοῦ in six books (F1–22), Περὶ τῶν παρὰ Πλάτωνι ἀπορρήτων (F23), Περὶ τῆς τῶν' Ἀκαδημαϊκῶν πρὸς Πλάτωνα διαστάσεως (F24–28), Περὶ ἀφθαρσίας ψυχῆς (F29). The remaining fragments are impossible to place at present (F30–59) or of doubtful authenticity (F60).

The most important of these works for our purposes is *On the Good*. In the first book Numenius appears to have argued that diverse oriental religions concur with Platonism in their affirmation of the incorporeal nature of God. Eusebius cites Numenius as follows:

> After having spoken to this point and sealing it with the testimonies of Plato, it will be necessary to return and connect it to the teachings of Pythagoras; and to summon the most reputable nations, introducing their rites and doctrines, and the setting up of temples, all carried out in agreement with Plato, whatever the Brahmans, Jews, Magi, and Egyptians have determined (F1a).

Here we have an unambiguous statement affirming the presence of a common truth.

What makes Numenius' work doubly important for us is that the fragments which have come down to us frequently mention his efforts to use Jewish and even Christian material in his system.[81] Like the other

---

[79] The standard critical edition is E. des Places, *Numénius Fragments*, Budé (Paris 1973). All references are to this edition. There is an older collection with English translation, K. Guthrie, *The Neoplatonic Writings of Numenius* (London 1917; reprint ed., Kansas 1987). Standard discussions include: R. Beutler, 'Numenios', PW Sup. 7 (1940) 664–78; , P. Merlan, 'Greek Philosophy from Plato to Plotinus', in A. H. Armstrong (ed.), *The Cambridge History of Later Greek and Early Medieval Philosophy* 96–106; Dillon, *The Middle Platonists* 361–79; M. Frede, 'Numenius', ANRW II.36.3 (Berlin 1987) 1034–75. I have also found Lamberton's treatment of Numenius' handling of the Homeric material helpful, *Homer the Theologian* 54–77. For a recent bibliography see Deitz, 'Bibliographie du platonisme impérial antérieur à Plotin', 155–57. Numenius is frequently called a Pythagorean in ancient sources. I have followed Dillon's lead in considering Numenius a Platonist with strong Pythagorean tendencies.

[80] So Des Places, *Numenius* 125, following E. R. Dodds.

[81] This treatment may have comprised the third and fourth books of the work (F9–15). The Jewish material is conveniently collected in M. Stern, *Greek and Latin Authors on Jews and Judaism*, 3 vols. (Jerusalem 1974–84) CX (2.206–16) (hereafter *GLAJJ*). For Numenius' use of the OT see F9 (Moses vs. Jannes and Jambres), 10a (Moses vs. Jannes and

figures which we have examined, Numenius used allegory as the means for uncovering the hidden truth within these oriental texts. Origen tells us that unlike Celsus: 'he did not hestitate to use the prophetic works in his writing and to interpret them allegorically' (F1b).[82] His understanding of Judaism is best captured in his celebrated *dictum*: τί γάρ ἐστι Πλάτων ἢ Μωσῆς ἀττικίζων;[83] An example of how he used Judaism is evident in the controversial F13. Numenius argues that just as there is a relation between the cultivater and the planter, so there is between the first God and the Demiurge: ὁ μέν γε ὢν σπέρμα πάσης ψυχῆς σπείρει εἰς τὰ μεταλαγχάνοντα αὐτοῦ χρήματα σύμπαντα. There is a long-standing debate over how to understand ὁ μέν γε ὤν. E. R. Dodds, Thillet, and J. Dillon have all proposed emendations.[84] The difficulty which they have felt is the need to have a predicate after ὤν. There is, however, an alternative which makes good sense of the text as it stands: ὁ ὤν may be a reflection of the LXX rendering of Exod 3:14: 'Ἐγώ εἰμι ὁ ὤν. The phrase could therefore be understood absolutely and rendered: 'the Self-Existent plants the seed of every soul in everything that has a share in him'. Apparently either Numenius—or more probably—a source before him identified the τὸ ὂν ἀεί of Plato with the ὁ ὤν of the LXX.[85] The question of a possible source raises the issue of whether Numenius knew the work of Philo.[86] In this instance there is no doubt that Philo made this

---

Jambres), 13 (Exod 3:14), 30 (Gen 1:2), 56 (the God of the Jerusalem temple and cult). For the Christian material see F10a.
[82] Cf. also F1c and 30.
[83] F8 (Eusebius, *PE* 11.10.14 (*GLAJJ* 363c)). The proverb is reported at least four other times: Clem. Alex., *Str.* 1.22.150.4 (*GLAJJ* 363a); Eusebius, *PE* 9.6.9 (*GLAJJ* 363b); Theodoret, *Graecarum Affectionum Curatio* 2.114 (*GLAJJ* 363d); Souda, s.v. Νουμήνιος (*GLAJJ* 363e). John G. Gager, *Moses in Greco-Roman Paganism* (Nashville 1972) 66–68, has convincingly defended the authenticity of the saying.
[84] Dodds, 'Numenius and Ammonius', in *Les Sources de Plotin*, Entretiens sur l'Antiquité Classique 5 (Genève 1960) 15, suggested ὁ μέν γε α' ὤν (= πρῶτος ὤν); Thillet, *apud* Des Places, *ap. crit.* proposed ὁ μὲν γεννῶν; and Dillon, *The Middle Platonists* 368 n. 1, emended it to ὁ μὲν γεωργῶν.
[85] I am following the lead of A. J. Festugière, *La Révélation d'Hermes Trismégiste*, 4 vols. (Paris 1945–54) 3.44 n. 2; J. Whittaker, 'Moses Atticizing', *Phoenix* 21 (1967) 196–201 and 'Numenius and Alcinous on the First Principle', *Phoenix* 32 (1978) 144–54, both reprinted in J. Whittaker, *Studies in Platonism and Patristic Thought*, CSS 201 (London 1984); and Merlan, 'Greek Philosophy from Plato to Plotinus' 100.
[86] Among those who think he did are E. R. Dodds, *Pagan and Christian in An Age of Anxiety* (Cambridge 1965) 95–96, who argues that Numenius served as a bridge between Philo and Plotinus; J. H. Waszink, and 'Die sogenannte Fünfteilung der Träume bei Chalcidius und ihre Quellen', *Mnemosyne* 3.9 (1940) 84, and 'Porphyrios und Numenios', in *Porphyre*, Entretiens sur l'Antiquité Classique 12 (Genève 1966) 49–53. Those who prefer to consider it a possibility, but unprovable include Whittaker, 'Moses Atticizing' 201 n. 28; Dillon, *The Middle Platonists* 378–79; and Lamberton, *Homer the Theologian* 75–76.

connection.[87] The problem is that we can not be sure that only Philo made the connection. The other *comparanda* are similar, intriguing but inadequate. Whether Numenius knew Philo's work or not, I think it fair to say that he would have found it of worth.

One of the most interesting aspects of scholarship on Numenius is the debate over whether we should consider him an orientalist. Did Numenius interpret the Occident in light of the Orient? Henri-Charles Puech thought that he might even be a Jew.[88] I see no reason to go this far. It is better to view Numenius as a later witness to the conviction that both Hellenic philosophy and Eastern religions testify to the same conception of God. Since this appears to be the thrust of book one, it is *a priori* likely that this conviction served as the *point d'appui* for his larger argument of identification.

Conclusions

Those who study world religions—as the discipline is commonly called today—have distinguished three major postures towards the religions of the world. First, most religions begin with an *exclusivistic* stance, i.e., adherents are convinced that their own particular tradition offers the truth to humanity. This truth is absolute in the sense that it is independent of all other traditions. Second, those who become familiar with other religious traditions often move to a more *inclusivistic* position, i.e., they maintain the claim that their tradition represents the ultimate truth, but no longer insist that it is absolute. They concede that other traditions may constitute alternative approaches to the same truth. Finally, those who push *inclusivism* to its logical end embrace a *pluralistic* posture, i.e., they are convinced that the major religious traditions represent different perceptions of the same ultimate reality. Some pluralists are thoroughgoing relativists who argue against any hierarchical scale of value; others recognize validity in each tradition but are

---

[87] *Det.* 160.
[88] Henri-Charles Puech, 'Numénius d'Apamée et les théologies orientales au second siècle', *Mélanges Bidez: Annuaire de l'Institut de Philologie et d'Histoire Orientales* 2 (1934) 745–78, esp. 754; Dodds, 'Numenius and Ammonius' 4–11, who did not think that Numenius was Jewish but concluded: 'M. Puech is right: there *was* an oriental baby in the bathwater, probably a whole litter of babies... But because he was, as Macrobius says, *occultorum curiosior* (F39 (= F55 in Des Places)), he welcomed all the superstitions of his time, whatever their origin, and therely (*sic*) contributed to the eventual degradation of Greek philosophical thought' (p. 11); Gager, *Moses in Greco-Roman Paganism* 68–69, leaves the issue of whether Numenius was a Jew open. Merlan, 'Greek Philosophy from Plato to Plotinus' 103, is less enthusiastic about his orientalism. For a summary see Des Places, *Numénius* 21–23.

unwilling to grant each equal value. They are convinced that some religious traditions offer more insight than others.[89]

If I were to use these perspectives to locate different groups or figures from second temple Judaism, I would place the Essenes among the *exclusivists*, Aristobulus and most Jewish apologists among the *inclusivists*, and Philo among the *pluralists*. I would not categorize Philo as a thoroughgoing relativist, but as a pluralist who had a distinct hierarchy of values by which he measured all efforts to understand what is Real. Philo's hierarchy was bifid: he was thoroughly convinced of the validity of Platonism—more specifically, of the Middle Platonism of his native Alexandria—and of his ancestral faith. All other systems of thought were measured by these. I do not mean to imply by this anachronistic analogy that Philo thought of the two socially distinct entities as separate systems of thought. I have argued that one of the major purposes of his tractates was to demonstrate the unity of the two. For Philo they were two ways of expressing a single vision of truth.

What led Philo to such an understanding? Although an adequate answer to this question would involve the analysis of social as well as intellectual concerns, I am convinced that one of the most important factors was the presence of similar efforts within the philosophical tradition of the first two centuries CE. Philo was by no means the only figure who attempted to demonstrate the unity of oriental and occidental thought: Chaeremon, Plutarch, and Numenius all undertook the same enterprise. What they shared in common—with varying degrees of flexibility—was the conviction that no one tradition had a monopoly on the correct perception of reality. Their works were attempts at demonstrating where the unity lay.

Philo's relationship to philosophy is thus complex. From *his* perspective he was a devoted follower of Moses. Yet Philo's Moses was not a Hebrew Moses; he was a Middle Platonist. It is from this perspective that I think *we* can speak of Philo as a representative of Middle Platonism. By this I do not mean that we should consider him a Middle Platonist *tout court*, anymore than I would argue that he is Jewish *tout court*. For Philo, Plato and Moses are intellectually one. I think that he would have been pleased with both Numenius' witticism as well as with its reversal: τί γάρ ἐστι Μωσῆς ἢ Πλάτων ἑβραΐζων.[90]

University of Notre Dame

---

[89] The three positions are clearly sketched by J. Hick, 'Religious Pluralism', *The Encyclopedia of Religion* 12 (1987) 331–33, esp. 331.
[90] I want to thank the members of the seminar for their suggestions and criticisms.

WAS PHILO A MIDDLE PLATONIST?
A difficult question revisited

DAVID T. RUNIA

It is nearly exactly ten years ago that I completed my study *Philo of Alexandria and the Timaeus of Plato*, written as a doctoral dissertation at the Free University of Amsterdam under the supervision of Professors A. P. Bos (Amsterdam) and J. C. M. van Winden (Leyden). A third scholar closely associated with the project was Professor V. Nikiprowetzky (Sorbonne, Paris), who read the entire work in manuscript. In this work I explicitly raised the question of whether Philo was a Middle Platonist (it is the title of section III 3.5), and was bold (or rash) enough to answer the question with a qualified but clear negative. In revisiting this question as part of our seminar on Philo's relationship to Middle Platonism, I would like to begin with a retrospective look at my dissertation and how it was received. This exercise may seem at first a little self-indulgent. It will emerge, however, that, because my response to the above-mentioned question was embedded in a wider view of how we should evaluate Philo's achievement, such a retrospective glance will be a suitable way to introduce our theme. So my paper will fall in two halves. Firstly, I will look at a number of general aspects of my dissertation which I would like to reconsider and sometimes revise in response to pertinent criticisms. Secondly, I narrow the focus of the paper by turning to the specific question of whether Philo can and should be called a 'Middle Platonist', taking once again my own earlier conclusions as starting point.

I

Firstly it should be pointed out that my study appeared in two different versions. The dissertation was written with a view to publication, but for practical reasons I could not postpone the doctoral ceremony for too long. So it first appeared in a typewritten version, dated 1983.[1] The typeset version was not published until 1986.[2] This double form of

---

[1] *Philo of Alexandria and the Timaeus of Plato*, doctoral dissertation Free University of Amsterdam, VU Boekhandel Amsterdam 1983, 2 volumes, x + 592p.
[2] *Philo of Alexandria and the Timaeus of Plato*, revised edition E. J. Brill Leiden 1986,

publication had its drawbacks. It was to be expected that there would be confusion between the two editions.[3] In time, no doubt, references to the provisional edition will die away. But there was also another problem. The date of publication of the 'definitive' edition was three and a half years after the completion of the manuscript. By that time quite a lot of fast-flowing water had passed under the bridge of scholarship.

It could in fact be argued that the period from 1983 to the end of the decade was a very fertile period for Philonic scholarship, as shown by the following list of 16 monographs.[4]

1983   Y. Amir, *Die hellenistische Gestalt des Judentums bei Philon von Alexandrien*
       J. Cazeaux, *La trame et la chaîne*, volume 1
       R. Sorabji, *Time, Creation and the Continuum*
       T. H. Tobin, *The Creation of Man: Philo and the History of Interpretation*
       D. Winston–J. Dillon, *Two Treatises of Philo of Alexandria: a Commentary on De Gigantibus and Quod Deus Sit Immutabilis*
1985   D. Winston, *Logos and Mystical Theology in Philo of Alexandria*
1986   J. P. Martín, *Filon de Alejandría y la génesis de la cultura occidental*
       A. Méasson, *Du char ailé de Zeus à l'Arche d'Alliance: Images et mythes platoniciens chez Philon d'Alexandrie*
1987   R. Goulet, *La philosophie de Moïse: essai de reconstruction d'un commentaire philosophique préphilonien du Pentateuque*
       C. Kraus Reggiani, R. Radice and G. Reale, *Filone di Alessandria. La creazione del mondo secondo Mosè*
       L. A. Montes-Peral, *Akataleptos theos: der unfassbare Gott*
1988   H. Burkhardt, *Die Inspiration heiliger Schriften bei Philo von Alexandrien*
       L. Grabbe, *Etymology in Early Jewish Interpretation: the Hebrew Names in Philo*
       A. Mendelson, *Philo's Jewish Identity*
1989   J. Cazeaux, *La trame et la chaîne*, volume 2
       R. Radice, *Platonismo e creazionismo in Filone di Alessandria*

It goes without saying that, had I been able to learn from these works before I wrote my study, it would have been a much better and more balanced work.[5] In the case of the first five, it was theoretically possible to include their results into the revised edition. But in practice this proved well-nigh impossible. The dissertation had been written as an integrated whole; confronting the radical new insights of Cazeaux and Tobin would have led to an undesirable chain reaction. It was particularly disappointing to me that I heard of Tobin's work too late, since it has been available in dissertation form since 1980. The least we can say is

---

Philosophia Antiqua 44, xiii + 617p.
[3] Not least because the author had two slightly differing names. It was mandatory to publish the dissertation under the Dutch (Frisian) name Douwe Theunis Runia.
[4] For further details on these works see the bibliographical works of Radice, Runia *et al.*
[5] This applies less to the two Italian works, which to some degree build on my own study.

that contacts between scholars working in the area of Philo have greatly improved since then! I would also dearly have loved to have been able to consult Winston's monograph before I wrote my book. But by that time the work was already in proof.

It is six years since the definitive edition appeared, and it may be assumed that most reviews that will be written have by now seen the light of day. Those known to me are the following (I do not list those which merely announce the book and give a brief indication of its contents):[6]

Provisional edition, 1983:

Ch. Lefèvre, *Mélanges de Science Religieuse* 40 (1983) 207.
J. den Boeft, *Philosophia Reformata* 49 (1984) 92-95.
R. Radice, *Rivista di Filosofia Neo-scolastica* 76 (1984) 32-41.
P. W. van der Horst, *Nederlands Theologisch Tijdschrift* 39 (1985) 247.
A. Solignac, *Archives de Philosophie* 48 (1985) 475-477.

Definitive edition, 1986:

N. E. Emerton, *Vetus Testamentum* 37 (1987) 498-500.
J. Moulder, *South African Journal of Philosophy* 6 (1987) 68-69
R. Radice, *Elenchos* 8 (1987) 480-485
A. Sheppard, *Classical Review* 37 (1987) 222-224.
J. Dillon, *Journal of the History of Philosophy* 26 (1988) 658–660
A. Hilhorst, *Journal for the Study of Judaism* 19 (1988) 258-259
R. Joly, *L'Antiquité Classique* 57 (1988) 364-365
E. N. Lee, *Canadian Philosophical Reviews* 8 (1988) 417-422
D. M. Hay, *Mnemosyne* 43 (1990) 490–493.
B. Rosenstock, *The Studia Philonica Annual* 2 (1990) 195-201
J. P. Martín, *Methexis* 5 (1992) 135–143
D. Winston, *Ancient Philosophy* 12 (1992) 222–227.

On the whole it has to be said that the reviewers were benevolent and complimentary. Many remarked on the book's length, but it is some comfort to the author to note that none complained that it was *too* long.[7] No doubt every author feels on occasion that he or she has not been properly understood, and that the reviewer has not read the book carefully enough. It seemed to me that this also happened on a number of occasions in my own case. But the blame for this I would lay at least in part at my own door. On difficult questions I tended to adopt rather nuanced or qualified positions, and it is too much to ask of a reviewer to report these accurately every time. After all reviewing is often as much a journalistic as a scholarly activity. In response to these reviews there are five areas in which I feel that some remarks can be made.

---

[6] It is regrettable that no German reviews have appeared. In the remainder of the paper I shall refer to these reviews by name and page number only.

[7] Cf. Dillon 659 on the relation between parts II and III: 'there is a certain amount of repetition involved in this, but it is worth it.'

1. *Methodology*. It was generally agreed that the method used was carefully thought through, and suitable for the subject in hand. Appreciation was shown for the full use of the Philonic corpus, including the often neglected Armenian works. A problem was located in the commentary format (i.e. of Part II), i.e. the difficulty of 'distinguishing passages where Philo may genuinely be said to be commenting on the *Timaeus* or making use of it from those where there is only a distant echo of Plato's works or a general influence of Platonic thought.' The same reviewer felt that the discussion at pp. 502–505 on the formal characteristics of Philo's exegesis suffers from comparing Philo's procedures only with Platonist commentators, ignoring the broader context of discussion of ἀπορίαι in both philosophers and poets.[8] I could not agree more with this perception. Insufficient account is taken of the method of Philo's exegesis and the structure of the individual treatise.[9] This was the first subject I turned to after having completed the book (inspired by the monographs of Cazeaux and Winston–Dillon),[10] and even now it seems to me that there is much more to be learnt about the techniques of Philo's exegesis, and the formal manner in which he draws on his knowledge of Greek philosophy in the process of commenting on scripture. Quite a different comment is found in the most critical of all the reviews, by the philosopher Edward Lee, who affirms that the book's 'analytical procedures tend to predetermine the limits of [its] portrait of Philo's thought'. The method used is painstaking, but also 'somewhat positivistic', resulting in a predictably shallow picture of Philo.[11] I return to this comment below in my fifth comment.

2. *The Alexandrian background*. The question of Philo's place in the development of Alexandrian Judaism was not ignored in the study. It of course had been place on the Philonist agenda long ago by Bousset, but in the early 80's was receiving new focus in the ambitious proposals of Burton Mack's Claremont Research Project and the more modest but important results of David Hay. Here the research of Tobin and Goulet has uncovered a good deal of (admittedly mostly speculative) new material. My study would have been greatly improved if I had been able to take this evidence into account. On p.527 I concluded that 'the exploitation of the *Timaeus* on a large scale may well have been a *personal contribution* on the part of Philo'. The studies of Tobin and Goulet do not—for the most part—challenge this conclusion, I believe, but rather would

---

[8] Sheppard 223–224.
[9] Also noted by Hay 493.
[10] Cf. the articles in *VChr* 1984, 1986 and 1987, now reprinted as IV–VI in *Exegesis and Philosophy: Studies on Philo of Alexandria* (London 1990).
[11] Lee 419.

have allowed it to be more precisely delineated.[12] Goulet's splendid study shows beyond any doubt that Philo has absorbed previous exegetical 'systems' which did not have Platonism at their core, but rather a form of immanentist Stoicism. Philo superimposes on this traditional base his own form of Platonist exegesis, but does this more effectively than Goulet wishes to admit.[13] In his review Martín perceptively remarks that insufficient attention was paid to Philo's only predecessor whose name we still know, Aristobulus.[14] The important conclusion on p.527 that the Platonic option used by Philo was not open in the same way to Aristobulus a century of more earlier still, I believe, stands firm. But it should be have been demonstrated in a more satisfactory way. The fact that the discussion of Aristobulan evidence was confined to the small print on p.103 shows that it was not taken sufficiently seriously.

3. *Other forms of Judaism, Gnosticism*. In the past decade awareness of the diversity of pre-Rabbinic Judaisms (the plural is deliberate) has steadily increased. So it would hardly surprise if my study was found to fall short in this area. Right at the beginning I disclaimed any intention of presenting a portrait of Philo 'in the round' (p.6). An implicit distinction is made between a 'concentration on the philosophically orientated aspects of Philo's work' and other 'aspects of Philonic studies', including 'his relation to Palestinian Judaism'. The implication is that these two areas have little to do with each other. In his review Rosenstock cast a searching beam of light on this aspect of the study. He agrees that the paucity of evidence on differing strands of Hellenistic Judaism makes further progress in this area difficult. But, he continues, 'almost no attention has been paid to the Rabbinic exegetic tradition for which our evidence is better preserved, though questions of chronology are considerable'.[15] I agree that there is more chance of progress in this area than in that of Hellenistic Judaism. Much research remains to be done on the possible connections, for example, between the material in the early chapters of Genesis Rabbah and earlier exegetical traditions, including those of Alexandria.[16] Obviously it will be advisable to try to

---

[12] If I had to reformulate my comments on Tobin's thesis, I would now use a less critical tone than I did in Appendix II (557–558), mainly on account of its further corroboration in Goulet's book.

[13] This is my chief quarrel with his thesis, as indicated in the review in *JThS* 1990 (reprinted in *Exegesis and Philosophy*, study VII). My impression is that this study has not been given the attention by Philonists that it deserves. Admittedly its immense amount of material is presented in such as way as to daunt all but the most persevering reader.

[14] Martín 139–140; cf. also Rosenstock 198.

[15] Rosenstock 199; the same point at Hay 493.

[16] An exceptional case is Rabbi Hosha'ia's image of the king and architect in the

avoid reinventing the wheel; starting point should be the studies of Bacher, Hegermann, Weiss and others. Two problems, however, will surely dog efforts in this direction. Firstly, as Rosenstock recognizes, the question of chronology continues to pose fundamental problems. Secondly there is the problem of whether we should consider that the Rabbis are 'doing philosophy'. If this question is already problematic with regard to Philo himself (see below, my fifth comment), what about other authors who stand at a much greater remove from the Greek philosophical tradition? Rosenstock illustrates the problem splendidly when he questions my assumption that Philo's reading of Genesis 1 in terms of a rational structure is 'peculiarly Greek and ... ultimately derived from the *Timaeus* (230)'. Can one not say that the presupposition of rationality is already present in the biblical author?[17] To this one might respond that the presupposition might be present, but that it is not articulated in a philosophical or 'scientific' way. One might add that Philo's philosophical training encouraged him to expand this basic assumption in a particular way. The attempt to read Gen. 1:14–19 and *Tim.* 38–40 through the eyes of a fictional contemporary reader (p.223) was a useful exercise, but the foundation on which these parallels were built could have been further thought through.

A further consideration might be that the *Sitz im Leben* furnished in the Introduction (pp.32–37) is too limited in its ambition. Philo's Alexandrian base is of course secure. For his relation to the Greek philosophical tradition that is by far the most important *datum*. But are there not further lines of enquiry possible with diaspora Judaism, particularly in relation to its 'home base'? I think particularly here of the possible relation of Philo to the Sadducee party, as suggested by Daniel Schwartz.[18]

A more complex question is that of Philo's relation to Gnosticism. Van der Horst in his brief review of the provisional edition pointed out a weakness in this area, namely that I had not made use of Alan Segal's classic study *Two Powers in Heaven*, available since 1977.[19] Consultation of this work would have allowed a more focused discussion of Philo's relation to incipient Gnosticism and to 'non-orthodox' Jewish thought.

---

commentary on Gen. 1:1, where a direct line to Philo via Origen is to my mind almost certain. See *Exegesis and Philosophy*, study III, with further references.

[17] Rosenstock 200.

[18] D. R. Schwartz, 'Philo's Priestly Descent', in F. E. Greenspahn, E. Hilgert and B. L. Mack (edd.), *Nourished with Peace: Studies in Hellenistic Judaism in Memory of Samuel Sandmel*, Scholars Press Homage Series 9 (Chico, California 1984) 155-171; see also the important analysis of the Jewish αἱρέσεις in Josephus recently given in S. N. Mason, *Flavius Josephus on the Pharisees: a Composition-critical Study*, SPB 39 (Leiden 1991).

[19] Van der Horst 247.

Segal puts forward a good case for the possibility of viewing Philo or thought like Philo's from the other side, i.e. from the predecessors of the Rabbinic movement. The brief remarks in Appendix II indicate lines of future research that have so far remained largely unexplored.

4. *The use of Middle Platonist evidence.* Most reviewers were pleased with the efforts to relate Philo to what we know about Middle Platonism, an area in which I unashamedly follow the paths already laid out by Theiler, Boyancé, Dörrie, and in particular John Dillon. But there is a dissenting voice, which in its remarks can draw on some exciting, if controversial, developments in the past few years. Martín points to a seemingly paradoxical aspect of my presentation of Philo and Middle Platonism, namely that most of the evidence that I use to locate Philo's interpretation of the *Timaeus* within the Middle Platonist ambit actually post-dates him.[20] This takes up the more general observation made by Radice on the way scholars, convinced of Philo's philosophical unoriginality, make use of the evidence he supplies:[21]

> What this amounts to is that Philo becomes his own source, inasmuch as his ideas, lent to others, are used to demonstrate his non-originality. This hermeneutic procedure is methodologically incorrect—in effect it tries to explain the anterior by the posterior—and above all unproductive in that it offers a large number of mutually incompatible explanations...

Both Martín and Radice are convinced that it is one-sided to see Philo as strongly influenced by Middle Platonism without considering that there may also have been movement in the other direction. Radice in his recent monograph has argued that the theory of the Ideas as thoughts of God was *devised* by Philo, from whom it was *taken over* by the Middle Platonists, commencing with the report in Seneca, *Ep.* 65. This makes him into an important *catalyst* in the process that led to the establishment of the Middle Platonist school.[22] If this were true, then the use of 2nd century Platonists to shed light on Philo would indeed be culpable. One is strongly reminded of the controversy engendered by Wolfson's view that Philo was the originator of the doctrine of the unknowability of God. Here Philo certainly makes claim to being the first witness.[23] As I

---

[20] Martín 141–142.
[21] R. Radice, 'Observations on the Theory of the Ideas as the Thoughts of God in Philo of Alexandria', in D. T. Runia, D. M. Hay and D. Winston (edd.), *Heirs of the Septuagint. Philo, Hellenistic Judaism and Early Christianity: Festschrift for Earle Hilgert*, BJS 230 [= *The Studia Philonica Annual* 3 (1991)] (Atlanta 1991) 128.
[22] *Ibid.* 133.
[23] As recognized by J. Dillon, *The Middle Platonists: a Study of Platonism 80 B.C. to A.D. 220* (London 1977) 155. The counter-example usually cited, Cicero *DND* 1.30, is not strong; although it refers to Plato, it comes from a non-Platonist source, and may be intended in a

have formulated it elsewhere, the question is whether Philo is 'witness or participant' in the Platonist tradition.[24] The danger must be recognized of a *petitio principii*, i.e. assuming rather than proving that Philo cannot be a participant in the development of Platonism. I shall briefly return to this issue in the second half of this paper. At this point, however, it is worth pointing out that we are not entirely helpless when it comes to gaining glimpses of early Middle Platonism and reconstructing connections between that Platonism and the better attested (and more fully developed) later form in the 2nd century. Take, for example, the table illustrating the terminology used for the concept of the intelligible world on p.160. Of the eight witnesses invoked as 'Middle Platonists', four are probably earlier than or approximately contemporary with Philo (Arius Didymus, Timaeus Locrus, Diogenes Laertius' *Vita Platonis*, Aëtius). The remaining four (Albinus—or as I now prefer, Alcinous—, Hippolytus' doxography on Plato, Nicomachus, Atticus) are probably to be dated to the 2nd century, but only the last-named *has to be* dated in its second half; for the other three a late 1st century date is far from impossible.[25] On p.501 I express some dissatisfaction at my inability to 'uncover the clear lines of influence and dependence which the *Quellenforscher* aims to find'. This attitude was, I now believe, a mistake. In a situation where there was a broad scholastic tradition resulting an amorphous but easily recognizable 'vulgate', it is illusory to think that such clear lines can be found. They may indeed never have existed.

Martín further remarks that, if 2nd century Middle Platonists are used to shed light on Philo, why not adduce early Christian authors from the same period?[26] I believe that this was done more than the reviewer gives me credit for (see the *index locorum*). But the relation between Philo's Platonism and that of the early Christian fathers is really the subject of a further study. The final sentence of the entire book was intended to be programmatic.[27]

---

polemical rather than a technical sense.
[24] 'Witness or Participant? Philo and the Neoplatonic Tradition', in A. Vanderjagt and D. Pätzold (edd.), *The Neoplatonic Tradition: Jewish, Christian and Islamic Themes*, Dialectica Minora 3 (Köln 1991) 36–56.
[25] Cf. J. Whittaker's attempt to date Alcinous in his recent edition (Paris 1990) xii–xiii, where he leaves a date earlier than the 2nd century open as a possibility. J. Mansfeld, *Heresiography in Context: Hippolytus' Elenchos as a Source for Greek Philosophy* Philosophia Antiqua 56 (Leiden 1992) 3, rightly regards the Hippolytan text as related to the 'Middle Platonist vulgate', but this need not entail a late date.
[26] Martín 141.
[27] See now *Philo and Early Christian Literature: a Survey*, CRINT III 3 (Assen-Minneapolis 1993).

5. *Is Philo to be regarded as a philosopher?* Although there is a long tradition of regarding Philo as a philosopher, I did not think this was a position that could simply be *assumed*. One of the challenges of the investigation was to keep a relatively open mind on the issue—if this is being 'positivistic', then so be it—and see what the outcome was. Many reviewers noted a marked preference for the view of Nikiprowetzky that Philo should primarily be seen as an exegete rather than a philosopher.[28] For Rosenstock the French scholar was the 'hero of the book'. Joly in contrast considers Nikiprowetzky's emphasis on Philo as exegete of the Law to be a simplification of Philonic thought. He thought that I stayed too close to my teacher, although I did show more awareness of the complexity of the material and the importance of Hellenism in Philo's thought. This comment overlooks the pages where I take issue with Nikiprowetzky's thesis and attempt to modify it in such a way as to do more justice to the profound impact of the basic assumptions of Greek philosophy on Philo's thought (p.538–542). Other reviewers did note these revisionary pages. Nevertheless in retrospect I wonder whether I did not underline my indebtedness to the views of my teacher in stronger tones than was prudent, especially on p.536, where I claim that 'it is ... the interpretation of Philo's achievement put forward by Nikiprowetzky in his magisterial study that has been corroborated by the results of our particular area of research'.

On the other hand it might be asked whether Nikiprowetzky's position has been fully understood by all concerned. His aim was certainly not to downplay the philosophical element in Philo's thought, which was in fact his main interest. He rather wished to overcome the antithesis between Philo the Jew and Philo the Greek philosopher, which in his view had had a debilitating effect on Philonic research.[29] I cannot entirely agree with Dillon's portrayal of his position when he observes:[30]

> He would see Philo, not primarily as a philosopher, *but rather as* an exegete, who *used* Greek philosophy as it suited him, but did not adopt any consistent philosophical stance. The force of such an antithesis entirely escapes me. How can one become an exegete in an intellectual vacuum? What stimulus would prompt one to such an activity? Obviously, Philo is constrained by the nature of his source-material, as anyone must be who decides to do philosophy through the medium of commentary (the Neoplatonists are under just the same constraint, both in commenting on Plato,

---

[28] See Lefèvre 207, Solignac 476, Joly 364, Rosenstock 195, Hay 491, Dillon 195, Winston 223. Radice's review article (1984) places my study in the 'scuola' of Nikiprowetzky!
[29] See esp. the posthumous article, 'Thèmes et traditions de la lumière chez Philon d'Alexandrie', *SPhA* 1 (1989) 6-33.
[30] In a most interesting review of C. Kraus Reggiani, G. Reale and R. Radice's *La filosofia mosaica* in *SPhA* 2 (1990) 177–182, quote on 179.

and, more acutely, in commenting on Aristotle), but this merely exercises his ingenuity, calling for tactical variations in his basic philosophical position, not vacillation or incoherence... (his emphases)

It is readily to be granted that Nikiprowetzky does place the brunt of his emphasis on Philo's role as exegete. But the distinction made *between* an exegete and a philosopher seems to me to go just that little bit too far. I think that Nikiprowetzky would be ready to subscribe to my description of Philo as 'philosophically orientated exegete' (p.545). The attractiveness of his emphasis on Philo's exegetical approach is twofold. It makes greater allowance for the *contextuality* of individual passages. Philo is not prepared to constrain every text into the Procrustean bed of a 'coherent intellectual system' (Dillon's phrase[31]). It explains how the interpreter can regard himself as subordinate to the authority of the text. Such subordination need not entail 'vacillation or incoherence' (Dillon's terms again), but does explain how it happens that the interpreter does not claim the last word on the subject. It is worth considering whether there is a difference here between Philo's practice and that of commentators in the various Greek scholastic traditions.

My conclusion was, therefore, that Philo is to be regarded as a 'philosophically orientated exegete'. How persuasive and how attractive is this view? Emerton concluded that the result of the book's investigations is 'a more convincing exposition of Philo's thought than most writers manage to achieve'.[32] Lee's reaction is more complex. Because of the inherent interest and relative inaccessibility of this highly intelligent and insightful review, it will be worth citing a few passages at some length. In response to the final evaluative section he writes (I leave out or shorten some of the asides):[33]

> Runia wants to rescue Philo from what he sees as inflated speculative interpretations that would discover in him the building of a Philonic 'System' (Wolfson) or the workings of a mystical philosophy involving the doctrines of eternal creation (Winston...). Yet he is not happy, either, with Philo as merely an eclectic compiler of Platonic parallels, and does not see his own project as a mere description of such parallels. Somewhat caught between two stools, he remains eager to defend Philo 'as a *philosopher* in his own right' (543–5) — though, on his own showing, I believe, Philo doesn't turn out to be *much* of one... The picture of a rather conservative, non-speculative, non-mystical Philo is a reasonably plausible, if rather uninspiring, one...
>
> For readers of this journal, a special interest will attach to the discussion of Philo as 'a philosopher in his own right' (543). It is no doubt understandable that 'Philo's primary allegiance was not to Pythagoras and Plato, but to the lawgiver Moses' (22),

---

[31] *Ibid.* 178.
[32] Emerton 499.
[33] Lee 418–421.

as well as that the 'Mosaic commentator must, it appears, reserve his attention for more pressing subjects' (455) — 'more pressing', that is, than sundry philosophy topics like the epistemological distinction between knowledge and belief, ontological issues like the precise status of nature of 'matter', or difficult metaphysical matters like Plato's odd and obscure account of the creation of, and nature of, the soul. My own impression, I must say, is that with regard to any philosophical question in Plato's *Timaeus* that one might pursue, Philo has nothing innovative nor even very interesting to say. No doubt that fact [I thought it was an impression, DTR] in part results from the particular rhetorical, political or literary concerns of his treatises, but I suspect it is as much an accurate indicator of his generally dogmatic, non-aporetic cast of mind. A fuller comparison with St. Augustine's Biblical exegesis would be instructive here and it is regrettable, I think, that the book shows such limited acquaintance with Augustine... Augustine of course had the advantage over Philo of having access to a later, more mature and probing form of Platonism than the sort that Philo had available, but Augustine's exegeses are by no means merely a matter of culling convenient parallels from Neoplatonic sources. A large part of Augustine's writing toils through the process of considering and *rejecting* interpretations that, as he believes (and argues!), will *not* work, making him labor to bring forth a philosophically, as well as doctrinally, satisfying understanding. ('*Fides quaerens intellectum*' turns out to involve a lot of analytical and argumentative *work*.) Philo, by contrast, seems content to present what he feels to be sufficiently parallel doctrines as the allegorical meaning of Scriptural texts, but shows very little of the Augustinian 'labor of thought'. That is a limitation the author might usefully have recognized, and his failure to do so shows some severe limitations in his own conception of 'philosophy'. He notes on p.222 that Philo never offers any 'substantial and penetrating discussions on the nature of time, nothing even remotely resembling Augustine's reflections in Book XI of the *Confessions*,' yet he feels unnecessarily compelled to go on and defend his subject author from any negative implication of this fact; 'on the other hand it is unwarranted to conclude that Philo has never taken the trouble to think through the question of what time is, for in that case the consistent views which emerged in our analysis could not be explained.' But they *could*, of course, be explained merely by Philo's having not-very-reflectively taken over his views on time from the established, and at least reasonably consistent, tradition of the *Timaeus*. Many minor or derivative philosophical minds work in just that manner and, for this reviewer, Runia's Philo emerges as just such a mind. It is no disgrace, after all, to be a lesser philosopher than the greatest ones in our history, but it is important, I believe, for those who write about them to recognize the difference: where one's subject-author suffers by comparison with some other, it seems more useful to explore that comparison so as to recognize a limitation or to define a difference than to defend against taking it seriously. Philo was no doubt a figure with enormous, even world-historical importance for the Alexandrian strategy of negotiating a rapprochement between pagan philosophy and the Judaic (or Judaeo-Christian) tradition. Surely that is enough. Runia's view that we should also see him as a 'philosopher in his own right' does not seem to me to be a defensible verdict.

It will be agreed that these remarks are of enormous interest for anyone wishing to reflect on Philo's status as a philosopher, and raise far more issues than it would wise to discuss in this context. I do feel compelled, however, to respond to the *ad hominem* character of some of the remarks. The upshot of Lee's evaluation seems to be that he is in basic agreement with my portrait of Philo, but finds it uninspiring, and so disagrees with my attempt nevertheless to present Philo as a serious philosopher, which shows a lack of insight into what philosophy really is. Lee, as is evident from the tenor of the entire piece, is an eminent exponent of the (Vlastossian) method which attempts—often with great success—to apply the techniques of modern analytical philosophy to giants of the ancient past. Augustine (virtually alone among all the Church Fathers, I suspect) gets a good press among such philosophers.[34] I respect this method, but it differs from my own background in the continental tradition. Moreover it is incumbent on the analytic philosopher, no less than anyone else, to read the text in front of him carefully. I do *not* defend the position that Philo is 'a philosopher in his own right', but rather *pose the question* as to whether this is the case. Once again one might comment that my position is too nuanced for my own good. However this may be, the response was: from Philo's own viewpoint the answer is in the affirmative, but from *our* viewpoint we must have misgivings, which on further examination brought me to the conclusion that Philo is a 'philosophically orientated exegete'. Indeed the problem that Lee raises about Philo's lack of argument troubled me all the way through my research. It is a fundamental problem that must confront everyone who turns to Philo for philosophical illumination. Rather than pursue this question further in the general terms set out by Lee, I would prefer now to turn to the more specific topic to be dealt with in the second half of this paper: are we justified in regarding Philo as a Middle Platonist? The connection is obvious. No one doubts that the Middle Platonists were philosophers, though in some quarters it has been felt that they too were not very good ones. What we have to ask ourselves is whether Philo should be regarded as one of their number.

---

[34] Cf. the recent study in the series The Arguments of the Philosophers by C. Kirwan, *Augustine* (London 1989), who writes in his preface (vii): 'The excuse for this book is rather that it observes Augustine from a stance outside that Christian theological tradition, the stance of an analytic philosopher, who happens also to be an atheist (though that should make little difference)...'

II

It was certainly the case that when I was preparing my study the issue of whether Philo should be called a Middle Platonist or not had a certain topicality. This was mainly the result of the excellent research that had just been done by Dillon and Winston. They had for the first time managed to persuade a large number of scholars that Philo's thought was basically Platonist in its orientation. Due to their efforts the view that Philo's philosophical perspective was primarily Stoic, or a Platonizing form of Stoicism, was most definitely on the retreat. It would, however, have been premature to pronounce it dead. Given the subject of my thesis, the issue of Philo's Platonism had to be tackled head on.

This I did in the third chapter of the 'synthetic' part of my study, in which I look at the sources of Philo's use of the *Timaeus*. Various influences were examined at some length, notably the Academy, Aristotelianism, Stoicism, and finally Middle Platonism. An aspect to be borne in mind here is that the background of the discussion was first of all the use of the *Timaeus* in Philo's cosmology, theology and anthropology. There was a risk here of which I was aware, namely that from this particular perspective the Platonist background was going to loom larger than it might otherwise do. In spite of this awareness, however, the conclusion was unavoidable, namely that the Platonist influence delineated in the study was very strong indeed. For this reason the final section of the chapter (§5, pp. 505-519) was devoted to the question which I used as its title: is Philo a Middle Platonist? Four considerations were outlined which pointed towards a negative answer:

(a) Philo does not show any particular *loyalty* towards Plato or his doctrines; this is reserved for Moses and 'Mosaic philosophy'.

(b) In his *technique of philosophical explanation* Philo differs from Middle Platonist counterparts such as Plutarch and Alcinous, most strikingly in the fact that he declines to give clear answers to some of the standard scholastic controversies.

(c) Various *doctrinal divergences* indicate Philo's independence of mind if his views are compared with those of Middle Platonist authors;

(d) Philo reveals a *different set of priorities* and reveals a *different direction in his interests* compared with the Middle Platonists that we know.

My final conclusion was double-edged. On the one hand I argued that 'the profound influence of Plato's writings and their interpretative tradition must be recognized for what it is, a pillar of Philo's thought which, if removed, would cause the whole edifice to totter and collapse' (p.518).

On the other hand it would be wrong to conclude from this that Philo *himself* is a Platonist, the reason being that 'he is doing his own thing' (p.519), i.e. constructing a Mosaic philosophy. It is this conclusion which will have to be reviewed in the remainder of this paper.

It will be helpful, it seems to me, to start our discussion with a *typology*. Theoretically there are a number of positions that one can take on the issue of how one wishes to evaluate Philo's relation to contemporary currents of Greek philosophy. For the sake of illustration I take the following six:
(1) that Philo is a *de iure* Middle Platonist, i.e. belongs to the school or αἵρεσις in the manner of a Plutarch or an Albinus;
(2) that Philo is a *de facto* Middle Platonist, i.e. does not belong to the school, but has a philosophical stance which is fundamentally Platonist and might well make him welcome in such circles;
(3) that Philo is a Platonizing expositor of scripture, showing a marked preference for using Middle Platonist doctrines in his exegesis;
(4) that Philo is an eclectic philosophical expositor of scripture, who appropriates various school doctrines as it suits his exegetical purposes;
(5) that Philo is an independent philosopher who argues with and against the great Greek philosophers from a fundamentally Jewish viewpoint;
(6) that Philo is a Jewish religious thinker, who does not understand philosophy very well, and uses philosophical doctrines of various kinds exclusively for apologetic purposes.
Needless to say this typology should not be taken too seriously. On reading the list insiders will have had their suspicions about which familiar names might lurk behind the various positions. Let us elucidate the typology a little further by means of some explanatory comments.

Ad (1). This view is purely theoretical, for no one would wish to subscribe to it. Philo may have had contact with a Middle Platonist 'school' or group in Alexandria—about such things we know nothing—but was surely not a member in the active sense.[35] It does raise the question, however, of how important matters of school or αἵρεσις are in Philo's situation, to which I shall return directly.

Ad (2). This is approximately the view of Winston (with of course allowance for Philo's Jewish situation). In my study I associated both Winston and Dillon with this point of view. But here there is an impor-

---

[35] Scholars have often postulated that Philo's career may have run parallel to that of Justin Martyr, i.e. that he was first a Platonist and then *converted* to Judaism. There is no evidence for this. An essential difference is that Justin was born a pagan, Philo a Jew.

tant rectification I have to make. The section on Dillon's view in the *status quaestionis* was headed 'Philo as a Middle Platonist' (p.20). Although I almost immediately pointed out that Dillon does not actually call Philo a Middle Platonist in so many words, when I summarized my results on p.519 I reiterated 'his thesis that Philo is a Middle Platonist' and pronounced that it was 'in the final analysis unconvincing'. Dillon was quite right to protest against this portrayal in his review. Indeed he argues that in our basic position we are 'in fact in agreement'.[36]

Ad (3). This is approximately the view which I defended in my study, and with which Dillon wishes to be associated. We recall, however, the risk noted above, that the concentration on the *Timaeus* may lead one to overestimate the importance of the Platonist component.

Ad (4). This is approximately the viewpoint of Nikiprowetzky, as formulated in his view that Philo uses philosophy as 'a language of reason' for the purposes of commenting on scripture. The key term here is 'eclectic', but it is not necessarily meant in a negative sense.

Ad (5). Wolfson's position will be immediately recognized here. Criticism must be directed both at his notion of Jewish philosophy and at his 'timeless' portrait of Philo, entirely divorced from the contemporary philosophical scene (including Middle Platonists). Impressive though Wolfson's portrait is, few will be prepared to defend it as he presented it.

Ad (6). I have in mind something like Völker's view, and also scholars of Greek philosophy such as Dodds who find Philo simply incompetent. But Philo's stocks have risen during the past decades. Most of those who have taken the trouble to read Philo carefully have rejected this position, as was even the case for Lee in the long quote cited above.

My conclusion is that in this typological spectrum from Greek philosopher to Jewish religious apologist, it is above all positions (2), (3) and (4) that demand our attention. I turn now to a number of issues that may clarify the situation further.

1. *The question of loyalty.* In my argument denying that Philo should be called a Middle Platonist the notion of *loyalty* played a central role. The discussion was not, however, in all respects satisfactory. To start with, the notion of loyalty was presented in terms that were too vague. Philo's loyalty to the Jewish community and the Jewish religion is unquestioned. But I overlooked the fact that also in terms of the organization of Greek philosophy loyalty is an important factor. As John Glucker has shown, by the time of Philo philosophers for the most part

---

[36] Dillon 659. We note that the same position as Dillon is taken by P. L. Donini in hi excellent handbook on the period from Antiochus to Plotinus, *Le scuole l'anima l'imperc la filosofica antica da Antioco a Plotino* (Turin 1982) 101.

did not belong to schools in the *institutional* sense, but rather were *affiliated* to a particular αἵρεσις. The term affiliation he chooses deliberately because it denotes 'a free adoption into a society of a member who is thereafter free to end his membership or 'change his affiliation''.[37] He does consider another term, 'allegiance', which he finds too medieval and does not stress the aspect of free choice as well. Semantically we are close to the notion of loyalty. There are a number of indications that Philo regards 'Mosaic philosophy' or groups of its practitioners as a kind of αἵρεσις, even if he does not use the term as freely as Josephus does.[38] A telling text here is his description of the Therapeutae as having τῆς αἱρέσεως ἀρχηγέται ('leaders of the school') who have shown them the way in allegorical exegesis (*Contempl.* 29).[39] I believe that Philo quite deliberately presents his philosophy of Moses in such a way that it is parallel to Greek 'schools' or αἱρέσεις. If this is the case, there can be no question of allegiance to more than one school of thought at a time. As Glucker emphasizes, one is by definition a devotee, but can change one's affiliation.

There are, however, other aspects to do with loyalty that have to be taken into consideration. A possibility that I failed to take into account in my thesis was that one can also demonstrate loyalty in a *subversive* way, whether this be judged as such by others from the outside or by oneself. Philo's apologetic motives have been universally recognized. But it is possible to conclude that he was defending Judaism in a way that undermined its own identity. This was clearly the conclusion of the later Rabbis, who condemned him to silence. They will have thought that he professes loyalty to Moses and Judaism, but his real allegiance is to Greek philosophy and Platonism in particular. The further question immediately follows: how can *we* reach a judgment on this issue? what can we use as a standard of reference? I am not sure that an appeal to a *normative* view of Judaism (as employed by the Rabbis, for example) will work very easily here. More fruitful might be a conception of a *biblical* (or Judaeo-Christian) tradition which differs in fundamental ways from Greek thought. I shall return to this suggestion in our case-study below. The other possibility is that *Philo himself* was aware of the subversive na-

---

[37] J. Glucker, 'Cicero's Philosophical Affiliations', in J. M. Dillon and A. A. Long (edd.), *The Question of "Eclecticism"* (Berkeley 1988) 34–69, quote at 34; cf. also his *Antiochus and the Late Academy*, Hypomnemata 56 (Göttingen 1978) 174–185.
[38] I hope to return to this subject elsewhere, but cf. already A. Le Boulluec, *La notion d'hérésie dans la littérature grecque IIe-IIIe siècles*, 2 vols. (Paris 1985) 37–38; the remarks on Josephus by Mason, *op cit.* (n. 18) at 125–128 are somewhat disappointing.
[39] Note also the way Philo frequently speaks of the γνώριμοι or θιασῶται or φοιτηταί of Moses.

ture of his activity as a commentator of Moses who draws on the tradition of Greek philosophy.[40] I myself consider this view unlikely. One of my reasons is that I do not think that Philo deliberately sets out to reconcile Judaism and Greek thought, but rather discerns fundamental Greek philosophical assumptions within scripture itself. One might also ask whether such a strategy is compatible with the notion of belonging to a 'school of thought', as outlined above. To delve further into these issues, however, would take me beyond the scope of the present paper.

What then about the other side of the coin? Does Philo show any form of loyalty to the Greek philosopher Plato? I thought not: great respect and a recognition of indebtedness certainly, but not loyalty. Winston in his review takes issue with this conclusion: 'what greater devotion and loyalty could Philo show towards his beloved Plato than to read his Platonic convictions into the Mosaic Torah?'[41] In response one might appeal to the way that Philo refers to Plato—often anonymously—, which does not differ from the way he treats other Greek philosophers whom he esteems (except perhaps that the references to Plato are greater in number). But such a response cannot settle the matter, because the issues involved go deeper than the surface of the text. We need to move on.

2. *Scripture and the status of the scriptural commentary*. Just as the Middle Platonists produced extensive commentaries on Plato's writings, so Philo wrote his lengthy sequence of treatises commenting on the books of Moses. *Prima facie* this is a strong argument for not identifying Philo with the Platonists, but rather for seeing them as engaged in parallel activities. Again Winston strongly disagrees with such a conclusion: 'The key to gauging Philo's true intentions lies in the peculiar nature of his exegesis, namely, its midrashic/allegorical character.' Citing P. S. Alexander he argues that midrash is as much a means of imposing ideas upon scripture as deriving ideas from scripture. Right throughout Jewish tradition it has been regarded as legitimate to align 'non-biblical' ideas with the sacred text. It is therefore 'not difficult to see why Philo would wish to read his Platonist views into the Biblical text and thus achieve his goal of preserving his ancestral tradition while yet filling it with a new content... Since in the Judaism of his day it was not systematic exposition, but the commentary that was the legitimate form

---

[40] This is the view to which David Winston inclines, although the term 'subversive' is certainly stronger than he would use. Cf. his comparison of Philo with Spinoza in *Philo of Alexandria: The Contemplative Life, The Giants and Selections*, The Classics of Western Spirituality (New York-Toronto 1981) 36, and his conclusion in 'Judaism and Hellenism: Hidden Tensions in Philo's Thought', *SPhA* 2 (1990) 19.
[41] Winston 223.

through which the truth could be developed, he [Philo] chose to Platonize his Jewish heritage through the medium of Biblical commentary.'[42] Winston is right to conclude that there is a fundamental difference of opinion here. It is clear that he regards the form of the commentary as *extrinsic*—or even an impediment—to Philo's aims, imposed on him by his cultural context. I regarded Philo's use of the exegetical method as *intrinsic* to his own conception of his role. In both cases scripture is regarded as an *authoritative* text, but in significantly different ways. Winston emphasizes that in Jewish tradition scripture is God-given, but the midrashists are well aware that they are developing interpretations that go well beyond the literal text (cf. the story of Moses and Rabbi Akiva which he cites). In my view Philo too regards scripture as God-given, but above all as revealed to 'God's friend', the prophet Moses. The task of the commentator is to attempt to extricate the revealed truth, which he can never do in more than a partial and incomplete way. If Platonic doctrines are used to explicate the text by means of the commentary, that is because they are regarded as *inherent* in that text.[43] Paradoxically, perhaps, this conception of Moses as lawgiver and philosopher *par excellence* is in fact strongly influenced by Hellenistic conceptions of the role of the philosopher and of tradition. The fundamental assumption is the 'proof from antiquity', in which Moses is presented as superior to both later Greek philosophers *and* the 'modern' commentator.[44] For Philo non-literal interpretation is *explication of* the text, not *imposition on* the text, no matter how we may wish to view it.

3. *Self-definition versus historical perspective*. At this point the reader may wish to interrupt and say to me: in your arguments on allegiance and foundations of thought, and on extrinsic and intrinsic views of the role of commentary you are in fact talking at cross-purposes. It is above all a matter of *perspective*. The view that Philo is not a Middle Platonist but a Platonizing exegete of scripture represents above all *Philo's* view of himself, or his 'self-definition', to use a term much in vogue during the past decade. The view that the foundations of Philo's thought are Middle Platonist, so that he deserves to be given that epithet, is the way that the

---

[42] Winston 224–225.
[43] This view has been strengthened by the monograph on Philo's view of the inspiration of scripture by H. Burkhardt cited above at n. 4. Winston's own important interpretation of the role of Moses in 'Two Types of Mosaic Prophecy according to Philo', *JSP* 4 (1989) 49-67, to my mind does not exclude this interpretation.
[44] On this subject the remarks in my study have been refined and supplemented in P. Pilhofer, *Presbyteron kreitton: Der Alterbeweis der jüdischen und christlichen Apologeten und seine Vorgeschichte*, WUNT 2.39 (Tübingen 1990) 173-192. I would dispute, however, the claim that Philo's remarks at *Sacr.* 76–79 undermine the entire argument.

matter appears to *us* when looked at from our modern, historical perspective. When you distinguish between Platonism as an indispensable pillar of Philo's thought but refuse to allow him the title of Middle Platonist, you are trying to have it both ways, without making the necessary distinction outlined above.

It seems to me that there is certainly an element of truth in this response. Certainly the distinction envisaged might have added clarity to the discussion. But it would not have altered my view. I still maintain that it is more helpful to describe Philo as a 'Platonizing devotee of Mosaic scripture' than a 'Middle Platonist' *tout court*. Platonism provides Philo with fundamental convictions in his philosophical views, for example in his doctrine of two worlds, and in how creation should be understood. Other convictions are broader, above all his appropriation of the central role of rationality, which can be said to be fundamental to the entire Greek philosophical tradition. But not enough of Philo's thought is covered in this way. Other facets, such as his views on God's transcendence and relation to man, and his views on man's relation to man, are strongly controlled by Jewish or biblical convictions. If we take the standard dichotomy between Philo the Greek and Philo the Jew, which since Nikiprowetzky most students of Philo try to overcome, we might think of the image of an *ellipse*, where the path traced out is always tied to *both* poles, no matter how close it comes to the side of one or other of them. This one might illustrate with the following diagram:

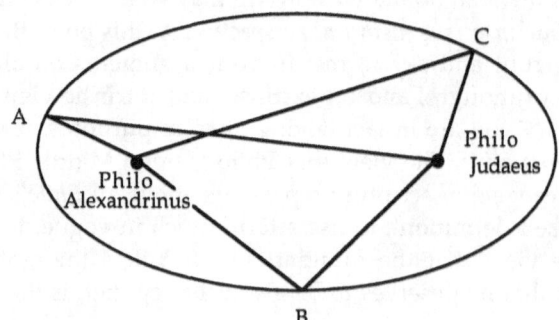

The Philonic Ellipse

A: Philo at his 'most Greek', e.g. in the doctrine of the κόσμος νοητός
B: Philo with both Greek and Jewish elements, e.g. in his presentation of Moses as prophet
C: Philo with a Jewish slant, e.g. his view of God's 'personal' relation to his people

If we say that Philo is a Middle Platonist, one of the poles to my mind becomes regrettably obscured.

4. *The question of eclecticism.* There remains the fine but real distinction between positions (3) and (4) in our typology. In my study I addressed the question of eclecticism at various stages, but most pointedly at p. 519. Here too it is possible to advance the discussion. I wrote:

> There is clearly a consistent rational behind his [Philo's] procedure. It resembles the procedure of the Middle Platonists, but is not wholly the same. For Philo is explaining the words of Moses and owes no particular loyalty to the teachings of Plato. If an Aristotelian or Stoic doctrine is useful in illuminating the intentions of Moses he will not reject it simply because it is not Platonic.

This could be argued much more clearly. As is well known, the Middle Platonists too would not reject an Aristotelian or Stoic doctrine if it was useful in illuminating the intentions of Plato. For this reason doctrines such as the ten categories and the theology of the unmoved mover are attributed to Plato, because they are seen to explicate views that are already present in the Platonic dialogues. Dillon has reasoned successfully that one should be careful in arguing that this is 'eclecticism'.[45] My remark would have had much more point if I had asked whether Philo would have adopted Aristotelian or Stoic doctrines that are not only not Platonic, but are *incompatible with* Platonist views. This is a move that Platonists obviously would not make. What about Philo? It is clear from Philo's exegetical practice that he has no compunctions on this score.

Discussion on the problem of eclecticism received an important stimulus through the collection of papers published by Dillon and Long in 1988. Philo's practice is analysed by Mansfeld in an intelligent and informative article. Of particular interest is a thought experiment that he puts forward. Having stated that he does not wish to disagree with the modern consensus that 'much of Philo's philosophizing reflects the re-interpretative system of his so-called Middle Platonist contemporaries', he goes on to add:[46]

> However, there are other works which cannot, by any stretching of the term, be called Middle Platonist. For instance, if his only surviving works were *Quod omnis probus liber* and *De animalibus*, would we not say that 'if he had made a few little changes', Philo could be designated a 'most genuine Stoic', even more so, perhaps, than Antiochus, for whom the sobriquet was coined by Cicero (*Acad.* 2.132)... It may therefore be of some importance to point out that Philo's contemporary and fellow-Alexandrian, Chaeremon, who was a notorious enemy of the Jews, was a Stoic. Chaeremon interpreted Egyptian religion in the terms of Greek philosophy, just as Philo did for the Jewish religion...

---

[45] Dillon, *op. cit.* (n. 28) xiv–xv and *passim*.
[46] J. Mansfeld, 'Philosophy in the service of scripture: Philo's exegetical strategies', in Dillon and Long, *op. cit.* (n. 37) 70-102, quote on 76–77.

Mansfeld only mentions two works. Others might be added, most notably the fragment *De Deo*, which has a pronounced Stoicizing slant.[47] In his paper Mansfeld is able to advance the position of Nikiprowetzky, to which he refers with approval, by examining the 'sceptical' aspect of Philo's thought. Philo uses the sceptical method of balancing opinions of the philosophers, but unlike the Sceptics he believes that the scales should be tipped. 'With the backing of the books of Moses and supported by the religious traditions of his people which are grounded in these books, the studious exegete is in a position to lord it over the Greek philosophers.'[48] This, as Mansfeld further observes, inevitably will make an eclectic impression. Inasmuch as we find, however, that the scales are consistently (though not exclusively) tipped in favour of Platonic rather than other doctrines, we may be justified in adopting position (3) rather than (4) in our typology, even if the distinction between them remains, as I said above, rather fine.

5. *A historical case-study*.[49] The example of Chaeremon that Mansfeld cites as a parallel to Philo is worth pursuing a little further (even if not all aspects can be discussed).[50] Chaeremon is explicitly called a 'Stoic' or a 'Stoic philosopher' in a number of sources.[51] Two testimonia in the *Souda* assign him a place among professional philosophers in Alexandria, where he is said to have had a pupil who became his successor.[52] He wrote a book *On Comets* (probably with astrological rather than scientific emphasis), and most likely also a work on grammatical aspects of logic.[53] On the other hand, he was also well-known as an Egyptian priest who wrote a book or books on Egyptian history and culture, in which Egyptian tradition was presented as ancient wisdom and the hieroglyphics were interpreted in terms of philosophical allegory.[54] Chaeremon's theological and religious concerns are evident. As Frede

---

[47] As emerges in the recent full study of the work, F. Siegert, *Philon von Alexandrien Über die Gottebezeichnung "wohltätig verzehrendes Feuer" (De Deo): Rückübersetzung des Fragments aus dem Armenischen, deutsche Übersetzung und Kommentar*, WUNT 46 (Tübingen 1988), esp. 2.
[48] *Ibid.* 102. Pilhofer in an interesting comparison with Cicero, *op. cit.* (n.44) 191f., notes Philo's sense of superiority.
[49] On this subject see further the discussion in Sterling's paper above. Remarkably the two accounts were drafted completely independently of each other.
[50] Testimonia and fragments collected in P. W. van der Horst, *Chaeremon, Egyptian Priest and Stoic Philosopher*, EPRO 101 (Leiden 1984); philosophical aspects recently discussed at length by M. Frede, 'Chaeremon', *ANRW* 36.3 (Berlin-New York 1989) 2067–2103.
[51] Test. 9–10, fr. 3, 10–11, 14.
[52] Test. 3–4.
[53] Fr. 3, 14.
[54] Fr. 5–12.

points out,⁵⁵ he appears to anticipate trends to be found among later Platonists, who showed a modest interest in him. But Porphyry explicitly informs us that Chaeremon refused to accept any form of incorporeal being, and interpreted Egyptian theology wholly in terms of physical existents such as the celestial beings.⁵⁶

Can Philo be called a Platonist in the way that Chaeremon is called a Stoic? None of the sources speaks of Philo as ὁ Πλατωνικός.⁵⁷ But our second earliest witness, Clement of Alexandria, twice speaks of him as ὁ Πυθαγόρειος.⁵⁸ The description is puzzling. On what is it based? Surely it is not meant as an assertion that Philo belongs to the Pythagorean αἵρεσις. Nor does Philo show a particular partiality for Pythagorean above Platonist doctrines. I wonder whether it may be the result of Clement's observation that Philo makes such extensive use of arithmological doctrine in his exegesis.⁵⁹ But this is purely speculative. In his biographical sketch of Philo Eusebius introduces him as distinguished in both sacred and profane learning. The latter aspect is expanded in the statement that Philo 'showed zeal for the Platonic and Pythagorean school of thought'.⁶⁰ It seems to me that the Christian schema of the two types of learning is already making its presence felt here. There are two further differences between the two men. Philo does not write books on as technical matters as grammatical aspects of logic.⁶¹ Philo is not described as belonging to the 'professional philosophical establishment'. Although other parallels involving the apologetic use of the notion of ancient wisdom and of the allegorical method are strong, I conclude that Philo is not a Platonist in the way that Chaeremon was a Stoic. Later sources recognize his interest in and knowledge of Platonism, but fall short of identifying him with the Platonist school (of thought).

---

⁵⁵ *Art. cit.* 2103.
⁵⁶ Fr. 5.
⁵⁷ We cannot be sure that Philo could have been called this in his contemporary situation, since the epithet does not appear until the end of the 1st century in our evidence, as I show in a brief note at ZPE 72 (1988) 241–243.
⁵⁸ *Str.* 1.72.4, 2.100.3 (texts at C-W 1.lxxxvff.). I have found remarkably little discussion of this epithet. In her recent study on Clement's use of Philo A. van den Hoek makes no effort to explain it; cf. *Clement of Alexandria and his Use of Philo in the Stromateis: an Early Christian Reshaping of a Jewish Model*, VChr.S 3 (Leiden 1988) 179, 184.
⁵⁹ Especially in the *Quaestiones*, which Clement knew very well.
⁶⁰ HE 2.4.3, ὅτε μάλιστα τὴν κατὰ Πλάτωνα καὶ Πυθαγόραν ἐζηλωκὼς ἀγωγήν. For the meaning of the term ἀγωγή cf. Glucker, *op. cit.* (n. 37) 191, 196f., who argues that its place is usurped by αἵρεσις. A little later Eusebius uses the same word in the more common sense of 'way of life' (2.16.2). Is he following an earlier source in the previous passage?
⁶¹ Philo's most 'technical' works are his philosophical treatises. But, as has often been noted, these works too are not divorced from the concerns that predominate in his exegetical works.

6. *A doctrinal case study.* This paper has been long on general discussion and short on specific analysis of doctrine and philosophical argument. I no longer have the space to rectify this shortcoming, but can at least present one theme which may illustrate these issues raised so far. A first subject that springs to mind is the contentious issue of Philo's conception of creation, and whether it should be interpreted as *creatio aeterna* or *creatio continua vel temporalis* (i.e. κατὰ χρόνον). I took the latter position. In his review Winston cannot resist the temptation to set out the reasons why he feels impelled to choose the former option.[62] We can all be in agreement that the evidence in Philo's various works does not allow for a straightforward interpretation. Two other scholars have worked through the evidence carefully. Sorabji's conclusion stands not so far from mine, Sterling's position corroborates the Winstonian view.[63] A possible compromise is suggested by Dillon in his review:[64]

> If he stoutly maintains that the world is created, that is to establish its absolute *dependence* on God, not its creation at any point in time. Certainly Philo makes confusing noises on occasion, but all he really wants to claim, I would suggest, is that the universe, both physical and intelligible (the *kosmos noētos*), is dependent on God as its *arché*, or first principle, and, in the case of the physical cosmos, that it is continually in a state of coming-to-be, and so <is *genētos*. What it is not is> *agenētos*, as the Peripatetics would have it, and it is against this position that his polemic is directed.

But this view, attractive though it is, surely raises a further problem: what sort of a philosopher is Philo if he leaves such a vital question as this without a clear answer?

In the present context I wish to set this question aside. Instead I wish to take a brief look at the doctrine of the Ideas as God's thoughts, the issue that was briefly raised in connection with Radice's new thesis on the relation between Philo and Middle Platonism.[65] I present now only the main lines of discussion.

In the strongly theologized interpretation of Plato's thought that we find in Middle Platonist authors the relation between God as source and first cause of physical reality and the world of the Ideas as its intelligible pattern and model is a central issue. In most authors we encounter a solution that may in rather simple terms be described as 'the Ideas as God's thoughts'. It might be useful, however, for the sake of clarity to

---

[62] Winston 224–226.
[63] R. Sorabji, *Time, Creation and the Continuum* (London 1983), esp. 203–209; G. E. Sterling, 'Creatio Temporalis, Aeterna, vel Continua? an Analysis of the Thought of Philo of Alexandria', *The Studia Philonica Annual* 4 (1992) 15–41.
[64] Dillon 660 (I have tried to repair the obvious case of parablepsis in the printed text).
[65] See above part I, section 4 of this paper.

distinguish between two strands in this issue. In mainly early sources we find a presentation in terms of two principles, God and matter. In a very early (and often neglected) source, Theophrastus attributes to Plato the view that God is equated with the idea of the Good:[66]

Πλάτων ... τὴν πλείστην πραγματείαν περὶ τῆς πρώτης φιλοσοφίας ποιησάμενος, ἐπέδωκεν ἑαυτὸν καὶ τοῖς φαινομένοις ἁψάμενος τῆς περὶ φύσεως ἱστορίας· ἐν ᾗ δύο τὰς ἀρχὰς βούλεται ποιεῖν τὸ μὲν ὑποκείμενον ὡς ὕλην ὃ προσαγορεύει πανδεχές, τὸ δὲ ὡς αἴτιον καὶ κινοῦν ὃ περιάπτει τῇ θεοῦ καὶ τῇ τοῦ ἀγαθοῦ δυνάμει.

(Plato ... made the study of first philosophy (= metaphysics) his chief concern, but also devoted himself to the appearances and took up the study of nature, in which he wished to make the principles two in number, the substrate as matter, which he names 'all-receiver', the other as cause and mover, which he assigns to the power of God and the power of the Good.)

In another early and this time heavily Stoicized source, the somewhat confused Platonic doxography at Diog. Laert. 3.67–80, we also find two principles θεός–νοῦς and ὕλη (§69, 76). Here God is again implicitly equated with the Good (§72) and the Ideas play a very subordinate role, being merely intelligible exemplars of physical things (§77). In Timaeus Locrus—a work probably contemporary with Philo—a system of two principles also seems implied. Because the author adheres rather closely to the *Timaeus*, he speaks first (§1) of two αἰτίαι (νοῦς–θεός and ἀνάνκα) and then of two ἀρχαί, εἶδος and ὕλη (§5). From the opening of the work it is clear (§1–2), however, that the Idea (the author only speaks in the singular) is subordinated to God as first cause.[67]

At some stage, probably in the first century AD it was decided by some (for us anonymous) Middle Platonists that a systematic presentation in terms of two principles did not do justice to Plato's intentions. Hence the move to the doctrine of the three principles.[68] A succinct but typical formulation is found in the doxographer Aëtius (fl. ± 50 AD), who uses Middle Platonist formulations to present his Platonic doxai:[69]

Πλάτων Ἀρίστωνος Ἀθηναῖος ... τρεῖς ἀρχάς, τὸν θεὸν τὴν ὕλην τὴν ἰδέαν. ἔστι δὲ ὁ θεὸς ὁ νοῦς ⟨τοῦ κόσμου⟩, ὕλη δὲ τὸ ὑποκείμενον πρῶτον γενέσει καὶ φθορᾷ, ἰδέα δ' οὐσία ἀσώματος ἐν τοῖς νοήμασι καὶ ταῖς φαντασίαις τοῦ θεοῦ.

---

[66] Fr. 230 in the new edition of Theophrastus' fragments, W. W. Fortenbaugh–P. M. Huby–R. W. Sharples–D. Gutas, *Theophrastus of Eresus: Sources for his Life, Writings, Thought, and Influence*, 2 vols., Philosophia Antiqua 54 (Leiden 1992) 1.422.
[67] If we agree with M. Baltes, *Timaios Lokros Über die Natur des Kosmos und der Seele*, Philosophia Antiqua 21 (Leiden 1972) 34 that τὰ ξύμπαντα in §2 picks up τῶν συμπάντων in §1.
[68] Which is not to say that there were not antecedents, e.g. the Varronian text at Augustine *DCD* 7.28.
[69] At Ps.Plut. *Placita Philosophorum* 1.3, 59.8 Mau.

Plato the Athenian, son of Ariston... [posits] three principles: the god, matter, the idea. God is the mind of the cosmos; matter is the prime substrate underlying becoming and destruction; the idea is the incorporeal being in the thoughts and representations of the god.

For Alcinous (formerly known as Albinus) in his handbook presentation of Plato's doctrine the Ideas are the παραδειγματικὴ ἀρχή, standing beside God and matter:[70]

ἔστι δὲ ἡ ἰδέα ὡς μὲν πρὸς θεὸν νόησις αὐτοῦ, ὡς δὲ πρὸς ἡμᾶς νοητὸν πρῶτον, ὡς δὲ πρὸς τὴν ὕλην μέτρον, ὡς δὲ πρὸς τὸν αἰσθητὸν κόσμον παράδειγμα, ὡς δὲ πρὸς αὐτὴν ἐξεταζομένη οὐσία.

Examined in relation to God the idea is his thinking; in relation to us it is the first object of thought; in relation to matter it is a measure; in relation to the sense-perceptible cosmos it is a model; in relation to itself it is a being (or substance).

In the following chapter Alcinous returns to the relation between the Ideas and the first theological principle:[71]

ἐπεὶ δὲ ὁ πρῶτος νοῦς κάλλιστος, δεῖ καὶ κάλλιστον αὐτῷ νοητὸν ὑποκεῖσθαι, οὐδὲν δὲ αὐτοῦ κάλλιον· ἑαυτὸν ἂν οὖν καὶ τὰ ἑαυτοῦ νοήματα ἀεὶ νοοίη, καὶ αὕτη ἡ ἐνέργεια αὐτοῦ ἰδέα ὑπάρχει.

Since the first mind is supremely fair, it is necessary that the object of thought that subsists in him be supremely fair also. Nothing is more fair than himself. Therefore he always thinks himself and his own thoughts, and this activity of his constitutes the idea.

The presentation of the Ideas as God's thoughts is here clearly influenced by the Aristotelian portrait of the first unmoved mover. For this reason there is no direct relation to the doctrine of the creation of the cosmos as based on the *Timaeus*. This we do find, however, when Alcinous turns from the first principles proper to the φυσικὸς τόπος (natural realm) at §12.

The two schemas that I have outlined furnish an evident interpretative difficulty. In a schema of two principles the Ideas must be subordinate to God and thus regarded as 'his thoughts'. In a schema of three principles the Ideas would appear to regain a measure of independence. It would seem better to formulate this position as 'the Ideas as objects of God's thought'. Nevertheless they are often enough described, as in the case of Aëtius, as being *in* God's thoughts or *in* God.[72] A solution here might be to suggest that there are two issues involved here: (1) the onto-

---

[70] §9, 20.14 Whittaker.
[71] §10, 22.27 Whittaker.
[72] Cf. also Seneca *Ep.* 65.7 *haec exemplaria rerum omnium deus intra se habet numerosque universorum quae agenda sunt et modos mente complexus est.*

logical *status* of the Ideas, which are now on a level equal with God, and (2) the question of the *location* of the Ideas, which are commonly regarded as being found *in* God, without necessarily implying subordination.[73]

But let us turn back to Philo. In his exegesis of 'day one' of the Mosaic creation account Philo basically interprets the biblical text in terms of the Middle Platonist doctrine of the *genesis* of the cosmos. It is true to say, as I noted in my study,[74] that Philo's emphasis on the *creation* of the κόσμος νοητός goes further than we generally find in Middle Platonist texts, esp. in the formulation of the aspect of *pre-creational reflection*. We might compare two little-known texts in the *Introductio arithmetica* of Nichomachus of Gerasa (fl. ±100):[75]

1.4.2 ἔστι δὲ αὕτη ἡ ἀριθμητικὴ, οὐ μόνον, ὅτι ἔφαμεν αὐτὴν ἐν τῇ τοῦ τεχνίτου θεοῦ διανοίᾳ προυποστῆναι τῶν ἄλλων ὡσανεὶ λόγον τινὰ κοσμικὸν καὶ παραδειγματικόν, πρὸς ὃν ἀπερειδόμενος ὁ τῶν ὅλων δημιουργὸς ὡς πρὸς προκέντημά τι καὶ ἀρχέτυπον παράδειγμα τὰ ἐκ τῆς ὕλης ἀποτελέσματα κοσμεῖ καὶ τοῦ οἰκείου τέλους τυγχάνειν ποιεῖ...

And this [the method to learn first] is arithmetic, not solely because we said that it existed before all the others in the mind of the creating God like some universal and exemplary plan, relying upon which as a design and archetypal example the creator of the universe sets in order his material creations and makes them attain to their proper ends, but also...

1.6.1 πάντα τὰ κατὰ τεχνικὴν διέξοδον ὑπὸ φύσεως ἐν τῷ κόσμῳ διατεταγμένα κατὰ μέρος τε καὶ ὅλα φαίνεται κατὰ ἀριθμὸν ὑπὸ προνοίας καὶ τοῦ τὰ ὅλα δημιουργήσαντος νοῦ διακεκρίσθαι τε καὶ κεκοσμῆσθαι βεβαιουμένου τοῦ παραδείγματος οἷον λόγον προχαράγματος ἐκ τοῦ ἐπέχειν τὸν ἀριθμὸν προυποστάντα ἐν τῇ τοῦ κοσμοποιοῦ θεοῦ διανοίᾳ, νοητὸν αὐτὸν μόνον καὶ παντάπασιν ἄυλον, οὐσίαν μέντοι τὴν ὄντως τὴν ἀίδιον, ἵνα πρὸς αὐτὸν ὡς λόγον τεχνικὸν ἀποτελεσθῇ τὰ σύμπαντα ταῦτα, χρόνος, κίνησις, οὐρανός, ἄστρα, ἐξελιγμοὶ παντοῖοι.

All that has by nature with systematic method been arranged in the universe seems both in part and as a whole to have been determined and ordered in accordance with number, by the forethought and the mind of him that created all things; for the pattern was fixed, like a preliminary sketch, by the domination of number preexistent in the mind of the world-creating God, number conceptual only and immaterial in every way, but at the same time the true and the eternal essence, so that with reference to it, as to an artistic plan, should be created all these things, time, motion, the heavens, the stars, all sorts of revolutions.

---

[73] The question of the 'place' of the ideas was a hot topic in Middle Platonism; in his article 'Idee/Ideenlehre', soon to be published in *RAC*, M. Baltes outlines 7 different solutions, of which the one mentioned in the text is the most common. Philo refers to this question explicitly at *Opif.* 17.

[74] At p. 164–165, 445–446, but insufficiently at 515–516 when I discuss the relation to Middle Platonism.

[75] Text at R. Hoche (Leipzig 1866). I cite the translation of M. L. D'Ooge, F. E. Robbins and L. C. Karpinski, *Nichomachus of Gerasa Introduction to Arithmetic* (New York 1926). Note that as a Neopythagorean Nichomachus places more emphasis on the mathematical nature of the ideas.

There is much of interest in these texts (including the double reference to a λόγος). For our purposes now we note that by means of the prefix προ– the author emphasizes the pre-existence of the model no less than four times, but he does not insist on its createdness. We cannot be sure whether the Idea was pre-existent as idea, or whether it was made by the creating Deity.[76] Philo on the other hand is quite unambiguous in his formulation: 'God struck out in advance' (Opif. 16, προεξετύπου). It might well be argued, however, that Philo's insistence on the creation of the κόσμος νοητός as 'day one' is the result of exegetical constraint. As the model in or as the Logos it is clearly eternal. The emphasis on createdness may intend no more than to indicate its ontological dependence on God as creator of all things that exist.

A more promising line of Philonic distinctiveness might be thought to be suggested by the famous text at Opif. 8, where Philo writes:

Μωυσῆς ... ἔγνω δή, ὅτι ἀναγκαιότατόν ἐστιν ἐν τοῖς οὖσι τὸ μὲν εἶναι δραστήριον αἴτιον, τὸ δὲ παθητόν, καὶ ὅτι τὸ μὲν δραστήριον ὁ τῶν ὅλων νοῦς ἐστιν εἰλικρινέστατος καὶ ἀκραιφνέστατος, κρείττων ἢ ἀρετὴ καὶ κρείττων ἢ ἐπιστήμη καὶ κρείττων ἢ αὐτὸ τὸ ἀγαθὸν καὶ αὐτὸ τὸ καλόν, τὸ δὲ παθητὸν ἄψυχον καὶ ἀκίνητον ἐξ ἑαυτοῦ...

Moses ... understood that it was most essential that among the things that exist there be an active cause and a passive object, and that the former is the mind of the universe, supremely pure and undefiled, superior to excellence and superior to knowledge, and even superior to the God itself and the Fair itself, whereas the passive object was without its own source of life and movement...

The formulation, I have always thought, is rather awkward (especially the phrase ἐν τοῖς οὖσι). Nevertheless Philo here emphasizes the transcendence of the first cause in a manner that goes beyond anything we find in Middle Platonist authors. One might call the 'subordination' of the Good to God as a rhetorical flourish, but this would simply be to prejudge the seriousness of Philo's philosophizing. What, however, does God's superiority over the Ideas mean? Is the divine will sufficient to create its own values in a—from the human viewpoint—arbitrary fashion, or does what it wills conform to rationally determined values of goodness and excellence? I have to agree with Winston against Radice that Philo could not have meant the former option, since it is a central aspect of his appropriation of the ideal of Greek rationality that God in his relation to created reality works along rational lines laid down in his Logos.[77] Where I believe that Philo departs from his Middle Platonist

---

[76] The same ambiguity is inherent in the phrase πρότερον νοῆσαι at Atticus fr.9.37 Des Places.
[77] See Winston's review of Radice's monograph (above n. 4), SPhA 4 (1992) 163, and cf.

colleagues is in his very deliberate placement of God 'above' the noetic cosmos in the Logos (the distinction between the king and the architect in the image at *Opif.* 17–18). God's being is not exhausted by his relationship to created reality via the Logos. In a sense this view might be thought to anticipate the gods at three levels in Numenius or even the hypertranscendence of the Plotinian One. But differences remain: Philo's conception of divine transcendence is not so much 'hierarchical' (i.e. involving more than one level of deity) as 'aspectual'. It is also not prompted by logical considerations, but rather through an awareness of the overwhelming superiority and sublimity of the Divine Being.[78]

Finally, it has always struck me that in the above text, which despite certain clumsy aspects, surely was not written without careful thought, Philo refrains from speaking in the terms we noted earlier in Theophrastus, Diogenes Laertius and Timaeus Locrus, namely that there are *two* principles or causes in reality. There is God, first and highest cause, and there is matter which undergoes action. The suppression of a doctrine of two causes, which for a (early) Middle Platonist was simply par for the course, is deliberate.[79] This may mean that Philo is thinking ultimately in monistic terms, as Winston has suggested. My own view remains, however, that he has something like a 'monarchic dualism' in mind.[80]

This all-too-brief case-study points to a double conclusion. The very real affinities between Philo and Middle Platonism in the case of the doctrine of the 'Ideas as God's thoughts' to my mind do not point to any form of influence by Philo on the developing Platonist tradition, as Radice would wish. There are enough early witnesses to render his theory highly vulnerable on purely historical grounds. Philo's debt to contemporary Platonist theories of creation is great. Certain emphases *do* differ, however, and it is an important task to determine why this is so. My estimation is that his native Jewish tradition, with its biblical conception of God's nature and his relation to the world and its human inhabitants, is responsible for accents that a Middle Platonist would immediately recognize as foreign to his 'school of thought'.

---

my remarks at p.445.
[78] I cannot hope in this context to justify these sweeping considerations.
[79] Also at *Prov.* 1.22 Philo appears to be careful on this point.
[80] A term I introduce rather too hesitantly at p. 454, n. 264.

III

What is the upshot? The two sections of this paper appear to lead to parallel conclusions. In the case of the retrospective glance at my earlier study we may conclude that there was room for considerable improvement. To the extent that this awareness is the result of subsequent advances in research I need have no qualms. This is exactly what one hopes when one engages in research. I for one do not wish to have the last word on any subject. It is pleasing to think that my study may have contributed to moving the controversy about Philo 'into a newly refined and sophisticated phase', as my most critical reviewer predicted.[81]

What about the question of whether Philo is a Middle Platonist or not? Here too there were shortcomings in my arguments. Nevertheless I remain glad that I reached the opinion I did, and feel no impulse to diverge from it, even after ten years. Here too increasing sophistication is apparent on all sides. May it continue in the discussion of this paper, which has been written for no other purpose than to carry our combined researches further forward.

University of Leiden

---

[81] Lee 422. I repudiate the suggestion that I might regard the controversy about Philo as 'settled'.

Response to Runia and Sterling

DAVID WINSTON

In outlining his typology of the various positions one can take on how to evaluate Philo's relationship to Greek philosophy, Runia asserts that it is more helpful to describe Philo as a 'Platonizing devotee of Mosaic Scripture', than as 'a Middle Platonist *tout court*' (p. 130). Although he proceeds to identify the latter formulation as representing my own view, I would not in fact describe Philo in such a manner, and this for two reasons. First, Philo does not presume to be an original philosopher who seeks to leave his own distinctive imprint on the development of Platonic thought.[1] As Runia himself has correctly noted, the supporting argumentation for much of Philo's philosophical expositions is largely non-existent. More important, however, is the fact that Philo's primary task, as he sees it, is only to link his Platonic convictions to Hebrew Scripture. He is thus quite content to employ the conceptuality of Middle Platonism, with which he is in fundamental agreement, but whose cogency he does not attempt formally to demonstrate, in order to preserve the Mosaic Torah both for himself and other like-minded Jews, who were unable to accept the validity of that sacred text unless it could be shown to be compatible with philosophical reason. That he is nonetheless prepared to make what he considered to be minor adjustments in his Platonism in order to reconcile it with Scripture is not to be denied. How deep these modifications actually go depends on how one interprets certain key Philonic doctrines.

As to the question of loyalty, Runia now considers the possibility that 'one can also demonstrate loyalty in a subversive way, whether this be judged as such by others from the outside or by oneself. It is possible to conclude that Philo was defending Judaism in a way that undermined its own identity. This was clearly the conclusion of the later rabbis, who

---

[1] It is interesting to compare Maimonides' admission that his *Guide for the Perplexed* was not composed as a purely philosophical work: 'Know that my purpose in this treatise was not to compose something in the natural sciences [physics], or to make an epitome of notions pertaining to the divine science [metaphysics] ... For the books composed concerning these matters are adequate. If, however, they should turn out not to be adequate with regard to some subject, that which I shall say concerning that subject will not be superior to anything else that has been said about it. My purpose in this Treatise ... is only to elucidate the difficult points of the Law and to make manifest the true realities of its hidden meanings.' (*Guide* 2.2, Preface, trans. Pines, p. 253)

condemned him to silence.' Although it is impossible to know how the rabbis would have reacted to Philo's thought if his works had been written in Hebrew, it seems to me that the main reason for their ignoring him was the fact that they were essentially uninterested in speculative philosophy. In any case, it is certainly not my view that Philo thought of his activity as subversive, for he was undoubtedly convinced that his philosophical reading of Scripture was entirely legitimate.

A glance at Jewish mystical exegesis may be instructive here. Although there was some sporadic rabbinic opposition to the mystical interpretation of Scripture, this was generally not the case, and many of the mystics were themselves great rabbinic authorities. Moreover, the kabbalists know how 'to renew ancient words every day.' As Daniel Matt has pointed out, 'the oxymoron 'new-ancient words' appears perhaps a dozen times in the Zohar, but the dialectical relationship between new revelations and their ancient source is a constant subtext.' The task of the author of the Zohar, like that of Philo, is paradoxical. 'He must convey secrets without dissipating the aura of secrecy [cf. *Abr.* 147]. The kabbalist Jacob b. Sheshet insists that 'it is a miẓvah for every sage to innovate in the Torah according to his capacity,' and he concludes an innovative teaching on the Tetragrammaton with the following comment: 'Do not think this is far-fetched. If I had not invented it in my mind, I would say it was transmitted to Moses at Sinai.' This conveys his conviction that his creative interpretation is as authoritative as revelation itself. [Like Philo], the Zohar rails against those who are blind to the gems within Torah and think its words are defective or worthless (Zohar 1.63a) [cf. *Mut.* 60–61]. There is not a single word or letter in the Torah that does not contain sublime and precious secrets' (Zohar 3.265a) [cf. *Spec.* 3.178]. If a verse sounds strange, it probably contains a secret' (Zohar 2.217b) [cf. *Conf.* 190].

Both Philo and the kabbalists are keenly aware of the highly innovative character of their exegesis, yet they are convinced that this is precisely what the inspired sacred texts demands of them. 'According to the Zohar, God himself is sure to be present when new words are spoken. Mystical innovations ascend to the height of the sefirot and these privileged new words are themselves adorned by the Ancient of Days' (1.4b).[2]

---

[2] For all this see D. C. Matt, "New-Ancient Words': The Aura of Secrecy in the Zohar,' (forthcoming). I am indebted to Matt for providing me with an advance copy of his fascinating study. Cf. also *Merkabah Shelemah*, ed. R. S. Musayev (Jerusalem, 1921) 8, on which passage Lieberman comments as follows: 'He who does not know how to make new deductions (καινοτομῆσαι) will die, and he who knows how to make new deductions will be summoned at the end of his days to the world to come, and in the words of *BT Baba Metzia* 86a: Rabbah b. Nahmani was summoned to the celestial academy, i.e. in order to

In short, just as Moses is transformed into a mystagogue in the Zohar (he is the only mortal vouchsafed mystical union with the *Shekhinah*: 1.21b–22a), Philo transforms the great prophet into a symbol of the ideal philosopher-sage, thereby converting the Mosaic Torah into an exposition of universal philosophical wisdom. Since Philo is personally convinced that Platonism is the true philosophy he has no compunctions about infusing the biblical text with its content. Moreover, since he is equally convinced that wisdom is infinite (*Post.* 151–52), he never claims to have exhausted all the possible meanings of Torah, and leaves open the possibility of uncovering ever deeper layers of signification. Analogously, for the great sixteenth century Safed kabbalist Moses Cordovero, every sefirah has an infinite number of aspects. The rise of the notion that Torah has an infinite number of significations had already been a major development in the kabbalistic thought of the last third of the thirteenth century.[3]

Runia maintains that Philo's choice of the exegetical genre as his mode of exposition is intrinsic to his own conception of his role, and if Plato's doctrines are used to explicate the biblical text by means of a commentary, that is because they are regarded as inherent in it. The fact is, however, that those who choose to compose a midrashic or allegorical commentary, whether it be of the homiletical, mystical, or philosophical variety, rather than a straightforward philological one, must be presumed to be especially motivated to do so. No one, I think, would wish to claim that the various midrashim of the rabbis, whether halakhic or homiletical, based as they are on what scholars have sometimes designated 'creative' philology or far-fetched hermeneutical rules, were meant to represent meanings believed to be literally inherent in the Biblical text. Not even the rabbis themselves seem to have thought so.[4] As G. Bruns has put it, 'the rabbis saw themselves in dialogue with each other and with generations of wise men extending back to Solomon and beyond to Moses and to God himself, who is frequently pictured as studying his own texts ... Midrash means the interpretation of texts that are not kept like museum pieces under glass. They are always entering

---

decide the controversy in matters of leprosy' (Saul Lieberman, *Texts and Studies* (New York 1974) 13.
[3] See M. Idel, 'Infinities of Torah in Kabbalah,' in G. H. Hartman and S. Budick (edd.) *Midrash and Literature*, (New Haven 1986) 152. Cf. Sirach 24:28–29; *Song Rabbah* 1.11 and *Pesiktah Rabbati*, piska 14.9, according to which Solomon had three hundred parables to illustrate each verse of Scripture, and one thousand and five interpretations for each parable, computing to a total of three million fifteen thousand interpretations for every scriptural verse.
[4] Cf. *Numbers Rabbah* 19.6: 'Matters that had not been disclosed to Moses were disclosed to R. Akibah and his colleagues.'

into new situations requiring that they be resituated in languages and forms of life differing from the ones in which they were originally composed.'[5] When Runia says that in Philo's exegesis 'the primacy is given to the actual text which the commentator is obliged to follow wherever it leads',[6] he is construing the midrashic-allegorical approach much too narrowly.

Kabbalistic midrash is even more exuberantly free than rabbinic midrash. R. Eleazar of Worms, for example, in his *Sefer ha-Hokhma* (1217), systematically interprets the first verses in Genesis in dozens of ways, and in his introduction lists the 73 'gates of wisdom,' which are in fact 73 methods of midrashic interpretation.[7] Eleazar, as Joseph Dan points out, was not bothered by the contradictions involved in such multiple interpretation, 'since the truth hidden within these verses was regarded as rich enough to be revealed in countless ways. But if everything is true, asks Dan, why bother with midrash? The answer lies in the fact that this was the only way to relate new ideas to a traditional authoritative source. 'The nature of the midrashic form facilitated the acceptance and integration of the Kabbalah in Jewish culture.'[8] As Idel has noted, the kabbalistic hermeneutical methods whereby innovations are injected into the text are wholly indeterminate and superflexible techniques whose looseness is counterbalanced solely by doctrinal inhibitions.[9] Since the same may be said of Philo, Runia's assertion that 'the Mosaic law is for Philo the indispensable touchstone for determining what the highest philosophy is,' fails, in my opinion, to appreciate the enormous flexibility of his allegorical exegesis and its true motivation.

Philo and Chaeremon

Both Runia and Sterling observe that the Egyptian priest and Stoic philosopher Chaeremon wrote works in which Egyptian tradition was presented as ancient wisdom and the Egyptian priests as Greek philosophers. Moreover, Chaeremon states that the more ancient Egyptian scribes, wishing to conceal the theory about the nature of the gods, wrote

---

[5] 'Allegory,' says Bruns, 'presupposes a cultural situation in which the literal interpretation of a text would be as incomprehensible as a literal translation of it.' See Gerald L. Bruns, 'Midrash and Allegory: The Beginnings of Scriptural Interpretation,' in F. Kermode and R. Alter (edd.), *The Literary Guide to the Bible* (Cambridge Mass. 1987) 630, 636.
[6] *Philo of Alexandria and the* Timaeus *of Plato* (Leiden 1986) 544.
[7] J. Dan, 'Midrash and the Dawn of Kabbalah,' in *Midrash and Literature, op. cit.* (n. 3) 130.
[8] *Ibid.* 138.
[9] *Ibid.* 152.

by way of allegorical symbols and characters ' (T12, F12, Van der Horst). Sterling concludes that the evidence points to the presence in first century CE. Alexandria of Egyptian priests and Jewish exegetes using Stoic and Platonic philosophy to forge a rapprochement between their ancestral traditions and Hellenistic thought.

Runia, however, raises the question of whether Philo can be called a Platonist in the way that Chaeremon is called a Stoic. He points out that none of the sources speak of Philo 'the Platonist', but that Clement of Alexandria twice speaks of him as 'the Pythagorean'. Runia finds this designation puzzling and observes that 'surely it is not meant as an assertion that Philo belongs to the Pythagorean αἵρεσις'. Nor does Philo show a particular partiality for Pythagorean above Platonist doctrines. Two further differences between Philo and Chaeremon are that Philo does not write books on technical matters such as the grammatical aspects of logic. Nor is Philo described as belonging to the 'professional philosophical establishment'.' Runia concludes that Philo is not a Platonist in the way that Chaeremon was a Stoic.

It may be instructive, however, to compare the case of Numenius of Apamea. According to Numenius, only Plato understood Socrates correctly, since, as a Pythagorean, he knew the origins of Socrates' teaching (fr. 24.57, Des Places). Plato, however, declined to represent this teaching in a univocal manner, and thus exposed it to a progressive falsification. If we should succeed in freeing the original teaching from the later distortions, Plato will have emerged as a pure Pythagorean (24.70). Numenius' reconstruction of Plato's philosophy was for the purpose of laying hold of the true philosophy, Pythagoreanism. This, as Michael Frede has pointed out, is the basis for the usual designation of Numenius as a Pythagorean. Frede further notes that Numenius was called a Pythagorean by Clement (*Str.* 1.150.4), Origen (*C. Cels.* 1.15; 4.51), Eusebius (*PE* 9.7.1), and Nemesius (*Nat. hom.* 17.17 Morani). This did not restrain Eusebius, however, from introducing Numenius as a representative of Platonic teaching. It is striking, moreover, that only Christian writers called him 'Pythagorean', whereas the Platonists themselves avoided that designation. Once, Porphyry lists Numenius along with Cronius among the Pythagoreans (Eusebius *HE* 6.19.8), but this appears to mean only that Numenius 'Pythagorized' and not to exclude him from being a Platonist. Moreover, Porphyry counted Numenius and Cronius among the Platonic authors studied by Plotinus, beside Severus, Gaius, and Atticus (*VP* 14.1–12). It is thus clear that the expression 'Pythagorean' does not preclude one from being a Platonist.[10] Clement's designation of

---

[10] See M. Frede, 'Numenius,' in *ANRW* II 36.1 (Berlin 1989) 1034–75, esp. 1046–47.

Philo as a 'Pythagorean' was therefore probably not meant to preclude his being a Platonist, but was used only to indicate that both he and Plato had 'Pythagorized'.

Graduate Theological Union
Berkeley

Was Philo a Middle Platonist?
Some suggestions

THOMAS H. TOBIN, S.J.

I want to begin by thanking David Runia and Gregory Sterling for papers that are both well argued and well written. The question each offered an answer to is important if one is ever to understand what Philo was about. As I read each of the papers, I found that both Runia and Sterling made very good cases for their different positions on the question. Of the six possible positions listed by Runia (Runia, p. 125), Sterling takes the position that Philo is a *de facto* Middle Platonist (position two) while Runia himself takes the position that Philo is a Platonizing expositor of scripture but not a Middle Platonist as such (position three). I agree with Runia and Sterling that these are the only two really plausible positions of the six listed. While in many ways the two positions are close together, nevertheless, whether Philo was a Middle Platonist or not is significant because of what it says about who Philo is and what he is about in his scriptural interpretations. In my response, however, I should prefer not to answer the question directly. Rather, I want to make several suggestions to provoke discussion and add several other angles to it.

The first suggestion concerns the milieu in which Philo was writing. A common goal in Hellenistic Jewish literature was to establish a communality of viewpoint with the best of the Greek world plus specific differences which showed the superiority of Judaism over that world. One finds this already in earlier Hellenistic Jewish texts (e.g. *Letter of Aristeas* and the fragments of Aristobulus). The same is true of Philo. But this complicates the question of how to identify Philo. There is little doubt that Philo's overall construal of reality is Platonic in one form or another. Yet he does this by interpretations of the *Jewish* scriptures and not by interpretations of *Platonic* texts as did other Middle Platonists. Does this make Philo a Middle Platonist or not? One can at least wonder what Philo would have made of this question. He may well have taken it as a sign that he had succeeded in his efforts.

My second suggestion concerns the question of who should be considered a Middle Platonist at all. When one reads what are commonly accepted as Middle Platonic texts or when reads histories of Middle Platonism, one is struck by the differences among these writers. For example, should 'Neopythagoreans' such as Moderatus of Gades, Nicomachus of Gerasa, and Numenius of Apamea be considered Middle Platonists? Should even Eudorus, who is often connected with the origins of Middle Platonism, be considered a Middle Platonist or a Neopythagorean? If one wants to understand what was happening philosophically during this period, one might be better advised to think in terms of 'family resemblances'. Are there significant elements many or most of which these writers share? No one writer may have all of the elements and no single element may be found in all of the writers. Yet the significant elements which are commonly found in them, their 'family resemblances,' may entitle them all to be thought of as Middle Platonists. Can the same thing be said about Philo? Does Philo have enough of these family resemblances to be called a Middle Platonist? Can Philo be seen as a Middle Platonist in the same way that Chaeremon can be seen as a Stoic? Both Runia and Sterling use Chaeremon as examples supporting their positions. It seems to me that the example of Chaeremon is worth more discussion.

My third suggestion has to do with the place of Philo in the history of Middle Platonism. Philo comes comparatively early in the history of Middle Platonism. This too may affect the way in which one evaluates the extent of his Middle Platonism. An example of this may well be Philo's use of the λόγος concept, a concept obviously derived from Stoicism.[1] Philo depicts the λόγος in a variety of ways, and the figure has a number of different functions. One of those functions (e.g. *Opif.* 24–25) is cosmological. The λόγος is the image of God, the highest of all beings who are intellectually perceived, the one closest to God, the only truly existent (*Fug.* 101). This image, the λόγος, also serves as the paradigm or model for the ordering of the rest of the universe (*Somn.* 2.45). The λόγος is the archetypal idea in which all of the other ideas are contained (*Opif.* 24–25). But the λόγος is not simply the image or paradigm according to which the universe was ordered, it is also the instrument (ὄργανον) through which the universe is ordered (*Cher.* 127; *Spec.* 1.81). The λόγος is both the power through which the universe was originally ordered and the power by which the universe continues to be ordered. While some sort of intermediate reality between the transcendent God and the world is common in Middle Platonism, Philo is distinguished from most later Middle Platonists by his use of the term λόγος to identify this intermediate reality.[2] Interestingly enough and for reasons which are not entirely clear, this reinterpretation of the Stoic λόγος as an inter-

---

[1] For a treatment of λόγος in Stoicism see A. A. Long, *Hellenistic Philosophy* (London 1986²) 144–47, 149–50, 154–6.
[2] See J. Dillon, *The Middle Platonists* (Ithaca 1977) 46.

mediate reality in the intelligible realm seems to have taken place primarily in Alexandria and at an early stage in Middle Platonism.³ Eudorus of Alexandria may have referred to the demiurgic combination of the Monad, which represented form, and the Dyad, which represented matter, as the thought (λόγος) of the essentially transcendent God, the First or Supreme One.⁴ The λόγος as an intermediary figure appears in the *Poimandres* 10–11, a first or second century AD treatise from Egypt which, although not Jewish, draws on both Plato's *Timaeus* and the early chapters of Genesis.⁵ The most important passage in which the λόγος appears as an intermediate figure is in Plutarch (c. 50–120 AD) (*De Is. et Os.* 53–54, 372E–373C). The λόγος, which was identified with the Egyptian God Osiris, was that which ordered and made manifest the material world and at the same time served as the intelligible paradigm for that world. Both the myths about Osiris and Plutarch's interpretations of the myths are probably to be located in first-century AD Alexandria.⁶ Philo's use of the λόγος concept derived from Stoicism in the creation of the world probably reflects at this point an element from the early stages of Alexandrian Middle Platonism, an element that was not, on the whole taken up by subsequent Middle Platonic writers. My point in giving this example is simply to suggest that in asking the question of Philo's Middle Platonic identity, one must be aware of the fact that Philo comes quite early in the history of Middle Platonism and that this awareness may affect our evaluation of him.

My fourth and final suggestion has to do with the question of 'school' or αἵρεσις. Runia points out that, while most philosophers by the time of Philo did not belong to schools in an *institutional* sense, they were *affiliated* with a particular philosophical αἵρεσις (p. 126–127). Would Philo have considered himself affiliated with the Platonic or, more

---

³ In his paper (pp. 138) Runia points to the use of λόγος by Nicomachus of Gerasa (*Introductio arithmetica* 1.4.2; 1.6.1). Yet in both instances the term seems to be simply 'plan' or 'sketch' and has none of the complex functions assigned to it by Philo. The connection of the λόγος as an intermediate figure with early Alexandrian Middle Platonism, however, cannot be pressed too far. Both John 1:1–18 (the Prologue of John) and what may be first-century AD sections of the *Trimorphic Protennoia* (46.5–6; 47.5–22; 49.22–49; 50.9–12; 18–20) cannot be traced to any particular place, although Alexandria cannot be excluded. Yet it is worthwhile noting that both are beyond the realm of Middle Platonism. For the *Trimorphic Protennoia*, see John D. Turner, 'Trimorphic Protennoia', in J. M. Robinson (ed.)*The Nag Hammadi Library* (SanFrancisco 1988³) 511–13.
⁴ Dillon, *The Middle Platonists*, 128.
⁵ For introductions to the *Poimandres* and the Hermetic Corpus see A. D. Nock and A.-J. Festugière, *Corpus Hermeticum* (Paris 1972) 1.1–28 and B. Layton, *The Gnostic Scriptures* (Garden City 1987) 447–51.
⁶ See J. G. Griffiths, *Plutarch's De Iside et Osiride* (Cardiff 1970) 41–48; T. H. Tobin, *The Creation of Man:Philo and the History of Interpretation* (Washington 1983) 73–76.

exactly, the Academic αἵρεσις ? Runia thinks not, and I agree with him. If anything, Philo would have considered himself affiliated with a Mosaic αἵρεσις. Yet given how strongly Philo's own basic construal or reality reflects Platonic or Middle Platonic outlooks can we stop there? I wonder whether two concepts drawn from the social sciences may not be helpful at this point. Social scientists often distinguish between an 'emic' and an 'etic' analysis. An 'emic' analysis is an analysis of phenomena in terms of internal structures of a particular system. An 'etic' analysis is of phenomena considered in relation to predetermined general concepts. In 'emic' terms, Philo would not be considered a Middle Platonist because, on his own terms, he is an interpreter of the Jewish scriptures and not of Platonic texts; he affiliates himself with the Mosaic, not the Platonic or Academic, αἵρεσις. In 'etic' terms, however, one might want to call him a Middle Platonist because he reflects so many of the basic positions associated with the more general category of Middle Platonism.

These remarks admittedly do little actually to answer the question of whether or not Philo was a Middle Platonist. I hope, however, that they will be of some help in furthering discussion of the question, especially the discussion of two very well done papers.

Loyola University
Chicago

A Response to Runia and Sterling

JOHN DILLON

This note is by way of a brief reply to, or comment upon, the papers of David Runia and Gregory Sterling in the present collection. I was sorry not to be able to attend the meeting in November 1992 in San Francisco when they were first delivered, but am glad to have had the chance to read them subsequently. I am also glad to say that I find myself in substantial agreement with them both.

I wonder, indeed, if it is not too optimistic to discern a broad consensus emerging on the subject of the true nature of Philo's philosophy. Can we take it now as agreed by all reasonable people that what he is engaged in is a creative adaptation of the Platonist tradition as it presented itself to him in Alexandria at around the turn of the Common Era? Even if this be granted, however, this does not of course make him a Platonist. For one thing, he seems prepared to turn also directly to Stoic or to Pythagorean sources if they suit his purposes better, although we cannot be sure, in the wake of, first Antiochus (for the Stoics) and then Eudorus (for the Pythagoreans), how much of this had not been done by Platonists already).

For another thing, there is a certain element of distinctively Jewish piety discernible in Philo which leads him, I think, to favour the Stoic concept of the Logos over the more Platonist system of Demiurge and/ or World Soul (though the logos-doctrine could well be an inheritance from Antiochus), and to indulge in rather more negative theology and down-grading of human capacities (even to the extent of making use, on at least one occasion, of the sceptical tropes of Aenesidemus, *Ebr.* 162–205) than I would expect of the average Platonist of this era. But this, I think, does not alter the fact that his basic orientation is Platonist.

As I read over my own treatment of him in *The Middle Platonists* back in 1977 (henceforth *MP*), I am struck by a certain tendency to naive simplification in defining his position. For a start, including Philo as a major part of a chapter in a book entitled *The Middle Platonists*, in close proximity to the Platonist Eudorus, was asking for misinterpretation. I don't, of course, feel that I was wrong to do this, since I still regard him as our best evidence for Middle Platonism at the earliest stage of its development (if we regard Antiochus as a forerunner of Middle Platonism, as I would prefer to do, rather than as the founder of the movement), but such an inclusion does undeniably lead to difficulties. It is good, therefore, to have yet another opportunity here to set the record straight.

I was of course concerned, as I specified at the conclusion of my study of him (*MP* p. 182), primarily with Philo as a witness to contemporary Platonism, and thus indulged in a 'deliberately partial study', but I cannot be too surprised that people tend to ignore that disclaimer, since I tended to forget it myself in the course of my study of him, caught up as I was in the fascination of the subject-matter.

Since 1977 a good deal of attention has been given to the question of Philo's philosophical allegiances and strategies, well summarised here by David Runia. I find the typology which he sets out on p. 125 of his paper most useful. I would agree that it is his position (3) that on reflection I would most favour—'that Philo is a Platonizing expositor of scripture, showing a marked preference for using Middle Platonist doctrines in his exegesis.' Of course, as Runia says, if we are trying to probe how Philo would have defined himself, as opposed to how we would best define him, then we would have to see him as constructing a 'Mosaic' philosophy, rather than admitting allegiance to anything Greek.

If Philo were cross-questioned closely about remarkable similarities to, say, Plato's *Timaeus* in the *De Opificio Mundi*, or about close analogies, amounting frequently to identity, between many of his philosophical formulations and those of the Stoics, he would doubtless maintain in his defence that the whole tradition of Greek philosophy descending from Pythagoras to Plato to Aristotle and then to the Stoics, together with the insights of such thinkers as Heraclitus and Parmenides, are simply borrowed from the teachings of Moses and his followers, and that he is quite entitled to borrow them back; but this does not commit him to allegiance to any Greek *hairesis*.

However, we do not have to take Philo at his own valuation, if we do not accept the basic foundation-story of which he has persuaded himself. I do not in fact see how any serious student of Philo can adopt any position outside the range of Runia's (2), (3) and (4), though each of those positions could be defended with some plausibility. As I say, however, (3) seems to me nearest to the truth, as it does to Runia, and to Gregory Sterling also.

Sterling's adducing of the parallels of Chaeremon (adduced also by Runia), Plutarch and Numenius is, I think, helpful and illuminating in various ways. The situations of each of the three are different, of course. Chaeremon is an Egyptian priest who has adopted Stoicism as a key to understanding, and proving the philosophical superiority of, his native traditions; Plutarch is a Platonist who sees great philosophical wisdom in both Egyptian (Isis and Osiris) and Persian (Ormuzd, Ahriman

Mithras) traditions; and Numenius is a Pythagoreanizing Platonist, who both wishes to establish Pythagoras as the true father of the Platonist tradition, and is hospitable, to an even greater degree than Plutarch, to the wisdom of the East (which, however, he wishes to bring into conformity with Platonic-Pythagorean principles). Of these, Philo's position is closest to his enemy Chaeremon, and rather the converse of that of Plutarch and Numenius. He is convinced of the superiority of his own traditions, and is using the tools of Greek philosophy to demonstrate that superiority. In this connection, it seems to me that Sterling's characterizing of Philo, in his conclusion (p. 111), as a 'pluralist', but one 'with a distinct hierarchy of values', is fair enough, though it is not, of course, how Philo would have seen himself.

That said, I would like to turn now, first, to certain details of Runia's paper, and then to some reflections on a line of investigation not represented in these two papers, but one which seems to me incorrect in an interesting way, which deserves much further consideration.

By way of illustration of the ways in which Philo's Jewish sensibility might be thought to result in positions at variance with contemporary middle Platonism Runia adduces, first (p. 134), his doctrine of the 'createdness' of the world, and then (p. 134–139) his doctrine of the forms as thoughts of God. In relation to the former I am grateful to him, first of all, for correcting a printing error in the text of my review of his *Timaeus* book, which very much obscured my argument. As regards the position I advance, I still think I am on the right lines: what Philo wishes to combat, as a 'Peripatetic' heresy, is the notion that the world could have an existence independent of God, and in that sense it cannot be ἀγένητος. He seems already to be acquainted with a fairly sophisticated Platonist tradition of debate about the various possible meanings of γενητός, such as we only find evidence for much later, in the second century CE, in the formulations of Calvenus Taurus, and Alcinous in the *Didaskalikos* (cf. *MP* pp. 242 & 286–7).

Again, on the matter of the forms as thoughts of God, Runia is surely right to assume that Philo is drawing upon existing Platonic doctrine, rather than that he himself had any influence on the formulation of subsequent Platonic doctrine, while at the same time drawing attention to Philo's significant ranking of God as 'superior to the Good Itself and the Beautiful Itself', as going further than a contemporary Platonist would go in the assertion of God's transcendence.

Finally, however, I would like to turn to another issue not raised in these papers, but which has been given a very full airing in the recent vast and admirably learned monograph of Richard Goulet, *La Philosophie de Moïse* (Paris 1987), to which Runia makes reference on p. 116 of his essay. He says there, 'Goulet's magnificent study shows beyond any doubt that Philo has absorbed previous exegetical 'systems' which did not have Platonism at their core, but rather a form of immanentist Stoicism. Philo superimposes on this traditional base his own form of Platonist exegesis, but does this more effectively than Goulet wishes to admit.'

As he goes on to remark in a footnote, 'My impression is that this study has not been given the attention by Philonists that it deserves.' He suggests its vast bulk (578 pages and text) and rebarbative format as an explanation of this, and to this I can testify, since I am still working my way through it myself. However, I have read enough to derive the strong impression that I am not going to agree with its conclusions at the end of the day much as I admire its scholarship. My problem is that the alleged non-Platonist, non-literal predecessors do not really add up to anything coherent. In his chap. 10, Goulet proposes to identify these earlier Jewish allegorists with the syncretist Platonist tradition, taking in much Peripateticism and especially Stoicism, of the School of Antiochus. But who were these men?

It is these people who, for instance, Goulet maintains (pp. 53–7), will have identified Cain and Abel with irrational soul and intellect respectively (as in *Agr.* 27–66), instead of with 'the theory which attributes everything to the (human) intellect', and 'that which attributes everything to God', as did Philo himself (e.g. at *Sacr.* 2–3). I just do not see that this is a necessary explanation of such apparent discrepancies of interpretation as there are. In both these passages Philo is undoubtedly presenting the doctrine as his own, and I think that he would have seen them as compatible, especially if one bears in mind that the basic opposition that he wishes to make between Cain and Abel is between the mind that attributes everything to itself, and that which attribute everything to God.

At such a passage as *Abr.* 99–102, however, we find a different situation (discussed by Goulet on p. 34ff.). Here Philo first reports a view he has heard from certain φυσικοὶ ἄνδρες who have offered as allegorical interpretation of Abraham and Sarah's adventures in Egypt in Gen. 12: 10–20, to the effect that Abraham represents the σπουδαῖος νοῦς and Sarah ἀρετή. This interpretation, however, Philo himself demurs at (101), suggesting that these learned persons have perhaps been deceived by the genders of the principal characters, and have not reckoned that in fact Virtue is *male*, in that it takes an active role in instilling noble thoughts into the mind, which correspondingly takes on a *female* role in this process. On the other hand, it is by no means clear in this passage what his own position is, because in general his view is that Abraham *does* represent the νοῦς (cf. *Cher.* 7; *Mut.* 66, etc.), and Sarah ἀρετή (*Cher.* 3–10; *Congr.* 1–13, *Mut.* 61, etc.), so that it is conceivable that, despite the turn of phrase he uses, he may just be introducing a modification to his own exegesis here.

On the other hand, he does seem here to refer to 'physical philosophers' who indulge in biblical exegesis, and this sort of passage gives Goulet an opening for wide-ranging speculations. I am not in a position to disprove definitively his views, but I would like to take each controverted passage one by one, and dispute with him on it. I do not deny that there were Jewish Alexandrian intellectuals who indulged in scattered allegorical exegeses of Scripture based on an acquaintance with Greek philosophy, but I very much doubt that there was anything like Philo's comprehensive enterprise before Philo. I would be much readier to believe that in many passages Philo is simply *inventing* predecessors, on the model of the Greeks, just by way of 'keeping up with the (Hellenic) Joneses.' This is not too difficult to imagine him doing, I think. Greek philosophers also did this to a certain extent, postulating a series of oversimplified or wrong-headed positions on a given question, whether or not anyone had ever advanced them, simply in order to shoot them down, thus making one's own position clearer. Even Aristotle does this, to a certain extent, and the later Platonist commentators certainly do so on occasion. So why not Philo?

I would persist, then, as seeing Goulet's enterprise as leading down a wrong path, though I second David Runia's praise of the book as a monument of scholarship, and am quite sure that I will learn a lot from it. I may even be induced, by the time I have reached p. 578, to change my present views.

Trinity College
Dublin

INSTRUMENTA

REVERSE INDEXES TO PHILONIC TEXTS IN THE PRINTED FLORILEGIA AND COLLECTIONS OF FRAGMENTS

JAMES R. ROYSE

As an appendix to my *The Spurious Texts of Philo of Alexandria*,[1] I provided lists of the Philonic texts found in the printed florilegia and collections of fragments. In his review of this work David T. Runia observed that these lists could be usefully supplemented by a reverse index, which would allow one to find all the texts cited which come from a particular work of Philo.[2] And, as Runia suggests, the Instrumenta section of *SPhA* is an appropriate place for such a reverse index.

In fact, several such reverse indexes seem to be warranted, since the texts cited fall into several distinct groups: (1) texts which have been located within the existing works of Philo, (2) the Fragmenta spuria, (3) other non Philonic texts, and (4) unidentified texts. (For convenience in future references the members of the last group are numbered.) For each text cited, references are given to the lists as provided in *The Spurious Texts*, using the abbreviations and methods of citation used there (see 148–151),[3] with the following exceptions. Texts found in both Tischendorf's edition of 1855 and his edition of 1868 are referenced here, using the abbreviations 'Tis 1855' and 'Tis 1868'. The occasional cross-references to other works (Cramer, etc.) are omitted here, since they will be found using the references here. However, it seemed useful to include all references to the lists themselves, even though this does involve some reduplication.[4]

Finally, it should be noted that the works of Philo are cited here by the abbreviations of *SPhA*, whereas the earlier lists used those of *SPh*.[5]

---

[1] ALGHJ 22 (Leiden 1991) 152–223.
[2] 'Confronting the Augean stables: Royse's *Fragmenta Spuria Philonica*', *SPhA* 4 (1992) 78–86.
[3] As Runia notes (Review 83, n. 25), the date of Petit's edition should be corrected at p. 150 to 1978. Other (self-evident) abbreviations used here are Sac = *Sacra Parallela*, Max = Maximus, Ant = Antonius, Joh. Geo. = Johannes Georgides.
[4] E. g., one will find here a reference to both Mangey and Harris, whereas under Harris's list one will also find the reference to Mangey.
[5] I use the standard order of Philo's works as found, for example, in Mayer's *Index Philoneus*, with the Armeniaca added (first the *Quaestiones*, then the other works).

1. Identified Philonic Texts

Opif. 23	οὐχ ὡς πέφυκεν — αὐτῶν	Pitra 305.III; Harris 84.2
Opif. 28	καλὸν οὐδὲν — ἐπινοίαις	Harris 89.6
Opif. 61	οὐ πάντα — γνώριμα	Mangey 661.6; Harris 81.7
Opif. 103	κατὰ — παραιρεῖσθαι	Sac 314 (1108D1–12)
Opif. 105	ἰατρὸς — γέρων	Sac 314 (1108D12–9A13)
Opif. 124	τὰ κατὰ — δυναμένων	Sac 407 (1313C14–D3); Harris 89.7
Opif. 135	τοῦ τεχνίτου — ἡμῶν	Harris 90.1
Opif. 138, 139	ὁ δημιουργὸς — μίμημα	Harris 90.2
Leg. 1.46	ὥσπερ γὰρ — σκεδάννυσιν	Pitra 310.Ib; Harris 103.3b; PCW 1:lix
Leg. 1.52	οἴησις ἀκάθαρτον φύσει (ἐστίν)	Sac 629 (216D6), 704 (384A4); Mangey 652.10, 668.2; Mai 105a (2088D1); Harris 81.2
Leg. 1.58	ἡ θεωρία — περιμάχητος	Ant 10 (793C6–7); Mangey 670.3b; Harris 95.3
Leg. 1.73	ἀνάγκη — διασῴζεσθαι	Max 584 (821C9–11); Ant 87 (1032D8–10); Tis 1855 174.30
Leg. 1.89	πολλοὶ — ἑκάστην	Ant 116 (1117D11–20A3)
Leg. 1.91	ὁ νοῦς — ἀσώματον	Harris 90.3
Leg. 1.102	σπάνιον — ἀναρίθμητον	Harris 90.4
Leg. 2.65	ἀναισχυντία — ἀσυγκαταθέτως	Max 633 (916A9–12) (— ἀσυνκαθέτως); Ant 135 (1169D1–3); Mangey 672.4, 692; Tis 1855 174.29; Harris 95.2
Leg. 2.79	ἡδονῇ ἐναντίον — ἀρετή	Pitra 311.IIIb; Harris 87.3
Leg. 2.79	οὐ παντὸς — θεοφιλοῦς	Pitra 311.IIIa; Harris 87.2
Leg. 2.101, 102	ὄντως ὑπὸ — εὐδαιμονήσει	Pitra 311.IV; Harris 87.4
Leg. 3.4	πάντα — πανταχοῦ	Sac 301 (1080C2–6); Harris 90.5
Leg. 3.10	ἀξίως — τούτους	Sac 427 (1357C12–D3); Max 603 (860A11–14); Tis 1855 172.16; Harris 90.6
Leg. 3.10	τοῖς — οἷόν τε	Sac 663 (293A3–4); Ant 92 (1049B5–6); Joh. Geo. 84 (1141A5–6)
Leg. 3.16–17	αἱ συνεχεῖς — νοῦν	Ant 151 (1213A9–14)
Leg. 3.47	εἰ ζητεῖς — ἀναζήτει	Sac 304 (1085D5–6); Harris 90.7
Leg. 3.73	τὸ κύριος — ὄνομα	Sac 784 (532C9–12)
Leg. 3.79	βασιλεὺς — εἰσηγητής	Mai 107b (2096A3–4); Harris 83.4
Leg. 3.81	τύραννος — εἰρήνης	Ant 77 (1004B12–13)
Leg. 3.86	ἡ χαρὰ — χαρά	Harris 90.8
Leg. 3.89	ἡ τυχοῦσα — γέννημα	Mangey 663.2a; Harris 100.6

Leg. 3.105	θεοῦ — ἐπάγειν	Sac 710 (397A9–10); Joh. Geo. 47 (1104D1–5A1); Pitra 306.IV; Harris 80.2, 84.4
Leg. 3.106	(οὐδὲ) τοῖς — ἐπανόρθωσιν	Sac 710 (397A11–13); Ant 22 (832C9–11); Joh. Geo. 47 (1105A1–3); Pitra 306.V; Harris 80.1
Leg. 3.158	τὰ μὴ σὺν — κόσμια	Sac 397 (1293C1–2); Ant 13 (801D11–12); Joh. Geo. 84 (1141A3–4) (τὰ μὴ συλλόγων —); Mangey 650.4; Harris 78.6
Leg. 3.160	οὐκ ἔστι τῶν — ἐᾷ	Harris 110.5
Leg. 3.167	νόμος οὗτος — τιμᾶν	Harris 109.6
Leg. 3.182	οὐκ ἂν — κολακεία	Sac 564 (77C9–10), 715 (408D5–6); Harris 79.7
Leg. 3.182	νόσος — κολακεία	Max 565 (789B1); Ant 58 (941A4)
Leg. 3.205	ὅρκος — ἀμφισβητουμένου	Ant 129 (1156D2–3); Harris 97.1[6]
Cher. 24	τὸ σὺν θεῷ — φευκτόν	Pitra 306.VII; Harris 84.6
Cher. 29	ὦ διάνοια — θεοῦ	Harris 109.11
Cher. 83	οἱ λεγόμενοι — ὀνομάζονται	Sac 434 (1373C4–5); Ant 97 (1064B6–7)
Cher. 98	ἐπειδήπερ — θεός	Ant 150 (1209C11–D2); Mangey 672.5a; Harris 97.7
Sacr. 35	ἀρχήν — συνιστάμενον	Ant 117 (1124A5–8)
Sacr. 35, 40	ἀρχήν, εἰ δεῖ — δεδώρηται	Harris 96.7
Sacr. 40	θνητῷ — δεδώρηται	Ant 117 (1124A9–10)
Sacr. 86	ἡ συνεχὴς — ἀμελετησία	Sac 405 (1312A5–6); Mangey 650.7a; Harris 79.1a
Sacr. 86	ἡ συνεχὴς — ἐξέλυσαν	Ant 119 (1128C3–5)
Sacr. 86	μυρίοι γοῦν — ἐξέλυσαν	Harris 79.2
Sacr. 111	ἄγευστον — σπανιώτατον	Pitra 308.XVIa; Harris 85.2
Sacr. 114	χαλεπόν — φύσει	Sac 711 (400B1); Harris 81.3
Sacr. 124	ἐγὼ οὖν — δωρούμενον	Ant 112 (1105C6–12); Harris 96.4

[6]This text was cited as *Decal.* 86 in the printed lists (see p. 167, n. 13), contrary to Harris's identification of it as *Leg.* 3.205, and contrary to PCW's identification of it as *Spec.* 2.10. It now seems to me that Harris is correct: this text agrees with *Leg.* 3.205 in reading πράγματος ἀμφισβητουμένου and in having ὅρκος (ὅρκον) at the beginning, whereas *Decal.* 86 reads πραγμάτων ἀμφισβητουμένων and has ὅρκος at the end. And *Spec.* 2.10 differs in having the addition of οὐδὲν ἄλλο ἤ. (I take the shift from the accusative of *Leg.* 3.205 to the nominative in the text as required in an excerpt, and as a coincidental agreement with the nominative of *Spec.* 2.10.) Now, the citation at Ant 129 (1157C11–D2) = Harris 97.4 is certainly from *Decal.* 86. So we must grant (contrary to my earlier view) that indeed "two excerpts were made independently of almost the same phrase from two of Philo's works."

REVERSE INDEXES TO ROYSE'S *SPURIOUS TEXTS* 159

Sacr. 135	κακίας — (ἐπ)εισέρχεται	Sac 438 (1381B9–11); Max 530–31 (725C7–9); Ant 10 (793C1–3); Tis 1855 174.35; Tis 1868 154.9; Harris 89.2
Det. 4	ἐν ᾗ μὲν — ὑπείληπται	Mai 107a (2093C9–12); Harris 83.3
Det. 61	ἔκθεσμος — παρορᾶν	Sac 301 (1080C6–7)
Det. 136	κυρίως — ἀβέβαιον	Sac 326 (1136B1–9); Mai 96a (2064C3–10); Harris 82.3
Post. 11	καθάπερ — ἀκούσια	Mai 102a (2080D7–9); Harris 103.1
Post. 14	οὐκ ἐν χρόνῳ — χρόνου	Pitra 307.IX; Harris 85.1
Post. 21	ἀναζητοῦσιν — αὐτῆς	Pitra 306.VI; Harris 84.5
Post. 24	πέφυκεν — εἶναι	Max 670 (984B1–3); Ant 144 (1193B7–8); Tis 1855 174.39; Tis 1868 155.15; Harris 89.5
Post. 24–25	πέφυκεν — ἔχουσα	Sac 448 (1404C10–12); Max 670 (984A10–12); Tis 1855 174.38
Post. 24–25	πέφυκεν — πραγμάτων	Sac 750 (476A6–12); Mai 100a (2076B6–12); Harris 72.2
Post. 59	ὁ νοῦς — ἀψευδέστατος	Sac 349 (1188A12–B1); Mangey 649.2; Harris 78.1
Post. 97	παιδείας — ἀμήχανον	Sac 435 (1376A12–B1); Mai 99b (2073B1–3); Harris 82.4
Post. 138 (+ gloss)	φρόνησις — δεσπότας	Ant 11 (797B13–C2); Tis 1855 172.8
Post. 138	μόνος — δεσπότας	Sac 693 (361A4–5); Harris 91.1
Post. 141	εὐήθεις — δίδωσιν	Mai 99b (2073B3–C2); Harris 82.5
Post. 142, 142–43, 145	οὐ πάντα — σταθμᾶται	Pitra 306.VIII; Harris 84.7
Post. 152	πάνυ εὐήθεις — ὑφηγητήν	Mai 107b (2096A14–B5); Harris 83.5
Post. 158	αὕτη — ὑπολαμβάνειν	Ant 118 (1124A11–12); Harris 110.12
Deus 27	ἀνθρώποις — ἐχθρῶν	Sac 776 (516D1–5); Mangey 657.5; Harris 69.8; Marcus QG no. 5
Deus 46–47	τῆς ψυχῆς — δέξασθαι	Harris 9.4; Harris 95.1
Deus 61	τῷ ἄριστα — ἐντυγχάνοντας	Harris 9.5
Deus 64	καὶ — νουθετοῦνται	Ant 97 (1064B3–5); Mangey 673.2
Ebr. 6	τοῦ ληρεῖν — ἀπαιδευσία	Wendland 20.1b
Ebr. 6	ἀλήθεια — δύναμις	Ant 26 (844A9–10); Harris 109.1
Ebr. 12	ἀπαιδευσία — χρησομένοις	Wendland 20.1c
Ebr. 26	τῷ ὄντι — ἀγαθόν	Wendland 21.2a
Ebr. 26	πολύχουν — ἀγαθόν	Ant 20 (824D8–10)
Ebr. 26	ἐσταλμένον — ἀγαθόν	Sac 688 (348C6); Harris 91.2; Wendland 21.2b

Ebr. 30	πατρὸς — ἀπέτεκεν	Ant 91 (1044D1-8)
Ebr. 32	τῶν θείων — οἴσομεν	Wendland 25.11
Ebr. 48–49	τοῖς ἀσκηταῖς — ἐντυχεῖν	Wendland 21.3
Ebr. 56–58	οὐ δύναται — αὐτομολοῦμεν	Pitra 309.XVIII; Harris 85.4; Wendland 21.4a
Ebr. 57	τίς τιμῆς — παράπαν	Ant 140 (1184C3–5); Harris 110.11; Wendland 21.4b
Ebr. 71	λόγου θεοῦ — ψυχῶν	PCW 2:xxvii, n. 1
Ebr. 100	(ὁ) σοφὸς — ζωήν	Sac 754 (484B3–5); Max 599 (852B4–6); Ant 143 (1192A4–6); Mangey 656.2; Harris 99.5
Ebr. 125	τὰ ἀκούσια — καταβαρούμενα	Wendland 21.5
Ebr. 141	νόσου — ἀπαιδευσία	Sac 363 (1217B11); Mangey 649.7; Harris 78.5; Wendland 20.1a
Ebr. 160	ὁ ἰδὼν καὶ — ἐπιβουλεύεται	Wendland 21.6
Ebr. 162	χαλεπὸν — ἐπαιρόμενος	Wendland 22.9
Ebr. 174	γίνεται — δυσθήρατον (εἶναι)	Sac 531 (1584B6–12); Harris 91.3; Wendland 21.7
Ebr. 176–77	οὐ μόνον — νομισθῆναι	Wendland 21.8a
Ebr. 179	οὐ γὰρ — γεγηρακόσιν	Wendland 21.8b
Ebr. 188	τὸ μὴ — πίστιν	Ant 27 (845A11–12); Mangey 671.8
Sobr. 43	τοῦ πυρὸς — ἀνακαίεται	Pitra xxiii.IV; Harris 84.1
Sobr. 49–50	ἔτι ἐν τῷ — σωτήριον	Pitra 313.X; Harris 87.5
Her. 6–7	πότε ἄγει — ἐβασίλευσε	Harris 91.4
Her. 9	μέγιστον — κατορθοῦν	Ant 98 (1065D1–4); Mangey 673.3; Harris 96.2
Her. 21	πᾶς σοφὸς θεοῦ φίλος	Sac 693 (361A6); Mangey 652.8; Harris 99.2
Her. 56–58	φησὶν ὁ νομοθέτης — τούτου	Harris 91.5
Her. 105	μυρίοι — καταχρησάμενοι	Harris 91.6
Her. 105–6, 110	σοὶ λέγεται — διαγγέλλῃ	Mangey 660.3; Harris 99.7
Her. 112–13	βουληθεὶς — βίον	Mangey 669.2; Harris 102.6
Her. 261	ἡ τῶν μελλόντων — ἀνθρώπῳ	Mangey 661.5; Harris 100.2a
Her. 302, 303	οἱ πιθανῶν — συνεπιγράφεται	Harris 92.1
Congr. 162	τὰ πλεῖστα — περιγίνεσθαι	Ant 118 (1124B2–3); Mangey 668.5
Fug. 14	βλαβεραὶ — εἴδωλα	Sac 692 (357A3–5); Ant 109 (1096D6–8); Joh. Geo. 17 (1073C8–10); Mangey 652.7, 671.3a; Harris 81.1

Fug. 153	δυσεύρετον — καλόν	Ant 144 (1193C8–9); Joh. Geo. 26 (1084C1–2); Mangey 671.6b; Harris 97.6
Mut. 10	τί θαυμαστόν — εἶδεν	Sac 784 (532C12–15)
Mut. 11	οὐχ ὁρᾷς — λέγεσθαι	Sac 784 (532C15–D3)
Mut. 13	περὶ δὲ τοῦ — αὐτοῖς	Sac 784–85 (532D3–6)
Mut. 14	οὕτω καὶ — εὐφημήσεις	Sac 785 (532D6–9)
Mut. 22	κύριος — ἡγεμών	Sac 434 (1373C5–8); Ant 97 (1064B8–10); Harris 92.2
Mut. 36	ἀδύνατον — ἐνδεδεμένον	Pitra 308.XVIb; Harris 85.3
Mut. 37	ἔστι — συνέρχεσθαι	Ant 143 (1192A7–10)
Mut. 39–40, 42, 45	τῷ 'Αβραάμ — γενομένου	Harris 92.3
Mut. 49	ἄπειρα — ἀμήχανον	Ant 154 (1224C4–8)
Mut. 55 (+ gloss?)	ὁ μηδέποτε — φίλοις	Harris 109.5
Mut. 169	τὸν φαῦλον — βίον	Ant 104 (1084B12–C3); Harris 96.3 (τῶν φαύλων —)
Mut. 170	οὐδενὶ — ἐστι(ν)	Ant 128 (1153A14–B1); Harris 110.8
Mut. 170	πόνος — ἀπεχθάνονται	Ant 119 (1128B14–C2); Harris 110.1
Mut. 213	τοῦ κατ' ἀρετὴν — ζῆσαι	Harris 92.4
Mut. 218	οὐχ ἃ δοῦναι — δωρεάς	Pitra 309.XIX; Harris 85.5
Mut. 239–40, 243	χαλεπὸν — βλαβερώτερον	Harris 92.5
Somn. 1.11	ἀνθεῖ(ται) — μαραίνονται	Sac 404 (1308C9–10); Max 635 (917C4–5) (— περαίνονται); Ant 94 (1056B9–10); Harris 92.6
Somn. 1.150–52	ἀνώμαλον — καθελών	Ant 115 (1116B1–C3); Harris 96.6
Somn. 1.176	ὥσπερ — φύσεως	Ant 56 (933C8–10); Harris 95.6
Somn. 1.177, 176	ἐάν τις — ὠφέλειαν	Sac 750 (473C2–76A2); Mangey 655.2; Harris 69.6; Marcus QG no. 4; Petit QE no. 28
Abr. 271	ὁ ἀληθείᾳ — θεωρεῖται	Max 635 (917B11–12); Ant 94 (1056B1–2); Tis 1855 174.36
Abr. 271	ὁ ἀληθείᾳ — παιδευθέντας	Sac 404 (1308C11–D4); Harris 93.1
Abr. 271	τοὺς — παιδευθέντας	Ant 95 (1057B2–5)
Abr. 272, 274	τῷ ὄντι — μετιών	Sac 693 (361A7–13); Harris 80.3
Jos. 144	πλούτου — ἐπικουρίᾳ	Sac 481 (1473D14–15), 502 (1520D6–7); Max 568 (793D7–8); Ant 38 (884B9–10); Tis 1855 172.13; Harris 93.2
Mos. 1.35	οἱ ξένοι — γραφέσθωσαν	Harris 93.3
Mos. 1.59	(τὸ) καλὸν τότε — γνωρίσματα	Ant 102 (1080A3–5); Mangey 670.7

Mos. 1.62	ἀμήχανον — παιδευθῆναι	Sac 363 (1217B12–C1); Max 584 (821C12–13); Ant 56 (933C6–7); Tis 1855 172.15; Harris 87.6
Mos. 1.160–61	ἐπειδὰν ἡγεμὼν — εἰσίν	Harris 108.3
Mos. 1.174	ἴδιον θεοῦ — χειρός	Pitra 305.II; Harris 84.3
Mos. 1.230	ὀλισθηραὶ — ἐνσφραγιζόμεναι	Harris 93.4
Mos. 1.285	βέλτιον — ἡσυχία	Joh. Geo. 14 (1072A10–11); Mangey 661.8; Harris 82.1
Mos. 1.304	τὸ μέγιστον — δῶρον	Ant 132 (861B8–9); Mangey 671.10 (— ἔργον); Harris 108.6
Mos. 2.27	τὰ καλὰ — ἀναλάμπει	Max 658 (960C14–D1); Mangey 672.7 (τὰ κᾶν —); Tis 1855 171.2; Tis 1868 152.2; Harris 89.1
Mos. 2.108	ἡ ἀληθὴς — κόσμῳ	Ant 3 (773B5–8); Mangey 666.4; Harris 101.12
Mos. 2.184	ὁ μὲν τὸν — μακαριότητα	Max 620 (889C3–5); Ant 118 (1124A13–B1); Tis 1855 173.23; Harris 96.8
Mos. 2.218	διατί — παρανόμημα	Tis 1868 152; Harris 88.3
Decal. 6	τιμὴ τίς ἂν — τίμιον	Harris 93.5
Decal. 52–53	πλάνος τις — παρεκαλύψαντο	Harris 93.6
Decal. 82–83	οὐ λήψῃ — παρήγγειλεν	Pitra 309.XX; Harris 85.6
Decal. 84	φασί τινες — ὑπονοεῖται	Ant 129 (1157C9–10); Harris 97.3
Decal. 86	ὅρκος — ἀμφισβητουμένου	see under Leg. 3.205
Decal. 86	μαρτυρία — ἀνοσιώτατον	Ant 129 (1157C11–D2); Harris 97.4
Decal. 87	ὁ ἑκάστη ψυχῇ — ἀπορρήξῃ	Harris 93.7
Decal. 92	ἐκ πολυορκίας — φύεται	Ant 129 (1157C8); Joh. Geo. 34 (1092B11) (ἐκ πολυλογίας —); Harris 97.2
Decal. 94	οἶδά τινας — ἀσέβειαν	Harris 94.1
Decal. 110	οἱ γονέων — ἀνθρώπους	Ant 93 (1049D6–7); Harris 95.10
Decal. 112	τίνα ἕτερον — δυνάμενον	Tis 1855 173.19
Decal. 113	καλὸν — ἐλπίδα	Ant 108 (1093C7–8); Joh. Geo. 49 (1105C1–2); Mangey 670.8; Harris 88.1 (ὅσον δοκεῖ —)
Decal. 137	ἐγχρονίζον — (συν)αυξάνοντα	Max 674 (989C15–D3); Ant 145–46 (1200A1–3); Mangey 674.8; Tis 1855 172.4; Tis 1868 152.4; Harris 82.2
Spec. 1.100	τὸ περὶ θεὸν — ἀφορητότερον	Harris 108.5

Spec. 1.120	μεταδοτέον — συγχύσεως	Mai 103a (2081D7–11); Harris 83.1a
Spec. 1.121	εἰ γὰρ ἴσον — κακῶν	Harris 83.2
Spec. 1.121	τὰ ὅμοια — κακῶν	Mai 103a (2081D13–14); Harris 83.1b
Spec. 2.225	οἱ γονεῖς — ἀθανατίζουσιν	Tis 1855 172.17
Spec. 2.225	ὅπερ, οἶμαι — ἀθανατίζουσιν	Ant 91 (1044C1–5); Harris 95.9
Spec. 2.253	τὸν ὀμνύντα — τιμωρίας	Ant 129 (1157D3–6); Mangey 672.6; Tis 1855 173.18 (— οὐδέποτε); Harris 97.5
Spec. 3.194	δοκεῖ γάρ — λογισμοῦ	Tis 1855 174.33; Tis 1868 155.13; Harris 104.2
Spec. 4.55	ἄτοπον — ἐξισοῦντας	Ant 88 (1037B1–2)
Spec. 4.55, 63	ἄτοπον γάρ — πονηρευομένων	Tis 1855 174.32; Tis 1868 155.12; Harris 89.3
Spec. 4.221	εἰρήνη κἂν — πολέμου	Sac 356 (1204B3–4); Ant 132 (861B5–6); Harris 78.2
Spec. 4.223	καὶ τοῖς ἑτέρων — σωφρονεῖν	Harris 98.7b
Virt. 9	ὁ φαῦλος — τείνει	Sac 378 (1252D10–53A2); Harris 94.2
Virt. 9	ὁ σπουδαῖος — ἀθανασίας	Sac 365 (1224B12–C1), 613 (181C6–9); Max 574 (805A8–11); Ant 38 (881A4–7); Tis 1855 172.14; Harris 94.3
Virt. 177	τὸ μὲν μηδέν — ἀγνοήσαντος	Ant 22 (832C5–8); Harris 95.5 (— εἰς ἀπάθειαν ἔρχεται)
Praem. 5	οἱ ἄνανδροι — γίνονται	Mangey 663.3; Harris 100.7
Praem. 51	μετὰ τόν — καλόν	Ant 94 (1056B3–8); Harris 96.1
Praem. 51	χωρὶς θεωρίας — καλόν	Sac 397 (1293C3–4); Ant 13 (801D13–14); Joh. Geo. 98 (1153B8–9); Mangey 671.5a; Harris 78.7, 94.4
Praem. 63	παντός — φαντασιούμενον	Harris 94.5
Praem. 69	(οἱ) ἄνθρωποι — ἀρχή	Sac 730 (441A5–7); Tis 1855 174.26
Praem. 72	ἐλπίδα — δράσαντες	Ant 8 (789A3–5); Mangey 673.9
Praem. 104–5	οἷς ὁ ἀληθινός — κτῆσις	Harris 94.6
Praem. 123	οἶκος — βασιλείῳ	Ant 150 (1209D3–5); Mangey 672.5b; Harris 97.8
Prob. 4–5	λέγω δέ — ζῶσιν	Pitra 311.II; Harris 87.1
Contempl. 16	αἱ μὲν (ἐκ) — καλόν	Max 568 (796A1–3); Tis 1855 171.1; Tis 1868 152.1; Harris 88.4

Contempl. 16	χρόνου φείδεσθαι καλόν	Sac 563 (76A7); Mangey 651.7; Harris 79.6
Flacc. 1	οἷς — κατορθοῦσι(ν)	Ant 149 (1208B14–15); Mangey 671.2
Flacc. 5	τῷ στρατιώτῃ — φυλάττειν	Sac 688 (349B1–3); Harris 99.1
Flacc. 7	τῷ μὲν — ἔχει	Max 610 (869C7–9); Tis 1855 173.20
Flacc. 7	τῷ μὲν — δικαστηρίῳ	Sac 520 (1560C1–4); Ant 151 (1213A15–B3); Harris 79.4, 94.7
Flacc. 17	ὅταν — ἀνερεθίζεσθαι	Ant 87 (1033A3–6); Harris 95.8
Flacc. 34	αἰσχροὶ — προχειρότατοι	Sac 379 (1253D6–9); Mangey 650.3; Harris 10.2
Flacc. 41	ἡ ἐξ ἔθους — ἐπίβουλον	Ant 119 (1128C6–7); Joh. Geo. 39 (1097A7)
Flacc. 99	ἀλήθεια αὐταρκέστατος ἔπαινος	Harris 109.2
Flacc. 109	ἀβέβαιοι — πάσχοντες	Ant 104 (1084C4–6) (— πασχόντων); Mangey 666.5; Harris 101.13
Flacc. 154	χρήσιμον — σωφρονίζεσθαι	Sac 683 (337C12–13); Mangey 652.5; Harris 98.7a
Legat. 1	μέχρι — νήπιοι	Ant 95 (1057B6–8)
Legat. 2	ὀφθαλμοῖς — μέλλοντα	Ant 150 (1209D6–8); Mangey 672.5c; Harris 97.9
Legat. 7	ἡ κόλασις — παθεῖν	Sac 683 (337D1–4); Mangey 652.6; Harris 80.4
Legat. 14	ἐγκρατείας — θανάτῳ	Max 612 (873D6–76A2); Ant 46 (908B13–14), 48 (913C6–7); Tis 1855 174.34; Tis 1868 155.11; Harris 89.4
Legat. 17	ὦ πόσα — φόβοι	Sac 359 (1209C6–8); Mangey 649.4; Harris 78.3
Legat. 18	φήμης οὐδὲν ὠκύτερον	Sac 711 (400C3)
Legat. 36	τὴν αἰδῶ — πολλοῖς	Sac 378 (1252A3); Ant 128 (1156A9)
Legat. 39	δεινὸν — γίνεται	Ant 107 (1089D13–92A2); Harris 96.5
Legat. 47	ἄξιον — ἀναπέμπουσι	Sac 551 (49C6–9); Mangey 651.3; Harris 98.4
Legat. 50	βασιλεῦ — εὐεργετεῖν	Ant 77 (1004C1–5); Harris 95.7
Legat. 60	τοιοῦτον — εὐεργετήσασιν	Ant 101 (1073C1–3)
Legat. 68	εἰρήνη — φύεται	Ant 132 (861B7)
Legat. 72	δεσμὸς — μετάγουσαι	Ant 16 (812C8–9); Harris 95.4
Legat. 85	ἰσότης πηγὴ δικαιοσύνης	Sac 556 (60D9)
Legat. 140	τὰς τῶν — πλεῖστοι	Sac 564 (77C11–12); Max 565 (789B1–3); Ant 58 (941A5–6); Harris 79.8

Legat. 147	ὁ τῆς εἰρήνης — βίῳ	Harris 109.3
Legat. 190	νεότης — γίνεται	Sac 776 (516A3–5); Ant 80 (1012B6–7), 97 (1061D3–4); Harris 81.5
Legat. 195	τοῖς — δημιουργοῦσι	Harris 109.10
Legat. 233	οὐδεὶς — δεσπότῃ	Sac 448 (1401D8–9), 567 (84B7–8); Ant 98 (1068B11–12); Harris 94.8
Legat. 245	τοῖς — ὠφεληθήσονται	Ant 102 (1077D12–13); Harris 109.13
Legat. 247	οὐκ ἀσφαλὲς — πράγματα	Harris 94.9, 109.4
Legat. 287	τί ἂν — ἄμεινον	Ant 77 (1004C6–7)
Legat. 319	ἀσθενέστεραι — καταλαβεῖν	Sac 777 (517B7–9); Ant 105 (1088A9–11); Harris 81.6
Legat. 360	ὅταν — σιωπᾶν	Ant 88 (1037B3–4); Harris 109.8
Legat. 369	ἃ πρέσβεις — ἀναφοράν	Sac 367 (1229A3–4); Harris 78.4
Hypoth.	τὸν μὲν παλαιὸν — πολυανδρίαν	Mangey 626.1
Hypoth.	ἀνήρ γε μὴν — πεισθῆναι	Mangey 627.1
Hypoth.	ἆρά τι τούτων — ἁπανταχοῦ	Mangey 628.1
Hypoth.	ὅλην δὲ ἡμέραν — λόγος	Mangey 630.1
Hypoth. (Apol.)	μυρίους δὲ τῶν — σεμνοποιοῦσι	Mangey 632.1
Hypoth.	φίλαυτον — ἀνδρός	Ant 107 (1092A3–4)
Hypoth.	φίλαυτον γυνὴ — παραλῦσαι	Harris 76.4
Hypoth.	φίλαυτον γυνὴ — πράττειν	Sac 777 (517B13–C8); Harris 76.5
QG 1.1	διὰ τί τὴν — γεγονότα	Lewy 75.1
QG 1.3	μήποτε ὡς ἵππος — δεῖται	Wendland 36
QG 1.17 (a)	φίλον ἡγητέον — δύνηται	Max 548 (757C11–12); Ant 28 (849A6–7); Tis 1855 172.9
QG 1.17 (a), (b)	φίλους — ἐγώ	Sac 788 (540B9–14); Mangey 659.6
QG 1.20	ἀνδρὸς — εὐκλείας	Sac 748 (469B9–C6); Mangey 653.2b
QG 1.21	ἤγαγεν — προσέταττεν	Sac 748 (469A13–B9); Mangey 653.2a
QG 1.24	ὁ ὕπνος — ὑπεκλέλυνται	Mangey 667.5
QG 1.27	ἀποικίαν — τῶν νόμων	Lewy 75.2
QG 1.28	καὶ θεασάμενος — γέννησιν	Sac 748 (469C6–10); Mangey 653.2c
QG 1.29	διό φησιν — ἥδεσθαι	Sac 748 (469C11–D1); Mangey 653.2d
QG 1.41 (b)	δοκεῖ μὲν — ἔστι(ν)	Ant 19 (824B4–5); Mangey 674.1; Wendland 140, n. 1
QG 1.49	τοῦ φαύλου — ἀνακέκραται	Sac 782 (528B11–C1); Mangey 659.2; Harris 73.7; Marcus QE no. 8; Petit QE no. 33
QG 1.51	τί ἐστιν — προσενεμήθη	Sac 748 (468D11–69A8); Mangey 653.1
QG 1.55 (a)	οὔτε ἐνδοιασμὸς — ἐστιν	Mangey 669.7

QG 1.63	σημεῖον δὲ — τεθυκότι	Wendland 39
QG 1.64 (b), (c), (d)	τὸ εὐχαριστεῖν — εἰσηγουμένη	Mangey 668.3
QG 1.65	τὸ μὴ — ἔχοντες	Sac 751 (476C12–D2); Mangey 655.5
QG 1.70	τί δ' ἐστιν — ἐγκατώρυξαν	Lewy 75.3
QG 1.77	ὁ μὲν Κάϊν — δεκάσω	Sac 776–77 (516D9–17A7); Mangey 658.1a
QG 1.79	ἐλπίς — προσδοκία	Ant 8 (789A1–2)
QG 1.82	συγγνώμη — γεννᾶν	Ant 125 (1145A12); Mangey 672.3
QG 1.85	ἤδη τινὲς — νόσον	Sac 784 (532B9–11); Ant 116 (1120A4–6); Mangey 659.4
QG 1.89	ἀεὶ φθάνουσι — προγενέσθαι	Mangey 670.2
QG 1.92	πνευματικαὶ (-κὴ) — μεταμορφούμενοι	Sac 309 (1097B2–4), 772 (505D11–13); Mangey 656.3
QG 1.93	ἔνιοι νομίζουσι — γῆς	Mangey 669.6
QG 1.94	διὰ τί ἄνθρωπον — γέγονε	Mangey 675.1
QG 1.98	σωτήριον — οὐρανοῦ	Mangey 664.4; Harris 101.1
QG 1.100 (a)	οὐδὲν ἐναντίον — ἀδικία	Sac 751 (476C6–7), 787 (537A14–B1); Mangey 655.4; Harris 70.8
QG 1.100 (c)	ὡς ἀμέτοχος — θεός	Pitra 307.XI
QG 2.5 (b)	δυνατὸν — γεννᾶν	Sac 314 (1109B1–5)
QG 2.10	τί ἐστιν — τῇ κτήσει	Lewy 76.5
QG 2.12 (c)	ἡ ἐν τῷ φαύλῳ — φονώντων	Mangey 663.4
QG 2.12 (d)	ἠθικώτατον — ἐστίν	Lewy 77.6
QG 2.15 (b)	θεοπρεπῶς — δίκαιον	Pitra 313.VIII
QG 2.17 (c)	εὔλογον — δυνατόν	Lewy 77.7
QG 2.22	καλῶς — σωτηρίας	Wendland 55–56; Marcus 192
QG 2.34 (a), (c)	αἱ αἰσθήσεις — σῴζει	Mangey 665.6
QG 2.34 (b), (c)	ἀμήχανον — σῴζει	Mangey 669.1; Harris 70.4
QG 2.41	ὁ καλὸς — δόγμασιν	Mangey 662.7; Harris 100.5
QG 2.54 (a)	ἡ πρότασις — βεβαιοτάτου	Pitra 304.I
QG 2.54 (c), (d)	ἴσον — τεινόμενον	Mangey 663.2b
QG 2.59	τί ἐστιν — αἵματι	Mangey 668.7
QG 2.62	διὰ τί ὡς — ἐξομοιοῦσθαι	Mangey 625.1
QG 2.68 (b)	διττὸν τὸ — πίπτει	Mai 104a (2085A15–B2)
QG 2.74	νεώτερον — κακία	Wendland 61, n. 4
QG 3.3 (a)	ἀτόπως — στερούμενα	Sac 774 (512C13–D8); Mangey 657.1
QG 3.3 (b)	συγκρύπτεται — δοκιμώτατον	Mai 103b (2084C7–8); Harris 71.3; Marcus QG no. 13; Petit QG no. 7
QG 3.7	πᾶσα ἡ — ξένων	Mai 98b (2072B4–5)
QG 3.8	ἕνεκα — ὠφελεῖν (ὠφελεῖσθαι)	Ant 112 (1105D1–6); Mangey 661.3

QG 3.30 (a)	τὸ ὑποτάττεσθαι — ὠφελιμώτατον	Sac 359 (1209A11), 567 (84B6), 657 (280C7) (— ὠφέλιμον); Ant 154 (1224C3); Mangey 652.2 (— ὠφέλιμον); Mai 103a (2084A14)
QG 3.30 (b)	ὁ μαθών — ἄρχεσθαι	Sac 359 (1209A7–10); Max 646 (937C2–5); Ant — (968A1–4); Mangey 649.3
QG 3.38 (b)	μακαρία — γινομένοις	Sac 372 (1240B11–14), 675 (321A9–12) (— γενομένοις); Joh. Geo. 59 (1116C15–D2); Mangey 650.1; Harris 97.10
QG 3.48	οἴησις — ἀνέχεται	Sac 629 (216D3–5), 704 (384A1–3); Mangey 652.9; Harris 99.3
QG 3.52	οὐδὲν — τιμωρία	Mangey 675.2a
QG 4.8 (c)	τοῖς ἀμυήτοις — τελετῆς	Sac 782 (525D8–10); Mangey 658.4c; Harris 69.4c
QG 4.30	τῷ μὲν ᾽Αβραὰμ — σκότει	Pitra xxiii.I
QG 4.33 (a)	στενοχωρεῖται — διάγειν	Sac 363 (1217B5–8); Mangey 649.5b, 674.6
QG 4.33 (b)	πάγκαλον — πάθους	Lewy 78.9
QG 4.40	νόμος — ἀορασίας	Sac 341 (1169D2–4), 518 (1556C5–7), 774 (512D9–11); Mangey 657.2
QG 4.43	οἱ ἐν ταῖς — τίθενται	Mai 101b (2080B4–11)
QG 4.47 (a)	ὁ σοφὸς — ἐπιτύχῃ	Sac 376 (1245D9–48A2) (— ἐντύχῃ), 754 (484A9–10); Max 599 (852B1–3); Ant 143 (1192A3–4); Mangey 650.2 (— ἐντύχῃ), 655.8
QG 4.47 (b)	ὁ φαῦλος — ἀτιμότατον	Ant 144 (1193C3–7); Mangey 671.6a
QG 4.51 (a)	διὰ τί ἐξῆλθεν — ἐχόντων	Mangey 675.3
QG 4.51 (b), (c)	ἐκ τοῦ — βαρύτατα	Lewy 78.10
QG 4.52 (b)	χαίρειν ἐπὶ — ἀνθρώπινον	Sac 509 (1536A10–11); Max 588 (832A3–4); Mai 102a (2080C9–10); Tis 1855 174.41; Tis 1868 154.10
QG 4.64	(οὐχ) ὡς τὸ — δικαιοσύνης	Sac 520 (1560B6–10); Max 660–61 (965A13–B3); Mangey 651.1; Mai 102a (2080D12–81A3); Tis 1855 172.5
QG 4.67	οὐ πάντα — ὀνομάτων	Mai 106b (2092D1–3)
QG 4.69	τὸ δὲ — δύνανται	Mai 106b (2092D3–11)
QG 4.74	οὕτως γὰρ — λέγεται	Sac 754 (484A11–B2); Mangey 656.1; Harris 69.7

QG 4.76 (a)	τῶν μὲν — θεοφιλής	Sac 396 (1292C2-4)
QG 4.76 (a), (b)	τῶν μὲν — ἐπιστήμονα	Sac 775-76 (513D2-16A2); Mangey 657.4
QG 4.99	ἀναιδὲς βλέμμα — σώματι	Sac 658-59 (284B11-C4); Max 633 (916A13-B3); Ant 155 (1225A5-9); Mangey 652.3; Tis 1855 173.24; Tis 1868 154.7
QG 4.100	φυσικώτατα — ὑπονόστησιν	Mangey 667.2; Harris 102.3
QG 4.102 (a), (b), (c)	ἄξιον ἀποδέχεσθαι — ἴσον	Mai 106a (2089D11-92A5)
QG 4.104	οὐχ ὡς — δυνάμεως	Sac 435 (1376B2-5); Mai 99b (2073C4-7)
QG 4.110 (a)	ἀκοῦσαι — πρᾶξαι	Mai 99b (2073C7-9)
QG 4.130	δεῖ γὰρ — δῶρα	Pitra 314.XI
QG 4.131	μετανενοήκασιν — ἀπότρεχε	Lewy 79.11
QG 4.168	καὶ τὸ ῥητὸν — λαβόντων	Pitra 311.V
QG 4.179	μεῖζον — ζημιωθέντι	Sac 363 (1217B9-10); Max 670 (984A13-14); Mangey 649.6; Tis 1855 171.3; Tis 1868 152.3; Harris 69.2
QG 4.184	διὰ τί λέγει — νόμου	Lewy 79.12
QG 4.191 (b), (d)	οἱ βασκανίᾳ — χάριτας	Mai 108b (2097B7-12)
QG 4.191 (c), (d)	διὰ τί ἃ — χάριτας	Lewy 79.13
QG 4.193	φιλάνθρωπος — βλάπτειν	Ant 102 (1077D8-11); Mangey 670.6
QG 4.195.7*	κατάσκοποι — αὐτῶν	Mangey 675.4
QG 4.195.8*	οὐ διὰ τὸν — μετάνοιαν	Mangey 676.2
QG 4.195.9*	ἀμήχανον — θεῷ	Mai 107b (2096B7-10)
QG 4.198	δυοῖν — κακοδαιμονέστατος	Mangey 676.3
QG 4.202 (a)	ἄξιον καὶ — ἄξω	Mangey 676.4a
QG 4.204	ὥσπερ τὰς — ὑβριστής	Mai 106b (2092D13-93A10)
QG 4.206 (b)	λεγέτω καὶ — δρωμένων	Mai 106b (2093A10-B1)
QG 4.211	τὰ αὐτὰ — πλεονεξίαν	Mai 100b (2076D14-77A3); Harris 70.5
QG 4.227	οὐκ ἐπὶ τῷ — πάτερ	Mangey 676.5
QG 4.228	ἀλλ' εἴ γε — σπουδαῖος	Mangey 676.6
QG 4.228	οὐ πᾶς δόλος — ἴδιον	Sac 367 (1228C14-D5); Mangey 649.8
QE 1.1	ὅταν οἱ — ὦσιν	Sac 789 (540D10-15); Mangey 660.1
QE 1.6 (a)	ὑπερβολαὶ — ἄγαν	Mai 106a (2092A7-12)
QE 1.6 (b)	ἡ αὐτάρκεια — καθαιρεῖν	Ant 38 (881A8-9) (— βίον); Mangey 666.2; Harris 101.10
QE 1.7 (a)	λέγεται — ἄρσεν	Sac 777 (517B4-6); Ant 105 (1088A7-8); Mangey 658.3
QE 1.7 (b)	ἔνιοι — (ἀντ)εναπέθετο	Sac 343 (1176A1-5); Ant 116 (1117D6-10); Mangey 648.3

REVERSE INDEXES TO ROYSE'S *SPURIOUS TEXTS* 169

QE 1.19	αἱ μὲν γάρ — ἐπιθυμιῶν	Pitra 313.IX; PCW 2:xv, no. 1
QE 1.21	ἄνδρες — πολιτείας	Ant 102 (1077D14–80A2); Ant 112 (1105D7–9); Mangey 661.2
QE 2.1	τί ἐστι — δεόμενα	Mangey 677.1
QE 2.2	ἐμφανέστατα — ὑπογράφεται	Mangey 677.2
QE 2.3 (a)	χήραν — ἀναπληροῦσθαι	Mangey 677.3
QE 2.3 (a)	οὐ δυναμένου — γονεῖς	Mai 104b (2085D14–88A4)
QE 2.3 (b)	ψυχαὶ δέ — κηδεμονίας	Pitra 308.XIV
QE 2.6 (b)	τῷ ἀγαθῷ — εὐφημία	Lewy 79.14
QE 2.6 (b)	οὐδέν — εὐφημία	Max 556 (773A12–13); Ant 100 (1072D8–9), 126 (1149A9–10); Mangey 671.7; Tis 1855 172.11
QE 2.9 (a), (b)	μάταιόν φησιν — ἀκοῇ	Mangey 677.4
QE 2.9 (a)	μάταιον οὐδέν — ζημίαι	Harris 75.3; Marcus QE no. 22
QE 2.9 (b)	παρ' ἐνίοις — ἀκοῇ	Sac 754 (481C11–13); Mangey 655.7
QE 2.10 (a), (b)	πενία — ἐστι	Mangey 678.1
QE 2.11 (a)	διὰ τί τόν — ἰδίᾳ	Lewy 80.15
QE 2.13 (b)	ὁ πεινῶν — οἰκίας	Sac 613 (184B3–6); Mangey 651.10
QE 2.13 (c)	τῷ ἔνδον — ἁλίσκεται	Ant 151 (1213B4–5); Harris 109.12
QE 2.14	ἀντὶ τοῦ — ἔγγονα	Mangey 678.2
QE 2.14	τὸ αἷμα — ὅσιον	Mangey 678.3
QE 2.15 (b)	ψυχὴ πᾶσα — εὐφροσύνης	Mangey 664.6; Harris 101.3
QE 2.16	φωνὴν θεοῦ — καθαιρεῖν	Mangey 678.4
QE 2.17	στῆλαί εἰσι — καλοῖς	Mangey 678.5
QE 2.19 (a)	ἀγονίαν — διαμονήν	Mai 105b (2089B9–14)
QE 2.19 (b)	εὔπαιδες — ἐπιστήμονες	Ant 93 (1052B2); Mangey 673.5b; Lewy 82.24
QE 2.21	τὸ μὲν ῥητόν — προσγενομένης	Pitra 313.VII
QE 2.24 (b)	σύμβολον — παράπαν	Mangey 679.1
QE 2.25 (b), (c), (d)	ἐὰν τοῦ — ἐμποιεῖ	Mai 100a (2073D8–76A7)
QE 2.25 (b), (c)	ἐὰν ἄρτι — αἴτιον	Mangey 663.1; Pitra 312.VIa
QE 2.25 (d)	ἀγαθός — ἐμποιεῖ	Sac 557 (61C1–6); Mangey 651.5
QE 2.26	ὥσπερ οἱ — τελευτῶσα	Sac 774 (512A12–B5); Mangey 656.5
QE 2.28	οὐχ ὁρᾷς — ἀναλώσῃ	Sac 749 (472C1–5); Mangey 654.1f
QE 2.37	οὐδεὶς αὐχήσει — ἀλογιστίᾳ	Mangey 662.3
QE 2.38 (a)	τὸ μὲν ῥητόν — διαφωνεῖν	Mangey 679.3
QE 2.38 (b)	τὸ ἐμμελές — πειρωμένους	Sac 774 (512B13–C1); Mangey 656.7a; Harris 73.3a; Marcus QE no. 4a
QE 2.40	ἐνίοις — παλινδρομοῦντες	Sac 784 (532B5–8); Mangey 659.3
QE 2.44	ὁ τοῦ σοφοῦ — κάλλος	Sac 774 (512C1–3); Mangey 656.7b; Harris 73.3b; Marcus QE no. 4b
QE 2.45 (a)	ἐναργέστατα — νομοθετεῖσθαι	Mangey 679.5

QE 2.45 (b)	ἄβατος — ἐπιψαῦσαι	Sac 748 (469D5–8); Mangey 654.1a
QE 2.47	τὸ δὲ εἶδος — διάνοιαν	Mangey 679.6
QE 2.49 (a)	ὅτι ἔμελλε — ἀχάριστον	Mangey 680.1
QE 2.50 (a)	τὴν καρδίαν — γραφή	Mai 103a (2084A9–10)
QE 2.50 (b)	ὁ μὴ ἐκ προαιρέσεως — ἀπαρχή	Mangey 670.1
QE 2.55 (a)	οἱ ἀστέρες — ἐξαιρέτοις	Mangey 669.5
QE 2.55 (b)	ὁ τῶν — πνευμάτων	Sac 506 (1529B10–14) (— πραγμάτων); Mangey 674.4
QE 2.62–68	τίνα τὰ Χερουβὶμ — κόσμον	Tis 1868 144–52; PCW 1:xxvii (reference)
QE 2.64	τὸ εὔνομον — ὄντων	Mangey 665.4 (ἔννομον); Harris 101.7 (ἔννομον); Wendland 24.9
QE 2.65	αἱ τοῦ θεοῦ — ἐφιέμεναι	Sac 772 (505D14–8A2); Mangey 656.4; Pitra xxiii.II
QE 2.71	αἱ τοῦ — ἀπόλαυσιν	Sac 789 (541A1–3); Mangey 660.2; Harris 73.8; Marcus QE no. 9
QE 2.99	οὔτε πλοῦτον — ἀποστρέφεται	Pitra 308.XIII
QE 2.105	οὐδὲν οὔτε — θεῷ	Sac 775 (513C8–12); Mangey 657.3
QE 2.107	δόξα — ἀβέβαιος	Mai 102a (2080C2–3)
QE 2.110	τὸ λέγειν — ἀτελές	Harris 108.4; Petit QE no. 27
QE 2.115	θυμῷ μάλιστα — σῶμα	Ant 137 (1173C13–D2); Harris 110.6
QE 2.118	οἱ λάλοι — ἄξια	Sac 576 (104B5–7); Mangey 651.8

References to the fragments of *Prov.* in Eusebius

	(Greek not cited)	Harris 75
Prov. 2.3	πρόνοιαν εἶναι — ταπεινοί	Mangey 634.1; Aucher 45–46; Harris 75.6
Prov. 2.15–33	οὐ τύραννος — εἰσόμεθα	Mangey 634.2; Aucher 53–72; Harris 75.7
Prov. 2.15	βασιλεῖ — πατρός	Mangey 635, n. b, cites; Harris 76.3
Prov. 2.15	ὅπερ — θεός	Sac 637 (236A9–11)
Prov. 2.15	φίλων καί — πταίσματα	Mai 107a (2093D2–3); Harris 71.5
Prov. 2.31	ὠμῆς — κακία	Ant 111 (1101D13); Joh. Geo. 104 (1160B5); Harris 76.1
Prov. 2.39	ἀεὶ πρὸς — κρειττόνων	Harris 76.2
Prov. 2.50–51	περὶ δὲ τοῦ — φύσει	Mangey 625.2; Aucher 80–82; Harris 75.8
Prov. 2.51	σοφιστείας — ἀποδοχῆς	Joh. Geo. 79 (1136B5–7); Harris 108.2
Prov. 2.99–112	ἀνέμων καί — πραγμάτων	Mangey 642.1; Aucher 107–20; Harris 75.9
Anim. 6	τὸ ζητεῖν — ἀνυσιμώτατον	Sac 613 (184B1–2), 693 (361B1–2); Mangey 651.9; Harris 11.2

Anim. 7	διδάσκουσι — ἀπαγγέλλοντες	Mai 99b (2073C11–13); Harris 11.3
Anim. 100	τὸ νέμειν — ἀδικίας	Sac 556 (60D10–11), 569 (88C3–4); Ant 90 (1041C5–6); Mangey 651.4; Mai 102b (2081D1–2); Harris 11.4

2. Fragmenta spuria

(cited in alphabetical order)

ἄγγελος ἦν — ἀποστείλω	Fr. sp. 39 = Harris 107.4
ἀδύνατον οἶμαι — δοκῇ	Fr. sp. 31 = Mangey 662.5; Pitra 309.XVII; Harris 9.1
ἀκύμαντος λιμὴν πολιά	Fr. sp. 47 = Sac 404 (1308D4); Mangey 650.5; Harris 97.11
ἀλγεῖν — ἀπαιδαγώγητον	= οὐ μὴ — ἀπαιδαγώγητον
ἀμήχανον — σκότος	Fr. sp. 30 = Sac 370 (1233C4–6), 382 (1260C2–4); Mangey 649.9; Mai 98b (2069D1–3); Harris 7.1
ἀνδρείας ἐστὶ — θάρσος	Fr. sp. 6 = Mangey 665.1; Harris 9.2
ἀπὸ ἑνὸς — πόλις	Fr. sp. 21 = Sac 693 (360C7); Max 689 (1017A5); Ant 112 (1105B8); Harris 110.9
ἀποστρέφου — κρείττονα	Fr. sp. 50 = Max 567 (792C5–9); Ant 59 (941D11–44A3); Mangey 671.9; Tis 1855 172.12; Lewy 81.20
ἀσκητέον — μακροτάτω	Fr. sp. 3 = Ant 38 (881A10–11); Mangey 666.3; Harris 101.11
ἄτοπόν ἐστι — τιμαί	Fr. sp. 40 = Sac 518 (1556C3–4), 713 (401D13–14) (— γίνεσθαι); Max 621 (889D1–2); Ant 86 (1029A1–2); Mangey 668.6; Harris 81.4 (— γίνεσθαι)
αὕτη — ἀρετή	= ἡ Φίλωνος γυνὴ — ἀρετή
αὐτὸς πάντα — μόνος	Fr. sp. 27 = Pitra 310.XXIII; Harris 85.7
εἰ βούλει — ἐπιτίμα	Fr. sp. 53 = Max 685 (1012A1–3); Mangey 670.4; Lewy 82.23
εἷς μὲν — βούλεται	Fr. sp. 58 = Ant 51 (921A1–5); Mangey 672.2b
ἐκ χρυσοῦ — ἐστιν	Fr. sp. 8 = Max 548 (757D1–2); Ant 29 (852C13–D1); Mangey 673.6a
ἐσχάρα ἄνθρακι — μάχης	Fr. sp. 20 = Pitra xxiii.III; Harris 83.6
ζητοῦσιν βρῶσιν — οὐρανοῖς	Fr. sp. 33 = Pitra 310.Ia; Harris 103.3a; PCW 1:lix
ἡ τῆς ἀρχῆς — γαλήνη	Fr. sp. 48 = PCW 1:lix
ἡ Φίλωνος γυνὴ — ἀρετή	Fr. sp. 18 = Max 632 (912C1–4) (αὕτη —); Ant 105 (1088A12–B2); Mangey 673.4; Tis 1855 174.27

ἡ χάρις — φαίνεται   Fr. sp. 17 = Max 556 (773B7–8); Joh. Geo. 41
                                       (1097C6–7)
ἡμερήσιοι — σημαίνουσιν   = οἱ ἡμερήσιοι — σημαίνουσιν
κακόσιτος — φάρμακον   Fr. sp. 16 = Max 670 (984B12–14)
λάλει ἃ δεῖ — ἃ μὴ δεῖ   Fr. sp. 41 = Sac 357 (1205C6–7), 563 (76A6–7);
                                       Max 647 (940B10–11); Ant 135 (1168D3–4);
                                       Mangey 651.6; Harris 79.5
λεία ὁδὸς — γίνεται   Fr. sp. 43 = Sac 481 (1473D6–7); Harris 105.2
μέγα τῷ — συμφορᾶς   Fr. sp. 38 = Sac 679 (329A8–10); Max 589
                                       (832B1–3); Ant 70 (981B7–9)
μεγίστη — κείμενον   Fr. sp. 36 = Max 588 (832A7–8); Ant 8
                                       (788C10–11), 70 (981B1–2); Joh. Geo. 57
                                       (1113C10–11)
μὴ δοξάζου — αὐτῶν   Fr. sp. 23 = Ant 93 (1049D4–5)
μήτε — ἀπαιδαγώγητον   = οὐ μὴ — ἀπαιδαγώγητον
νεότης — κακοπραγεῖ   Fr. sp. 19 = Ant 97 (1061D5–6); Mangey 673.7
ὁ γὰρ ὕπνος — χρόνον   Fr. sp. 29 = Max 616 (881B5–6); Ant 51
                                       (920D12–13) (ὁ ὕπνος —)
ὁ μὲν θεὸς — ἀναξίους   Fr. sp. 55 = Max 559 (777D4–80A1); Ant 77
                                       (1004B7–11) (— αἰτήσεις); Tis 1855 174.37; Tis
                                       1868 155.14; Harris 104.3
ὁ ὕπνος — χρόνον   = ὁ γὰρ ὕπνος — χρόνον
οἱ ἐλαφροὶ — εἰσίν   Fr. sp. 15 = Max 670 (984B10–11); Mangey 671.4b
οἱ ἡμερήσιοι — σημαίνουσιν   Fr. sp. 1 = Max 616 (881B12–13); Ant 51
                                       (921A9–11) (ἡμερήσιοι —)
οἱ μὲν — φύονται   Fr. sp. 10 = Max 548 (757D5–6); Mangey 673.6c
ὄντως πληγή — κακοπάθεια   = πληγή — κακοπάθεια
ὅταν ἄνθρωπος — ᾄδου   Fr. sp. 49 = Sac 343 (1176A6–11), 597
                                       (148C9–D1); Mangey 648.4; Harris 77.4
οὐ μὴ — ἀπαιδαγώγητον   Fr. sp. 35 = Max 580 (817A4–5) (μήτε —), 588
                                       (832A5–6); Ant 70 (981A12) (ἀλγεῖν —)
οὐ ποιεῖ — συνδιατριβή   Fr. sp. 4 = Ant 109 (1096D9–10); Mangey 671.3b
οὐ τὸ — κολάσεως   Fr. sp. 26 = Sac 349 (1188A3–4); Max 642
                                       (932B5–6); Mangey 673.8
οὔτε — εὐλαβεῖσθαι   Fr. sp. 14 = Max 670 (984B4–5); Ant 134
                                       (1165B13–14); Mangey 671.4a
οὐκ ἔστιν — ψυχῆς   Fr. sp. 22 = Sac 693 (360D1); Max 582
                                       (820A10–11); Ant 55 (932C7–8); Harris 110.10
περισσὸς — ὁμόνοια ᾗ   Fr. sp. 24 = Ant 128 (1153B2–3); Mangey 671.5c
πέφυκε τοῖς — φθόνος   Fr. sp. 25 = Mangey 668.4; Harris 9.3
πλέον ἀγάπα — σκοπόν   Fr. sp. 54 = Max 556 (773A14–B6); Tis 1855
                                       174.40; Tis 1868 155.16; Harris 105.1
πληγή — κακοπάθεια   Fr. sp. 37 = Sac 674 (317C8–10) (ὄντως πληγή
                                       —); Max 588–89 (832A9–10); Ant 70 (981B3–4)
πλοῦτος — ὑπηρέτης   Fr. sp. 5 = Sac 418 (1340A4–5); Ant 39 (885A6–7),
                                       40 (889A1–2)
πολλοὶ — ἕκαστον   Fr. sp. 12 = Max 548 (760A1–2); Mangey 673.6e

πολλοί — πλουτοῦντας   Fr. sp. 11 = Max 548 (757D7–8); Ant 28
                              (849B3–4); Mangey 673.6d
primum — testimonium   Latin version of Fr. sp. 61 = PCW 2:xv, n. 2
πρὸς τὰς — ἀνατυπούσης   Fr. sp. 45 = Lewy 81.19
πρότερον — ψευδομαρτυρήσῃς   Fr. sp. 61 = PCW 5:xvi, n. 1; 5:173, app.
σκεύη — παλαιοτέρα   Fr. sp. 9 = Max 548 (757D3–4); Ant 28 (849B1–2);
                              Joh. Geo. 82 (1140A9–10); Mangey 673.6b
συγγνώμην — ἀπαλλαγή   Fr. sp. 56 = Max 681 (1004B6–10); Ant 123
                              (1137C4–8); Mangey 670.5; Tis 1855 174.31
τέκνων — πατέρων   Fr. sp. 34 = Sac 701 (377D6); Ant 93 (1052B1);
                              Mangey 673.5a
τῇ μὲν — ἁπλότητα   Fr. sp. 51 = Max 561 (781C5–12); Ant 80
                              (1012B8–C1); Mangey 673.1
τὴν — ἀποτίθεσθαι   Fr. sp. 32 = Pitra xxiii.V; Harris 103.2; PCW 2:xviii
τὸ ἔντιμον — ἔσεσθαι   Fr. sp. 42 = Max 635 (917C1–3); Lewy 83.29
τὸ μὴ — ὑπερβολή   Fr. sp. 7 = Max 633 (916B8–9); Ant 135 (1169D8);
                              Harris 106.2
τοιοῦτος — ἀντιλάβωμεν   Fr. sp. 52 = Max 554–55 (769C1–6); Ant 35
                              (872D1–5); Mangey 672.1; Tis 1855 172.10; Tis
                              1868 153.5; Harris 104.1
τῶν ἀπορρήτων — ἀνατίθη   Fr. sp. 60 = Mangey 674.3; Harris 102.8
ὕπνος ἐστὶ — ἀργία   Fr. sp. 57 = Ant 51 (920D14–15); Mangey 672.2a
ὑπὸ γυναικὸς — ἐσχάτη   Fr. sp. 2 = Max 631 (912B6–7); Ant 107 (1089D12)
φεύγειν — διάθεσις   Fr. sp. 13 = Max 548 (760A3–4); Ant 30 (853A11)
φοβηθῶμεν — σώματος   Fr. sp. 28 = Sac 341 (1169C12–D1), 751
                              (476B11–13) (— νόσος); Max 610
                              (869C10–72A2); Ant 19 (824A12–14); Mangey
                              674.5; Tis 1855 173.21; Harris 77.3
ψεῦδος — ὑπάρχοντος   Fr. sp. 46 = Ant 27 (845A13–B2)
ὥσπερ — ἰάσασθαι   Fr. sp. 59 = Ant 51 (921A6–8); Mangey 672.2c

3. Other non-Philonic texts

(cited in alphabetical order)

ἀνθρωποπρεπῶς — ἔχει   text cited by Wendland 47, n. 1 (p. 24, n. 44)
αὗται αἱ — μετῴκησαν   gloss to *QG* 4.195.7* (p. 20) = Mangey 676.1;
                              Wendland 86
δῆλον δὲ — ἡμάρτανον   gloss to *QG* 1.100 (p. 19) = Harris 107.2;
                              Wendland 51–52
ἑβδόμῃ — ἑορτάζειν   gloss to *QG* 2.47 (p. 19) = Harris 106.4; Wendland
                              49 (— ἀριθμούμενον)
ἐθάρρει μὲν — θεοῦ   gloss to *QG* 4.202 (p. 20) = Mangey 676.4b;
                              Wendland 86

έθέλει δὲ — περιστοιχίζεται gloss to *QE* 2.25 (a) (in part) (p. 20) = Wendland 100
ἐκ τούτου — ἔκτισεν gloss to *QG* 1.94 (a) (p. 18) = Wendland 47; Marcus 191–92
ἰδοὺ τοῦτο — τούτοις gloss to *QG* 2.10 (p. 19) = Harris 107.3
ἡ τρυφή — ἀφαιρεῖται Pseudo-Plutarch = Max 612 (876A3–5) (see p. 44, no. 2)
ἦν γνωσιμαχῶν — ἑαυτοῦ gloss to *QG* 1.77 (p. 18) = Sac 777 (517A7); Mangey 658.1b; Marcus 190
καὶ τὰ τῶν παθῶν θηρία κοιμίζει gloss to *Leg.* 1.46 (p. 101, under Fr. sp. 33) = Pitra 310.Ic; Harris 103.3c; PCW 1:lix, 1:72, app.
μία δὲ — πλημμελεῖν text cited by Wendland 40 (p. 24, n. 44)
νεώτερον — Χάμ gloss to *QG* 2.71 (p. 20) = Harris 28
ὁ μὲν ἁπλούστερός φησι ὅτι κτλ. gloss to *QG* 1.94 (b) (p. 18) = Harris 19
ὁ φρόνιμος ὥσπερ — ἀναηκαιότερα Pseudo-Plutarch (see p. 44, no. 1)
οὐκ ἐπειδὴ — πληρουμένου gloss to *QG* 3.52 (p. 20) = Mangey 675.2b
οὐκ ἐπειδὴ — προσαγορεύονται gloss to *QG* 2.15 (p. 19) = Harris 106.3
πρὸς τούτοις — ἐχθρῷ gloss to *QE* 2.25 (a) (p. 20) = Pitra 312.VIb; Harris 103.4; Marcus *QE* no. 23
σωτηρίαν τὴν — ἔχοντες gloss to *QG* 4.195.8* (p. 20) = Marcus 272, n. c
ταῦτα μὲν — Βηρσαβεέ gloss to *QE* 2.25 (b) (p. 21) = Mangey 679.2; Wendland 101, n. 2
τόξον — ὑπερθήσομαι gloss to *QG* 2.64 (p. 19) = Harris 106.5
τοὺς ἑβδομήκοντα — ἀπελείφθη gloss on Exod 24:11 (p. 21) = Mangey 679.4

4. Unidentified texts

(cited in alphabetical order and numbered)

1 ἀδυνατήσει — μαρμαρυγῶν Sac 749 (472B12–C1); Mangey 654.1e; Harris 72.3d; Marcus *QE* no. 1d; Petit *QE* no. 6
2 αἱ πάντων — δυνάμεις Sac 681 (333B7–9); Mangey 652.4; Harris 98.6; Wendland 24.10
3 αἱ περὶ τῶν — ἀλήθειαν Sac 774 (512B6–12); Mangey 656.6; Harris 73.2; Marcus *QE* no. 3; Petit *QE* no. 7
4 αἱ φιλοσοφίαι — διώσασθαι Sac 749 (472A12–B6); Mangey 654.1c; Harris 72.3b; Marcus *QE* no. 1b; Petit *QE* no. 4
5 ἀκερδὴς — μετάμελος Ant 13 (804A1–2); Mangey 662.6; Harris 100.4
6 ἀμήχανον — ὄψεται Sac 748–49 (469D8–72A12); Mangey 654.1b; Harris 72.3a; Marcus *QE* no. 1a; Petit *QE* no. 3
7 ἀνελεύθερον — ἔχον Mangey 664.1; Harris 100.9
8 ἀρεταὶ μόναι — ἐπίστανται Ant 10 (793C4–5); Mangey 670.3a; Harris 109.7b; Lewy 81.21
9 ἀρετὴ προηγούμενον — ἀρχαῖον Harris 109.7a
10 ἄσπονδος — ἀπειλεῖν Mangey 664.3; Harris 100.11; Petit *QE* no. 30

11	ἄτοπον ἐν μὲν — ἐκρίπτειν	Sac 782 (528A1–5); Mangey 658.5a; Harris 99.6; Petit QE no. 13
	αὔξει τὴν — τριβή	= unidentified no. 40
12	ἄχρις ἄν — ἀμώμητα	Sac 782 (525D5–8); Mangey 658.4b; Harris 69.4b; cited by Marcus as QG 4.8; Petit 147, n. b, and QG no. 2b
13	γονέας τίμα — φυσικός	Sac 663 (293A5–6); Harris 110.7
14	δεῖ τὸν — προθέσεως	Sac 749 (472B6–12); Mangey 654.1d; Harris 72.3c; Marcus QE no. 1c; Petit QE no. 5
15	διάβολοι — ἀλλότριοι	Sac 436 (1377B5–8); Mangey 650.9; Harris 98.2
16	διδύμους — αὐτοῦ	Harris 107.1; Wendland 37, n. 1 (τινὲς — δηλοῦν)
17	δυσεκρίζωτος — χρόνῳ	Joh. Geo. 27 (1084C3–4) (— πολλῷ); Harris 105.5
18	ἐὰν δόξαις — ἐκτραχηλισθῇς	Ant 139 (1180C1–4) (εἰ δόξαις —); Mangey 667.4; Harris 102.5
19	ἐὰν πολὺς — τέλματος	Mangey 666.1; Harris 101.9
20	εἰ βούλει — θεοῦ	Sac 341 (1169D5–7); Mangey 648.2; Harris 77.2
	εἰ δόξαις — ἐκτραχηλισθείς	= unidentified no. 18
21	εἴ τις πάσας — τυγχάνοι	Sac 438 (1381B11–C1); Mangey 650.11; Harris 79.3
22	εἰκότως — ὁλοκλήρου	Max 615 (881A9–13); Ant 51 (920D7–11); Mangey 667.6; Tis 1855 173.22; Harris 7.3
23	εἰώθασιν — καιροί	Mai 101b (2080A3–B1); Harris 70.6; Marcus QG no. 9; Petit QG no. 5
24	ἐν θεῷ — μεμαθημένως	Mangey 667.1; Harris 70.3; Marcus QG no. 8; Petit QG no. 16
25	ἐν νυκτὶ βουλή· — ἀπόλιπος	Mai 102b (2081A12–14); Lewy 80.16 (— ἀποπόμπιμον); Petit QE no. 20
26	ἐνέχυρον — θεόν	Harris 110.2; PCW 4:287–88, app.
27	ἐντὸς φέρει — ψυχῇ	Sac 782 (528B7–10); Mangey 659.1; Harris 73.6; Marcus QE no. 7; Petit QE no. 32
28	ἐπειδὴ πρὸς — ὁδηγίαν	Mangey 666.7; Harris 70.2; Marcus QG no. 7; Petit QG no. 15
29	ἐπίσταται — αἰσθάνονται	Wendland 23.4
30	ἐπιστήμη — καλόν	Ant 13 (801D14–15) (— πάντων); Joh. Geo. 98 (1153B9–10); Mangey 671.5b (— πάντων); Harris 78.8
31	ἐπίστησον — σοφίας	Sac 435 (1376B6–11); Mai 100a (2073D2–6) (— προέσθαι); Harris 98.1
32	ἐπιχαιρεκακία ἀλλότριον σοφῶν	Ant 111 (1105A7)
33	ἔστω οὖν — ἀμφισβητουμένου	Harris 110.3; latter part = Harris 97.1 (Leg. 3.205); PCW 4:287–88, app.
34	εὐδαιμονιστέον — τοιούτου	Ant 112 (1105C13–15); Mangey 671.1
35	ἔχουσιν — μεμφθῆναι	Sac 521 (1561D5–6); Lewy 82.25
36	ἡ εὐφυΐα — περικόπτειν	Mai 106a (2092B12–C3); Harris 74.7; Marcus QE no. 17; Petit QE no. 25
37	ἡ πρὸς τοὺς — ποιεῖσθαι	Mangey 674.2; Harris 102.7
38	ἡ φορὰ — τυφλουμένην	Sac 751 (476C1–C5); Mangey 655.3; Harris 73.1; Marcus QE no. 2; Petit QE no. 31

39	ἰδοὺ δέδωκα — γενητοῦ	Mai 95b (2061D2–64B6); Harris 8.1
40	καὶ πάλιν — τριβή	Sac 405 (1312A6–7); Mangey 650.7b; Harris 79.1b; Lewy 82.22 (αὔξει τὴν —)
41	καλὰ ἑκάστοις — πάθει	Lewy 81.18
42	καλόν ἐστιν — μνήμην	Mangey 664.5; Harris 101.2; Petit QE no. 9
43	κοινωνικὸν — ἄνθρωπος	Harris 105.3; PCW 3:163, app.
44	μακρὰν — ἐπακολουθοῦντα	Mangey 664.7; Harris 101.4; Petit QE no. 10
45	μεγίστη — ἀνακτησομένου	Max 589 (832A11–12); Ant 70 (981B5–6)
46	μείζονα — πτωχεύσαντας	Sac 481 (1473C10–D4), 575–76 (101C8–12); Max 568 (796A4–8); Ant 41 (892D5–9); Mai 104a (2085A8–12); Harris 75.4
47	μελέτη τροφὸς (ἐστιν) ἐπιστήμης	Sac 405 (1312A7–8); Mangey 650.8; Mai 99a (2072D1); Harris 69.3; Marcus QG no. 2; Petit QG no. 4
	μέχρι μὲν — φρονεῖν	= unidentified no. 109
48	μή σε — πράγματα	Joh. Geo. 59 (1116C12–14); Harris 108.1
49	μὴ τοῖς (τοὺς) — βλάπτοντας	Sac 565 (77D1–3); Lewy 80.17
50	μηδαμῶς — ποιεῖ	Max 674 (989D4–5); Ant 146 (1200A4–5); Harris 88.2, 105.4
51	μηδενὶ συμφορὰν — εὑρεθῇς	Sac 630 (220B5–7); Mangey 652.1; Harris 98.5
52	μία ἀνάπαυσις — πράξεων	Mangey 669.3; Harris 73.10; Marcus QE no. 11a; Petit QE no. 11
53	μυρία γε — νοῦν	Mangey 662.2; Harris 73.9; Marcus QE no. 10; Petit QE no. 2
54	ὁ εὐλαβέστερος — κακοπαθῇ	Mai 107a (2093D6–9); Harris 71.6; Marcus QG no. 15; Petit QG no. 9
55	ὁ σοφιστικός — σημεῖα	Mai 108a (2096C11–D6); Harris 74.8; Marcus QE no. 18; Petit QE no. 26
56	οἱ ἑαυτῶν — θεοφιλής	Sac 721 (420D5–21A5); Max 686 (1012D5–6) (— ἐπιτηδεύουσιν); Ant 141 (1188A1–2) (— ἐπιτηδεύουσιν); Mangey 662.1; Mai 108b (2097D6–2100A2) (— ποιητῇ); Tis 1855 172.6 (— ἐπιτηδεύουσιν); Harris 71.1; Marcus QG no. 11; Petit QG no. 10
57	οἱ οἰκέται — ὕβρις	Lewy 82.26
58	οἱ ὑπηρέται — θεοῦ	Mangey 664.2; Harris 100.10; Petit QE no. 29
59	ὅρασις παρὰ — εἰσδύεται	Mai 109b (2100A11–B5); Harris 74.9; Marcus QE no. 19; Petit QE no. 21
60	ὅρκον περίφευγε καὶ δικαίως ὀμνύειν	Ant 129 (1156D4)
61	οὐ θέμις — ἀμυήτοις	Sac 533 (9B10–11), 782 (525D4–5); Mangey 651.2, 658.4a; Aucher 1822, 75, n. 2; Harris 69.4a; cited by Marcus as QG 4.8; Petit 147, n. b, QG no. 2a
62	οὐ πάντων — θέμις	Sac 782 (528A5–B3); Mangey 658.5b; Pitra 307.XII; Harris 75.1; Marcus QE no. 20; Petit QE no. 14
63	οὐ ποιήσετε — αἴτιον	Mangey 661.9; Harris 100.3

64	οὐκ ἐπὶ φιλίας — χάριτος	Harris 77.1
65	οὐκ ἔστι(ν) — θεόν	Sac 349 (1188A5–11); Max 642 (932A11–B4); Mangey 649.1; Tis 1855 173.25; Tis 1868 154.8; Pitra 310.XXII; Harris 10.1; PCW 6:l
66	οὐχ ἡ — εἰλικρίνεια	Sac 570 (89B13–14); Max 669 (980C9–11); Ant 67 (972C7–8), 149 (1209C2–4) (— ἀκραιφνής)
67	οὐχ ἧττον(α) — ἐργάζεται	Mai 105b (2089C13–14); Lewy 76.4; Petit QE no. 23
68	πάντων μέν — κύριον	Sac 326 (1136B10–C3); Mangey 648.1; Harris 6.1; Petit QE no. 16
69	παρατηρητέον — ἐπιστήμην	Lewy 82.27
70	πέρας εὐδαιμονίας — στῆναι	Mangey 669.4; Harris 74.1; Marcus QE no. 11b; Petit QE no. 12
71	περιέχει — πεπλήρωκεν	Sac 752 (477C3–6); Mangey 655.6; Harris 73.5; Marcus QE no. 6; Petit QE no. 1
72	πολλὰ ἀσωμένοις — ἐστι(ν)	Mai 96b (2065B9–11); Harris 74.2; Marcus QE no. 12; Petit QE no. 17
73	προσήκει — ὑπολαμβάνοντες	Mai 107a (2093B3–C5); Harris 8.2
74	πρότερον — λαχεῖν	Lewy 77.8
75	πῶς οὐκ ἔστιν — ἔργα	Wendland 23.6
76	σώματος — παθῶν	Sac 404 (1308D4–5); Mangey 650.6; Harris 97.12
77	τὰ βουλήματα — ζώντων	Mai 101a (2077A13–14); Harris 74.4; Marcus QE no. 14; Petit QE no. 19
78	τὰ γὰρ τοῦ — ἐστίν	Harris 72.1; Marcus QG no. 17; Petit QG no. 17
79	τὰ μέτρα — θρασύτητα	Mai 106a (2092A14–B2); Harris 74.6; Marcus QE no. 16; Petit QE no. 24
80	τὰ τῶν προτέρων — σωτήρια	Mangey 665.5; Harris 101.8
81	τὰς ἐπηρείας — μεῖζον	Wendland 22.3
82	τὴν εὐταξίαν — γνωρίζομεν	Mangey 674.7; Harris 102.9
83	τῆς εὐδαιμονίας — θεοῦ	Mangey 668.8; Harris 8.3
	τῆς καρτερίας — ἀτυφίας	= unidentified no. 102
84	τί ἂν γένοιτο — γένηται	Sac 436 (1377B9–C1); Mangey 650.10; Harris 98.3
85	τί γὰρ — χρῆται	Wendland 22.1
	τί οὖν — ἐγχειρήσεως	= unidentified no. 98
86	τίνας γὰρ — ἐλπίζομεν	Pitra 310.XXI; Harris 11.1
	τινὲς ἀπὸ μιᾶς — δηλοῦν	= unidentified no. 16
87	τίς οὐκ οἶδεν — δυνατά	Wendland 23.5
88	τίς ἐξαμαρτὼν — ἐλέγχῃ	Mangey 666.6; Harris 102.1
89	τίς ἔχει — γλωσσαλγίας	Harris 105.7; PCW 4:290, app.
90	τὸ ἄνισον — ὠφέλειαν	Mangey 665.3; Harris 101.6; Wendland 24.8
91	τὸ δ' εὐδαιμονεῖν — μέλη	Lewy 83.30
92	τὸ δὲ ἀγ. — διαφαίνουσιν	Lewy 83.28
93	τὸ δὲ μάννα — διασῴζεσθαι	Harris 106.1; PCW 1:civ (τὸ μάννα —)
94	τὸ εἰδέναι — δικαιοσύνης	Sac 613 (184B7–8), 693 (360D7–8); Max 583 (821C3–4), 662 (968C12–13); Ant 56 (933D5–6); Mangey 651.11; Harris 80.5
95	τὸ ἐπαισθάνεσθαι — ἀνδρός	Sac 777 (517A8–11); Mangey 658.2; Harris 70.1; Marcus QG no. 6; Petit QG no. 12

96	τὸ ἐπιορκεῖν — ἀλυσιτελέστατον	Sac 784 (532C6); Mangey 659.5; Harris 70.7; Marcus QG no. 10; Petit QG no. 14
	τὸ μάννα — διασῴζεσθαι	= unidentified no. 93
97	τὸ μὲν — παρθενίας	Mai 105b (2089C3–10); Harris 74.5; Marcus QE no. 15; Petit QE no. 22
98	τὸ οὖν — ἐγχειρήσεως	Pitra 307.X (τί οὖν —); Harris 71.7 (τί οὖν —); Marcus QG no. 16 (τί οὖν —); Petit QG no. 3
99	τὸ τέλος — μόνος	Mangey 661.7; Harris 100.2b
100	τὸ τῶν φαύλων — ἑαυταῖς	Mai 100b (2076C1–4); Harris 74.3; Marcus QE no. 13; Petit QE no. 18
101	τὸ φιλότιμον — κατεσκωμμένον	Sac 716 (409C3–4); Ant 35 (not in PG)
102	τὸν καρτερίας — ἀτυφίας	Ant 139 (1180B11–14); Mangey 667.3 (τῆς καρτερίας —); Harris 102.4
103	τόπος — περιπολοῦσιν	Mangey 661.4; Harris 100.1
104	τοῦ (μὴ) προθύμως — αἰώνιος	Mangey 667.7; Harris 10.3
105	τοῦ φαύλου — πολέμιος	Max 530 (725C4–6) (— μαχόμενα); Ant 104 (1084B6–11); Mangey 663.5; Tis 1855 172.7 (— μαχόμενα); Tis 1868 153.6 (— μαχόμενα); Harris 100.8
106	τοὺς ἄρξαντας — πέρας	Mai 105b (2089B1–6); Harris 71.4; Marcus QG no. 14; Petit QG no. 8
107	τοὺς ἐντυγχάνοντας — συνᾴδουσιν	Sac 774 (512C5–12); Mangey 656.8; Harris 73.4; Marcus QE no. 5; Petit QE no. 8
108	τρεπτοὶ — ὑπολαμβάνομεν	Mai 102a (2081A6–8); Harris 71.2; Marcus QG no. 12; Petit QG no. 6
	τῷ μὴ ἐφεδρεύει — λέλυται	= unidentified no. 118
109	τῶν πολιτικῶν — φρονεῖν	Max 623 (896B8–9) (— ἔχοντα); Ant 87 (1032D11–14) (μέχρι μὲν —), 87 (1033A1–2) (— ἔχοντα), 140 (1184C1–2) (— ἔχοντα); Mangey 661.1; Tis 1855 174.28 (— ἔχοντα); Harris 7.2
110	τῶν φαύλων — πένητες	Sac 362–63 (1217B3–5); Mangey 649.5a; Harris 69.1; Marcus QG no. 1; Petit QG no. 11
111	φασί τινες — ἡττᾶσθαι	Ant 140 (1184B12–15); Mangey 668.1; Harris 7.4
112	φεῦγε (φεύγετε) — παρακαλεῖ	Ant 19 (824B6); Harris 110.4
113	φησὶ Μωυσῆς — βούλεται	Lewy 83.31; Petit QG no. 13
114	φθαρτὸν καλῶ — βίος	Pitra 308.XV; Harris 75.2; Marcus QE no. 21; Petit QE no. 15
115	φιλόσοφος — ἐπιδεικνυμένη	Lewy 84.32
116	φιλοῦσι — τίκτεσθαι	Sac 507 (1532A1–2); Harris 109.9
117	φιλοῦσιν — ἐξάπτουσιν	Harris 105.6
118	ᾧ μὴ ἐφεδρεύει — λέλυται	Ant 74 (996A1–2); Joh. Geo. 104 (1160A12–13); Mangey 666.8 (τῷ μὴ —); Harris 102.2
119	ὡς ἂν ἔχουσιν — ἐστι	Harris 10.4
120	ὡς δεινὸν — παραδοθέν	Mai 109a (2100A7–8); Harris 75.5

121	ὥσπερ <βλάπτει> — ἐξαπιναῖος	Wendland 22.2
122	ὥσπερ κίονες — γένος	Sac 749 (473A6–8); Mangey 655.1, 662.4; Harris 69.5; Marcus QG no. 3; Petit QG no. 1
123	ὥσπερ τὸ — πάντα	Sac 711 (400B2–6); Mangey 652.11; Harris 99.4
124	ὥσπερ τῶν — ἰσότητος	Mangey 665.2; Harris 101.5; Wendland 24.7

San Francisco

BIBLIOGRAPHY SECTION

PHILO OF ALEXANDRIA:
AN ANNOTATED BIBLIOGRAPHY
1990

D. T. RUNIA AND R. RADICE

1990*

Y. AMIR, 'The Decalogue according to Philo', in B. Z. SEGAL and G. LEVI (edd.), *The Ten Commandments in History and Tradition*, Publications of the Perry Foundation for Biblical Research: The Hebrew University of Jerusalem (Jerusalem 1990) 121–160.

    English translation of the article earlier published in German and Hebrew; see R-R 8307, 8604. (DTR)

B. BELLETTI, 'Il logos come immagine di Dio in Filone di Alessandria', *Sapienza* 43 (1990) 311–320.

    This article discusses one of the most important and central themes in Philo's thought, the relation between God and Logos. Indeed, this theme determines the general nature of Philo's metaphysics, which can be characterized as *exemplaristic* and *imaginistic*. Belletti analyses the various relations between Logos, God, and 'Man in God's image', and reaches the following conclusions. 'Man in God's image' signifies both the Logos and the ideal man. The prevailing hierarchy in Philo's writings is that of God-Logos-Intellect. It follows that 'Man in God's image' is man's reason and that there is a clear difference between the ideal man and sensible man (319). By 'man's reason' Belletti means 'the reason which is in each of us and which constitutes the "model" and guide for our lives, containing the imprint of the divine' (320). (RR)

---

* The principles on which this annotated bibliography is based have been outlined in *SPhA* 2 (1990) 141–142, and are largely based on those used to compile the 'mother work', R-R. One deviation is that all language restrictions have been abandoned. The compilers would like to thank a number of scholars for generously giving assistance when called upon, notably P. W. van der Horst, N. G. Cohen, G. E. Sterling. The summaries of R. Radice were translated from the Italian by A. P. Runia (Groningen). Due to pressures of time it proved impossible to gain access to a number of items from 1990. These will be summarized in next year's bibliography. Regrettably there is no contribution from our Jerusalem correspondent this time. Hebrew items will be given more attention in the next volume.

G. CARRAS, 'Philo's *Hypothetica*, Josephus' *Contra Apionem* and the Question of Sources', *SBLSP* 29 (1990) 431-450.

A revised and expanded version of this paper is found in the present volume, pp. 24–47.

N. G. COHEN, 'Agrippa I and *De Specialibus Legibus* IV 151-159', *SPhA* 2 (1990) 72-85.

Argues that Philo's intention in composing the passage headed 'On the appointment of rulers' was not so much to recapitulate the relevant halakha from an academic point of view, but rather to express his views on a burning political issue of his day, namely the suitability of Agrippa I to be king of Judea from the viewpoint of *kashruth*. By means of his 'homiletic hermeneutic' Philo contends that Agrippa's appointment by the Roman authorities is legitimate. The article concludes with some remarks on the relation between scriptural commentary and topical political comment. (DTR)

N. G. COHEN, '"Contemporary" Political Overtones of Philo's *Specialibus Legibus* IV 151-159', in D. Assaf (ed.), *Proceedings of the 10th World Congress of Jewish Studies*, Division A: The Bible and its World (Jerusalem 1990) 253–260.

A shortened presentation of the article cited above. (DTR)

C. COLPE, 'Von der Logoslehre des Philo zu der des Clemens von Alexandrien', in *Das Siegel der Propheten: historische Beziehungen zwischen Judentum, Judenchristetum, Heidentum und frühem Islam*, Arbeiten zur neu-testamentliche Zeitgeschichte 3 (Berlin 1990) 141-164.

Reprint of article first published in 1979 (= R-R 7907). (DTR)

G. PATERSON CORRINGTON, 'Philo *On the Contemplative Life: or, On the Suppliants* (The Fourth Book on the Virtues)', in V. L. WIMBUSH (ed.), *Ascetic Behavior in Greco-Roman Antiquity: a Sourcebook*, Studies in Antiquity and Christianity (Minneapolis 1990) 131-155.

As part of a source book for the study of asceticism in the ancient world, a new translation of *De vita contemplativa* has been produced. It is prefaced by a brief introduction, accompanied by brief notes. The chapter ends with a brief list of suggested further literature. Both translation and accompanying material are marred by frequent errors. See my review in *SPhA* 4 (1992) 133–136. (DTR)

B. DECHARNEUX, 'Mantique et oracles dans l'œuvre de Philon d'Alexandrie', in A. MOTTE (ed.), *Oracles et mantique en Grèce ancienne: Actes du colloque de Liège (Mars 1989)*, = *Kernos* [Revue internationale et pluridisciplinaire de religion grecque antique] 3 (Liège 1990) 123-133.

Philo's views on divination are especially important because he is the first to interpret divination in a monotheistic context, whereas the usual context of soothsaying is polytheism. Decharneux underlines two aspects: (1) Philo rejects technical divination by means of his allegorical exegesis of Balaam. (2) He accepts and approves of divination which works via the interpretation of dreams (124). The underlying position is that Philo accepts forms of divination in which the initiative is left to God or the word of God and rejects forms which rely on human devices. These lead to false knowledge and ultimately to impiety. The same position allows Philo to establish a hierarchy of inspired forms of divination, in which dreams are more significant the more they come from God, and the interpreter is more faithful the closer he is to the mystic state. In the latter case 'the philosopher is transformed into a kind of anti-philosopher, *alogos* ... totally dedicated to God', to being the mouthpiece of his word (132). (RR)

B. DECHARNEUX, 'Interdits sexuels dans l'œuvre de Philon d'Alexandrie dit «le Juif»', in J. MARX (ed.), *Religion et tabou sexuel*, Université Libre de Bruxelles Institut d'étude des religions et de la laïcité: Problèmes d'Histoire des Religions 1 (Brussels 1990) 17–31.

The basic thesis of the author is that the sexual prohibitions of the Bible are transformed in Philo, by means of the allegorical process of interpretation, into philosophical concepts. 'Les austères interdits sexuels de la Bible se trouvaient ainsi transposés dans le champ infini, de Dieu, du Monde, de l'âme et du philosophe. A l'interdit l'effort de rationalisation de l'Alexandrin voulait substituer la philosophie (27).' Within this framework a number of themes are analysed: the practice of circumcision (including the relation to the doctrine of the Logos tomeus and its metaphysical foundations), the episode of Abraam and Sarah, that of Joseph and Potiphar's wife, and also the praise of virginity which is expressed in arithmological terms, with reference to the hebdomad. (RR)

V. DESPREZ, 'Jewish Ascetical Groups at the Time of Christ: Qumran and the Therapeuts', *American Benedictine Review* 41 (1990) 291-311.

As part of a series of articles outlining Jewish roots of Christian monasticism the author discusses the communities of Qumran and the Therapeutae. The method is largely descriptive, but some evaluative comments are given by way of conclusion. The piety of both groups is authentically biblical, but in both cases there are also problems. At Qumran it is the tendency towards excessive particularism, while in Alexandria it is the 'excessive idealism, due in great part to the bias of our historian, Philo. The Therapeuts seem like intellectuals lost in allegory, living on air (311).' This is in marked contrast to later Egyptian Christian monks who had their feet firmly on the ground. (DTR)

A. J. DEWEY, 'A Re-hearing of Romans 10:1–15', *SBLSP* 29 (1990) 273–282.

As the title is meant to indicate, the article concentrates on the oral aspect of Paul's address to the Romans, in which an utopian perspective is presented. The quotation of scripture in the form of Deut. 30:11–14 is an act of power, to which the congregation has access through the oral experience of reading aloud. Philo is then introduced for comparative purposes, with special attention paid to his use of the same Pentateuchal text. Philo uses the best available technologies and tries to promote utopian possibilities in a gradual and irenic manner, whereas Paul may well represent a counter-cultural position. A slightly more expanded version of the same article was earlier published under the title 'Acoustics of the Spirit: a Hearing of Romans 10 (Deut 30:11–14)', in T. Callan (ed.), *Proceedings Eastern Great Lakes and Midwest Bible Society vol.* 9 (1989) 212–230. (DTR)

F. G. DOWNING, 'Ontological Asymmetry in Philo and Christological Realism in Paul, Hebrews and John', *JThS* 41 (1990) 423-440.

Starting-point of this rich but difficult contribution on Philo's theological thought is the monograph of J. D. G. Dunn, *Christology in the Making* (London 1980), in which it is argued that for Philo the Logos bridges the gulf that exists between God and creation. But, according to Downing, Philo never speaks of such a 'gulf'. God as transcendent Being exists in a way that man can acknowledge but not apprehend. This constitutes what Downing describes as an 'asymmetry of knowing', asymmetrical precisely because God knows man, but man is not in a position to know God. Moreover one can also argue that there is an 'asymmetry in being', as seen in the statement in *Legat.* 118 that it would easier for God to become human than for a human to become God. The article concludes with reflections on the status of the Logos. 'The Logos is real, because it/he is less distinct from God than any other reality of which we can conceive (439).' This Philonic background implies that some intellectuals at least were much more ready for the notion of a 'pre-existent' Christ than Dunn allows. (DTR)

H. EILBERG-SCHWARZ, *The Savage in Judaism* (Bloomington 1990), esp. 154–155, 175.

In providing his controversial interpretation of early Judaism from the viewpoint of cultural anthropolgy, the author is struck by Philo's recognition of the centrality of procreation in God's covenant with Abraham. (DTR)

C. ELSAS, 'Argumente zur Ablehnung des Herrscherkults in jüdischer und gnostischer Tradition', in C. ELSAS and H. G. KIPPENBERG (edd.), *Loyalitätskonflikte in der Religionsgeschichte: Festschrift für Carsten Colpe* (Würzburg 1990) 269–281, esp. 279–281.

Argues that the positive attitude towards monarchic imperial rule (conditional upon there being no threat to monotheism) represented by Philo and Hellenistic Judaism may have contributed to the Gnostic revolt against both earthly rulers and the God of Judaism. (DTR)

J. FERGUSON, 'Epicureanism under the Roman Empire', *ANRW* II 36.4 (Berlin-New York 1990) 2257–2327, esp. 2273–74.

Brief and regrettably superficial treatment of Philo's knowledge of Epicureanism, which is described as 'accurate and detailed'. (DTR)

P. GILABERT I BARBERÀ, "... Però la dona ho esguerrà tot': El De opificio mundi de Filó d'Alexandria (LIII–LXI) o els fonaments grecs d'una fita en la història da la misogínia occidental', *Anuari de Filologia: Studia Graeca et Latina* (Barcelona) 13 (1990) 55–84.

Gilabert i Barberà analyzes the main passages of *Opif.* relating to the theme of woman and the creation. A translation is given of §§136–138, 140–142, and 151–166, together with the crucial Greek terms and comments on the attitude to women which emerges from these passages. In the author's view Philo is strongly influenced by Platonism on this point. Indeed, the role of woman in the creation is of fundamental allegorical significance in explaining man's fall from the perfect condition in the World of ideas (corresponding to the biblical paradise) to the world of becoming (cf. 57, 67). Perhaps Philo has also been unconsciously influenced by the myth of the ages of the world (cf. Hesiod, *Works and Days*, 106-201; cf. 62ff.), but the closest reference for Philo is most certainly Plato's ontological and moral dualism. In any case Philo's text expresses the patently misogynous view (76) that man's 'progressive degradation' goes hand in hand with the 'increasing sexualization of the story of the fall' (73, 79). The connections with Greek culture (lyric poetry, tragedy, philosophy) show that Philo, too, takes a negative view of the love of women, which is seen as sensual (76) and as conflicting with the love of God (59). These ideas were widely used by the Church Fathers, who in the end took a saner view of these 'obsessions'. (RR)

P. J. GRABE, *Dunamis in the Sense of Power in the Main Pauline Letters* (diss. University of Pretoria 1990)

Although δύναμις is used by Paul in his main letters for a whole range of meanings, this investigation deals with δύναμις in the sense of power. Section A has been devoted to a lexico- and conceptual-historical survey of δύναμις in which the Hellenistic (profane Greek) use of δύναμις, the Old Testament basis for Paul's use of δύναμις, as well as concepts of power in early Judaism, Philo and Qumran are discussed. It is concluded that Hellenistic influence on Paul's use of δύναμις can be observed in a passage such as Romans 1:20, which is only to be understood against the background of a Hellenistically influenced Jewish apocalyptic tradition. By and large, however, the lexico- and conceptual-historical background of Paul's use of δύναμις is to be found in the Old Testament. (DTR, based on DA 52-04A, p.1388)

J. T. GREENE, 'Balaam as Figure and Type in Ancient Semitic Literature to the First Century B.C.E., with a Survey of Selected Post-Philo Applications of the Balaam Figure and Type', *SBLSP* 29 (1990) 82-147.

Continuing the research initiated in 1989 (see *SPhA* 4 (1992) 103f.), this study aims to present—in a fairly exhaustive manner—preliminary materials for an interpretation of Balaam in Philo. Thirteen pre-Philonic and six post-Philonic interpretations are set before the reader, allowing him or her 'to not have to study Philo's consideration of Balaam within a hermeneutical vacuum (143)'. But no discussion is actually given of Philo's contribution. See now also the monograph on the same subject published in 1992 (details in Supplement below). (DTR)

C. W. GRIGGS, *Early Egyptian Christianity from its Origins to 451 C.E.*, Coptic Studies 2 (Leiden 1990, 1991²), esp. 19–20.

The use of Philonic evidence in the discussion of the origins of the Alexandrian church is disappointingly limited. (DTR)

A. J. GUERRA, 'The One God Topos in *Spec. Leg.* 1.52', *SBLSP* 29 (1990) 148-157.

The affirmation that 'there is One God' is a prominent feature of Jewish, and later Christian, exclusivism, and plays an important role in the relation of both groups to the Hellenistic gentile world. As used in literary works, this theme can be described as a topos. The author first briefly examines some uses of the topos in the Sybilline Oracles and Josephus, which are useful for comparative purposes when he turns to Philo. In the text examined in detail, *Spec.* 1.52, it emerges that Philo is above all concerned to promote the acceptance and even privileged treatment of proselytes. A contrast is drawn between 'Hellenistic Judaism and ... Hellenistic philosophy at large' in which 'the primary concern was the pursuit of a theoretical basis of unity' and Philo, who 'was far more concerned to articulate the social implications for unity which the shared acceptance of One God afforded (157)'. (DTR)

R. A. HARRISVILLE III, *In the Footsteps of Abraham: the Figure of Abraham in the Epistles of Saint Paul* (diss. Union Theological Seminary in Virginia 1990)

A chapter on Abraham in Philo is included as part of an investigation on Paul's use of the patriarch Abraham. (DTR, based on DA 51/12A, p. 4162)

W. E. HELLEMAN, 'Philo of Alexandria on Deification and Assimilation to God', *SPhA* 2 (1990) 51-71.

Philo's views on man's deification and assimilation to God form an important background to the Patristic view of salvation as 'deification' of man. The author concentrates above all on Philo's use of the Platonic motif of ὁμοίωσις θεῷ as employed by Philo in passages in *Fug.*, *Spec.*, *Virt.*, *Opif.*, *Migr.*, and *QE*. On the basis of this material the following aspects are further analysed: (a) assimilation as a process of transition; (b) the 'god' to whom man is assimilated, namely the divine Logos; (c) the kinship between God and man, as indicated above all by Gen. 1:26; (d) the divine nature of the human mind; (e) the special status of Moses as a 'god', but only in a derivative sense. Helleman concludes that Philo on the one hand recognizes assimilation to god as a legitimate and proper goal of human life, involving a choice based on knowledge and reason, but that on the other hand man cannot become God nor gain a true vision of who God is. The contradictory nature of these two positions can only be resolved if we take into account the flexibility with which he uses the word θεός. Against this Philonic background it should come as no surprise that the Church Fathers assigned to Christ the Logos the pivotal role in the process of salvation as deification. The patristic view of *sharing* in the divine nature, however, finds no support in Philo. (DTR)

A. VAN DEN HOEK, 'How Alexandrian was Clement of Alexandria? Reflections on Clement and his Alexandrian Background', *Heythrop Journal* 31 (1990) 179-194.

Concludes that Clement must have had a good Christian library at his disposal, in which a prominent place was given to Philo. 'The multitude of sources that reached him —whether in the form of extracts or complete works—proves how richly endowed his immediate environment was. His borrowings are often literal, and he often mentions his source by name. Philo remains strangely unacknowledged, but this omission is an exception rather than the rule (190).' (DTR)

P. W. VAN DER HORST, 'Nimrod in the Jewish Haggada', in A. KUYT, E. G. L. SCHRIJVER and N. A. VAN UCHELEN (edd.), *Variety of Forms: Dutch Studies in Midrash* (Amsterdam 1990) 59–75, esp. 61–63; reprinted in Dutch version in *idem, Studies over het Joden in de Oudheid* (Kampen 1992) 108–126.

A shorter version of the article published together with K. van der Toorn in *HThR*. For a summary see below under Van der Toorn – Van der Horst. (DTR)

L. D. HURST, *The Epistle to the Hebrews: its Background of Thought*, SNTSMS 65 (Cambridge 1990), esp. 7–42.

During the last century a number of differing backgrounds have been exploited in order to explain the *Sitz im Leben* of the Letter of the Hebrews. To a remarkable degree each seems convincing when considered in isolation from the rest. The study's aim is to examine these various backgrounds in order to determine their strengths and weaknesses. The first chapter gives an excellent analytic survey of various attempts to privilege the Philonic, Alexandrian and Platonist background. The author concludes that the various aspects of Platonist dualism, both in motifs and vocabulary, have been exaggerated, and that apocalyptic themes are more important. We quote the chapter's final words (42): 'Enough indications exist to point to a reasonable conclusion that *Auctor* [i.e. the anonymous author] developed certain OT ideas within the Jewish apocalyptic framework, while Philo developed the same themes within a Platonic framework. Both writers ... probably go back independently to a common OT background. The Platonic/Philonic background for Hebrews is therefore "not proven", and as such it must give way to an examination of other possible backgrounds.' (DTR)

S. ISSER, 'Two Traditions: the Law of Exodus 21:22–23 Revisited', *CBQ* 52 (1990) 30–45, esp. 37–38.

The article examines the two different traditions of the law on injury done to a pregnant woman and the child she carries represented by the MT and the LXX. Philo's exegesis is evidence for the understanding of the Septuagint version. (DTR)

R. A. KRAFT, 'Tiberius Julius Alexander and the Crisis in Alexandria according to Josephus', in H. W. ATTRIDGE, J. J. COLLINS and T. H. TOBIN S.J. (edd.), *Of Scribes and Scrolls: Studies on the Hebrew Bible, Intertestamental Judaism, and Christian Origins presented to John Strugnell on the occasion of his Sixtieth Birthday*, College Theology Society Resources in Religion 5 (Lanham 1990) 175-184.

Independently of D. R. Schwartz *SPhA* 1 (1989) 63–69 the author looks at the career of Philo's nephew as described by Josephus and poses the question whether a connection can be made between Philo's account of the 'Sabbath crisis' in *Somn.* 2.123–132 and Josephus' story of the Alexandrian confrontation with Tiberius Julius Alexander in 66 AD. There are chronological difficulties involved (Philo would have to be in his 70's or even 80's), but in the author's view 'it is an attempt worth considering' (184). See also his article in the Koester Festschrift, edited by B. A. Pearson (full reference in Supplement) (DTR)

C. KRAUS REGGIANI, 'Tradizione e innovazione nel giudaismo ellenistico', in *La tradizione: forme e modi: XVIII Incontro di studiosi dell'antichità cristiana (Roma 7–9 maggio 1989)*, Studia Ephemeridis Augustinanum 31 (Rome 1990) 93–117.

Approaches the subject of tradition and innovation in Hellenistic Judaism by looking at those passages of Sapientia Salomonis and IV Maccabees which show substantial innovations with regard to the Old Testament tradition of eschatological themes, such as the doctrine of retribution and the immortality of the soul. Reggiani's third and most important example is Philo, all of whose philosophical elaborations are innovative in relation to traditional Hebrew thought. Yet man's journey to God, which Philo deals with in a masterly manner, does not provide an eschatological conclusion, but fully adheres to the Jewish conception of perfect happiness which can be achieved in this world by the wise and virtuous, who gain it as a reward for the spiritual union which they have achieved with God, together with the Jewish conception of retribution in this life for the wicked, whose punishment is to have a soul dead to virtue and knowledge. Consequently, Philo shows little interest in the eschatological problem. Nevertheless, on the few occasions when he does touch on the subject, it is clear that—like the author of Sapientia and IV Maccabees—he does not regard immortality as an ontological fact, but as the fruit of a personal achievement reserved for a few elected souls. (RR)

J. A. LOADER, *A Tale of Two Cities: Sodom and Gomorrah in the Old Testament: Early Jewish and Early Christian Traditions*, Contributions to Biblical Theology and Exegesis 1 (Kampen 1990), esp. 86-96.

Philo's evidence furnishes important material for the *Wirkungsgeschichte* of the exegesis of Genesis 18–19 in Jewish and Early Christian traditions, but because it is so copious the discussion has to be abridged and reduced to 'some basic tenets'. These are summarized at the end of the discussion as: (1) Philo's treatment is determined by the scriptural background; (2) he is acquainted with the familiar motifs of wickedness, wealth, punishment, with special concentration on the ideas of barrenness and blindness; (3) these motifs determine his allegorical treatment; (4) this treatment has an anti-hedonistic focus and breathes the spirit of a stern Stoicizing ethic; (5) the story symbolizes the destruction of what is bodily as opposed to what is spiritual; (6) the story is used not only to extol Abraham, but also to expound theological views. (DTR)

J. MAIER, *Zwischen den Testamenten: Geschichte und Religion in der Zeit des zweiten Tempels* (Würzburg 1990), esp. 83–88, 128–130.

Two sections deal with Philo in this book. On pp. 82-88 Maier discusses the written sources of Jewish literature in the period of the Second Temple and briefly presents Philo's works (list of writings and summary of contents) and fundamental bibliographical aids (editions, translations, lexicons, bibliographies, critical literature). On pp. 128-130 he succinctly describes the relation between the Jewish Halakah and Philo's allegorical method and highlights the analogies that can be detected in them. (RR)

F. MANNS, *Le Midrash, approche et commentaire de l'Ecriture* (Jerusalem 1990), esp. 60–69.

A modest contribution designed to introduce students to an aspect of the world behind the New Testament. The author emphasizes the balance in Philo's exegesis between literal and allegorical interpretation, and also his use of midrashic techniques. (DTR)

J. P. MARTÍN, 'Filon Hebreo y Teofilo Cristiano: la continuidad de una teologia natural', *Salmanticensis* 37 (1990) 302-317.

Theophilus of Antioch at *Ad Autolycum* 3.9 follows the five points of Philo's teaching at *Opif.* 170–172 very exactly in order to develop a natural theology based on a biblical and stoicizing perspective. On the other hand he systematically criticizes the Platonic concepts of Philo's exegesis of Genesis to the extent that they contain either cosmological or anthropological dualism. Antecedents of the Antiochean school of biblical exegesis are thus to be found in both dependence and criticism of Philo. (RR; based on author's abstract)

J. P. MARTÍN, 'Filon y la historia del platonismo: un dialogo con R. Radice', *Methexis* 3 (1990) 119-127.

Martín emphasizes the important points of agreement between his work *Filón de Alejandría y la génesis de la cultura occidental* (1986) and R. Radice's *Platonismo e creazionismo in Filone di Alessandria* (1989). Briefly, these are: (1) the way of reading Philo's text; (2) the interpretations of its content; (3) the attempt to determine Philo's place in the history of philosophy. The article discusses these subjects and also dwells on the problem of *creation ex nihilo* (122-124), which is dealt with at length in Radice's book. (RR)

J. P. MARTÍN, 'Ontologia e creazione in Filone Alessandrino: dialogo con Giovanni Reale e Roberto Radice', *Rivista de Filosofia Neoscolastico* 82 (1990) 146-165.

Starting from the generally similar positions of Reale and Radice on the way in which Philo's thought should be interpreted, Martín sets himself two aims in this article. First, he wants to show that there are no grounds for assuming that Philo is philosophically inferior to the Greek tradition. This assumption prevents us from properly understanding the philosophy of the first centuries (148ff.). To show this he follows a different route from that of Reale and Radice, concentrating on the relations between Theophilus of Antioch and Philo. His second aim is to find the core of Philo's thinking. This core has been located in four different areas by Philonic scholars (151ff.): (a) in the theory of Ideas (Wolfson); (b) in the theory of creation, particularly in that of the Ideas as thoughts of God (Reale-Radice); (c) in the concept of migration (Nikiprowetzky); (d) in the polarity self-love–love of God (Harl). Martín agrees with the second view, but extends it in such a way as to incorporate the others (165) and to include his own view of the 'centrality of the ontological exegesis of Ex. 3:14'. Like Reale and Radice, he concludes that in the light of the new interpretation of Philo 'we need to rewrite the history of Middle Platonism and the precursors of Neoplatonism' (165). (RR)

M. MILLS, *Human Agents of Cosmic Power in Hellenistic Judaism and the Synoptic Tradition*, JSOT Supplement Series 41 (Sheffield 1990), esp. 42–46.

The starting point of this study on human agents of cosmic power is Jesus the exorcist. Various literary traditions on wonder-workers are examined, including Moses. The two documents used for the Moses tradition are the magical text *The Sword of Moses* and Philo's *De vita Moysis*. The similarity in both texts is that Moses is 'regarded as an extremely significant human being because he is able to channel divine energy to human situations' (46). (DTR)

B. A. PEARSON, *Gnosticism, Judaism, and Egyptian Christianity*, Studies in Antiquity and Christianity 5 (Minneapolis 1990).

Reprints a important selection of articles with themes covered by the title, published in various journals and collections of essays during the past two decades. Specifically devoted to Philo are 'Friedländer Revisited: Alexandrian Judaism and Gnostic Origins' (1973, = R-R 7333), and 'Philo, Gnosis, and the New Testament' (1983, = R-R 8359). See further the review of G. E. Sterling in *SPhA* 4 (1992) 175–178, which lists all the references to Philo and also gives an *Index locorum Philoneorum*. (DTR)

S. PÉTREMENT, *A Separate God: the Christian Origins of Gnosticism* (San Francisco–London 1990), *passim*.

English translation of earlier voluminous French study (*Le Dieu séparé: les origines du gnosticisme*, Paris 1984), in which the author argues a Christian origin for the Gnostic movement. Extensive use is made of Philonic material (see index, p. 540), even if it is argued that (41): 'But, heretic or not, Philo is still very far from being a Gnostic.' The translation was prepared by Carol Harrison. (DTR)

M.-J. PIERRE, 'Philon, gnose, patristique et apocryphes chrétiens', *Revue Biblique* 97 (1990) 296–301.

A review of three recent works on Philo: R. Goulet, *La philosophie de Moïse* (Paris 1987) (cf. *SPhA* 2 (1990) 155–6); J. Ménard, *La Gnose de Philon d'Alexandrie* (Paris 1987) (cf. *SPhA* 2 (1990) 161–2); and R. M. Berchman, *From Philo to Origen* (Chico, California 1984) (cf. R-R 8408). (RR)

P. PILHOFER, *Presbyteron kreitton: Der Altersbeweis der jüdischen und christlichen Apologeten und seine Vorgeschichte*, WUNT 2.39 (Tübingen 1990), esp. 173–192

By 'Altersbeweis' the author means the apologetic argument or proof founded on the axiom that 'what is old is good', which is then extended to the view that 'what is older is better' (the title of the book is derived from a concise formulation of this position in Timaeus Locrus 7). The study of the theme is divided into four parts: Greek literature, Roman literature, Hellenistic-Jewish literature, and the Christian apologetic literature of the 2nd century (excluding Clement). In the third part an extensive chapter is devoted to Philo. In 1880 Joel, attacking the authenticity of the Aristobulan fragments, had claimed that few statements claiming the greater antiquity of Judaism were to be found in Philo. Pilhofer argues that he could not have read the complete Philo when making this claim, and sets out to present the evidence as thoroughly as possible. To be sure, Philo's attitude towards the relation between old and new is complex, and cannot be reduced to a single formula (his emphasis on the validity of the new in a theological context—in the case of God nothing is old, but rather timeless—is quite unusual). Pilhofer then proceeds to enumerate and discuss all the texts in which Philo asserts the antiquity of the Judaism compared with Greek culture. It is true, however, that on a number of occasions Philo does not use the argument when we might expect it, e.g. in the *De vita Moysis*. In many aspects, it is concluded, Philo's approach shows similarity with that of Cicero, the former as apologist *pro Ioudaeis*, the latter *pro Romanis*. But Philo has the easier task: Moses was after all of venerable antiquity... (DTR)

M. PUCCI BEN ZEEV, 'New Perspectives on the Jewish-Greek Hostilities in Alexandria during the Reign of Emperor Caligula', *JSJ* 21 (1990) 227-235.

Some interesting critical comments provoked by two articles published about a decade earlier. Polaček's description of the Alexandrian pogrom in 38 AD as a 'holocaust' is misleading and methodologically unsound. Cracco-Ruggini's interpretation of the same event in terms of a 'class struggle' raises interesting issues. The assumption that the Jewish population represented a homogenous group that can be described as a 'politically evolved social stratum of petty bourgeois' is questioned. It would seem that socio-economic differences within the Jewish community were extensive and profound. A task for future research is to unravel the political, social and religious factors at work in Alexandria in the first century of our era. (DTR)

G. REALE, *A History of Ancient Philosophy*, vol. 4 The Schools of the Imperial Age, edited by J. R. CATAN (Albany, N.Y. 1990), esp. 169-204.

Reale's chapter on Philo, the longest to be presented in a general history of Greek philosophy (cf. R-R 7839), is now available in English translation. (DTR)

H. Graf REVENTLOW, *Epochen der Bibelauslegung I: von Alten Testament bis Origenes* (München 1990), esp. 44-49.

Brief general presentation of Philo's allegorical method as part of an account of biblical interpretation 'zwischen den Testamenten'. (DTR)

J. RIAUD, Art. 'Thérapeutes', *DSp* fasc. 95 (1990) 562-570.

Discusses the controversial topic of the historical identity of the community which established itself on the mountains above Lake Mareotis and which Philo describes in *Contempl*. Philo uses two names to designate these monks: 'Therapeutae' and 'Suppliants'. The first term indicates that they 'regarded themselves as priests and worshippers of the one true God and as moralists and philosophers who healed the body by curing the soul. The name 'Suppliants', on the other hand, suggests a connection with the Levites and the great allegorical theme of the migration from the dominion of the body and from the 'Egypt' of the passions (565). Riaud describes the characteristics of the Therapeutae (average age, social origin, way of life, etc.), their relations with the priesthood of Jerusalem (568), their use of allegory (565 ff.), and their links with Christian monasticism (568 ff.). The article ends with a useful bibliography. (RR)

D. T. RUNIA, *Exegesis and Philosophy: Studies on Philo of Alexandria*, Variorum Collected Studies Series (London 1990).

Collection of 11 articles and 2 reviews on Philo published between 1981 and 1989. The pagination of the original publication is retained. The first article, 'Philo, Alexandrian and Jew' is an English translation of an article first published in Dutch (cf. *SPhA* 4 (1992) 110). Some brief addenda and a short index (restricted by the format of the series) conclude the volume. (DTR)

D. T. RUNIA, 'How to Search Philo', *SPhA* 2 (1990) 106-139.

Since the writings of Philo are by any standard voluminous, it will be useful for the Philonist to develop techniques that enable him or her to carry out searches. This article outlines and illustrates five different techniques for searching Philo: Leisegang's Indices, Mayer's *Index Philoneus*, Borgen and Skarsten's KWIC concordance, and using the TLG database on the IBYCUS and Macintosh personal computers. In each case an example is used, namely the phrase ἀντίμιμος οὐρανοῦ. This phrase is of interest because it is used by the 4th century writer Heliodorus in a passage that must be dependent on Philo *Mos.* 2.195. Some research shows that the parallel was probably first discovered by the great Frisian classical scholar Tiberius Hemsterhuys. The article concludes that computer searches should be a supplement of, not a substitute for, wide reading (134). (DTR)

D. T. RUNIA, R. RADICE and D. SATRAN, 'Philo of Alexandria: an Annotated Bibliography 1986-87', *SPhA* 2 (1990) 141-175.

First continuation in the pages of this Annual of R-R after its publication in 1988. On pp. 141-142 the principles of the continuation are outlined.

E. P. SANDERS, *Jewish Law from Jesus to the Mishnah* (London–Philadelphia 1990), esp. part IV, 255–308.

Extensive use of Philonic evidence in an penetrating examination of the extent to which Diaspora Judaism was dependent for its practice in the area of purity, food and offerings on rules formulated in Jerusalem. Philo yields important information on Diaspora practice. (DTR)

S. SCHWARTZ, *Josephus and Judaean Politics*, Columbia Studies in the Classical Tradition 18 (Leiden 1990), esp. 40-43, 51-54, 209–210.

Schwartz concedes that Josephus may have been indebted to Philo for some details of biblical exegesis (54), but for the most part strongly downplays any influence that Philo may have exerted. Josephus was 'not profoundly interested in or well-informed about the Hellenistic-Jewish intellectual tradition' (209). (DTR)

A. F. SEGAL, *Paul the Convert: the Apostolate and Apostasy of Saul the Pharisee* (New Haven–London 1990), esp. 43–45 and *passim*.

Evidence from Philo is used to furnish the background to Paul's 'mysticism'. (DTR)

P. SHULER, 'Philo's Moses and Matthew's Jesus: A Comparative Study in Ancient Literature', *SPhA* 2 (1990) 86-103.

Not persuaded by the frequently stated view that the Gospels do not share any affinities with genres of Greco-Roman literature, the author believes that they can be illuminated by looking at features of the encomiastic biography which they take over. For this purpose he compares Matthew's Gospel with Philo's *Life of Moses*. Both choose the genre of encomiastic biography, and this choice gives them the freedom to construct their portraits in such a way as to fulfil their purposes. In their desire to communicate they direct their message to both Jewish and Gentile readers. Moreover the two accounts share a similar topical arrangement. In both cases emulation of the portrayed hero is required. The various similarities discovered can only be explained if one takes into account the type of narrative used, i.e. encomiastic biography. (DTR)

D. SLY, *Philo's Perception of Women*, BJS 209 (Atlanta 1990).

This revised doctoral dissertation prepared at McMaster University under the supervision of Alan Mendelson is the first monograph specifically to address the question of Philo's perception of women and the place they occupy in both his social world and his thought as expressed primarily in his biblical exegesis (in many respects therefore the study is a continuation at a more specific level of Baer's study on the relation between male and female, R-R 7005). I give here the briefest synopsis of the contents; see further also the extensive review by R. Kraemer at *SPhA* 4 (1992) 168–173. Chapters one and two introduce Philo and place his views on women against the background of Jewish Alexandrian society (Sly thinks that Philo himself was probably married, but had no children). Chapter three examines the small amount of scholarship on the subject. Chapter four examines Philo's use of language with regard to the sexes, concluding that women are not inclusively designated in the terms ἄνθρωπος and ἀνήρ. In chapter five a crucial distinction is made in Philo's perception between women and virgins (based on remnants of blood taboo). This distinction is used to structure the following five chapters on Philo's presentation of biblical material involving the female sex. Biblical women are presented in chapters six (Eve) and seven (others); biblical virgins in chapters eight (general allegorical considerations), nine (Sarah and Rebecca) and ten (others). In chapter 11 the attention moves to women in Philo's own world (a direct connection is postulated with how he presents women in his exegesis). Here the main distinction seems to be between women under male control (good women) and women eluding male control (harlots). There is a discrepancy between Philo's ideals and the real social situation of women in his society, for most of whom virginity could not possibly be an option. Chapter twelve gives a summary and draws some conclusions. Philo's conviction that women need to be controlled stands in strong contrast to the spiritual freedom that he offered man in the Odyssey of the spirit. (DTR)

J. Z. SMITH, *Drudgery Divine: on the Comparison of Early Christianities and the Religions of Late Antiquity* (Chicago 1990), esp. 7–13.

Those intrigued how the proverb about Plato and Philo comes to be mentioned in correspondence between two early Presidents of the United States may wish to consult this astonishingly learned exposé entitled 'On the Origins of Origins'. (DTR)

G. STERLING, 'Philo and the Logic of Apologetics: an Analysis of the *Hypothetica*', *SBLSP* 29 (1990) 412-430.

The aim of the paper is to offer a basic reconstruction of this fragmentary and little studied work of Philo and to attempt to locate it within the context of Jewish-Egyptian relations. Sterling examines in turn the content, form and function of the work. Especially the title has been a source of much controversy. After rejecting other interpretations Sterling notes that ὑποθετικά is a terminus technicus in Stoic logic and explores the possibility that Philo may have meant by the title something like 'Hypothetical propositions', i.e. logically valid statements which will be apologetically effective. Thus Philo's apologetics in this case appeal to the authority of reason rather than of scripture. The choice of such a method is bound up with the work's purpose and historical context: it was written as a response to insinuations made against the Jews and Jewish culture by Greco-Egyptian intellectuals such as Lysimachus, Apion and Chaeremon. It is perhaps no coincidence that the latter two had ties with Stoicism. (DTR)

T. H. TOBIN, 'The Prologue of John and Hellenistic Jewish Speculation', *CBQ* 52 (1990) 252-269.

Distinguishing an original logos hymn from the rest of the Prologue to John's Gospel, the author seeks to determine its relation to Hellenistic Jewish wisdom speculation. Three themes are examined in turn: (1) the reality and functions of the Logos; (2) the contrast between light and darkness; (3) the Logos and Heavenly Man. Philo is the main point of comparison, which leads to the following conclusion (268): 'On the basis of the parallels between the hymn of the Prologue and some of the biblical interpretations of Philo of Alexandria, one is led to the conclusion that the hymn in the Prologue, like Philo of Alexandria, was part of the larger world of Hellenistic Jewish speculative interpretations of biblical texts... The argument is not that the author of the hymn had read Philo of Alexandria; the parallels are not close enough to maintain that kind of position. But the parallels do show that both the author of the hymn and Philo of Alexandria were part of the larger tradition of Hellenistic Jewish biblical interpretation and speculation. Both were making use of similar structures of thought and were expressing those structures through the use of similar vocabulary, even though the results were very different.' (DTR)

P. J. TOMSON, *Paul and the Jewish Law: Halakha in the Letters of the Apostle to the Gentiles*, CRINT 3.1 (Assen 1990), esp. 36-47.

In investigating Paul's relation to the halakha, the author notes that it is accepted that halakha occupied a central place in 'hebraizing Palestinian Judaism', but that its function in diaspora Judaism is far less clear. For this reason he turns to Philo and gives a critical survey of the literature on the subject from Ritter (1879) to N. Cohen (1987). After dealing at some length with *Migr.* 86-93 he concludes that 'the image we gain from Philo is that of enlightened piety, freely enriched with numerous elements from Hellenistic intellectual tradition, but organized along the lines of Jewish life' (45). Philo's evidence thus shows that the halakha was no less vital an element in diaspora Judaism, and therefore that it must have been a central factor for Paul, unless it can be shown that he effectively departed from the ways of Judaism. (DTR)

K. VAN DER TOORN AND P. W. VAN DER HORST, 'Nimrod before and after the Bible', *HThR* 83 (1990) 1–29, esp. 17–19.

Philo is the first post-biblical writer to mention Nimrod explicitly. In the two passages in which he is discussed, *QG* 2.81–82 and *Gig.* 65–66 a number of haggadic elements occur which return frequently in later haggadic developments. Moreover the interpretation that Nimrod was 'against' rather than 'before' the Lord recurs explicitly in Augustine *DCD* 16.4. This section was written by P. W. van der Horst (see also above under his name). (DTR)

A. UÑA JUAREZ, 'Antiqua et Mediaevalia. Sobre el significado teorico del platonismo en la historia del pensamiento', *La Ciudad de Dios* 203 (1990) 143–187.

Primarily a bibliographical notice. In section IV entitled 'Middle Platonism and the Platonism of Philo of Alexandria' (176–178) the author gives a rapid survey of recent scholarship covered by this title, concentrating particularly on *ANRW* II 36.1 (dedicated to Middle Platonism), II 21.1 (dedicated to Alexandrian Judaism), and the work of D. T. Runia, *Philo of Alexandria and the* Timaeus *of Plato* (Leiden 1986[2]), which is deemed to be a work of 'high quality' (p. 185). (RR)

R. WILLIAMSON, Art. 'Philo', in R. J. COGGINS and J. L. HOULDEN (edd.), *A Dictionary of Biblical Interpretation* (London-Philadelphia 1990) 542–544.

More than 5 columns devoted to Philo is rather generous in this single volume dictionary. Both the survey and the bibliographical information are idiosyncratic, but charmingly so. (DTR)

D. WINSTON, 'Judaism and Hellenism: Hidden Tensions in Philo's Thought', *SPhA* 2 (1990) 1-19.

Originally presented as a keynote address to the North American Patristic Society in 1989, the article takes as its starting point the assertion that 'it is in the nature of so vast an enterprise of conceptual adaptation [as undertaken by Philo], that inner tensions must inevitably work their way ever so subtly to the surface, thus creating elements of stress that only an exposition employing systematic ambiguity could contain' (3). Winston then proceeds to discuss several fundamental themes that illustrate such ambiguity as it emerges in Philo's commentary on Scripture. These themes are: repentance, the divine nature, Moses as sage, Moses as prophet, ecstatic and noetic prophecy and mystic vision. On the basis of these discussions Winston concludes that although Philo 'allows the Jewish side of his thought the dominant place in his presentation, he invariably tones it down by introducing some philosophical twist and by allowing the perceptive reader a glimpse of his true position... The philosophical portrait of Philo that thus emerges is that of a mind fully committed to a mystical form of Platonism. At the same time, it is the mind of a Jew who has remained loyal to his native religious tradition (18).' (DTR)

D. ZELLER, *Charis bei Philon und Paulus*, Stuttgarter Bibelstudien 142 (Stuttgart 1990).

Zeller's first concern in this book is to show that Philo and Paul operated in a similar context: they were contemporaries, both were familiar with the Judaism of the Diaspora, and both championed the monotheism of their faith against pagan polytheism. Whereas this position is all-important to Philo, for Paul it merely serves as a 'prelude' to his more important campaign on behalf of Christ (10). The two thinkers also express themselves in different ways: Philo mainly wrote allegorical, philosophically oriented treatises and is strictly an interpreter of Scripture. Paul, by contrast, is essentially a missionary (and a theologian) who writes letters, and though he is no stranger to philosophy, he is not conditioned by it to the same extent as Philo. On the basis of these similarities and differences Zeller compares Philo and Paul on the theological conception of grace. Though neither depends on the other, they do have common roots in the historical tradition. Zeller starts with a general lexical analysis of the term χάρις, and then looks at the meaning of the word in Greek antiquity, in the Septuagint, and in Hellenistic Judaism (13–32). The second part of the book analyzes the concept in Philo, with special reference to the relationship between grace and creation (33–48)—the main relationship in Philo—, that between grace and sin, and that between grace and moral perfection (49–103). In this ethical context the ultimate objective appears to be knowledge of God, which is identical to moral and spiritual perfection. Philo goes beyond Plato (and the Stoics) here in that man's understanding of God is not due to human virtue or merit but comes about by the initiative, i.e. in self-revelation, of God in the moment of ecstasy (103–105) and so, in the final analysis, by grace. Chapter 3 deals with χάρις in the New Testament and in the period immediately prior to Paul, while chapter 4 is devoted to χάρις in Paul. Paul shares with Philo the conviction that man cannot save himself. Like every pious Jew, Philo bases the possibility of man's salvation on the Bible and the Patriarchs. In his view, true faith culminates in the recognition of the Creator and the gratuitousness of his acts, in man's total dependence on God, and in the gift of grace, which extends not only to man but to all creation. The 'place' where grace is experienced is the created cosmos, and also the people of Israel, where the ecstatic knowledge of God is possible. For Paul, on the other hand, the principle of grace is Christ and his sacrifice for man, and this makes for a fundamental distinction between grace and human action, and between grace and law. For Philo, too, grace and moral perfection are gifts from God, but they are awarded only to those who lead a deserving life. In this way the gratuitousness of grace is given much less emphasis in Philo than in Paul, for whom the difference between the time before Christ (the era of sin) and the new dispensation brought by Christ constitutes a clean break, not only historically, but also in terms of individual salvation (this passage from sin to a state of grace is much more gradual in Philo). Zeller concludes: 'Even though the starting-points of Philo and Paul are so different, nevertheless we have been able to fix similar tendencies and consequences. The recognition—in the case of Paul, the demonstration—of χάρις brings man's pride to silence and leads him to thanksgiving' (199). See further also the review of David Hay in *SPhA* 4 (1992) 174–175. (RR)

Addenda 1986–89

P. ALLEN, 'Plato, Aristotle, and the Concept of Woman in Early Jewish Philosophy', *Florilegium* 9 (1987) 89–111, esp. 93–97.

Although there is no evidence that Philo was influenced by Aristotle's writings on the subject, his espousal of 'sex polarity' in the four categories of opposites, generation, wisdom and virtue are exactly parallel to Aristotle's theory. The polarity is indicated in a table on p. 97. The article is rather unclear on the extent to which Philo may have influenced later Jewish thinkers. Confusion occurs because Leone Ebreo introduces a character called Philo in his *Dialoghi d'Amore*, and the unsuspecting reader might think that the Jewish philosopher is meant (*quod non*, surely). (DTR)

A. A. BARRETT, *Caligula: the Corruption of Power* (London 1989), esp. 73–80, 214–216 and *passim*.

'This first major reassessment of Caligula's reign and violent death for over fifty years' (dustjacket) cannot fail to refer frequently to the Philonic evidence. (DTR)

G. J. BARTELINK, 'Die Beeinflussung Augustins durch die griechischen Patres', in J. DEN BOEFT and J. VAN OORT (edd.), *Augustiniana Traiectina: communications présentées au Colloque International d'Utrecht 13–14 novembre 1986* (Paris 1987) 9–24, esp. 13–14.

Concise but valuable discussion on the possible acquaintance of Augustine with the works of Philo. (DTR)

S. BELKIN, *The Midrash of Philo: the Oldest Recorded Midrash Written in Alexandria by Philo (c. 20 B.C.E. – 45 C.E.) before the Formulation of Tannaitic Literature. Vol. 1 Genesis II–XVII; Selected Portions from Philo's Questions and Answers and from his other writings, translated into Hebrew from the Armenian and Greek with a commentary. Based upon Parallels from Rabbinic Literature*, edited by E. HURVITZ (New York 1989) [Hebrew].

See the review of N. G. Cohen separately listed below.

J. COHEN, *"Be Fertile and Increase, Fill the Earth and Master It": the Ancient and Medieval Career of a Biblical Text* (Ithaca–London 1989), esp. 72–76.

Philo is touched upon in the course of this fascinating account of the interpretation of a crucial biblical text from its time of writing until the end of the medieval period. Like other Hellenistic writers Philo shows more interest in the dominion of the first humans over nature than in their reproductive fertility, and hardly makes any direct reference to Gen. 1:28. (DTR)

N. G. COHEN, 'Review of S. Belkin, *The Midrash of Philo* vol. 1', *JSJ* 23 (1992) 100–105.

Contrary to our usual practice we list this review separately (and two years ahead of time) because for the scholar unable to read modern Hebrew it is the best introduction to an extensive body of work on Philo in relation to his Jewish background, the publication of which began in 1989. The full title is given above under the name of its author, the distinguished Philonist and Rabbinic scholar Samuel Belkin. The review actually concerns volume 1 of a projected six-volume work presenting the material left unpublished by Belkin on his death and prepared for publication with great devotion by E. Hurvitz. It aims to reintroduce Philo to the traditional halakhic and midrashic corpus and thus enable a more positive evaluation of Philo in orthodox Judaism. Belkin does not argue for direct contact between Philo and Rabbinic midrash, but rather that they both drew from a common Palestinian tradition. In the first volume now published Belkin arranges Philonic midrash in the form of a commentary to selected passages from the *Quaestiones*. The reviewer argues that what we are presented with is more of a presentation of 'raw material' than any kind of scholarly comparison, but that it is nonetheless a valuable contribution, particularly on account of the relevance of Philo to modern religiously committed Jews. She ends by emphasizing the limited accessibility of the work. Not only is it published in Hebrew, but it also makes use of a number of conventions that only make sense to scholars versed in the Rabbinic tradition. (DTR)

R. ECHUARI, 'Dios y el ser', *Annuario Filosófico (Universidad de Navarra)* 19.1 (1986) 9-24.

Philo's interpretation of Ex. 3:14 is very important in that by identifying God's nature with his being (*Mut.* 21, 11, *Somn.* 1.230-232, *Mos.* 1.75) it proclaims God's eminence on the one hand and his unknowability on the other. Only God's existence, not his nature, can be demonstrated, precisely because he has no other determination apart from his being. This conception opens 'a new road which will be deeply explored by other illustrious philosophers' (10), in particular by Avicenna, Maimonides, and Aquinas (17). By contrast, Heidegger adopts an opposite position in that he distinguishes God's nature from his being (19 ff.). (RR)

B. SEPTIMUS, 'Biblical Religion and Political Rationality in Simone Luzzatto, Maimonides and Spinoza', in I. TWERSKY and B. SEPTIMUS (edd.), *Jewish Thought in the Seventeenth Century* (Cambridge Mass. 1987). 399–433, esp. 419–421

Isolated but interesting remarks on the 17th century Venetian Jew Simon Luzzatto's attitude to Philo. If only Philo had educated contemporary Jews instead of writing for the Greeks, rationality would not have been such a problem for Judaism. (DTR)

Universities of Leiden and Utrecht
Catholic University of the Sacred Heart, Milan

SUPPLEMENT

A Provisional Bibliography 1991–93

The user of this supplementary bibliography of very recent articles on Philo is once again reminded that it will doubtless contain inaccuracies and red herrings, because it is not in all cases based on autopsy. It is merely meant as a service to the reader. Scholars who are disturbed by omissions or keen to have their own work on Philo listed are strongly encouraged to take up contact with the bibliography's compilers.

1991

M. ALEXANDRE JR., 'The Art of Periodic Composition in Philo of Alexandria', in D. T. RUNIA et al. (edd.), *Earle Hilgert Festschrift* [= *SPhA* 3 (1991)] 135–150.

J. ASHTON, *Understanding the Fourth Gospel* (Oxford 1991).

J. N. BAILEY, 'Metanoia in the Writings of Philo Judaeus', *SBLSPS* 30 (1991) 135–141.

L. L. BELLEVILLE, *Reflections of Glory*, JSNTSupp 52 (Sheffield 1991).

B. L. BLACKBURN, *Theios Anēr and the Markan Miracle Traditions*, WUNT 2.36 (Tübingen 1991).

G. BOCCACCINI, *Middle Judaism: Jewish Thought 300 B.C.E. — 200 C.E.* (Minneapolis 1991).

P. BORGEN, 'The Sabbath Controversy in John 5:1–18 and Analogous Controversy Reflected in Philo's Writings', in D. T. RUNIA et al. (edd.), *Earle Hilgert Festschrift* [= *SPhA* 3 (1991)] 209–221.

A. P. BOS, *In de greep van de Titanen: Inleiding tot een hoofdstroming van de Griekse filosofie*, Verantwoording 5 (Amsterdam 1991), esp. 89–96.

S. B. BOWMAN, 'Art. Philo Judaeus', in A. P. KAZAKHAN, *Oxford Dictionary of Byzantium* (New York–Oxford 1991) 3.1655.

C. CARLIER, *La μήτροπολις chez Philon d'Alexandrie: le concept de colonisation appliqué à la Diaspora juive*, Mémoire pour l'Académie des Inscriptions et Belles-Lettres, Ecole Biblique et Archéologique Française de Jerusalem (Jerusalem 1991).

A. CHESTER, 'Jewish Messianic Expectations and Mediatorial Figures', in M. HENGEL and U. HECKEL (edd.), *Paulus und das antike Judentum*, WUNT 58 (Tübingen 1991) esp. 48–50.

A. D. DE CONICK and J. FOSSUM, 'Stripped before God: a New Interpretation of Logion 37 in the Gospel of Thomas', *VC* (1991) 123–150.

S. DANIEL-NATAF [דניאל־נתף :ס] (ed.), פילון האלכסנדרוני: כתבים [= *Philo of Alexandria: Writings*]: vol. 2, Exposition of the Law, Part One (Jerusalem 1991).

E. DASSMANN et al., *Reallexikon für Antike und Christentum*, Band XV = Lieferungen 113–120 (Stuttgart 1991)
G. O'DALY, Art. 'Hierarchie', 41–73, esp. 50–51 (hierarchy); A. LUMPE–H. BIETENHARD, Art. 'Himmel', 173–212, esp. 196–197 (heaven); J. ENGEMANN, Art. 'Hirt', 577–607, esp. 589 (shepherd); J. PROCOPÉ, Art. 'Hochmut', 795–858, esp. 824–825 (pride, arrogance); F. K. MAYR, Art. 'Hören', 1023–1111, esp. 1071–1074 (hearing); A. DIHLE–B. STUDER–F. RICKERT, Art. 'Hoffnung', 1159–1250, esp. 1177–1178 (hope).

E. DASSMANN et al., *Reallexikon für Antike und Christentum*, Lieferung 121 (Stuttgart 1991)
F.-L. HOSSFELD–G. SCHÖLLGEN, Art. 'Hohepriester' 4–58, esp. 19–23 (High priest); G. J. M. BARTELINK, Art. 'Homer' 117–147, esp. 125–126 (Homer).

J. DILLON, *The Golden Chain: Studies in the Development of Platonism and Christianity*, Variorum Collected Studies Series (London 1991).

L. H. FELDMAN, 'Nodet's New Edition of Josephus' Antiquities', *JSJ* 22 (1991) 88–113, esp. 90f.

F. FENDLER, *Studien zum Markusevangelium*, FRLANT (Göttingen 1991), esp. 62–69.

S. D. FRAADE, *From Tradition to Commentary: Torah and Its Interpretation in the Midrash Sifre to Deuteronomy* (Albany 1991).

Y. FRANKEL [פרנקל :י'], דרכי האגדה והמדרש [= *The Methods of the Aggadah and the Midrash*] (Jerusalem 1991), esp. 2.473–475.

I. GOBRY, 'La ténèbre (γνόφος): l'héritage alexandrin de Saint Grégoire de Nysse', *Diotima: Revue de Recherche Philosophique* 19 (1991) 79–82.

L. L. GRABBE, 'Philo and Aggada: a Response to B. J. Bamberger', in D. T. RUNIA et al. (edd.), *Earle Hilgert Festschrift* [= *SPhA* 3 (1991)] 153–166.

J. GRONDIN, *Einführung in die philosophische Hermeneutik* (Darmstadt 1991), esp. 33–36.

J. HALLMAN, *The Descent of God: Divine Suffering in History and Theology* (Minneapolis 1991).

R. G. HAMERTON-KELLY, 'Allegory, Typology and Sacred Violence: Sacrificial Representation and the Unity of the Bible in Paul and Philo', in D. T. RUNIA et al. (edd.), *Earle Hilgert Festschrift* [= *SPhA* 3 (1991)] 53–70.

D. M. HAY, 'Philo's View of Himself as an Exegete: Inspired, but not Authoritative', in D. T. RUNIA et al. (edd.), *Earle Hilgert Festschrift* [= *SPhA* 3 (1991)] 41–53.

D. M. HAY (ed.), *Both Literal and Allegorical: Studies in Philo of Alexandria's Questions and Answers on Genesis and Exodus*, BJS 232 (Atlanta 1991).

D. M. HAY, 'References to Other Exegetes', in *idem* (ed.), *Both Literal and Allegorical: Studies in Philo of Alexandria's Questions and Answers on Genesis and Exodus*, BJS 232 (Atlanta 1991) 81–97.

P. HAYMAN, 'Monotheism—A Misused Word in Jewish Studies', *JJS* 42 (1991) 1–15.

E. HILGERT, 'The *Quaestiones*: Texts and Translations', in D. M. HAY (ed.), *Both Literal and Allegorical: Studies in Philo of Alexandria's Questions and Answers on Genesis and Exodus*, BJS 232 (Atlanta 1991) 1–15.

E. HILGERT, 'A Review of Previous Research on Philo's *De Virtutibus*', *SBLSPS* 30 (1991) 103–115.

N. JANOWITZ, 'The Rhetoric of Translation: Three Early Perspectives on Translating Torah', *HThR* 84 (1991) 129–140.

D. N. JASTRAM, 'Philo's Concept of Generic Virtue', *SBLSPS* 30 (1991) 323–347.

R. A. KRAFT, 'Philo and the Sabbath Crisis: Alexandrian Jewish Politics and the Dating of Philo's Works', in B. A. PEARSON et al. (edd.), *The Future of Early Christianity: Essays in Honour of Helmut Koester* (Minneapolis 1991) 131–141.

J. LAPORTE, 'The High Priest in Philo of Alexandria', in D. T. RUNIA et al. (edd.), *Earle Hilgert Festschrift* [= *SPhA* 3 (1991)] 71–82.

S. LEVARIE, 'Philo on Music', *Journal of Musicology* 9 (1991) 124–130.

D. LÜHRMANN, 'The Godlessness of Germans Living by the Sea according to Philo of Alexandria', in B. A. PEARSON et al. (edd.), *The Future of Early Christianity: Essays in Honour of Helmut Koester* (Minneapolis 1991) 57–63.

B. L. MACK, 'Wisdom and Apocalyptic in Philo', in D. T. RUNIA et al. (edd.), *Earle Hilgert Festschrift* [= *SPhA* 3 (1991)] 21–40.

S. MACKNIGHT, *A Light Among the Nations: Jewish Missionary Activity in the Second Temple Period* (Minneapolis 1991).

J. W. MARTENS, 'Philo and the Higher Law', *SBLSPS* 30 (1991) 309–322.

J. P. MARTÍN, 'El *Sofista* de Platón y el platonismo de Filón de Alejandría', *Methexis* 4 (1991) 81–99.

J. P. MARTÍN, 'Philo and Augustine, *De civitate Dei* XIV 28 and XV: Some Preliminary Observations', in D. T. RUNIA et al. (edd.), *Earle Hilgert Festschrift* [= *SPhA* 3 (1991)] 283–294.

B. C. MCGING, 'Pontius Pilate and the Sources', *CBQ* 53 (1991) 416–438.

B. MCGINN, *The Presence of God: a History of Christian Mysticism; vol. 1 The Foundations of Mysticism* (New York–London 1991), esp. 35–41.

A. MÉASSON and J. CAZEAUX, 'From Grammar to Discourse: a Study of the *Questiones in Genesim* in Relation to the Treatises', in D. M. HAY (ed.), *Both Literal and Allegorical: Studies in Philo of Alexandria's Questions and Answers on Genesis and Exodus*, BJS 232 (Atlanta 1991) 125–225.

A. MENDELSON, 'Two glimpses of Philo in Modern English Literature: Works by Charles Kingsley and Francis Warner', in D. T. RUNIA et al. (edd.), *Earle Hilgert Festschrift* [= *SPhA* 3 (1991)] 328–343.

E. M. MORALES, 'De Fuga et Inventione: Filon de Alejandria', Notizario Centro di Studi sul Guidaismo Ellenistico 2 bis (1991) 1-7.

K. A. MORLAND, The Galatian Choice: Galatians 1:6-12 and 3:8-14 in the Light of Jewish Curse-Texts and Antique Rhetoric (dissertation Oslo/Trondheim, 1991).

J. VAN OORT, Jerusalem and Babylon: a Study into Augustine's City of God and the Sources of his Doctrine of the Two Cities, VCSup 14 (Leiden 1991), esp. 235-254.

J. PANAGOPOULOU, Η ΕΡΜΗΝΕΙΑ ΤΗΣ ΑΓΙΑΣ ΓΡΑΦΗΣ ΣΤΗΝ ΕΚΚΛΗΣΙΑ ΤΩΝ ΠΑΤΕΡΩΝ: ΟΙ ΤΡΕΙΣ ΠΡΩΤΟΙ ΑΙΩΝΕΣ ΚΑΙ Η ΑΛΕΞΑΝΔΡΙΝΗ ΕΞΗΓΗΤΙΚΗ ΠΑΡΑΔΟΣΗ ΩΣ ΤΟΝ ΠΕΜΠΤΟ ΑΙΩΝΑ, vol. 1 (Athens 1991).

B. A. PEARSON, 'Pre-Valentianian Gnosticism in Alexandria', in B. A. PEARSON et al. (edd.), The Future of Early Christianity: Essays in Honour of Helmut Koester (Minneapolis 1991) 455-466.

R. J. QUINONES, The Changes of Cain: Violence and the Lost Brother in Cain and Abel Literature (Princeton 1991), esp. 23-29.

R. RADICE, 'Observations on the Theory of the Ideas as the Thoughts of God in Philo of Alexandria', in D. T. RUNIA et al. (edd.), Earle Hilgert Festschrift [= SPhA 3 (1991)] 126-134.

J. RIAUD, 'Quelques réflexions sur les Thérapeutes d'Alexandrie à la lumière de De vita Mosis II, 67', in D. T. RUNIA et al. (edd.), Earle Hilgert Festschrift [= SPhA 3 (1991)] 184-191.

J. R. ROYSE, 'Philo, Κύριος, and the Tetragrammaton', in D. T. RUNIA et al. (edd.), Earle Hilgert Festschrift [= SPhA 3 (1991)] 167-183.

J. R. ROYSE, 'Philo's Quaestiones in Exodum 1.6', in D. M. HAY (ed.), Both Literal and Allegorical: Studies in Philo of Alexandria's Questions and Answers on Genesis and Exodus, BJS 232 (Atlanta 1991) 17-27.

J. R. ROYSE, The Spurious Texts of Philo of Alexandria: a Study of Textual Transmission and Corruption with Indexes to the Major Collections of Greek Fragments, ALGHJ 22 (Leiden 1991).

D. T. RUNIA, 'Philo and the Neoplatonic Tradition', in A. VANDERJAGT and D. PÄTZOLD (edd.), The Neoplatonic Tradition: Jewish, Christian and Islamic Themes, Dialectica Minora 3 (Köln 1991) 36-56.

D. T. RUNIA, 'Philo of Alexandria in the Letters of Isidore of Pelusium', in D. T. RUNIA et al. (edd.), Earle Hilgert Festschrift [= SPhA 3 (1991)] (Atlanta 1991) 295-319.

D. T. RUNIA, 'Secondary Texts in Philo's Quaestiones', in D. M. HAY (ed.), Both Literal and Allegorical: Studies in Philo of Alexandria's Questions and Answers on Genesis and Exodus, BJS 232 (Atlanta 1991) 47-79.

D. T. RUNIA, 'Underneath Cohn and Colson: the Text of Philo's De Virtutibus', SBLSPS 30 (1991) 116-134.

D. T. RUNIA, D. M. HAY and D. WINSTON (edd.), Heirs of the Septuagint.

Philo, Hellenistic Judaism and Early Christianity: Festschrift for Earle Hilgert, = The Studia Philonica Annual 3 (1991), Brown Judaic Studies 230 (Atlanta 1991).

D. T. RUNIA, R. RADICE and P. A. CATHEY, 'Philo of Alexandria: an Annotated Bibliography 1987–88', SPhA 3 (1991) 347–374.

K. G. SANDELIN, 'The Danger of Idolatry According to Philo of Alexandria', Temenos 27 (1991) 109–150.

E. P. Sanders, Judaism: Practice and Belief, 63 BCE – 66 CE (London–Philadelphia 1991).

G. SCARPAT, 'La Torre di Babele in Filone e nella Sapienze (Sap 10,5)', Rivista Biblica 39 (1991) 167–173.

M. SCHOFIELD, The Stoic Idea of the City (Cambridge 1991).

J. M. SCHOLER, Proleptic Priests, JSNTSupp 49 (Sheffield 1991).

A. B. SCOTT, Origen and the Life of the Stars, Oxford Early Christian Studies (Oxford 1991).

J. P. SCULLION, A Traditio-Historical Study of the Day of Atonement (Yom Kippur, Purification) (dissertation Catholic University of America, 1991).

T. SELAND, Jewish Vigilantism in the First Century C.E.: a Study of Selected Texts in Philo and Luke on Jewish Vigilante Reactions against Nonconformers to the Torah (diss. Trondheim 1991).

D. I. SLY, '1 Peter 3:6b in the Light of Philo and Josephus', JBL 110 (1991) 126–129.

D. I. SLY, 'Philo's Practical Application of Δικαιοσύνη', SBLSPS 30 (1991) 298–308.

G. E. STERLING, 'Philo's Quaestiones: Prolegomena or Afterthought?', in D. M. HAY (ed.), Both Literal and Allegorical: Studies in Philo of Alexandria's Questions and Answers on Genesis and Exodus, BJS 232 (Atlanta 1991) 99–123.

M. STERN [שטרן [מ: מחקרים בתולדות ישראל בימי הבית השני], [Studies in Jewish History: The Second Temple Period] (Jerusalem 1991) passim.

A. STROTMANN, "Mein Vater Bist Du!": zur Bedeutung der Vaterschaft Gottes in kanonischen und nichtkanonishcen frühjüdischen Schriften, Frankfurter Theologische Studien 39 (Frankfurt 1991).

L. TELESCA, 'Filone e Ambrogio: due testi a confronto', Notizario Centro di Studi sul Guidaismo Ellenistico 2 (1991) 1–13.

A. TERIAN, 'The Priority of the Quaestiones among Philo's Exegetical Commentaries', in D. M. HAY (ed.), Both Literal and Allegorical: Studies in Philo of Alexandria's Questions and Answers on Genesis and Exodus, BJS 232 (Atlanta 1991) 29–46.

A. TERIAN, 'Strange Interpolations in the Text of Philo: the Case of Quaestiones in Exodum', in D. T. RUNIA et al. (edd.), Earle Hilgert Festschrift [= SPhA 3 (1991)] 320–327.

T. H. TOBIN, 'Romans 10:4: Christ the Goal of the Law', in D. T. RUNIA et al. (edd.), *Earle Hilgert Festschrift* [= *SPhA* 3 (1991)] 272–280, esp. 277ff.

N. UMEMOTO, 'Die Königsherrschaft Gottes bei Philon', in M. HENGEL and A. M. SCHWEMER (edd.), *Königsherrschaft Gottes und himmlischer Kult im Judentum, Urchristentum und in der hellenistischen Welt*, WUNT 55 (Tübingen 1991) 207–256.

J. ROMNEY WEGNER, 'Philo's Portrayal of Women—Hebraic or Hellenic?', in A.-J. LEVINE (ed.), *"Women like this": New Perspectives on Jewish Women in the Greco-Roman World*, Early Judaism and its Literature 1 (Atlanta 1991) 41–66.

H. WEISS, 'Philo on the Sabbath', in D. T. RUNIA et al. (edd.), *Earle Hilgert Festschrift* [= *SPhA* 3 (1991)] 83–105.

H.-F. WEISS, *Der Brief an die Hebräer*, Kritisch-exegetischer Kommentar über das Neue Testament 15 (Göttingen 1991), esp. 100–103 and *passim*.

D. WINSTON, 'Aspects of Philo's Linguistic Theory', in D. T. RUNIA et al. (edd.), *Earle Hilgert Festschrift* [= *SPhA* 3 (1991)] 109–125.

J. ZANDEE, *The Teachings of Silvanus: a Commentary* (Leiden 1991).

1992

M. BARKER, *The Great Angel: a Study of Israel's Second God* (Westminster 1992), esp. chap. 7.

P. BILDE, T. ENGBERG-PEDERSEN, L. HANESTAD AND J. ZAHLE (edd.), *Ethnicity in Hellenistic Egypt* (Aarhus 1992).

G. BOCCACCINI, *Portraits of Middle Judaism in Scholarship and Arts: a Multimedia Catalog from Flavius Josephus to 1991*, Quaderni di Henoch (Turin 1992).

P. BORGEN, Art. 'Philo', in D. FREEDMAN (ed.), *Anchor Bible Dictionary* (New York 1992) 5.333–342.

P. BORGEN, 'Filo fra Aleksandria: Joedisk filosof og Jesu samtidige', *Midtoesten Forum* 7 (1992) 40–46.

P. BORGEN, Art. 'Judaism in Egypt', in D. FREEDMAN (ed.), *Anchor Bible Dictionary* (New York 1992) 3.1061–1072.

P. BORGEN, 'Overcoming Fear', in J. CHARLESWORTH (ed.), *Overcoming Fear* (New York 1992) 109–118.

P. BORGEN, 'Philo and the Jews in Alexandria', in P. BILDE et al. (edd.), *Ethnicity in Hellenistic Egypt* (Aarhus 1992) 122–138.

P. BORGEN, '"There Shall Come Forth a Man": Reflections on Messianic Ideas in Philo', in J. H. CHARLESWORTH (ed.), *The Messiah* (Minneapolis 1992) 341–361.

D. BOYARIN, 'Behold Israel According to the Flesh: on Anthropology and Sexuality in Late Antique Judaism', *Yale Journal of Criticism* 5 (1992) 27–57.

D. BOYARIN, 'This we know to be the Carnal Israel', *Critical Inquiry* 18 (1992).

F. E. BRENK, 'Darkly beyond the Glass: Middle Platonism and the Vision of the Soul', in S. GERSH and C. KANNENGIESSER (edd.), *Platonism in Late Antiquity*, Christianity and Judaism in Antiquity 8 (Notre Dame 1992) 39–60, esp. 46–51.

D. I. BREWER, *Techniques and Assumptions in Jewish Exegesis before 70 C. E.*, TSAJ 30 (Tübingen 1992), esp. 198–212.

G. L. BRUNS, *Hermeneutics Ancient and Modern* (New Haven-London 1992), esp. 83–103.

R. and C. CLARK KROEGER, *I Suffer not a Woman: Rethinking 1 Timothy 2:11–15 in Light of Ancient Evidence* (Grand Rapids 1992), esp. 146–148.

N. G. COHEN, 'Review of S. BELKIN, *The Midrash of Philo*: vol. 1', *JSJ* 23 (1992) 100–105.

E. DASSMANN et al., *Reallexikon für Antike und Christentum*, Lieferung 122 (Stuttgart 1992).

K. THRAEDE, Art. 'Homonoia (Eintracht), 176–289, esp. 238–239 (concord); K. HOHEISEL, Art. 'Homosexualität', 289–364, esp. 334–335 (homosexuality).

J. D. DAWSON, *Allegorical Readers and Cultural Revision in Ancient Alexandria* (Berkeley 1992)

D. DELIA, *Alexandrian Citizenship During the Roman Principate*, American Classical Studies 23 (Atlanta 1992).

C. DOGNIEZ and M. HARL, *La Bible d'Alexandrie: Le Deuteronome* (Paris 1992).

C. A. EVANS, *Non-canonical Writings and New Testament Interpretation* (Peabody 1992), esp. 80–86.

L. H. FELDMAN, 'Was Judaism a Missionary Religion in Ancient Times?', in M. MOR (ed.), *Jewish Assimilation, Acculturation and Accommodation: Past Traditions, Current Issues and Future Prospects* (Lanham 1992) 24–37.

R. FELDMEIER, *Christen als Fremden in 1 Petrusbrief*, WUNT (Tübingen 1992).

W. W. FORTENBAUGH, P. M. HUBY, R. W. SHARPLES and D. GUTAS, *Theophrastus of Eresus: Sources for his Life, Writings, Thought, and Influence*, 2 vols., Philosophia Antiqua 54 (Leiden 1992), esp. 1.342–355.

J. GLUCKER, 'Critolaus' Scale and Philo (Evidence for Critolaus' Scale Metaphor in Passages by Philo of Alexandria)', *CQ* 42 (1992) 142–146.

M. GOODMAN, 'Jewish Proselytizing in the First Century', in J. LIEU, J. NORTH and T. RAJAK (edd.), *The Jews among Pagans and Christians* (London 1992) 53–78.

L. GRABBE, *Judaism from Cyrus to Hadrian: Sources, History, Synthesis*, 2 vols. (Minneapolis 1992).

P. GRAFFIGNA, *Filone di Alessandria, La vita contemplativa*, Opuscula 47 (Genoa 1992).

J. T. GREENE, *Balaam and His Interpreters: a Hermeneutical History of the Balaam Traditions*, BJS 244 (Atlanta 1992).

D. M. HAY, 'Things Philo said and did not say about the Therapeutae', *SBLSP* 31 (1992) 673–684.

A. HILHORST, 'Was Philo Read by Pagans? The Statement on Heliodorus in Socrates *Hist. Eccl.* 5.22', *SPhA* 4 (1992) 75–77.

P. HOFRICHTER, 'Logoslehre und Gottesbild bei Apologeten, Modalisten und Gnostikern: Johanneische Christologie im Lichte ihrer frühesten Rezeption', in H.-J. KLAUCK (ed.), *Monotheismus und Christologie: zur Gottesfrage im hellenistischen Judentum und im Urchristentum*, Quaestiones Disputatae 138 (Freiburg 1992) 186–217, esp. 187–193.

L. P. HOGAN, *Healing in the Second Temple Period*, NTOA 21 (Freiburg–Göttingen 1992), esp. 168–207.

P. W. VAN DER HORST, "Gij zult van goden geen kwaad spreken': de Septuaginta-vertaling van Exodus 22:27 (28), haar achtergrond en invloed', *Nederlands Theologisch Tijdschrift* 46 (1992) 192–198; reprinted in *Studies over het Jodendom in de Oudheid* (Kampen 1992) 142–151.

C. LÉVY, 'Le concept de doxa des Stoïciens à Philon: essai d'étude diachronique', in J. BRUNSCHWIG and M. NUSSBAUM (edd.), *Passions and Perceptions: Proceedings of the Fifth Symposium Hellenisticum* (Cambridge 1992) 251–284.

J. MANSFELD, *Heresiography in Context: Hippolytus' Elenchos as a Source for Greek Philosophy*, Philosophia Antiqua 56 (Leiden 1992), esp. 313–315.

J. MARTENS, 'Unwritten Law in Philo: a Response to Naomi G. Cohen', *JJS* 43 (1992) 38–46.

G. MAY, *Creatio ex nihilo: the Idea of Creation in Early Christian Thought* (Edinburgh 1992).

P. A. MEIJER, *Plotinus On the Good or the One (Enneads VI,9)*, Amsterdam Classical Monographs 1 (Amsterdam 1992), esp. 326–328.

M. NIEHOFF, *The Figure of Joseph in Post-Biblical Jewish Literature*, Arbeiten zur Geschichte des Antiken Judentums und des Urchristentums 16 (Leiden 1992), esp. chap. 3.

F. PETIT, *La Chaîne sur la Genèse: Édition intégrale chapitres 1 à 3*, Traditio Exegetica Graeca 1 (Louvain 1992).

A. REINHARTZ, 'Philo on Infanticide', *SPhA* 4 (1992) 42–58.

C. J. ROETZEL, '*Oikoumene* and the Limits of Pluralism in Alexandrian Judaism', in J. A. OVERMAN and R. S. MACLENNAN (edd.), *Diaspora Jews* and Judaism: Essays in Honor of, and in Dialogue with, A. Thomas Kraabel, University of Florida Studies in the History of Judaism 41 (Atlanta 1992).

D. T. RUNIA, Platonisme, Philonisme en het begin van het christelijk denken, Quaestiones Infinitae 2 (inaugural lecture, Utrecht 1992).

D. T. RUNIA, 'The Language of Excellence in Plato's Timaeus and Later Platonism', in S. GERSH and C. KANNENGIESSER (edd.), Platonism in Late Antiquity, Christianity and Judaism in Antiquity 8 (Notre Dame 1992) 11-37, esp. 11-12, 34.

D. T. RUNIA, 'An Index to Cohn-Wendland's Apparatus Testimoniorum', SPhA 4 (1992) 87-96.

D. T. RUNIA, "Where, tell me, is the Jew...?': Basil, Philo and Isidore of Pelusium', VC 46 (1992) 172-189.

D. T. RUNIA, 'A Note on Philo and Christian Heresy', SPhA 4 (1992) 65-74.

D. T. RUNIA, 'Confronting the Augean stables: Royse's Fragmenta Spuria Philonica', SPhA 4 (1992) 87-96.

D. T. RUNIA, 'Philo and Origen: a Preliminary Survey', in R. J. DALY (ed.), Origeniana Quinta: Papers of the 5th International Origen Congress Boston College 14-18 August 1989, Bibliotheca Ephemeridum Theologicarum Lovaniensium 105 (Leuven 1992) 333-339.

D. T. RUNIA, 'Verba Philonica, ΑΓΑΛΜΑΤΟΦΟΡΕΙΝ, and the authenticity of the De Resurrectione attributed to Athenagoras', VC 46 (1992) 313-327.

D. T. RUNIA (ed.), The Studia Philonica Annual Volume 4, BJS 264 (Atlanta 1992).

D. T. RUNIA, R. RADICE, and D. SATRAN, 'Philo of Alexandria: an Annotated Bibliography 1988-89', SPhA 4 (1992) 97-124.

D. R. SCHWARTZ, Studies on the Jewish Background of Christianity, WUNT 60 (Tübingen 1992)

G. SELLIN, 'Gotteserkenntnis und Gotteserfahrung bei Philo von Alexandria', in H.-J. KLAUCK (ed.), Monotheismus und Christologie: zur Gottesfrage im hellenistischen Judentum und im Urchristentum, Quaestiones Disputatae 138 (Freiburg 1992) 17-40.

H. SHANKS (ed.) Christianity and Rabbinic Judaism: a Parallel History of Their Origins and Early Development (Washington 1992), esp. chapter 1 by L. FELDMAN.

F. SIEGERT, Drei hellenistisch-jüdische Predigten: Ps.-Philon, 'Über Jona', 'Über Jona' (Fragment) 'Über Simson'. II. Kommentar nebst Beobachtungen zur hellenistische Vorgeschichte der Bibelhermeneutik, WUNT 61 (Tübingen 1992)

D. SILLS, 'Vicious Rumours: Mosaic Narratives in First Century Alexandria', SBLSP 31 (1992) 684-694.

M. SIMONETTI, *The Early Church and the Word of God: an Historical Outline of Patristic Exegesis* (Edinburgh 1992).

G. E. STERLING, 'Creatio Temporalis, Aeterna, vel Continua? an Analysis of the Thought of Philo of Alexandria', *SPhA* 4 (1992) 15–41.

A. TERIAN, *Quaestiones et Solutiones in Exodum I et II e versions armeniaca et fragmenta graeca*, Les Œuvres de Philon d'Alexandrie 34c (Paris 1992).

M. THEOBALD, 'Gott, Logos und Pneuma: 'Trinitarische Rede von Gott im Johannesevangelium', in H.-J. KLAUCK (ed.), *Monotheismus und Christologie: zur Gottesfrage im hellenistischen Judentum und im Urchristentum*, Quaestiones Disputatae 138 (Freiburg 1992) 41–87, esp. 79ff.

T. H. TOBIN, 'Article 'Logos'', in D. FREEDMAN (ed.), *The Anchor Bible Dictionary* (New York 1992) 4.348–356.

UNKNOWN, 'Philo On the Life of the Therapeutae', *Parabola* 17 (1992) 57–60.

G. M. VIAN, 'Le Quaestiones di Filone', *Annali di Storia dell' Esegesi* 9 (1992) 365–388.

E. WILL and C. ORRIEUX, "Prosélytisme juif"?: histoire d'une erreur, Histoire (Paris 1992), esp. 81–101.

D. WINSTON, 'Philo's Conception of the Divine Nature', in L. E. GOODMAN (ed.), *Neoplatonism and Jewish Thought*, Studies in Neoplatonism Ancient and Modern 7 (Albany 1992) 21–42.

J. WHITTAKER, 'Catachresis and Negative Theology: Philo of Alexandria and Basilides', in S. GERSH and C. KANNENGIESSER (edd.), *Platonism in Late Antiquity*, Christianity and Judaism in Antiquity 8 (Notre Dame 1992) 61–82.

C. K. WONG, 'Philo's Use of Chaldaioi', *SPhA* 4 (1992) 1–14.

1993

D. CARABINE, *The Unknown God: Apophasis from Plato to Eriugena* (1993).

J. COHEN, *The Origins and Evolution of the Moses Nativity Story*, Numen Book Series 58 (Leiden 1993).

P. ELLINGWORTH, *Commentary on Hebrews*, New International Greek Testament Commentary (Grand Rapids 1993).

L. FELDMAN, *Jew and Gentile in the Ancient World* (Princeton 1993), passim.

H. W. HOLLANDER, and J. W. HOLLEMAN, 'The Relationship of Death, Sin and Law in 1 Cor. 15:56', *NT* 35 (1993) 270–291, esp. 275–8, 286.

D. LINDSAY, *Josephus and Faith: "Pistis" and "Pisteuein" as Faith Terminology in the Writings of Flavius Josephus and the New Testament*, ALGHJ 23 (Leiden 1993).

D. T. RUNIA, 'God of the Philosophers, God of the Patriarchs: Exegetical Backgrounds in Philo of Alexandria', in F. J. HOOGEWOUD and R. MUNK (edd.), *Joodse Filosofie tussen Rede en Traditie: Feestbundel ter ere van de tachtigste verjaardaag van Prof. dr. H. J. Heering* (Kampen 1993) 13–23.

D. T. RUNIA, *Philo in Early Christian Literature: a Survey*, CRINT III 3 (Assen–Minneapolis 1993).

P. J. TOMSON, *'Voor één dag genoeg' (Matt 6:34): het brood, het Woord en de wetenschap*, In Caritate 3 (inaugural address Brussels 1993).

W. C. van UNNIK, *Das Selbstverständnis der jüdischen Diaspora in der hellenistisch-römischen Zeit: aus dem Nachlaß herausgegeben und bearbeitet von P. W. van der Horst*, Arbeiten zur Geschichte des antiken Judentums und des Urchristentums 17 (Leiden 1993), esp. 127–137.

BOOK REVIEW SECTION

Folker SIEGERT, *Philon von Alexandrien. Über die Gottesbezeichnung 'wohltätig verzehrendes Feuer' ('De Deo'): Rückübersetzung des Fragments aus dem Armenischen, deutsche Übersetzung und Kommentar.* WUNT 46. J.C.B. Mohr, Tübingen 1988. viii + 190 pages. DM 89.

This volume is devoted to the fragment *Deo*, surviving from one of Philo's lost works, which has been preserved only in the sixth-century Armenian translation which includes (besides works extant in Greek) Philo's *QG, QE, Prov.*, and *Anim*. But this brief fragment has received very little scholarly attention. Indeed, apart from Aucher's 1826 edition of the Armenian text with Latin translation, only two articles have been devoted to it. In an earlier work Siegert had already provided a translation of *Deo* into German along with some textual notes, there classifying it among the pseudo-Philonic works.[1] But in the present work Siegert confidently takes it to be from Philo (as other scholars have done),[2] and gives it the critical attention which it deserves.

Siegert's approach is the following. First he reprints Aucher's Armenian text (but not Aucher's Latin, which would have been a valuable addition). Next he presents a reconstruction of Philo's original Greek from the Armenian, and then translates the Greek into German, where his earlier translation is revised. The bulk of the work then comprises a commentary on the Greek text. Here the reader will find comparisons with Philo's other works, elucidations of Philo's sources, and remarks on related or contrasting philosophical and theological ideas. Throughout Siegert presents his material clearly, with careful use of the original sources. Finally, Siegert concludes his work with a valuable bibliography and several quite useful indexes.

Siegert's commentary makes clear (as he says at 1) that *Deo* is a small compendium of Philonic theology, and includes Philo's fullest discussion of certain cosmological issues. The account of Abraham's visitors in Gen 18:2 leads Philo to consider God and the two chief powers of God. Siegert discusses the Jewish and Christian parallels to this subject, which

---

[1] *Drei hellenistisch-jüdische Predigten, Ps.-Philon, 'Über Jona', 'Über Simson', und 'Über die Gottesbezeichnung "wohltätig verzehrendes Feuer"', I: Übersetzung aus dem Armenischen und sprachliche Erläuterungen*, WUNT 20 (Tübingen 1980) 84-93.

[2] Siegert notes (2) that he had been led to consider the work pseudo-Philonic because it happens that in the excerpt the author appears to be more of a Stoic than Philo otherwise is.

of course is treated by Philo elsewhere (notably in *QE* 2.62–68). *Deo* continues with the only citation of Isa 6:1–2 in Philo's writings, and the mention there of 'seraphim' leads him to Deut 4:24. It is in fact this reference which is the basis of the title of the fragment, although Siegert claims (39, without citing any grounds) that this title does not come from Philo. And the reference to fire in Deut 4:24 leads Philo on to the four elements. Virtually every phrase of (the reconstructed Greek of) the text is discussed by Siegert, and there are also several valuable excursuses on background material.

While there is much in Siegert's volume which will reward the student of Philo, here I wish to examine in some detail his effort at reconstructing the Greek text which lies behind the Armenian.[1] The Greek text is only ten pages, but it is the result of much painstaking work, and is the basis for the commentary. However, despite being convinced of the importance of the Armenian for the study of the text of Philo, I am not as confident as Siegert is of the possibility of such a reconstruction. Siegert (7–10) says that his attempt to reconstruct Philo's Greek is made possible by the well-known literalness of the Armenian translation,[2] and by the assistance given by the Greek indexes of Leisegang and Mayer, the Armenian-Greek index of Marcus,[3] and the Armenian dictionary of 1836–37 (cited as ASA), edited by Aucher et al., which provides many Greek equivalents. But the evidence used by Siegert is not quite as conclusive as he suggests. For one thing, Siegert relies very heavily on ASA, although the equivalents there seem not always to be the best evidence on the usage in the Armenian translation of Philo. The index of Marcus, drawn from Philo only, is sometimes not reliable, since he often cites inferior Greek manuscripts for the Greek fragments. Also, additional relevant evidence on Armenian-Greek equivalents may sometimes be found in the index by Lucchesi to the fragments of *QG* 2.1–7 discovered by Paramelle,[4] in Reynders's index to

---

[1] A few of the points mentioned here can be found already in my briefer notice of Siegert's book in *Critical Review of Books in Religion 1990* (Atlanta 1990) 358-60. (I may note that in the top line of p. 360, the 'bu' should be 'but'.) Some observations from a different point of view may be found in the review by D. T. Runia in *VC* 43 (1989) 398-405, reprinted in his *Exegesis and Philosophy: Studies in Philo of Alexandria*, Variorum 332 (Aldershot 1990).

[2] Yet there is a slip in Siegert's criticism of A. Terian's more skeptical attitude. Siegert gives the Greek of *sermnakan bank^c* as λόγοι σπερματικοί; respect for the Armenian order would indicate rather σπερματικοὶ λόγοι.

[3] R. Marcus, 'An Armenian-Greek Index to Philo's *Quaestiones* and *De Vita Contemplativa*', *JAOS* 53 (1933) 251-82.

[4] J. Paramelle avec la collaboration de E. Lucchesi, *Philon d'Alexandrie, Questions sur la Genèse II 1-7, texte grec, version arménienne, parallèles latins, Interprétation arithmologique*

Irenaeus,[1] in Künzle's index to the Armenian Gospels,[2] and from elsewhere in Philo.[3] All of this is to say that sometimes Siegert has not used all the evidence which we have concerning the Armenian translation of Philo.[4] Of course, it is no easy matter to utilize all this evidence, and Siegert has certainly brought together much valuable material. But on occasion we could wish for more.

In any case, let us approach Siegert's work by considering some ways in which the Armenian has proved to be valuable in the textual criticism of Philo where we also have Greek evidence.[5]
1. The choice between competing Greek readings.
   a. *QG* 1.51. The fragment edited by Petit survives in four manuscripts of the *Sacra parallela*, SHAR.[6] As Petit tells us in her introduction,[7] there are two variations where the Armenian provides the decisive evidence:

   ἔλαχε SHA Arm : ἐλάμβανε R
   ἐζήλωσεν SHA Arm : ἐζήτησε R

   b. *Prov.* 2.27: ἀλλ' ὥσπερ οἱ τὰ ἄρρητα ὑπ' ἀνάγκης ἐκλαλοῦντες ἀφιᾶσι τὰς ἐκ πάθους ἀψευδεστάτας φωνάς. Here the Armenian provides decisive evidence for three readings where the manuscripts of Eusebius disagree:

   ἄρρητα I Arm : ἀρρωστήματα BON
   ἐκλαλοῦντες BIO Arm : ἐκκαλοῦντες ND
   ἀψευδεστάτας φωνάς I Arm : transp. BON

As the last case indicates, the Armenian is so literal that it can be cited even for variations in word order.

---

par J. Sesiano, *Cahiers d'Orientalisme* 3 (Geneva 1984) 247-53. See my review of this in *SPhA* 1 (1989) 134-44.
[1] B. Reynders, *Lexique comparé du texte grec et des versions latine, arménienne et syriaque de l' 'Adversus haereses' de saint Irénée*, 2 vols., CSCO 141-42, Subsidia 5-6 (Louvain 1954).
[2] B. O. Künzle, *Das altarmenische Evangelium, 1: Edition zweier altarmenischer Handschriften, 2: Lexikon* (Berne 1984).
[3] For my own use I have compiled an Armenian-Greek index for the Greek fragments of *Prov.*, and in connection with my planned edition of all the Greek fragments of Philo, I intend to produce an accompanying Armenian-Greek index and Greek-Armenian index.
[4] Perhaps this is the place to mention two other issues. First, Siegert regularly refers to the *Quaestiones* by citing Marcus's Loeb volumes as simply 'QG' or 'QE', followed by the page number. The reader must then convert to the usual system of referring to book and section. Secondly, Petit's much superior edition of the Greek fragments of the *Quaestiones* is not cited at all.
[5] My own interests have led me to choose examples from the Greek fragments.
[6] F. Petit (ed.), *Philon d'Alexandrie. Quaestiones in Genesim et in Exodum: Fragmenta Graeca*, PAPM 33 (Paris 1978) 52-53.
[7] *Ibid.*, 35. The reference to the Armenian is not, however, found in the apparatus itself (53).

Naturally, such uses of the Armenian are comparatively easy since there is no reconstruction occurring; the question is simply which of the two Greek readings it supports.[1]

2. Conjectures against the Greek evidence.

Unfortunately, not all variations will find the Armenian and some Greek witness in agreement. And in some of these cases we may reasonably believe that no Greek witness has preserved Philo's words.

a. *Prov.* 2.22, where the editions read: πάνθ' ὑπερβάντες τὰ περίστωα, τοὺς ἀνδρῶνας, τὰς γυναικωνίτιδας, γραφάς, ἄργυρον, χρυσόν, κτλ. This seems straightforward enough, but in fact only I Arm preserve γραφάς (BON omit), and whereas BON have ἄργυρον, I has the strange reading ἀνδριάργυρον. Here, though, the Armenian provides the crucial evidence, although only L. Früchtel seems to have appreciated it.[2] Following the word for γραφάς, the Armenian has z-patkerôk‛, z-arcat‛ (z- is a prefix which indicates the direct object), and Aucher's translation reads *imagines, argentum*. From this[3] Früchtel conjectured: ἀνδριάντας, ἄργυρον. This nicely explains the reading of I,[4] and is also supported by parallels where Philo mentions ἀνδριάντες. I have reported this at some length because we find the same Armenian term for ἀνδριάς (*patker*) in Deo, which will be discussed further below.

b. *Prov.* 2.15, where the Armenian has a phrase missing in all the Greek manuscripts of Eusebius: 'whence indeed in the most esteemed of poets, Homer, Zeus is called the father of men and gods'. Here we may suppose that Eusebius himself omitted these words (as not quite suitable to a preparation for the Gospel), and that the Armenian accurately reflects what Philo wrote.[5] We then have the problem of trying to reconstruct the Greek which the Armenian translator saw. In this case, we are aided by the fact that part of the phrase is itself a well-known citation from Homer, and by the fact that Philo introduces Homer in *Conf.* 4 by a similar phrase. Using fairly standard Armenian-Greek equivalences and these parallels, Wendland reconstructed Philo's Greek as: διὸ παρὰ τῷ μεγίστῳ καὶ δοκιμωτάτῳ ποιητῶν Ὁμήρῳ "πατὴρ ἀνδρῶν τε θεῶν τε" κέκληται Ζεύς.[6]

---

[1] Of course, in some cases the Armenian may not provide relevant evidence; for instance, it does not render the μέν of μέν ... δέ (even though Petit does cite it for the omission in her apparatus to *QG* 1.51).
[2] This is found in his manuscript collection of the Greek fragments of Philo.
[3] Früchtel knew the Armenian only from Aucher's translation; in this case fortunately the Latin accurately reflects the Armenian.
[4] The scribe leaped from the second α to the fourth.
[5] *Leg.* 2.165 cites the same Homeric formula.
[6] P. Wendland, *Philos Schrift über die Vorsehung* (Berlin 1892) 96, also notes: 'Die Erwähnung des Zeus war Eus. anstössig'. (Wendland says that he relied on Conybeare for

Now, whatever uncertainty attaches to such reconstructed phrases will increase as one attempts to render more words, words for which the Armenian rendering is not unique, or words for which no parallel in Philo can be found. Siegert's reconstruction is on a much larger scale than any others in the literature on Philo, and so in fact problems do arise.

To understand the nature of Siegert's reconstructed Greek of *Deo*, let us look in detail at the final sentence of section 6 (lines 86–88 (of the Greek)). The Armenian reads:[1]

ew šowrǰ hayec῾eal arowestakan z-ayn howr etes, or gorcê z-astowacayin patkers-n, oč῾ anšownč῾-n, ayl šnč῾awor ew banawor.

And Siegert's Greek for this is:

Κύκλῳ δὲ βλέποντα ἐκεῖνο τὸ τεχνικὸν πῦρ εἶδε τὸ ποιοῦν τὰς θείας εἰκόνας οὐκ ἀψύχους, ἀλλ' ἐμψύχους καὶ λογικάς.

This certainly gives a plausible equivalent of the Armenian,[2] but the Greek terms actually represent rather different levels of certainty. Here I cite the evidence from Marcus and from *Prov.*, followed occasionally by other evidence.

ew. Marcus: καί passim; δέ 15 times. *Prov.*: καί 235 times; δέ 50 times; a few others.

šowrǰ. Marcus says 3 cases of περι-; in fact we have:

šowrǰ ziwrew hayelev	περιαθρῶν	QG 2.72;
šowrǰ hayel gitel	περισκοπεῖν	QG 3.3;
šowrǰ yacmownk῾	περιπολήσεις	QG 4.51.

And we also have:

| gal šowrǰ | περιπολεῖν | Prov. 2.15. |

Siegert has followed ASA (2.491C) in giving κύκλῳ, although ASA (2.492A) also gives several compounds with περι-.

hayec῾eal (from *hayim*). Marcus: κατανοέω; ἀφοράω. *Prov.*: ἀφοράω 2.20. ASA (2.31A–B) gives 12 Greek words, including βλέπω. However, *šowrǰ hayim* is a combination that occurs several times. In the Gospels it renders περιβλέπω at Mark 3:34, 5:32; Luke 6:10. In Irenaeus it also renders περιβλέπω 3 times. The evidence indicates that *šowrǰ hayim* should definitely be taken as representing a verb with the prefix περι-, and that περιβλέπω is probably the best choice.

arowestakan. In the indexes mentioned this does not occur. However, the rendering as τεχνικός is confirmed by the renderings of related

---

advice on the Armenian.)

[1] Besides the z- prefix mentioned above, I have also marked the -n suffix, which roughly corresponds to the definite article.

[2] Aucher translates: 'Circumspiciens autem artificialem illum ignem vidit, qui efficit divinas imagines, non inanimes, sed animatas, et rationales'.

words: e.g. *arowest* corresponds to τέχνη in Marcus (5 times), *Prov.* 2.19, 2.50, 2.104.

ayn. Marcus: ἐκεῖνος; οὗτος. *Prov.*: ἐκεῖνος twice (2.18, 2.50); οὗτος twice (2.15, 2.32); a few others. It looks as though the Armenian could be either one.

howr. Marcus: πῦρ; φλόξ *QE* 2.15. *Prov.*: πῦρ twice (2.100, 2.100). Also πῦρ in both the Gospels and Irenaeus, as in ASA (2.125A).

etes (from *tesanem*). This renders many Greek verbs. Marcus: ὁράω; θεάομαι; θεωρέω 4 times in *Contempl.*; καθοράω *Contempl.* 66; καταθεάομαι *QG* 2.72; κατανοέω *QE* 2.66. *Prov.*: ὁράω 2.21, 2.23, 2.26, 2.27, 2.100, 2.103, 2.104, 2.108; θεάομαι 2.27; θεωρέω 2.25, 2.103, 2.105; βλέπω 2.18; περιαθρέω 2.17, 2.29; κατανοέω 2.26. The Gospels have: βλέπω; ἀναβλέπω; ἐμβλέπω; θεάομαι; θεωρέω; ὁράω. ASA (2.867B–C) gives 15 Greek words, including ὁράω.

or. Marcus: relative pronoun passim; relative pronoun + περ 10 times. *Prov.*: relative pronoun and article passim; a few others. So this should probably be a relative pronoun in Greek, as ASA (2.526B) also has.

gorcê (from *gorcem*). This also renders many Greek verbs. Marcus: δράω; ἐργάζομαι; ἀπεργάζομαι; ἐνεργέω; πράττω *QG* 4.228; *QE* 2.3, 2.25; misc. 3 cases. *Prov.*: εἴργω 2.99; ἐργάζομαι 2.32, 2.32, 2.112; δημιουργέω 2.27; συνεργέω 2.104; ἐπιτηδεύω 2.15; τελέω 2.24. In the Gospels, this is cited as representing ποιέω 30 times; ἐργάζομαι 10 times; πράσσω 4 times. ASA (1.576C) has: ἐργάζομαι, πράσσω, ἐνεργέω, and ἀπεργάζομαι. It appears that ποιέω is unlikely for Philo.

astowacayin. Marcus: θεῖος 20 times; ἱερός *QE* 2.15, *Contempl.* 26. *Prov.*: θεῖος 3 times (2.15, 2.26, 2.30); *mec ahagin ew astowacayin* = ἱερός 2.28. Also ἱερός in Irenaeus.

patkers (plural of *patker*). Not in Marcus. *Prov.*: ἀνδριάς 2.21, 2.22 (conj. by Früchtel, as discussed above). And so reconstructed by Siegert at *Deo*, l. 96 (with no note).[1] On the other hand, for εἰκών we would expect *kerparan*: *QG* 2.62; *QE* 2.66; *Deo*, l. 151.[2] This may be a place where the practice in the Armenian translation of Philo is peculiar. In the Gospels *patker* is in one-to-one correspondence with εἰκών (Matt 22:20; Mark 12:16; Luke 20:24). Also, in Irenaeus it corresponds to εἰκών at 6 places, and once renders εἴδωλον. The Latin of Irenaeus has *statua* 5 times, and the one place where the Greek is extant ἀνδριάς is used. Unfortunately,

---

[1] In this line we have also *patkeragorcê*, which is rendered with ἀνδριαντοποιός.
[2] Note, though, that this is not a one-to-one correspondence: *kerparan* is also used (according to Siegert) for μορφή at *Deo*, ll. 34, 78 (bis). Furthermore, Marcus reports its use for σχῆμα and εἴδωλον. ASA (1.1092B) cites twelve Greek equivalents (as Siegert notes at 139).

the Armenian is not extant at any of these five. ASA (2.612C) gives for *patker*: εἰκών, τύπος, ἄγαλμα, ἀνδριάς.
očʿ. Marcus: οὐ and μή passim. *Prov.*: οὐ and μή passim.
anšownčʿ. Marcus: ἄψυχος. *Prov.*: *anšownčʿew marg* = ἄψυχος 2.21. In Irenaeus it renders ἄπνους.
ayl. Marcus: ἀλλά. *Prov.*: ἀλλά 28 times; δέ 4 times (2.22, 2.30, 2.100, 2.106).¹
šnčʿawor. Not in Marcus or *Prov*. Renders ἔμψυχος once in Irenaeus. ASA (2.486A) gives ψυχικός, ἔμψυχος, and 3 other words.
ew. See above.
banawor. Marcus: λογικός *Contempl.* 9. Not in *Prov.* Renders φωνήεις once in Irenaeus. But Siegert's retroversion is confirmed by the regular use of *ban* for λόγος, as found in Marcus (23 times) and *Prov.* (6 times: 2.16, 2.28, 2.100, 2.104, 2.105, 2.111).

On a scale of A to D,² I would rank the certainty of Siegert's Greek words as follows:³

Κύκλῳ	C
δὲ	C (possible, but καὶ is more likely)
βλέποντα	B (probably this verb, but as part of a compound)
ἐκεῖνο	B (note the change in word order, also)
τὸ	A
τεχνικὸν	A
πῦρ	A
εἶδε	B (most likely, but could be one of several other verbs)
τὸ	C (likely a relative pronoun)
ποιοῦν	D (almost certainly not ποιέω)
τὰς	A
θείας	A
εἰκόνας	D (for Philo the Armenian suggests not εἰκών but ἀνδριάς)
οὐκ	A
ἀψύχους	A
ἀλλ'	A
ἐμψύχους	A
καὶ	A
λογικάς	B (could be a doublet in Arm)

---

[1] There is also another *ayl* in Armenian, which corresponds to ἄλλος, ἕτερος; but that meaning could not be present here.
[2] Following the usage in K. Aland, *et al.* (edd.), *The Greek New Testament* (New York 1975³) xii-xiii.
[3] For the sake of comparison, my own attempt at a reconstruction would be: Καὶ περιβλέποντα ἐκεῖνο τὸ τεχνικὸν πῦρ εἶδε ὃ ἐργάζεται τὰς θείας ἀνδριάντας οὐκ ἀψύχους ἀλλ' ἐμψύχους καὶ λογικάς.

This sentence is, I believe, more or less typical of what we find throughout Siegert's Greek. Some words (probably the majority) are quite certainly restored, in other cases some choice has to be made, and in yet others there is serious doubt. And from time to time a word about which there is serious doubt may be of great interest (as is εἰκών here; see Siegert's commentary). Of course, a similar range of certainty (or uncertainty) attaches to the Greek text of Philo as found in PCW. But there is the following difference. In PCW the evidence for the text (at least as then known) is generally presented accurately and completely in the apparatus. Serious students of Philo have that apparatus available, are able to evaluate its evidence, can see where there are textual problems, and can find further references in Greek or Latin (e.g. can trace the use of a Greek term in Philo and elsewhere). In the case of the Greek text of *Deo* as printed by Siegert, the evidence relating to the certainty of the equivalences is far from readily available, and we may suppose that very few students of Philo indeed would be able to use it effectively in any case. Naturally, all this is not Siegert's fault, and it is perhaps uncharitable to ask for even more from an author who has done so much to elucidate both the text and the content of the Philonic fragment. But I do feel that some additional textual guidance to the reader would have been most welcome, and that the importance of the text would justify a more involved presentation of the evidence for it.

I have also noted some other problematic reconstructions. These are:

passim: There are 24 occurrences of kʿanzi, which means 'because'. In the Greek fragments of Philo this word usually renders γάρ, but just within *Prov.* it also corresponds to διότι (2.29), ἐπειδή (2.27, 2.103), γοῦν (2.100), ἀλλὰ γάρ (2.51), καὶ γάρ (2.23), and οὖν (2.15). Now, of the 24 occurrences in *Deo*, Siegert chooses γάρ 20 times. But he also chooses διότι twice (ll. 32 and 73), ὅτι once (l. 52), and δήπου once (l. 35). Unless we simply print γάρ at each place (as the most likely equivalent) or have some very specific parallel phrase elsewhere in Philo, there seems to be no justification for making the kind of variation we find in Siegert's Greek. In fact it looks as though Siegert has simply chosen here to make his Greek text more literary by introducing these variations. But the reader of the Greek is not told this.

ll. 1 (title), 90, 93, 94, 96, 104-5, 108, 112: In all these places the Armenian verb *caxem* occurs. Siegert reconstructs ἀναλίσκω at all the places except 90, where it is an explicit citation of Deut 4:24. There we find καταναλίσκω. But the Armenian gives no justification for any shift in the Greek. It happens that this is the only citation of Deut 4:24 in Philo (as Siegert notes at 109), and that (according to G. Mayer's *Index Philoneus*) the compound verb otherwise occurs only at *Somn.* 2.212 and

Abr. 140, whereas the simple verb occurs 28 times, to which we may add *QE* 2.15, 2.28,[1] 2.47, and *Prov.* 2.32. If we look only at these figures, we will choose the simplex at all 8 occurrences in *Deo.* But if Philo cites the compound at l. 90, might he not use it throughout his discussion?[2] In any case, reading the compound at all these places would reflect the consistency of the Armenian. By the way, ASA (1.999C) cites ἐξαναλίσκω and καταναλίσκω, but not the simple form.

l. 41: Siegert chooses κοσμοποιός for *ašxarhastełc.* This is the only Greek cited in ASA (1.263C), but the evidence is not quite clear. Siegert refers us to 'QG 75. 89. 113'. What we find at those places is:

QG 75 (*QG* 2.5): In note *h* Marcus cites κοσμοποιός as his retroversion for *ašxarharar.*

QG 89 (*QG* 2.13): In note *t* Marcus cites κοσμοποιός as his retroversion for *ašxarhi araričᶜ.*[3]

QG 113 (*QG* 2.34): In note *a* Marcus cites κοσμοποιός from the Greek fragment as rendering *ašxarhagorc.*[4]

So the one instance of κοσμοποιός in a Greek fragment represents *ašxarhagorc* rather than *ašxarhastełc.* On the other hand, the *stełc* here generally corresponds to πλάζω and related words. E.g. Marcus cites διαπλάζω at *QG* 1.51 for *stełcanem,* and πλάσμα for *stełcowac* at *Contempl.* 63. The latter equivalence is found at *Prov.* 2.109, while at 2.21 we find πλαστῶν for *stełccᶜacᶜ.* I believe that all this indicates that at l. 41 *ašxarhastełc* more likely represents κοσμοπλάστης, which we find elsewhere only at *Plant.* 3 and *Congr.* 48.

ll. 48–49: The Armenian *paštpan,* which means 'protector', is used of the two chief powers of God. Siegert claims that the Greek original was δορυφόρος, and even discusses its background at the Persian court (71–73). However, Siegert cites no evidence for the claimed equivalence, and I have been unable to find such a case. On the other hand, at *QE* 2.67 the Armenian has instead *spasawor* ('attendant')[5] for δορυφόρος. Indeed, Siegert does note (26, n. 49) some evidence that the Armenian term might correspond rather to ὑπερασπιστής, but asserts that δορυφόρος better

---

[1] Petit, *Quaestiones: Fragmenta Graeca* 262, says of the Greek fragment here: 'Écho évident, mais dans une rédaction très remaniée'. And she prints the final ἀναλώσῃ in italics. Nevertheless, the use by Philo of this verb seems indicated by *caxeal lini* in Arm.

[2] Runia, Review 400, says: 'In the second passage [ll. 89-93] I am puzzled by the fact that the biblical text contains the verb καταναλίσκειν, but in his comments Philo repeatedly uses the word ἀναλίσκειν. This too seems contrary to his normal practice'.

[3] Procopius has κοσμοποιῶν here, but Petit believes the Armenian requires κόσμου ποιητής (*Quaestiones: Fragmenta Graeca* 92), which would be more literal.

[4] See the text in Petit, *Quaestiones: Fragmenta Graeca* 106.

[5] ASA (2.737A) gives several other Greek words for this; but for *spasaworak* it (2.737B) gives δορυφορικόν.

fits the context here. But this is in effect to override the Armenian. Siegert's reference to 'QG 42 und 494' points only to Marcus's retroversion from paštpan into Greek; no Greek fragment is present at either of these texts (QG 1.69, 4.201). On the other hand, Siegert's reference to 'QE 54' is to QE 2.16; there the Armenian does have paštpan while the Greek fragment has ὑπερασπιστής. Thus, what evidence there is suggests that the Armenian paštpan renders ὑπερασπιστής.[1] Of course, it may be that the Armenian is inconsistent in rendering δορυφόρος, but then a reconstruction of the Greek would be even less certain.

ll. 74, 146: At both places we find the Armenian araričʿ, and each time Siegert's German translation has 'der Schöpfer' (as Aucher used 'Creator'). However, in his commentary he distinguishes these two passages (see 97 and 134), using the difference in his reconstructed Greek: the first is ὁ Ποιητής, while the second is ὁ Δημιουργός. It is surprising that (as far as I have noted) Siegert does not tell the reader that we have the same word in Armenian. And that term can render either ποιητής (as at QG 2.15, 2.34; QE 2.66; Contempl. 90) or δημιουργός (as at QE 2.68 (3 times); Contempl. 5).[2]

l. 79: Siegert, citing no justification, chooses φθοροποιοῦ (modifying πυρός) as the equivalent of apakanacʿow. The Lucchesi index tells us that this Armenian term occurs twice for φθαρτόν in QG 2.7, and φθαρτοῦ πυρός would be paralleled by Abr. 157. And ASA 1.270A gives only φθαρτός as the Greek for apakanacʿow.

l. 83: Siegert chooses φλόγα for xančʿowmn. His note (28, n. 76) says: 'ASA gibt nur καῦσις und weniger Passendes'. But this is the *second* entry in ASA (1.922A) for the term. The *first* entry (1.921C) gives for the Greek: ὄγκημα, ὄγκος, οἴδημα. Moreover, Lucchesi's index reports that the Armenian renders ὄγκος at QG 2.2, and we find the same at Prov. 2.18. The resulting phrase, ὄγκος σώματος (for xančʿowmn marmnoy), has several Philonic parallels (e.g. Leg. 2.77; Congr. 97; Somn. 1.43; and an unidentified fragment of the Quaestiones[3]), and so ὄγκος seems certain here.

ll. 107–8: Siegert reconstructs several nouns as plurals (τὰς γὰρ παχυτέρας καὶ πυκνοτέρας καὶ βαρυτέρας). However, the Armenian terms are singular, and in his earlier translation Siegert translated them as singular in German.[4] There seems to be no reason cited for the shift to plurals.

In general Siegert maintains a high standard of accuracy, but there are

---

[1] And this is the only Greek cited for paštpan in ASA (2.598A), as Siegert notes.
[2] At Prov. 2.22, though, gorcak renders δημιουργός, while at Prov. 2.19 ararčʿakan renders an adjectival use of δημιουργός.
[3] Printed as QE, no. 15, by Petit, Quaestiones: Fragmenta Graeca 294-95.
[4] Drei hellenistisch-jüdische Predigten 1.90.

occasional misprints. Some of these he has now corrected,[1] but I may add the following. At 25, n. 44, read 'III' for 'II'. At 29, n. 104, read 'III' for 'IV'. And at 27, n. 61, the reference to 'QE 68' is not to a Greek fragment but to Marcus's citation of *Migr.* 169, which has no connection with the Armenian term being discussed by Siegert.

I would not wish to conclude without again emphasizing the value of Siegert's book. Although my suggestions here are sometimes negative in detail, Siegert has given us a meticulous work with insightful and provocative ideas throughout. His study of this difficult, valuable, but neglected Philonic text is an important contribution to Philo studies.

James R. Royse
San Francisco

Folker SIEGERT, *Drei hellenistisch-jüdische Predigten. Ps.-Philon, "Über Jona", "Über Jona" (Fragment) und "Über Simson", II: Kommentar nebst Beobachtungen zur hellenistischen Vorgeschichte der Bibelhermeneutik.* Wissenschaftliche Untersuchungen zum Neuen Testament 61. Mohr, Tübingen 1992. x + 416 pages.

It was in 1980 that Siegert published the first volume of his *Drei hellenistisch-jüdische Predigten* (WUNT 20). In that work he published his German translation of the Armenian text of the three pseudo-Philonic writings mentioned in the subtitle of the second volume *plus* his version of *De Deo*; he called the work *drei* instead of *vier* Hellenistic Jewish sermons because the fragment of the second sermon on Jona took only one page. In this second volume, however, the word *drei* does not have the same reference as in the first work, since it includes commentaries on the three works mentioned in the subtitle (i.e. also the tiny fragment on Jona) but *not* on *De Deo*. This has to do with the fact that in the intervening years Siegert changed his mind with regard to the authenticity of the latter treatise, which he now considers to be authentic, and rightly so, it would seem. It is for that reason that he decided to deal with *De Deo* in a separate work which appeared in 1988

---

[1] A few days before completing this review, I received a copy of Siegert's latest book, *Drei hellenistisch-jüdische Predigten, Ps.-Philon, 'Über Jona', 'Über Jona' (Fragment) und 'Über Simson', II: Kommentar nebst Beobachtungen zur hellenistischen Vorgeschichte der Bibelhermeneutik*, reviewed by P. W. van der Horst here below. While the pseudo-Philonic writings are Siegert's focus in this work, he does provide a list of corrections to the volume under review (359-60) as well as a discussion (64-91) of the hermeneutics of *Deo*. And in the course of the latter, he makes occasional emendations to the earlier volume, but not (I believe) to any of the passages discussed above.

in the same series (WUNT 46) with the title *Philon von Alexandrien. Über die Gottes Bezeichnung "wohltätig verzehrendes Feuer" (De Deo)*, in which, *inter alia*, he presents a retroversion of the Armenian text into Philonic Greek and an extensive commentary (see David T. Runia's review in *VC* 43 (1988) 398–405, reprinted in his *Exegesis and Philosophy. Studies on Philo of Alexandria* (London 1990), and also now James Royse's review in this volume). So in a sense this second volume is the third in the series.

The new volume begins with a lengthy introduction (1–54), in which the importance of these documents is sketched. They are in fact our only surviving specimens of ancient Jewish synagogue sermons in Greek (in 1955 H. Thyen published his *Der Stil der jüdisch-hellenistischen Homilie* without having even one instance of that genre at his disposal!). Explicit attention is paid by Siegert to the relevance of our texts for the 'Entwicklungsgeschichte' of the early Christian sermon. He also discusses the prose rhythm of the sermons, even though he now (wisely) refrains from a Greek retroversion, the occasion on which they may have been held, and their date and provenance (probably Alexandria, between the first century BCE and the second CE). The fascinating second chapter, 'Homer und Mose. Der Ursprung der jüdischen Schrifthermeneutik im Homer-Unterricht' (55–91), is given a programmatic title. 'Die jüdischen Theologen griechischer Sprache sind Nachahmer und Erben eines Bemühens, das der 'Entmythologisierung' in der Mitte unseres Jahrhunderts analog ist—nur daß der kanonische Text, um dessen Zeitgemäßes Verständnis es ging, Homer war' (55). Siegert tries to show that such remains of Hellenistic interpretation of Homer as we still have (Cornutus, Heraclitus the Stoic, but especially the unduly neglected treatise of Ps-Plutarch, *De vita et poesi Homeri*) clearly demonstrate that Greek-speaking Judaism borowed its hermeneutical principles of Bible interpretation from the (allegorical) interpreters of 'the Bible of the Greeks', Homer. Not only Philo and our pseudo-Philonic sermons, also Paul, the Rabbis and the Patres derive their hermeneutics from this 'Interpretationsuniversum der hellenistischen Welt' (63). In order to demonstrate this concretely Siegert presents a long 'Anwendungsbeispiel' (64–91), in which most interpretive elements in Philo's *De Deo* are shown to have their analogies in the Hellenistic interpreters of Homer (so that this chapter is in fact a valuable addendum to Siegert's 1988 commentary on the treatise). The heart of the book is of course the commentary on the two larger treatises, *De Jona* and *De Sampsone* (95–292). In these almost 200 pages Siegert not only gives a detailed interpretation of almost all elements in the text that require elucidation but he also inserts 15 valuable excurses on topics as widely varied as 'Zweifel und Leichtgläubigkeit in der Späntantike', 'Kann Gott lügen?', 'Können

Engel essen?', 'Das Zeichen des Jona', 'Herakles und Simson', etc. Here again Siegert demonstrates his 'considerable philological skills and remarkable breadth of knowledge' (cf. Runia (1989) 398) that also characterized his 1988 commentary. A final chapter (293-317) draws some threads together, deals with the sermons as 'Produkt der Rhetorenschule' (294), defines their mode of thought as 'eine Verbindung von alttestamentlichem und stoischem Denken' (299), and emphasizes that both Jews and Christians could have acquired these hermeneutical and rhetorical skills only in pagan schools so that they must have made 'einen praktischen Kompromiß mit dem Heidentum' (314; in this connection he rightly points out that the outspoken pagan Libanius still had both John Chrysostom and a son of the Jewish patriarch as his students). An extensive bibliography and exhaustive indices (including one of Greek terms) conclude this excellent book.

In spite of my admiration for Siegert's profound scholarship I find something ambivalent about the book. Siegert presents his discovery of exegesis of Homer as the background of Jewish Bible interpretation as one of the most important contributions his book makes to Judaic scholarship. This is certainly true, even though others had already pointed in that direction. But it is not acidental that he chose as his 'Anwendungsbeispiel' a short piece by Philo himself. After that demonstration, in the commentary on *De Jona* and *De Sampsone* the exegetical treatises on Homer play a much more modest role than in the 'Anwendungsbeispiel' and the emphasis is rather on the rhetorical aspects of the sermons, and rightly so. One of the most striking and essential characteristics of these treatises on Homer, namely their thoroughgoing allegorization of the 'canonical' text, is a feature that is completely lacking in both pseudo-philonic tractates. Therefore, I gradually got the impression that Siegert tries to do two different things in this book: (a) to write a commentary on the pseudo-Philonic sermons, and (b) to write a necessary supplement to his 1988 study of Philo's *De Deo*. These two goals have not always been perfectly attuned to one another.

I conclude with some minor points of criticism and addenda.

Although in most cases Siegert gives references to secondary literature in the footnotes, he also occasionally gives them in the text, which is not pleasant. Pervasive through the whole work is a comparison of these sermons with rabbinic literature, which in itself is worthwhile, but often the comparison reads like a value judgment in which rabbinic literature is invariably inferior to the sermons (see e.g. 238 and 309). There are many references to Samson haggada in Talmudic literature, but Siegert seems not to know the only monograph on the subject by J. S. Renzer, *Die Hauptpersonen des Richterbuches in Talmud und Midrasch, I: Simson* (Berlin 1902). Throughout the commentary Siegert compares the sermons' text with Chariton's novel and with the NT, but he does not refer to the collection of parallels in my essay on Chariton and the NT (*NovT* 25 (1983) 348–355); and for Nimrod as Babylonian tyrant in Jewish haggada (162) see now also my study of that topic in my *Essays on the Jewish World of Early Christianity* (Freibourg-Göttingen 1990, 220–232). The motif of the 'Schicksalsgemeinschaft zwischen Tier und Mensch' (193) in *De Jona* 145 probably has its biblical basis in Jona 4:11, 'Should I not be concerned about Nineveh, that great city, in which there are more than a hundred and twenty thousand persons who do not know their right hand from their left, *and also many animals?*' In the comments on *De Jona* 185 nothing is said on the motif of begrudging someone his salvation, on which see W. C. van Unnik, ΑΦΘΟΝΩΣ ΜΕΤΑΔΙΔΩΜΙ (Brussels 1971). There is no note on the use of φύσις for 'genital organs' in *De Sampsone* 13, on which see H. Herter in *RAC* 10, 2ff., nor on §23 where it is said that everything is possible to God, on which see again Van Unnik in *Verborum veritas. FS G. Stählin* (Wuppertal 1970, 27–36). I doubt Siegert's interpretation of *De Sampsone* 26 where he takes the subject of λέγει to be Scripture (280), whereas the context seems to me to indicate that it is the opponent of Scripture who is speaking here; his words are refuted in the same paragraph. *Ad* p. 336: there is a new edition of Ps-Justin by M. Marcovich (Berlin 1990). *Ad* p. 337: Kirk- Raven 1957 is now Kirk-Raven-Schofield 1983. Finally a warning: the commentary presupposes that the reader has volume I at hand.

Pieter W. van der Horst
Utrecht University

David M. HAY (ed.), *Both Literal and Allegorical: Studies in Philo of Alexandria's Questions and Answers on Genesis and Exodus*, Brown Judaic Studies 232. Scholars Press, Atlanta 1991. xiii + 256 pages.

The lack of attention on Philo's *Quaestiones et solutiones in Genesim et in Exodum* has long been a major lacuna in Philonic scholarship. Since the publication of Aucher's Armenian text in 1826,[1] scholarly opinions have been usually limited to brief, passing remarks on the work.[2] The problems are well known: couched in a literal Classical Armenian translation, the *Quaestiones* present comparatively bland exegetical comments that are at once similar to and yet different from those found in Philo's more discursive commentaries, the *Allegoriae* and the *Expositiones*. Now for the first time, a collaborative effort begins to fill that lacuna. Growing out of the Philo Seminar of 1985, *Both Literal and Allegorical* is a collection of four papers presented at that seminar and three invited contributions:

---

[1] J. B. Aucher, *Philonis Judaei paralipomena armena* (Venice 1826).
[2] Most recently see J. Morris, B. L. Mack, P. Borgen. Notable exceptions are the introductory article by Wolfgang Wiefel, 'Das dritte Buch über "Moses": Anmerkungen zum Quaestionenwerk des Philon von Alexandrien', *TLZ* 111 (1986) 865-82; see note 12 below.

Earle Hilgert, 'The *Quaestiones:* Texts and Translations'; James Royse, 'Philo's *Quaestiones in Exodum* 1.6'; Abraham Terian, 'The Priority of the *Quaestiones* among Philo's Exegetical Commentaries'; David Runia, 'Secondary Texts in Philo's *Quaestiones*'; David Hay, 'References to Other Exegetes'; Gregory Sterling, 'Philo's *Quaestiones:* Prolegomena or Afterthought?'; and finally a long essay (occupying nearly half the book) by Anita Méasson and Jacques Cazeaux, 'From Grammar to Discourse: A Study of the *Quaestiones in Genesim* in relation to the Treatises'. The book also includes a concise, helpful introduction by the editor, David Hay, and a cumulative bibliography of all the works cited in the seven essays.

Anything resembling a uniform approach in a collection like this is obviously an impossible ideal; it is therefore remarkable that five of the essays, with the exception of Hilgert and Royse's essays on the text, in one way or another are all concerned with the relationship of the *Quaestiones* to Philo's other works. This is owed in no small measure to the influence of Valéntin Nikiprowetzky, who in two substantial works demonstrated the importance of the question and answer technique in all three series of Philo's commentaries. In so doing, he raised the question whether there is a relationship between Philo's *Quaestiones* and his other two commentaries and, if there is, what that relationship might be.[1] Samuel Sandmel also speculated in a passing comment that the *Quaestiones* were 'preliminary notes' for the composition of the *Allegorical Commentary*. He repeated this comment 25 years later, accompanied this time by the claim of support from 'those who have seen it' without, however, naming his supporter.[2]

Although these five essays reflect a similar concern, they do not use the same method or draw the same conclusion. Runia investigates the use of secondary texts in the *Quaestiones* and concludes that the work is an independently composed commentary, not 'preliminary notes' for the *Allegoriae*, as Sandmel alleged. Runia's study is founded on the observation that there is a distinction between exegesis of 'primary biblical texts' and exegesis of 'secondary texts' (i.e., texts that deviate from the main discussion).[3] While Philo in the *Allegoriae* frequently launches

---

[1] *Le commenataire de L'Écriture chez Philon d'Alexandrie,* ALGHJ 11 (Leiden 1977), and 'L'exégèse de Philon d'Alexandrie dans le De gigantibus et le Quod Deus', in D. Winston and J. Dillon (edd.), *Two Treatises of Philo of Alexandria: A Commentary on* De gigantibus *and* Quod Deus sit immutabilis, BJS 25 (Chico, California 1983) 5-75.
[2] 'Philo's Environment and Philo's Exegesis', *JBR* 22 (1954) 249; *Philo of Alexandria: an Introduction* (New York 1979) 79, 181 n. 82.
[3] A distinction he made in two previous articles: 'The Structure of Philo's Allegorical Treatises', *VC* 38 (1984) 209-56; 'Further Observations on the Structure of Philo's Allegorical Treatises', *VC* 41 (1987) 105-38.

learned discussions based on secondary texts, according to Runia, he does so relatively infrequently in the *Quaestiones*. What secondary texts there are in the *Quaestiones*, furthermore, are rarely paralleled in his allegorical treatises. There is only one case in which the same secondary text is used in both commentaries in connection with the interpretation of the same primary text. From this Runia concludes that the *Quaestiones* are not notes for the *Allegoriae* but are a independent work.

Hay's study of references to other exegetes in the *Quaestiones* reaches a similar conclusion. Building on his own previous work,[1] Hay observes that in the *Quaestiones* Philo refers to the same class of exegetes and even ascribes to them the same interpretations as he does elsewhere in his corpus. But the references to other exegetes are so different in the *Quaestiones* than in the *Allegoriae* that Hay rejects Sandmel's hypothesis of 'preliminary notes' in favor of the alternative view that the two commentaries were independently composed. The *Quaestiones* are perhaps 'private notes' that circulated among Philo's fellow-exegetes, a suggestion that Hay himself admits to be hypothetical. Perhaps Philo in his treatises 'built on interpretations limned in the *Quaestiones*, but we need not infer that the latter were written simply as preliminary notes toward the composition of the former' (p. 96).

The data amassed by Hay, and for that matter by Runia as well, are by and large accurate. One may quibble with the specifics, as one always does, but the overall analysis seems sound. In spite of the judiciousness of Hay and Runia, however, one cannot help wishing that their conclusions had been based on broader examinations of the *Quaestiones*. Valuable as it is, a study of Philo's fellow-exegetes has the limited purpose of ferreting out Philo's intellectual environment, as Hay himself pointed out in his earlier study,[2] but does not plumb the depths of Philo himself. Though Philo could have included opinions of others in the *Quaestiones*, there is no reason why the exclusion of such references would make for lesser 'preliminary notes', if that is what they are. A similar *caveat* need be sounded in regard to Runia's study. No matter how lengthy and convoluted Philo's secondary discussion may be and how much it threatens to take over the main discussion, Philo always returns to the primary text eventually. In other words, despite its appearance, the *Allegorical Commentary* is still organized around the primary texts, perhaps even using these texts as κεφάλαια. If the *Quaestiones* are preliminary notes for the *Allegoriae*, one would *expect* them to be concerned more with the primary texts than with the secondary texts. A

---

[1] 'Philo's References to Other Exegetes', *SPh* 6 (1979-80) 41-76.
[2] *Ibid.*, 41f.

comparison between the *Quaestiones* and the *Allegoriae* only at the level of secondary exegesis, therefore, tells us why Philo seems less prone to distraction in the *Quaestiones* than elsewhere but does not answer the question of relationship. For this latter purpose a comparison in terms of primary texts may be more equal to the task.

A comparison of primary texts is precisely what Sterling does in his essay. But since he limits his scope of investigation to *Quaestiones in Genesim* Book 1, what conclusions he may draw from his analysis must necessarily be qualified. Sterling argues that since the *Quaestiones* and the *Allegoriae* are both organized by a common list of biblical lemmata and, even more important, by a common list of exegetical *topoi* arranged in the same order, some kind of relationship must exist between these two works. *Solutiones* to the questions in the *Quaestiones*, furthermore, are said to be found in the parallel passages of the *Allegoriae:* Sterling suggests, for example, that the answer to the *quaestio* of *QG* 1.1 is to be found in *Leg.* 1.19–20. Given the more sophisticated exegesis displayed in the *Allegoriae*, Sterling proposes that the *Quaestiones* be viewed as 'prolegomena' to the *Allegorical Commentary*. Here Sterling's conclusion may have advanced beyond his carefully marshalled evidence. The exegetical *topoi* used in the *Quaestiones* and in the *Allegoriae* probably owe their order of arrangement more to the biblical sequence than to anything else; similarity in this regard does not prove interdependency. It may likewise be hasty to call interpretations in the *Allegoriae* 'solutiones' to questions in the *Quaestiones*; questions in the *Quaestiones* are sometimes so general that any number of *solutiones* might fit them.

In their lengthy essay, whose lyricism and circuity would no doubt do Philo proud, Méasson and Cazeaux, like Sterling, also conduct an elaborate comparison between the Allegorical Treatises and the correspoding passages in the *Quaestiones*, but, unlike Sterling, arrive at the opposite conclusion, that the two commentaries represent independent efforts of Philo. Méasson and Cazeaux base their conclusion on the finding that exegetical passages in the *Quaestiones* are almost always static, elementary, and lacking in movement when compared to the full, dynamic treatments of the same biblical passages in the *Allegoriae*, a conclusion that accords well with the obvious difference in genre between the two works. The *Quaestiones*, in their estimation, are rather like 'catechism', offering the readers 'a simple work which is elevating and orthodox in thought', while the Treatises are 'theology', demanding their highest intellectual effort. The former have to do with 'faith'; the latter 'reason' (pp. 224f).

Méasson and Cazeaux thus part company with Nikiprowetzky, who suggested that the *Allegorical Commentary* was different from the *Quaes-*

tiones only in length and composition but not in kind (p. 135). To be fair, Nikiprowetzky's position on this is complex. In his earlier, more general work, he had suggested that the *Quaestiones* were an independent work to be set alongside the *Allegoriae* and the *Expositiones*.[1] In his later work, however, a work limited to a study of *QG* 1.89–99 and *Gig.-Deus* in parallel,[2] he argued for a closer relationship between the *Quaestiones* and the *Allegoriae* than his broader comparison had allowed.

In a different vein, Terian pursues the question of relationship in terms of chronology and argues strongly that the *Quaestiones* be taken as the earliest of the three series of commentaries. Ralph Marcus in a brief note suggested that *QG* 2.4; *QE* 2.34; and *QE* 2.113—to which one may add *QG* 4.123—contained references to the *Allegoriae*.[3] Terian suggests that it may be more natural to take all four cases as referring not to another work but to other sections of the *Quaestiones*. Terian's argument is based on solid lexical data; it is sure to put to rest Marcus's hypothesis that the *Quaestiones* were composed after the *Allegoriae* or the *Expositiones*. He is on shakier grounds, however, when he tries to show the inverse scenario, that in the *Allegoriae* are there are references to the *Quaestiones*. It is not clear that the three examples which Terian suggests, *Leg.* 3.139; *Sacr.* 51; and *Sobr.* 52, actually refer to the *Quaestiones*. In any case, it may be methodologically unwise to assume that such enormous works as the *Allegoriae* or the *Quaestiones* would be composed in an absolute sequence with no time overlap. The Allegorical Treatises, after all, were written individually, and sections of the *Quaestiones* might have been written as self-contained units (a good case, e.g. can be made for *QG* 2.1–8). It seems more reasonable to accept as a working hypothesis that parts of the *Allegoriae* may be earlier than the *Quaestiones* and parts later, which Méasson and Cazeaux also hold (pp. 126–27).[4]

To round out the volume, Hilgert and Royse offer essays on the text of the *Quaestiones*. Hilgert's survey of texts and translations on the *Quaestiones*, pursued with his characteristic thoroughness, is a helpful indicator of where Philonic scholarship currently stands on the *Quaestiones*. The Old Latin remains (*QG* 4.154–245) and the more than two hundred Greek fragments scattered throughout patristic sources have been recently edited with critical notes and apparatus, largely through the indefatigable efforts of Françoise Petit and James Royse. The latter, in

---

[1] *Le commenataire* 202.
[2] 'L'exégèse de Philon' 53f.
[3] Marcus, PLCL 11.x note a.
[4] Also the opinion of E. Schürer, *Geschichte des jüdischen Volkes* (Leipzig 1898³) 3.497 n. 33.

a series of articles including one in the present volume,[1] continues to enlarge our collection of Greek fragments. The Armenian text, by comparison, has not received the same, careful treatment. Nearly 170 years have passed and Aucher's 1826 uncritical text remains the only authoritative edition: there is as yet no critical text or tool. The lack of such basics bespeaks the relatively primitive stage in which students of the *Quaestiones* find themselves.

The singular focus on the relationship between the *Quaestiones* and the rest of the Philonic corpus may seem one-sided; one may with justification propose to compare the *Quaestiones* to non-Philonic materials (e.g. *midrashim*[2]) or to locate the work in the long and productive history of the genre ζητήματα καὶ λύσεις. But such criticism would overlook the pioneering spirit of this collection. Even if the present volume has generated more questions than answers, it has already made a major contribution by raising Philo's *Quaestiones* to the status of an independent commentary worthy of serious scholarly attention.

Sze-kar Wan
Andover Newton Theological
School

Geza VERMES and Martin D. GOODMAN, *The Essenes According to the Classical Sources*. Oxford Centre Textbooks 1. JSOT Press, Sheffield 1989. xi + 103 pages. $28.00.

This is the pilot volume for a new series of textbooks designed with the needs of students in mind. The series promises to offer collections of Hebrew, Aramaic, Greek, Latin, and Syriac texts. The format is modeled on two existing series: Kleine Texte für Vorlesungen und Übungen and the Loeb Classical Library. The former provides the inspiration for a collection with brief annotations and the latter for the arrangement of ancient texts with facing English translations. For the intial volume Geza Vermes contributed the main introduction and bibliography, while Martin Goodman supplied the treatments of the individual texts including the introductions, notes, and fresh translations except in the appendix where he adopts F. C. Conybeare's 1895 rendition of *Contempl*.

---

[1] And most recently in *The Spurious texts of Philo of Alexandria*, ALGHJ 22 (Leiden 1991).
[2] So Samuel Belkin, *Philo and the Oral Law* (Cambridge 1940) 18-19 n. 28; see also his articles in Hebrew, 'The Midrash Quaestiones et Solutiones in Genesim et Exodum of Philo of Alexandria and its relation to Palestinian Midrash', *Horeb* 14 (1960) 1-74, and 'Questions and Answers to Genesis and Exodus by Philo Judaeus: The Earliest Source for the Midrashim', in *idem* (ed.), *The Abraham Weiss Jubliee* (New York 1964) Hebrew Section, 579-633 (summarized at R-R 6003, 6402).

The texts are from standard critical editions, e.g., PCW, Niese, Mras.

Vermes sets out the basic data from the texts in the introduction without attempting to provide any extended critical discussions. He first presents the classical evidence in Philo, Josephus, and Pliny the Elder. Next, he sketches a picture based upon the Dead Sea Scrolls. He then compares the two and concludes that 'the theory identifying the Essenes with the 'monastic' brotherhood of Qumran has strong claims for general acceptance' (p. 13). He attributes the divergences to internal contradictions in the sources, the diverse nature of the sources, and the evolution of different practices at Qumran. He reaffirms this identification with a glance at the history of the Essenes and the Qumran settlement. He concludes with an appendix in which he argues that the Therapeutae 'represented an Egyptian offshoot of the Palestinian ascetic movement of the Essenes' (p. 17).

The remainder of the volume consists of the following texts arranged in chronological order: Philo, *Prob.* 75–91, *Hypoth.* (*ap.* Eus. *PE* 8.11.1–18 (Goodman's reference to 8.6–7 is to another fragment of the same work; he does not provide a reference to 8.11.1–18!)); Pliny the Elder, *NH* 5.73; Josephus, *BJ* 1.78–80; 2.113, 119–61, 567; 3.11; 5.145; *AJ* 13.171–72; 15.371–79; 18.18–22; *Vita* 10–11; Dio of Prusa (*ap.* Synes. of Cyrene, *Dio* 3.20); Hegesippus, *Hypomnemata* (*ap.* Eus. *HE* 4.22.7); Hippolytus, *Ref.* 9.18–28. Philo, *Contempl.* 1–2, 11–40, 63–90 is added in an appendix. The selection and arrangement is designed to provide access to the most credible historical evidence. The decision to limit the texts to the first three centuries, however, cuts off a significant number of texts which Alfred Adam and Christoph Burchard collected in *Antike Berichte über die Essener*, Kleine Texte 182 (Berlin 1972). Nor should a reader assume that all second and third century texts are included—they may not be if Solinus, *Collectanea* 35.9–12, belongs to the third rather than the fourth century.

One major limitation with the work as a student's textbook is the restricted scope of the notes which are limited primarily to text-critical matters or parallel references. So, for example, Goodman does not tell the reader that the threefold division of philosophy in Philo, *Prob.* 80 is the standard Stoic division which Philo repeatedly employs (e.g., Diogenes Laertius 7.39–41; and Philo, *Leg.* 1.57; *Agr.* 14–16; *Mut.* 74–75; *Spec.* 1.336). Even F. H. Colson's brief notes in the Loeb edition are more helpful. A second limitation is the presence of minor difficulties in the translations. I will limit my observations to examples from the Philonic texts. P. 21, *Prob.* 77: Goodman renders ἀχρήματοι, 'without goods', rather than 'without money'; p. 23, *Prob.* 80: ἀλείπταις χρώμενοι τοῖς πατρίοις νόμοις, 'constantly utilizing the ancestral laws', appears to omit ἀλείπταις = 'using the ancestral laws as trainers'; p. 79, *Contempl.* 16: αἱ γὰρ χρημάτων καὶ κτημάτων ἐπιμέλειαι τοὺς χρόνους ἀναλίσκουσι, 'for the cares of wealth and chattels consume the users thereof', should be 'consume time' which Philo goes on to discuss; p. 97, Contempl. 80: προσοδίων ὕμνων, 'professional hymns', should read 'processional hymns'; p. 99, Contempl. 87: ἐνθουσιῶντες should not be translated by 'were rapt with the Divine spirit' but 'were overwhelmed with divine ecstasy' ; and p. 99, Contempl. 87: τοὺς εὐχαριστηρίους ὕμνους εἰς τὸν σωτῆρα θεὸν ᾖδον, 'sang hymns of thanksgiving unto God', omits 'the Savior'. There are other places where the freedom of Goodman's translation (e.g., Prob. 87, p. 25; Hypoth. 3 = PE 8.11.3, p. 27) or the archaic nature of Conybeare's rendering (e.g., Contempl. 19, 'unhappy wights', p. 81; 20, 'solitary cots', p. 81) may present some difficulties, but the sense is defensible.

The concept of the series is solid: there is a need to have some inexpensive collections of texts. While this volume is most certainly a worthwhile collection of texts, the price and absence of notes restrict its usefulness as a student book. Hopefully the editors and publisher will modify the format and the price of future volumes.

Gregory E. Sterling
University of Notre Dame

Françoise PETIT, *La Chaîne sur la Genèse: Édition intégrale chapitres 1 à 3.* Traditio Exegetica Graeca 1. Peeters, Louvain 1992. xxxvii + 340 pages. Price BF 3800.

The Belgian scholar Françoise Petit is best known to Philonists on account of her two books devoted to aspects of the textual transmission of Philo's works. In 1973 she published an edition with commentary of the Latin translation of QG 4.154–245 (R-R 1601), an extremely difficult text, but of considerable interest not only because of its place in the dissemination of Philo's works, but also because it contains 12 sections missing in the Armenian translation. Five years later she produced what is up to now the definitive edition of the fragments of the *Quaestiones in Genesim et Exodum* that have survived in Greek (R-R 1814). This volume was taken up as part of the French translation of Philo's works, even though most of the fragments were left untranslated (only of those fragments whose origin could not be identified was a translation appended in small print). A considerable proportion of these fragments have their origin in the so-called *Catenae*. In her subsequent research Mme Petit has concentrated her attention on this particular form of exegetical literature, in which extracts of exegetical or homiletic works are appended to the biblical lemma which they discuss. In addition to a large number of Patristic authors from Irenaeus and Clement to Cyril of Alexandria, the Jewish authors Philo and Josephus are represented in these works. In two large volumes in the *Series Graeca* of the *Corpus Christianorum* Petit published collections of *Catenae* found in two important manuscripts, the *Catena Sinaitica* and the *Collectio Coisliniana*. (1977, CCSG 2 = R-R 1813; 1986, = CCSG 15, not in R-R). The volume under review represents the next step of her research. It is of particular importance because she has reached some significant new results, which have led her to revise earlier, more conventional views on the nature of the *Catena* tradition.

Briefly stated her thesis is as follows: the *Catena on Genesis* is not a collaborative work which reached its present form through the cumulative work of various contributors. A thorough analysis of the mss. tradition reveals that the work is the personal achievement of a single compiler, whose identity is unknown but whose intention can be clearly discerned, namely to present an objective and practical instrument of research for interested theologians (see p. xiv). The textual evidence for this work has to be sorted into a number of categories. There are four primary witnesses, the mss. in St. Petersburg (still given the abbreviation L for historical reasons), St. Catherine's monastery in the Sinai, Moscow and Basel. A second strand of the tradition is now identified by Petit as secondary rather than primary, namely the tradition derived from the *Collectio Coisliniana*, which is not a *Catena* in the direct sense, but rather a collection of exegetical material built up around the *Quaestiones* of Theodoret of Cyrrhus, among which a considerable number of extracts from the *Catena* tradition have been interspersed. These extracts can be shown to derive from the branch of the tradition represented by the Basel ms. A further complication is the relation to the *Commentary on the Octateuch* by Procopius of Gaza (c. 465–530). There is too much overlap between the two works for them to have been compiled in complete independence from each other, yet it is not possible at present to show the direction of the dependence. A major difference between the two works is that the exegesis in Procopius is always anonymous, whereas in the *Catena* the lemmata are introduced by the name of the exegete in the genitive. This means that much of the material it contains can readily be identified, even if many attributions are faulty.

On the basis of this stemmatic analysis of the tradition (see the diagram on p. xxxvii) Petit has concluded that it would be erroneous to continue to publish witnesses to the tradition as she has done so far. Instead it is possible to make a reconstruction of the work in its original form. In the volume under review she has done this for the first three chapters of Genesis, which has yielded a total of 478 exegetical extracts.

BOOK REVIEW SECTION   231

For each she gives the location in the primary and (some secondary) mss., the biblical lemma under which it falls, the text (with critical apparatus and sometimes the parallel text in Procopius), and lastly the source (with very brief explanatory notes). In my view more extensive notes and a translation of the text into French would have been welcome. But it would be churlish to complain when we have already been given so much. The typesetting of the book is of the highest standard, a feast for even the most critical eye. At a price of more than $100 one might expect no less. But at least here the expectations are fully realized (which is nowadays by no means always the case).

The hypothesis of a single redactor is certainly daring and to some extent counter-intuitive. One would expect an anonymous compilation such as this *Catena* to be highly susceptible to gradual accretion. The remarks on its origin, limited to a single paragraph on p. xiv, need to be further developed. We might, however, mention one small piece of evidence in its favour, based on the *Catena*'s Philonic components. In his recent monograph on the spurious fragments of Philo (reviewed in *SPhA* 4 (1992) 78–86) James Royse has pointed out that the *Catenae on Genesis and Exodus* use very specific segments of the Philonic corpus: the former uses only *QG* 1.55 – 4.228, the latter only *QE* 2.1–49 and a few passages from *Mos.* 1 (*The Spurious Texts of Philo of Alexandria* (Leiden 1991) p.16). This observation gives support to Petit's hypothesis, because it suggests the limitations of one particular collection of Philo's works. We shall now conclude our review with some brief comments on the Philonic material contained in this edition.

(i) **No. 194** contains an extract from *QG* 1.3, and so at first sight might appear to contradict Royse's conclusion cited above. But in fact, as he notes, the citation is *indirect*, for it is located in an interesting extract from the *Commentary on Genesis* of Eusebius of Emesa (c. 300–359). Eusebius cited a certain Ἑβραῖος (no doubt a rabbinic exegete) who contests the LXX version of Gen. 2:6, arguing that not a fountain springs up from the earth, but rather a 'form of mist or very thick collected ether'. In response Φίλων ὁ Ἑβραῖος is cited for an interpretation of πηγή taken in a collective sense. The juxtaposition of the two Ἑβραῖοι is intriguing. One suspects that Philo is being cited *as a Jew* in order to provide ammunition against Jewish exegesis that differs from Christian tradition.

(ii) **No. 361**. Petit notes that the exegesis of Gen. 3:9 given by Severian of Gabala (*ob.* c. 425) goes back to Philo *QG* 1.45. The Armenian version reads 'from what good hast thou removed thyself' (Marcus; Aucher *de quot bonis demutatus fuisti*, Mercier, 'de quels biens es-tu décbu'), the *Catena* ἀπὸ ποίας δόξης ἐξέπεσες). Is the Armenian translation inaccurate (perhaps reading δόξα as meaning 'glory'), or has Philo's ethical emphasis been 'doctrinalized'?

(iii) **No. 455**. This is the only direct citation from *QG* in this volume (found under *QG* 1.55 in Petit's *Fragmenta Graeca* mentioned above). The extract is very short, only about a fifth of what we find in Procopius, who quotes more than half of the *solutio*. In the *Catena* the lemma is cited under Φίλωνος ἐπισκόπου, the striking title which has often been cited to show how completely Philo was absorbed in the Christian tradition.

(iv) **No. 456.** In the very next section we find an anonymous extract on Gen. 3:22 which argues that Adam is prevented from eating from the Tree of Life because otherwise evil would be immortalized. The exegete then adds: καὶ τοῦτο ἔλεγεν ὁ Ἑβραῖος. Petit is quite right to point out that this exegesis is found in Philo *QG* 1.55 (as well as the statement that God is not subject to envy). She thus plausibly suggests that Philo may be the 'Hebrew' referred to. It should be noted, however, that it is risky to infer too quickly that Philo lurks behind the term Ἑβραῖος. For an interesting example of the problems here we might adduce the analysis of *Catena* material given by Wendland at *Neu entdeckte Fragmente Philos* (Berlin 1891) p. 111–113. Wendland argued that the mention of ὁ Ἑβραῖος by Origen at *Sel. Gen.* PG 12.108.38 was a reference to Philo, and pointed to *QG* 2.71 as the source. But the parallel is by no means clear, which led the German scholar to postulate a lacuna in the Armenian version! (For the problems caused by the expression ὁ Ἑβραῖος in the *corpus Origenianum* see N. de Lange, *Origen and the Jews* (Cambridge 1976) pp. 26–27.) When we read the term Ἑβραῖος in Patristic exegetical literature, we should in my view take into account the possibility that it refers to more or less contemporary Rabbinic exegesis.

The harvest of real Philonica in this first volume of Petit's projected complete edition of the *Catena in Genesim* is thus rather meagre. But even the few lines we have discussed above indicate how much interesting light this source can shed not only on the Philonic texts, but also on the way the Jewish exegete was received in the Patristic tradition. We congratulate Madame Petit on what she has already achieved, and wish her every success as she tackles the remaining 1800 texts contained in this remarkable document. Perhaps it would not be too outrageous to conclude with a final request. Since the standard accounts and descriptions of this complex material are considered no longer adequate (e.g. Devreesse in *DBSup* 1928 and Geerard *CPG* vol. 4, criticized at p. xiii and xxiii respectively), it would be most valuable to have a new synoptic survey of this enormously complex material. There can be no doubt that no one is better equipped to give us such a survey than Madame Petit herself.

David T. Runia
University of Leiden

Gabriele BOCCACCINI, *Middle Judaism: Jewish Thought, 300 B.C.E. to 200 C.E.* Fortress Press, Minneapolis 1991. xix + 289 pages. $24.95.

Boccacini's book is an intelligent and highly stimulating study of some of the central texts of what he prefers to call 'Middle Judaism'. Although the idea of many 'Judaisms' is no longer new, Boccaccini has made this approach the centerpiece of his presentation of Jewish thought in the Greco-Roman age, in which he provides detailed analyses of Ben Sira, Daniel, and Pseudo-Aristeas, including preliminary sketches of Philo of Alexandria, Josephus, and some New Testament writings (James and Paul). Moreover, he prefaces his account with a useful bird's-eye view of the biased perspectives that have dominated earlier scholarship on the religious corpora of the period in question.

Boccaccini points out that Judaism as an unchanging entity suited both Jewish traditionalists and Christian triumphalists, the former thus emphasizing their fidelity to an ancient unaltered tradition, the latter portraying Jesus' message as grafted onto a 'late' religion at the end of its role as a 'precursor'. Confessionally divided sources led to a confessionally divided scholarship, each religious corpus living its own hermetically sealed existence. 'The task of the historian', however, as Boccaccini correctly notes, 'is to describe an age in its complexity, using all the material available, canceling and verifying every traditional division without confessional presupposition' (p. 13). Judaism must be seen not as a homogeneous whole, but as a set of competing ideologies.

Boccaccini next raises the question of whether Christianity may legitimately be seen as a 'Judaism'. He notes that scholars such as A. F. Segal, A. Paul, D. Flusser, and H. G. Perelmuter, who have pointed out the fraternal relation between Christianity and Rabbinism, suggest that although one brother has remained in the parent's house, the other has gone away. (Interestingly, an analogous contrast was made long ago by Philo of Alexandria (*Deus* 31–32) and Plotinus (5.8.13.1), though for them the elder son who stays at home with his father is identified with the intelligible universe, and the younger son who appears 'without' is identified with the physical universe.) The departure of Christianity from its Jewish home is then readily placed at the junction of its abandonment of the Law and its conversion into a gentile movement. But the perspective from which Judaism is seen as linked to a defined people, undefiled by any alien cultural influence, argues Boccaccini, merely represents the rabbinical view of things. The fact remains that at the beginning of the common era, some varieties of Hellenistic and apocalyptic Judaism were already on the verge of becoming, as Christianity later did, multinational religions. Among the many possible

Judaisms, then, Christianity is one of those that was actually realized in history. The debate over whether it is Christianity or Rabbinism that represents the authentic development, i.e. the 'true Israel', belongs to confessional polemics (pp. 16–17). Finally, feeling the need for a comprehensive term that would encompass chronologically all the contemporaneous Judaisms of the period between the third century BCE and the second century CE without any ideological implication, Boccaccini proposes to use the term 'middle Judaism' for the bridge period that links ancient Judaism (sixth through third century BCE) with the distinct existence from the second century CE on of the two main Judaisms of modern times, Christianity and Rabbinism.

Boccaccini begins the body of his work with an insightful analysis of Ben Sira. He illuminates the latter's emphasis on free will by examining it against the background of the *Book of the Watchers* and *The Book of Astronomy* of *1 Enoch* (6–36; 72–82), which located the source of human evil in the actions of rebellious angels that involved their marriage with earthly women with its consequent procreation of giants who ultimately turned into demonic spirits, and their illicit revelations of secret sciences that led to human corruption. 'In these works', says Boccaccini, 'individual responsibility is gravely compromised. Salvation is entrusted to an extraordinary intervention by God and the idea of the covenant is emptied of all substance' (p. 79).

In his discussion of the relationship between wisdom and the Law, Boccaccini insists that Ben Sira's assertion that the Law is the historical manifestation in Israel of a pretemporal wisdom is far from an affirmation of identity (Sir 24:3–23). Unlike the Law, which has no function beyond the limits of the relationship between human beings and God, wisdom has a degree of autonomy as God's eternal possession, and is ultimately a gift not granted to all. The Law, which is the manifestation of wisdom in history, is in the cosmic context but one of the rules that God in his wisdom has established to govern creation. Moreover, the Law is not identified with wisdom but with the 'education' of wisdom. The observance of the Law is the pedagogical course that wisdom-seekers must undergo (Sir 6:18–37) (pp. 89–90, 94–95).

Boccaccini reads Ben Sira's emphasis on the immutable and above all uncorrupted laws of nature, as a counter to the apocalyptic tradition that immediately after their creation (the fourth day) the stars (that is, the angels who guide them) chose to refuse the role and place assigned them by God. This original sin overturned the order of the universe and was the beginning and cause of every sin (*1 Enoch* 18:14–16; cf. 21:3–6). There is no indication in this text, however, that the transgression of these seven stars has in any way subverted the ordered structure of the heavens. It was an exceptional act of a small group of disobedient stars whose punishment was summary. Boccaccini proceeds to cite *1 Enoch* 80:1–6 as confirming the fact that the original order of the universe 'does not exist any more, that it has been dramatically corrupted' (pp. 90–91). What this paragraph actually says, however, as James C. VanderKam has correctly put it, is that 'the heavenly luminaries will reflect (or cause) the eschatological chaos which will hasten upon the earth in the 'days of the sinners'. Prior to the end, natural laws, which are considered unchanging elsewhere in the *Astronomy Book* and in *1 Enoch* as a whole (e.g. 2:1), will no longer apply, just as humanity will violate moral and religious laws. The heavenly eschatological message of 80:2–8 is in starkest contrast to the scientific concerns of the original book'. Charles correctly saw that these lines were a later interpolation, but 'when and why they were spliced into the *Astronomy Book* remains an enigma' (*Enoch and the Growth of an Apocalyptic Tradition* (Washington D.C. 1984) 106–07).

As we have already seen, Boccaccini emphasizes Ben Sira's denial of an extraneous cause of human evil, citing 21:27, 'when an impious man curses the satan, he really curses his own soul'. 'The figure of "the satan"', he writes, 'the angelic being depicted in the *Book of the Watchers* as guilty of corruption of the world (I En 10:8) is thus radically demythologized'. Deterministic solutions, such as the reference to the 'heavenly tablets' in the *Book of Astronomy* (*1 Enoch* 81:2) are rejected. 'This is the first time in the history of Jewish Theology that we find the theme of free will conceptually developed'. For Ben Sira human ambivalence reflects the ambivalent structure of the cosmos, in which the opposites coexist but are 'annulled in the inscrutable unity of divine will' (pp. 105–09).

Although the above analysis is essentially correct, Boccaccini has failed to provide his readers with the Stoic context that illuminates Ben Sira's treatment of the paradox of freedom and determinism. As I have noted elsewhere, the older wisdom writers did not feel this contradiction too keenly and were content to assert that all was determined by the gods in advance and that nevertheless success and failure, punishment and reward, were conditioned by the individual's behavior. It has been pointed out that the Demotic wisdom Instruction known as *Papyrus Insinger* was the first such Egyptian writing to deal consciously and explicitly with the freedom/determinism dilemma. What we find here is very much like the paradoxical Stoic formulation that all is in accordance with *Heimarmene*, yet our actions are in our power. In light of the many Hellenistic elements in *Papyrus Insinger*, Lichtheim has concluded that it is very likely that in this case too we are dealing with such an influence. In view of the striking similarities between *Papyrus Insinger* and Ben Sira, it is reasonable to assume that their similar formulations of the freedom/determinism paradox were the result of their common use of Stoic sources. (See Miriam Lichtheim, *Late Egyptian Wisdom Literature in the International Context* (Freiburg 1983) 107–96.) It is thus the Stoic resolution of that dilemma that lies behind Ben Sira's espousal of a stark predestinarianism on the one hand, coupled with an emphatic teaching of human freedom on the other (See D. Winston, 'Theodicy in Ben Sira and Stoic Philosophy', in *Of Scholars, Savants, and their Texts*, ed. Ruth Link-Salinger (New York 1989) 243–46; and idem, *The Wisdom of Solomon* (Garden City 1979) 46–58).

Boccaccini offers a rather spirited account of the *Letter of Aristeas*, which he describes as 'testimony to an evolutionary possibility for Judaism that still seemed practicable at the end of the second century BCE' (p. 165). The banquet section, which forms the largest single unit of the book, may be characterized as a *summa theologica*. Boccaccini correctly notes that 'in the theological vision of the *Letter*, mercy is in fact God's attribute par excellence' (p. 169), but neglects to point out that the term used repeatedly by pseudo-Aristeas is not ἐλεήμων (which occurs only in 208), but ἐπιεικής, which means equitable or fair, and avoids (at least from the vantage point of the modified position of the middle and late Stoa) the embarrassment occasioned by the former term for one who is aware of the Stoic philosophical objection to its irrational character. This is especially striking, since even the author of the Wisdom of Solomon and Philo of Alexandria frequently speak of God's ἔλεος. Boccaccini also speaks of pseudo-Aristeas' 'theology of grace', but fails to acknowledge the fact that A. Jaubert had already indicated that in the *Letter* we see 'the first outlines of what we can call in Philo a theology of grace' (*La notion d'Alliance dans le Judaisme aux abords de l'ère chrétienne* (Paris 1963) 327; see also Harry A. Wolfson, *Philo: Foundations of Religious Philosophy in Judaism* (2 vols.; Cambridge, Mass. 1947) 1.449–50 and Jean Laporte, *Eucharistia in Philo* (New York 1983) 143–47). He correctly states that 'we find in the *Letter* that in addition to an individual's social status and success, moral being and action also depend on God', but when he says that 'from this perspective, the question 'Can good [the text says τὸ φρονεῖν, wisdom] be taught?' (236) is inevitably answered in the negative' (p. 172), he goes too far. As he himself points out, 'in our author's religious ideology "by nature" does not so much express a state of objective and impersonal necessity as it does a constituting act of the person-God... The two terms in the *Letter* are interchangeable' (p. 168). The good can be taught precisely because God has constituted human nature as he has. To say, as Boccaccini does, that for pseudo-Aristeas 'Nature is the result of God's "intervention"' is, in my opinion, to overinterpret his position, since his statements can probably be understood within an 'integrationist' scheme just as well as one that is 'interventionist'. Boccaccini concludes his analysis with the remark that 'when a comprehensive history of the many middle Judaisms—a history encompassing the winning and the losing movements, those that remained viable and those that did not— is written, an important place will be reserved for the *Letter of Aristeas* and its unique testimony' (p. 185).

Boccaccini's discussion of Philo's account of memory is brief but contains useful insights. He points out that Philo made use of Aristotle's *On Memory and Recollection*, and an excursus in pseudo-Aristeas (150–61) on the religious value of memory. He notes that even the mechanisms through which recollections are produced are described by Philo (*Deus* 43) in conformity to Aristotle (450a), but he ought to have added that Philo was influenced here by the account in Plato's *Theaetetus*, as were later Platonists in general, and also by Stoic doctrine. (See D. Winston and J. Dillon (edd.), *Two Treatises of Philo of Alexandria* (Chico, California 1983) 297.) For Philo memory is essentially memory of God and constitutes the greatest good (*Spec.* 1.133; 2.171). Of the Therapeutae it is said with great admiration that 'they keep the memory of God alive and never forget it' (*Cont.* 26). (Cf. the Sufi practice of *dhikr*, recollection [of God], which involved repeating the name of God without intermission.) Boccaccini points out that Philo draws an equivalence between recollection and repentance, for just as in bodies, health free from disease holds first place, so in the soul does remembering without lapse into forgetfulness. Recovery from disease, on the other hand, and recollection supervening on forgetfulness (defined by Philo as a πάθος) stand in second place. The latter, he adds, is akin to repentance, which also receives only the second prize (*Virt.* 175–6). Moreover, recollection is linked to learning, since the learner is very apt to forget, and learning is only a half-way stage, not a perfect achievement (*Mut.* 97–102; *Det.* 65). Beyond learning and recollecting, the mind must reach for the enduring memory of holy truths insusceptibe of forgetfulness, whose ultimate goal is the mystic encounter with God, when all other memories are relegated to total oblivion, and the mind remains fixed on Deity, 'alone [as Plotinus would later say] with the Alone'.

In short, Boccaccini's book is full of fresh and penetrating insights and is a pleasure to read.

David Winston
Graduate Theological Union
Berkeley

Hans CONZELMANN, *Gentiles-Jews-Christians: Polemics and Apologetics in the Greco-Roman Era*. Translated from the German by M. Eugene Boring. Fortress, Minneapolis, 1992. xxxviii + 390 pages. $37.95.

The final work of one of the most distinguished NT scholars of the second half of the twentieth century has received relatively little attention both inside and outside of Germany in the original edition, *Heiden-Juden-Christen: Auseinandersetzungen in der Literatur der hellenistisch-römischen Zeit*, BHT 62 (Tübingen 1981). M. Eugene Boring has attempted to redress the situation through this translation. Boring has, however, done more than translate Conzelmann's German: he has updated a number of the bibliographical references, supplemented the text with additional references to primary works, made corrections to the references—both ancient and modern, and provided standard translations of the ancient texts Conzelmann cited. In order to offer this work *in memoriam*, Boring included the addresses of Dietz Lange and Eduard Lohse given on the first anniversary of Conzelmann's death at Göttingen University.

One of the things which stamped Conzelmann's work was his combination of exegetical and theological sensitivity. This work is perhaps the clearest example of this synthesis. Conzelmann explicitly set out the *Sitz im Leben* of the present work and his intentions in the 'Introduction' (pp. 1–5). The work was a response to currents in Germany in the aftermath of the Six-Day War when theologians and pastors spoke favorably of the modern state of Israel under the theological rubric of 'salvation-history'. Conzelmann thought that this move replaced a 'theology of the Word' with 'a superficially christianized world view' which uncritically anointed the modern state of Israel (p. 2). He wrote this strictly historical work for modern Jewish-Christian dialogue because he was convinced that the issues raised in the ancient literature were similar to those which needed attention in contemporary discussions.

Conzelmann explicates the ancient material by examining the position of the Jews within the Greco-Roman world (chapters one-three) and then looking at how Christians situated themselves in the larger world vis-à-vis Judaism (chapter four). He opens with 'The Political Background' (chapter one) which addresses the issue of the political acceptance or non-acceptance of the Jews in the Greco-Roman world and the role the Jews themselves played in establishing their position. He begins each chapter with preliminary observations which frame his discussion. In this instance, he formulates the problem in terms of monotheism (p. 8) and restricts his coverage to c. 300 BCE–200 CE, the period of Hellenistic Jewish literature. The bulk of the chapter surveys the political status of Jews in Egypt and Cyrene and in the Roman Empire. With a reliable hand Conzelmann touches on all of the central historical issues, albeit briefly.

The second chapter, 'The Evaluation of Judaism in Greco-Roman Literature', is a summary of Greek and Latin authors' assessments of Judaism. It is like reading a summary of Stern's first two volumes, *Greek and Latin Authors on Jews and Judaism* (although Conzelmann did not have access to volume two, Boring has supplied the appropriate references). Conzelmann opens with some preliminary observations which address the issues of charges leveled against the Jews and developments in historiography including the issue of pagan knowledge of Jewish scriptures. He correctly points to the alleged Jewish 'hatred of the human race' as the principal critique. More importantly, he observes that it is a religious argument used by pagans for political purposes: the Jews are and should be subservient. He prudently argues that it is not until Numenius and Celsus in the second century CE that we have substantial evidence of pagan knowledge of the bible. He then surveys the Greek material from Herodotus through Porphyry and the Latin from Horace to Tacitus. He notes the fundamental shift in perspective from the Greek to the Latin material: Roman authors measured the Jews politically in a way that earlier Greek authors did not. His surveys focus on direct statements about the Jews, but also include occasional observations about specific authors, e.g., reconstructions of texts.

The third chapter, 'The Debate of Hellenistic Judaism with the Hellenistic-Roman World', examines the Jewish response to the perceptions surveyed in the previous chapter. Conzelmann frames his rehearsal of this material by setting out his understanding of the presuppositions of Jewish apologetic literature. The faith 'in the one God became the uncrossable boundary between Judaism and every form of non-Judaism and the basic theme of all its polemic' (p. 137). Jews could agree with Greek monotheists about the *existence* of God, but not about the *essence*. He considers Tcherikover's distinction between direct and indirect apologetic irrelevant. He does, however, accept Hengel's suggestion that literature which appears under the author's own name is *directly* addressed to the larger world (p. 142). He also discusses the 'proof for the antiquity of the Jews' argument. Using these presuppositions he works his way through the literature, first examining some of Greek texts within the LXX and then the literature outside the LXX. Among the latter, pride of place goes to Philo, Josephus, and the Jewish stratum of the Sibylline Oracles. Conzelmann discusses *Hypoth., Contempl., Decal., Spec., Flacc.* and *Legat., Ios.,* and *Mos.* within the Philonic corpus. He leaves the question of the authenticity of *Hypoth.* open and fails to make anything of the congruence of the law codes in this work, Pseudo-Phocylides, and Josephus *Ag. Ap.* 2 (pp. 190–91 (cf. my 'Philo and the Logic of Apologetics: An Analysis of the *Hypothetica*', *SBLSP* 29 (1990) 412–30 and George P. Carras' article elsewhere in this Annual)). He correctly considers the portrait of the Therapeutae to be the same literary form as Philo's presentations of the Essenes, i.e., they are 'exemplary forms of the ideal life' (p. 190; cf. now David M. Hay, 'Things Philo Said and Did Not Say About the Therapeutae', *SBLSP* 31 (1992) 673–83). He argues that the juxtaposition of *Decal.* and *Spec.* is 'probably the strongest proof that in Philo, "domestic policy" and "foreign policy" are inseparable' (p. 194). *Flacc.* demonstrates the harmony of Jewish and Roman ways of life while *Legat.* defends the loyalty of the Jews. *Ios.* underscores Jewish morality. *Mos.* is literarily unique in the Philonic corpus: it does not simply employ apologetic motifs, it is an historical, apologetic monograph. Conzelmann argues that the issue of Josephus' œuvre is how 'the fundamental Jewish confession "*One* God, *one* people, *one* temple"' can 'be concretely expressed in particular political decisions' (p. 204). He concludes with a brief analysis of *Sib. Or.* 3, 4, and 5, noting the development of an anti-Roman stance in 4 and 5. Jewish apologetic is therefore tied to Hellenistic Judaism. It offers 'an example of the association of Judaism with its environment on the foundation of monotheism and the law' (p. 233).

Against this background, Conzelmann works through Christian assessments of Jews in apologetic texts, 'Christians and Jews from the Beginnings of Christianity to the Time of Origen' (chapter four). The issue is what happens to Jewish monotheism when it is understood Christologically. In his preliminary comments he makes the distinction between *Urliteratur* and *Hochliteratur* that Franz Overbeck made famous ('Über die Anfänge der patristischen Literatur' *Historische Zeitschrift* 48 (1882) 417–72). The mid-second century shift to a more reflective stance forced Christians to address the issues of what they had in common with Judaism and what was specifically Christian. When salvation history is used as a solution to define Jewish-Christian relations, Conzelmann argues it obfuscates the basic issues. He defines salvation history as 'the transformation of faith into an objective, verifiable conception of the world, and that means a view of the world for which faith is not necessary' (p. 240; cf. also p. 297). The problem is that from this perspective the church can not claim to be the people of God without denying this status to Jews. Both lay claim to events which in their opinion actually occurred and thus set up an irreconcilable situation. With these stipulations, Conzelmann sketches the impact of the state on Christian self-understanding and the Jewish-Christian debate. He then surveys the early texts up until Justin and finally the fully developed apologetic literature from Justin to Origen. The touchstone of Conzelmann's analysis of all of these authors is whether they set the Jewish-Christian question within the framework of salvation history. For those who did, the Jews pose a problem, e.g. the polemic of Melito of Sardis against Israel in the *Passover Homily*. For those who did not, the Jews were not a problem, e.g. 'Tatian had peace with the Jews, the peacefulness found in a cemetery, purchased at the price of relinquishing the saving revelation' (p. 310). Origen is the exception: he understood the Jews on the basis of his biblicism. The problem with the Jews is that their literal interpretation of the law has failed them, only Christians understood it through allegorical interpretation. The issue is thus an issue of faith. It is no accident that Conzelmann concludes with Origen: this is the position he advocates. 'The only issue between Jews and Christains is the issue of faith' (p. 342). This means that all are justified before God in the same way, *sola fide*.

This work is a *tour de force*. The reader quickly realizes and never forgets that the author is an *homo eruditissimus*. This is true for both his survey of the ancient material as well as his summaries of modern discussions. He reliably guides readers through a great deal of difficult material. There is, however, a price to be paid: Conzelmann frequently summarizes without synthesizing. The result is that a reader often learns the views of others without ever hearing Conzelmann's own voice. It also means that the collection of texts often read more like a catalogue of observations than a sustained argument. This is compounded by the staccato and laconic style of his writing which continually forces a reader to pause and reflect on the connections of the thought. Although there are no serious lapses, one wonders whether the debilitating effects of Conzelmann's final illness do not surface in the manuscript, particularly toward the end of the book where, for example, the crucial discussion of Origen is limited to pp. 339–342. Readers should also be aware that several important monographs have appeared since the original date of publication which do not appear in the bibliography, e.g. R. Joseph Hoffmann, *On the True Doctrine: A Discourse Against the Christians* (New York 1987); Arthur Droge, *Homer or Moses? Early Christian Interpretations of Culture*, HUT 26 (Tübingen 1989); Peter Pilhofer, *Presbyteron Kreitton: Der Altersbeweis der jüdischen und christlichen Apologeten und seine Vorgeschichte*, WUNT 2.39 (Tübingen 1990).

We are indebted to Conzelmann for demonstrating how salvation history tended to a devaluation of Jews in early Christian literature. Any who would use it as a theological hermeneutic in contemporary Jewish-

Christian dialogue must be prepared to respond to his critique. Whether one accepts his classic Pauline/Lutheran statement of the importance of the Word depends on larger theological assumptions. One need not, however, share these to appreciate his magisterial control of ancient texts and to admire his ability to do theology in the form of exegesis.

Gregory E. Sterling
University of Notre Dame

H.-J. KLAUCK, (ed.), *Monotheismus und Christologie. Zur Gottesfrage im hellenistischen Judentum und im Urchristentum*. Quaestiones Disputatae 138. Herder, Freiburg-Basel-Wien 1992. 230 S.

Dieser Tagungsband verfolgt wenigstens in einem Teil der Beiträge die Spannung zwischen dem traditionellen Ein-Gott-Glauben Israels und dem christologischen Bekenntnis der Urkirche. Dabei geht es auch um die Frage, ob wenigstens das Diasporajudentum Ansätze für eine solche Auflockerung des Monotheismus bot. Die Antwort ist gespalten, wie der folgende Überblick über die beiden für den Philo-Liebhaber wichtigsten Aufsätze zeigt.

G. SELLIN, 'Gotteserkenntnis und Gotteserfahrung bei Philo von Alexandrien' (17–40). Der Autor ist den Philo-Forschern durch seine Arbeit *Der Streit um die Auferstehung der Toten*, FRLANT 138 (Göttingen 1986) bekannt. Er geht davon aus, daß der Schriftauslegung Philos ein durchaus systematischer Tiefen-Text zugrundeliegt. Hier läßt sich eine konsequente 'negative Theologie' erheben, die Sellin überzeugend zusammenfaßt (19–25). Im Unterschied zu dem in *SPhA* 2 (1990) 201–204 von mir besprochenen Buch *AKATALEPTOS THEOS* von L. A. Montes-Peral deutet er ihre philosophischen Wurzeln wenigstens an. Diese systematische Lehre von der Gotteserkenntnis breche aber zusammen, wo sie soteriologisch gedacht wird als durch Gnade und Inspiration ermöglicht. 'Hier wird der menschliche νοῦς in ein dualistisches Kräftefeld eingezeichnet, so daß die Erkenntnis, die dem natürlichen νοῦς möglich ist, geradezu zum Paradigma der Verblendung, Torheit, Hybris und Sündhaftigkeit wird' (25). Deutlicher als in seiner anfangs genannten Arbeit weist Sellin jetzt daraufhin, daß die Tendenz zur Esoterik und Offenbarungsreligiosität in der hellenistischen Philosophie selber schon angelegt ist.

Damit geht Sellin über zur anthropologisch-existentialen Ebene. Philon bringe im Weg der Erkenntnis von oben nach unten auch die alttestamentlich-jüdische Intention von der Heiligkeit Gottes, damit die Überzeugung von der Sündhaftigkeit des Menschen zur Geltung. Die

Erlösung geschieht gemäß alexandrinisch-jüdischer Weisheit als Einhauchen des göttlichen Pneuma (soteriologische Interpretation von Gen 2:7 in *Leg.* 1.32). Dahinter verberge sich 'die Transzendierung der Philosophie, der Wissenschaft, in ein demütiges Gottvertrauen'(28).

Sellin betrachtet nun die Stellen, an denen diese Erlösung als Selbstaufgabe des νοῦς in der Ekstase beschrieben wird, und kommt zu der kühnen Überschrift 'Der Mensch als Logos Gottes'. Diese überraschende Ineinssetzung wird dadurch möglich, daß die auf den vollendeten Weisen bezogenen Aussagen in *Somn.* 2.228–236 durch die früheren §§ 183–189 und *Fug.* 108 interpretiert werden. An letzterer Stelle ist der Hohepriester ausdrücklich als θεῖος λόγος gedeutet. Bei der ersteren Passage stellt Sellin einen Übergang vom vollkommenen νοῦς (§ 183 m.E. gar nicht sicher) zum Logos fest.

Ähnliches folgert Sellin aus *Conf.* 146–147, wo nicht nur der Logos Israel heißt, sondern auch der sonst peinlich beachtete Unterschied zwischen dem Logos als Bild Gottes und dem Menschen κατ' εἰκόνα verwischt werde. Wer auf der Spitze der Ideenpyramide, dem τόπος = Logos stehe, sei identisch mit ihm. Der an diese Spitze heraufberufene νοῦς bekomme auch aktive Funktionen des Logos. Dieser Exegese ist etwa *Conf.* 41 entgegenzuhalten, wo der gewöhnliche Sterbliche höchstens 'Sohn' des ἄνθρωπος θεοῦ = Logos werden kann.

In einem letzten Teil konfrontiert Sellin diese philonische Lehre mit der neutestamentlichen Rede von Gott und der Christologie. Einerseits sind die Grundlagen der theologischen Sprachlehre Philos auch für die christliche Theologie unverzichtbar (S. 37f.), andererseits erweist sich Philos Theo-Logie als unzulänglich, um die Personhaftigkeit Gottes und die leiblich-historische Dimension seiner Offenbarung auszusagen. Auf eine knappe Formel gebracht: 'Der philonische Logos-Mensch, der ἄνθρωπος θεοῦ, ist—jedenfalls im Zustand seiner Logos-Existenz—kein Mensch mehr. Christus aber ist gerade als Mensch das Antlitz Gottes' (36).

Dennoch meint Sellin die auffällige Tatsache, warum im Johannesprolog ein *Mensch* die Stelle der Hypostase Gottes eingenommen hat[1], durch die von Philo gebotene Logostheologie erklären zu können (35). M.E. läßt sie sich aber nicht ins Inkarnationsmodell überführen. Nur beim herabgehauchten Pneuma kennt Philo eine Abwärtsbewegung. Der Aufstieg des Menschen zu Gott verläuft in entgegengesetzter Richtung. Auch M. Theobald, der im selben Band über 'Gott, Logos und Pneuma' im Johannesevangelium (41–87) schreibt, meint: 'Vom philo-

---

[1] Vgl. auch meine Überlegungen in dem von mir hg. Band 'Menschwerdung Gottes–Vergöttlichung von Menschen', NTOA 7 (Freiburg/Schweiz -Göttingen 1988) 141-176, 154f.

nischen Logos her ergeben sich kaum Brücken zu diesem Spitzensatz, nach welchem der Logos, ohne seine Identität zu verlieren, in Jesus von Nazaret Mensch geworden ist' (83).

Mein Eindruck: Eine packende Zusammenschau, wobei aber die zugespitzte These vom 'Logos-Menschen' vielleicht doch nicht dem differenzierenden Denken Philos gerecht wird.

Max KÜCHLER, 'Gott und seine Weisheit in der Septuaginta (Ijob 28; Spr 8)' (118–143). Küchler ist durch seine monumentale Untersuchung *Frühjüdische Weisheitstraditionen*, OBO 26 (Freiburg Schweiz-Göttingen 1979) bestens dafür qualifiziert, die Modifikationen herauszuarbeiten, die die beiden Weisheitstexte Ijob 28 und Spr 8 in der griechischen Übersetzung erfahren haben. Mit philologischem Scharfsinn beobachtet er, wie die hebräischen Vorlagen zu neuen Gedichten mit bewußter, eigener Struktur umgestaltet wurden. Der Autor von Ijob 28 (LXX) habe die Relation zwischen der Weisheit und dem Gott Israels geklärt, indem er die Metaphorik der Begegnung zwischen Gott und der Weisheit vermied, eine klare Ortung der Weisheit in die göttliche Schöpfung[1] vornahm, dem gewöhnlichen Menschen die Pietas als Ort der Weisheit zuwies, sich selbst und seine Gruppe aber als privilegierte Seher und Hörer verstand.

Dabei wäre nur zu fragen, ob es tatsächlich im hebr. Text 'um eine überraschende Begegnung zweier vorweltlicher Wesen' geht (127). Die in V. 27 gebrauchten Verben sprechen doch eher von der Aufrichtung eines Ordnungsprinzips, um dessen vorherige selbständige Existenz der Verf. sich keine Gedanken macht, wie Küchler selbst bemerkt.

In Spr 8,21A–31 (LXX) werden die schöpferischen Tätigkeiten des Kyrios gegenüber den Ich-Aussagen der Weisheit in den Vordergrund gerückt, und zwar unter Vermeidung mythologischer Ausdrücke. Die Weisheit erscheint als Tochter Gottes, die die Harmonie der Welt sichert, so daß der Schöpfergott an der vollendeten Erde und den Menschenkindern seine Freude haben kann. Auch hier sind die Eingriffe des Übersetzers überzeugend gedeutet. Fraglich ist nur, ob erst er das umrätselte *ʾāmôn* in V. 30 auf die Weisheit bezogen hat. Der Bezug auf Gott als 'Werkmeister', den Küchler mit O. Keel für den Urtext annimmt, wäre doch ganz auf der Linie des Übersetzers.

Am Schluß dieses interessanten Beitrags vergleicht Küchler die Bearbeitung des vermutlich identischen Autors mit der Entwicklung der Weisheit in anderen Schriften des 2. Jh. (Sir 24; Bar 3f).

Drei neutestamentliche Aufsätze über den 'Gottesgedanken' bei den

---

[1] Zur Übersetzung S. 129: Das deutsche Präteritum von 'erschaffen' lautet 'erschuf', nicht 'erschaffte'.

Synoptikern (J. Gnilka), das Gottesbild in der Apostelgeschichte (K. Löning) und die Theologie im Kolosser- und Epheserbrief (R. Hoppe) kann der Philo-Forscher ignorieren. Dagegen weist P. Hofrichter in 'Logoslehre und Gottesbild bei Apologeten, Modalisten und Gnostikern' (186-217; S. 189-192) gegen neuerliche Bestreitung die Abhängigkeit Justins von Philo nach.

Dieter Zeller
Johannes-Gutenberg-Universität
Mainz

NEWS AND NOTES

Some recent Philo meetings

The 47th General Meeting of the Studiorum Novi Testamenti Societas was held in Madrid, Spain, 27–31 July 1992. The Society's Seminar on 'Philo of Alexandria and Christian Beginnings' met for three sessions, which were chaired by David Hay. The following papers were presented for discussion: R. McL. Wilson, 'Philo and Gnosticism' (Peter Hofrichter, respondent); Klaus Haacker, 'Paul's View of History in Romans 9–11 and Philo's Interpretation of Scripture' (Martin Rese, respondent); and José Pablo Martín, 'Philo and the Christian Literature of the Second Century' (Manuel Alexandre jr., respondent). Plans for the August 1993 in Chicago were discussed. The paper of R. McL. Wilson is published elsewhere in this volume (pp. 84–92).

The 'Philo of Alexandria Seminar' of the Society of Biblical Literature met at the Society's national meeting in San Francisco on November 22 and 24, 1992. Alan Mendelson presided at the first session, while Dorothy Sly did so at the second. The first session was devoted to 'Philo's Relationship to Middle Platonism.' Papers by Gregory E. Sterling ('Platonizing Moses: Philo and Middle Platonism') and David T. Runia ('Was Philo a Middle Platonist? a Difficult Question Revisited') were summarized; formal responses to them were presented by David Winston and Thomas H. Tobin, and general discussion followed. The papers and responses are published elsewhere in this volume (pp. 95–155). At the session on the 24th the following papers were summarized and discussed: David M. Hay, 'Things Philo Said and Did Not Say about the Therapeutae'; Peder Borgen, "Yes', 'No', 'How Far?': the Problem of Jewish and Christian Participation in Pagan Cults'. Plans were formulated for the continuation of the Seminar at the Society's next national meeting to be held in Washington D.C. in November 1993.

David M. Hay

Note on the Philo Collection at Yale

The Yale University Library has recently informed me that its special Philo Collection is now housed in 'Beineke', which contains Yale's collections of rare books and manuscripts. According to E. R. Goodenough, in an article in the *Yale University Library Gazette* 25:4 (April 1951), the collection includes 15 editions of the Greek text of Philo's works; two publications of the rare edition by Aucher of the Armenian translations (1822, 1826); and 10 editions of Latin translations.

David Winston

NOTES ON CONTRIBUTORS

George CARRAS is a Post-doctoral Fellow in Biblical Studies, Department of Near Eastern Studies, University of California, Berkeley, and a research scholar at the Center for Jewish Studies, Graduate Theological Union, Berkeley, California. His postal address is Department of Near Eastern Studies, Barrows Hall, UC Berkeley, Berkeley CA 94709, U.S.A.

Naomi G. COHEN has taught Jewish Philosophy and Thought for many years at Tel-Aviv and Haifa Universities. Her postal address is 26 Horeb Street, Haifa 34342, ISRAEL; her electronic address is rvolf01@haifauvm.

John DILLON is Regius Professor of Greek, Trinity College, Dublin. His postal address is Department of Classics, Trinity College, Dublin 2, IRELAND.

Louis FELDMAN is Professor of Classics, Yeshiva University, New York. His postal address is 69-11 Harrow St., Forest Hills NY 11375, U.S.A.

David HAY is McCabe Professor of Religion, Coe College, Cedar Rapids, Iowa. His postal address is Department of Religion and Philosophy, Coe College, Cedar Rapids IA 52402, U.S.A.; his electronic address is dmhay@umaxc.weeg.uiowa.edu.

Pieter VAN DER HORST is Professor of New Testament, Faculty of Theology, Utrecht University. His postal address is Faculty of Theology, Utrecht University, Postbus 80.105, 3508 TC Utrecht, THE NETHERLANDS; his electronic address is vdhorst@cc.ruu.nl.

Roberto RADICE is Lecturer in Ancient Philosophy at the Sacred Heart University, Milan. His postal address is Via XXV Aprile 4, 21016 Luino, ITALY.

David T. RUNIA is Professor of Ancient and Medieval Philosophy, Leiden University, and also C. J. de Vogel Professor Extraordinarius in Ancient Philosophy at Utrecht University. His postal address is Rijnsburgerweg 116, 2333 AE Leiden, THE NETHERLANDS; his electronic address is runia@rulcri.leidenuniv.nl.

NOTES ON CONTRIBUTORS 249

James R. ROYSE is a data processing consultant specializing in real-time financial applications. His postal address is 2200 31st Avenue, San Francisco CA 94116, U.S.A.; his electronic address is brt!jim@ uu.psi.com

Gregory E. STERLING is Assistant Professor in New Testament, Department of Theology, University of Notre Dame. His postal address is Department of Theology, University of Notre Dame, Notre Dame IN 46556, U.S.A.; his electronic address is gregory.e.sterling.1@nd.edu.

Thomas H. TOBIN S.J. is Professor of New Testament, Department of Theology, Loyola University of Chicago. His postal address is Department of Theology, Loyola University of Chicago, 6525 North Sheridan Road, Chicago IL 60626-5385, U.S.A.

Sze-Kar WAN is Assistant Professor of New Testament, Andover Newton Theological School, Boston. His address is Department of New Testament, Andover Newton Theological School, 210 Herrick Road, Newton Centre, MA 02145, U.S.A. His e-mail address is: andovrb@bcvms.bc.edu.

R. McL. WILSON is Emeritus Professor of Biblical Criticism at St Mary's College in the University of St Andrews. His postal address is 10 Murrayfield Road, St Andrews, Fife, KLY16 9NB, SCOTLAND.

David WINSTON is Professor of Hellenistic and Jewish Studies, Graduate Theological Union, Berkeley. His postal address is 1220 Grizzly Peak, Berkeley CA 94708, U.S.A.

Dieter ZELLER is Professor für Religionswissenschaft des Hellenismus at the Johannes-Gutenberg University of Mainz and Honorar-Professor at the Ruprecht-Karls University of Heidelberg. His postal address is Schillerweg 4, 6228 Eltville (Erbach), DEUTSCHLAND.

INSTRUCTIONS TO CONTRIBUTORS

Authors of articles and book reviews in *The Studia Philonica Annual* are asked to conform to the following guidelines.

1. *The Studia Philonica Annual* accepts articles for publication in the area of Hellenistic Judaism, with special emphasis on Philo and his *Umwelt*. Articles on Josephus will be given consideration if they focus on his relation to Judaism and classical culture (and not on primarily historical subjects). The languages in which the articles may be published are English, French and German. Translations from Italian or Dutch into English can be arranged at a modest cost to the author.

2. Since the Annual is being produced with a minimum of secretarial assistance, the editors request with some insistence that all articles and reviews be submitted on microdiskette. In the case of longer articles, contributions submitted as typescript will only be accepted by way of exception. For the formatting of submitted material the editors have the following order of preference:

(a) Apple Macintosh, formatted in MS-Word, using SMK Greek (or SuperGreek or Goulet-Corinthe) and SuperHebrew;

(b) MS-DOS on 5.25" (360K or 1.2M) or 3.5" (720K or 1.44M) diskettes, formatted in MS-Word or Word Perfect (preference for 5.1, but 4.2 and 5.0 accepted); users of Nota Bene are requested to submit a copy exported to DCA format.

In all cases it is **imperative** that a hard copy accompany the text on diskette, and that authors gives full details of the word processor used. No handwritten Greek or Hebrew can be accepted. Authors are requested not to vocalize their Hebrew and to keep their use of this language to a reasonable minimum. It should always be borne in mind that not all readers of the Annual can be expected to read Greek or Hebrew. Transliteration is permissible for incidental terms.

3. With regard to the citation of scholarly references the Annual will henceforth subscribe to the conventions embodied in the following examples (note (i) that no publishers' names are given, and (ii) that books and journals are italicized, series are not):

> A. Mendelson, *Secular Education in Philo of Alexandria*, Monographs of the Hebrew Union College 7 (Cincinnati 1982) 15–27.
>
> Y. Amir, 'The Transference of Greek Allegories to Biblical Motifs in Philo', in F. E. Greenspahn, E. Hilgert, B. L. Mack (edd.), *Nourished with Peace: Studies in Hellenistic Judaism in Memory of Samuel Sandmel*, Scholars Press Homage Series 9 (Chico, California 1984) 15–25.
>
> J. P. Martín, 'El encuentro de exégesis y filosofia en Filón Alejandrino', *Revista Biblica* 46 (1984) 199–211.

Mendelson *op. cit.* (n. 0) 23ff.
Amir, *art. cit.* (n.0) 16–18.
or Martín 'El encuentro' 199–201.

It is also possible to give references by author and date in the footnotes only, with full details presented in a bibliography at the end of the article (see the example on pp. 295–319 of volume 3).
For the abbreviations to be used, see further below. A sound guide to the way that Philonic scholarship should be cited will be found in R. Radice and D. T. Runia, *Philo of Alexandria: an Annotated Bibliography 1937–1986*, VCSup 8 (Leiden 1988). Note that with regard to the use of capitals in citing English references, both English-American and continental European conventions are permissible.

4. It is suggested that the following abbreviations be used (this **replaces** the guidelines set out in *SPh* 1 (1971) 92–96, 2 (1972) 77–80).
(a) Philonic treatises are to be abbreviated according to the following list. Numeration is according to Cohn and Wendland's edition, using Arabic numbers only (e.g. *Spec.* 4.123). Note that *De Providentia* should be cited according to Aucher's edition, and not the LCL translation of the fragments by F. H. Colson.

Abr.	*De Abrahamo*
Aet.	*De aeternitate mundi*
Agr.	*De agricultura*
Anim.	*De animalibus*
Cher.	*De Cherubim*
Contempl.	*De vita contemplativa*
Conf.	*De confusione linguarum*
Congr.	*De congressu eruditionis gratia*
Decal.	*De Decalogo*
Deo	*De Deo*
Det.	*Quod deterius potiori insidiari soleat*
Deus	*Quod Deus sit immutabilis*
Ebr.	*De ebrietate*
Flacc.	*In Flaccum*
Fug.	*De fuga et inventione*
Gig.	*De gigantibus*
Her.	*Quis rerum divinarum heres sit*
Hypoth.	*Hypothetica*
Ios.	*De Iosepho*
Leg. 1–3	*Legum allegoriae* I, II, III
Legat.	*Legatio ad Gaium*
Migr.	*De migratione Abrahami*
Mos. 1–2	*De vita Moysis* I, II
Mut.	*De mutatione nominum*
Opif.	*De opificio mundi*

Plant.	De plantatione
Post.	De posteritate Caini
Praem.	De praemiis et poenis, De exsecrationibus
Prob.	Quod omnis probus liber sit
Prov. 1–2	De Providentia I, II
QE 1–2	Quaestiones et solutiones in Exodum I, II
QG 1–4	Quaestiones et solutiones in Genesim I, II, III, IV
Sacr.	De sacrificiis Abelis et Caini
Sobr.	De sobrietate
Somn. 1–2	De somniis I, II
Spec. 1–4	De specialibus legibus I, II, III, IV
Virt.	De virtutibus

(b) Standard works of Philonic scholarship are abbreviated:

Aucher	*Philonis Judaei sermones tres hactenus inediti* (Venice 1822), *Philonis Judaei paralipomena* (Venice 1826)
G-G	H. L. Goodhart and E. R. Goodenough, 'A General Bibliography of Philo Judaeus', in E. R. Goodenough, *The Politics of Philo Judaeus: Practice and Theory* (New Haven 1938, reprinted Hildesheim 1967²) 125–321
PCH	*Philo von Alexandria: die Werke in deutscher Übersetzung*, edited by L. Cohn, I. Heinemann *et al.*, 7 vols. (Breslau, Berlin 1909–64)
PCW	*Philonis Alexandrini opera quae supersunt*, ediderunt L. Cohn, P. Wendland, S. Reiter, 6 vols. (Berlin 1896–1915)
PLCL	*Philo in Ten Volumes (and Two Supplementary Volumes)*, English translation by F. H. Colson, G. H. Whitaker (and R. Marcus), 12 vols., Loeb Classical Library (London 1929–62)
PAPM	*Les œuvres de Philon d'Alexandrie*, French translation under the general editorship of R. Arnaldez, J. Pouilloux, C. Mondésert (Paris 1961–)
R-R	R. Radice and D. T. Runia, *Philo of Alexandria: an Annotated Bibliography 1937–1986*, VCSup 8 (Leiden 1988)
SPh	*Studia Philonica*
SPhA	*The Studia Philonica Annual*

(c) Biblical books, Pseudepigraphical, Qumran, Rabbinic and Gnostic literature are to be abbreviated as recommended in the 'Instructions to Contributors' in the *Society of Biblical Literature Membership Directory and Handbook 1992*, pp. 209–226 (copies available on request). Note that biblical books are not italicized and that between chapter and verse a colon is placed (placement of a full stop after the abbreviation is optional, provided the author is consistent). Authors writing in German or French should follow their own conventions for biblical citations.

(d) Classical and Patristic authors should be cited in the manner recommended by the three Oxford lexica:

INSTRUCTIONS TO CONTRIBUTORS 253

H. G. Liddell, R. Scott, H. S. Jones (edd.), *A Greek-English Lexicon* (Oxford 1940⁹);
P. G. W. Glare (ed.), *The Oxford Latin Dictionary* (Oxford 1982);
G. W. H. Lampe (ed.), *A Patristic Greek Lexicon* (Oxford 1961).
Preferred abbreviations for Josephus, however, are *AJ*, *BJ*, *c. Ap.*, and *Vita*, but English abbreviations (*Antiquities*, *War*, etc.) are permitted. Once again consistency is the first requirement.

(e) Journals, monograph series, source collections and standard reference works are to be be abbreviated in accordance with the recommendation listed in the 'Instructions to Contributors' in the *Society of Biblical Literature Membership Directory and Handbook 1992*, pp. 217–226. The following list contains a selection of the more important abbreviations (adding a few abbreviations of Classical and philosophical journals and standard reference books not furnished in the list mentioned above.

AC	*L'Antiquité Classique*
ACW	Ancient Christian Writers,
AJPh	*American Journal of Philology*
AJSL	*American Journal of Semitic Languages*
ALGHJ	Arbeiten zur Literatur und Geschichte des hellenistischen Judentums
ANRW	*Aufstieg und Niedergang der römischen Welt*
AP	*L'Année Philologique (founded by Marouzeau)*
BAGD	*A Greek-English Lexicon of the New Testament and other Early Christian literature*, edited by W. Bauer, W. F. Arndt, F. W. Gingrich, F. W. Danker (Chicago 1979²)
BDB	*Hebrew and English lexicon of the Old Testament*, edited by F. Brown, S. R. Driver, C. A. Briggs (Oxford 1952)
BibOr	Bibliotheca Orientalis
BJRL	*Bulletin of the John Rylands Library*
BJS	Brown Judaic Studies
BZAW	Beihefte zur Zeitschrift für die alttestamentliche Wissenschaft
BZNW	Beihefte zur Zeitschrift für die neutestamentliche Wissenschaft
CAH	*The Cambridge Ancient History*, edited by J. B. Bury *et al.*, 16 vols. (Cambridge 1923–)
CBQ	*The Catholic Biblical Quarterly*
CBQMS	The Catholic Biblical Quarterly. Monograph Series
CChr	Corpus Christianorum, Turnhout
CIG	*Corpus Inscriptionum Graecarum*, edited by A. Boeckh, 4 vols. in 8 (Berlin 1828–77)
CIJ	*Corpus Inscriptionum Judaicarum*, edited by J. B. Frey, 2 vols. (Rome 1936–52)
CIL	*Corpus Inscriptionum Latinarum* (Berlin 1862–)
CIS	*Corpus Inscriptionum Semiticarum* (Paris 1881–1962)
CP	*Classical Philology*

CPJ	Corpus Papyrorum Judaicarum, ed. by V. Tcherikover and A. Fuks, 3 vols. (Cambrige Mass. 1957–64)
CQ	The Classical Quarterly
CR	The Classical Review
CRINT	Compendia Rerum Iudaicarum ad Novum Testamentum
CPG	Clavis Patrum Graecorum, edited by M. Geerard, 5 vols. (Turnhout 1974–87)
CPG	Clavis Patrum Latinorum, edited by E. Dekkers (Turnhout 1954)
DA	Dissertation Abstracts
DBSup	Dictionnaire de la Bible, Supplément (Paris 1928–)
DSpir	Dictionnaire de Spiritualité
EncJud	Encyclopaedia Judaica, 16 vols. (Jerusalem 1972)
EPRO	Études préliminaires aux religions orientales dans l'Empire romain
GCS	Die griechischen christlichen Schriftsteller, Leipzig
GLAJJ	M. Stern, Greek and Latin authors on Jews and Judaism, 3 vols. (Jerusalem 1974–1984)
GRBS	Greek, Roman and Byzantine Studies
HKNT	Handkommentar zum Neuen Testament, Tübingen
HNT	Handbuch zum Neuen Testament, Tübingen
HR	History of Religions
HThR	Harvard Theological Review
HUCA	Hebrew Union College Annual
JAAR	Journal of the American Academy of Religion
JAOS	Journal of the American Oriental Society
JbAC	Jahrbuch für Antike und Christentum
JBL	Journal of Biblical Literature
JHI	Journal of the History of Ideas
JHS	The Journal of Hellenic Studies
JJS	The Journal of Jewish Studies
JQR	The Jewish Quarterly Review
JR	The Journal of Religion
JRS	The Journal of Roman Studies
JSHRZ	Jüdische Schriften aus hellenistisch-römischer Zeit
JSJ	Journal for the Study of Judaism (in the Persian, Hellenistic and Roman Period)
JSNT	Journal for the Study of the New Testament
JSNTsup	Journal for the Study of the New Testament. Supplements Series
JSOT	Journal for the Study of the Old Testament
JSP	Journal for the Study of the Pseudepigrapha and Related Literature
JSS	Journal of Semitic Studies
JThS	The Journal of Theological Studies
KB	L. Koehler and W. Baumgartner, Lexicon in Veteris Testamenti libros, 3 vols. (Leiden 1967-83^3)
KJ	Kirjath Sepher
LCL	Loeb Classical Library
LSJ	A Greek-English lexicon, edited by H. G. Liddell, R. Scott, H. S. Jones (Oxford 1940^9)
MGWJ	Monatsschrift für Geschichte und Wissenschaft des Judentums
Mnem	Mnemosyne
NCE	New Catholic Encyclopedia, 15 vols (New York 1967)

INSTRUCTIONS TO CONTRIBUTORS 255

NHS	Nag Hammadi Studies
NovT	Novum Testamentum
NTA	New Testament Abstracts
NTOA	Novum Testamentum et Orbis Antiquus
NTS	New Testament Studies
OLD	The Oxford Latin dictionary, edited by P. G. W. Glare (Oxford 1982)
OTP	J. H. Charlesworth (ed.), The Old Testament Pseudepigrapha, 2 vols. (New York-London 1983-85)
PAAJR	Proceedings of the American Academy for Jewish Research
PAL	Philon d'Alexandrie: Lyon 11-15 Septembre 1966 (Paris 1967)
PG	Patrologiae cursus completus: series Graeca, edited by J. P. Migne, 162 vols. (Paris 1857-1912)
PGL	A Patristic Greek lexicon, ed. by G. W. H. Lampe (Oxford 1961)
PhilAnt	Philosophia Antiqua
PL	Patrologiae cursus completus: series Latina, edited by J. P. Migne, 221 vols. (Paris 1844-64)
PW	Pauly-Wissowa-Kroll, Real-Encyclopaedie der classischen Altertumswissenschaft, Stuttgart
PWSup	Supplement to PW
RAC	Reallexikon für Antike und Christentum
RB	Revue Biblique
REA	Revue des Études Anciennes
REArm	Revue des Études Arméniennes
REAug	Revue des Études Augustiniennes
REG	Revue des Études Grecques
REJ	Revue des Études Juives
REL	Revue des Études Latines
RGG	Die Religion in Geschichte und Gegenwart, 7 vols. (Tübingen 1957-65³)
RhM	Rheinisches Museum für Philologie
RQ	Revue de Qumran
RSR	Revue des Sciences Religieuses
SB	H. L. Strack and P. Billerbeck, Kommentar zum Neuen Testament aus Talmud und Midrasch, 6 vols. in 7 (Munich 1922-61)
SBLDS	Society of Biblical Literature. Dissertation Series
SBLMS	Society of Biblical Literature. Monograph Series
SBLSPS	Society of Biblical Literature. Seminar Papers Series
SC	Sources Chrétiennes
Sem	Semitica
SHJP	E. Schürer, The history of the Jewish people in the age of Jesus Christ, revised edition, 3 vols. in 4 (Edinburgh 1973-87)
SJLA	Studies in Judaism in Late Antiquity
SNTSMS	Society for New Testament Studies. Monograph Series
SR	Studies in Religion
StUNT	Studien zur Umwelt des Neuen Testaments
TDNT	Theological Dictionary of the New Testament, 10 vols. (Grand Rapids 1964-76)
THKNT	Theologischer Handkommentar zum Neuen Testament, Berlin
TRE	Theologische Realenzyklopädie, Berlin
TSAJ	Texte und Studien zum Antike Judentum

TU	Texte und Untersuchungen zur Geschichte der altchristlichen Literatur, Berlin
TWNT	Theologisches Wörterbuch zum Neuen Testament, 10 vols. (Stuttgart 1933–79)
VC	Vigiliae Christianae
VCSup	Supplements to Vigiliae Christianae
VT	Vetus Testamentum
WUNT	Wissenschaftliche Untersuchungen zum Neuen Testament
ZAW	Zeitschrift für die alttestamentliche Wissenschaft
ZKG	Zeitschrift für Kirchengeschichte
ZKTh	Zeitschrift für Katholische Theologie
ZNW	Zeitschrift für die neutestamentliche Wissenschaft
ZRGG	Zeitschrift für Religions- und Geistesgeschichte

www.ingramcontent.com/pod-product-compliance
Lightning Source LLC
Chambersburg PA
CBHW021806220426
43662CB00006B/201